BOOKS BY HENRY KISSINGER

Crisis: The Anatomy of Two Major Foreign Policy Crises

*Ending the Vietnam War: A History of America's
Involvement in and Extrication from the Vietnam War*

*Does America Need a Foreign Policy?:
Toward a Diplomacy for the 21st Century*

Years of Renewal

Diplomacy

Observations: Selected Speeches and Essays, 1982–1984

Years of Upheaval

For the Record: Selected Statements, 1977–1980

White House Years

American Foreign Policy: Three Essays

Problems of National Strategy: A Book of Readings (editor)

The Troubled Partnership: A Reappraisal of the Atlantic Alliance

The Necessity for Choice: Prospects of American Foreign Policy

Nuclear Weapons and Foreign Policy

*A World Restored: Metternich, Castlereagh,
and the Problems of Peace: 1812–22*

HENRY KISSINGER
CRISIS

*The Anatomy of
Two Major
Foreign Policy
Crises*

Simon & Schuster

NEW YORK LONDON TORONTO

SYDNEY SINGAPORE

SIMON & SCHUSTER
Rockefeller Center
1230 Avenue of the Americas
New York, NY 10020

SIMON & SCHUSTER and colophon are
registered trademarks of Simon & Schuster, Inc.

For information about special discounts for bulk purchases,
please contact Simon & Schuster Special Sales:
1-800-456-6798 or business@simonandschuster.com

Designed by Amy Hill

Manufactured in the United States of America

1   3   5   7   9   10   8   6   4   2

Library of Congress Cataloging-in-Publication Data
is available.

ISBN 0-7432-4910-0

To my grandchildren,
Sam, Sophie, Will, and Juliana

Contents

CRISIS

Introduction

While I served in the Richard M. Nixon and Gerald R. Ford administrations as National Security Adviser and then Secretary of State, holding both positions simultaneously from 1973 until the end of 1975, my secretaries transcribed the overwhelming majority of my telephone conversations. The original transcripts were never edited at the time they were typed. The purpose of making them was to enable me to follow up on promises made or understandings reached and to incorporate them into memoranda to the President or other records. In 1977, I deposited these working papers at the Library of Congress and, in 1980, made them available to review by the Department of State. Since 1997, these conversations have been used by the State Department's historical division for publication in its foreign policy series. In 2001, I turned over all the National Security Council conversations to the National Archives and the conversations as Secretary to the State Department to enable these agencies to process them with a view to their general availability.

These conversations convey the mood in which major decisions were made and the attitudes from which national policy was compounded. Since decisions on the telephone reflect the urgency of the moment, they do not always contain the full range of underlying considerations. A complete history would require a record of the various interagency meetings and transcripts of personal conversations with the President. Nevertheless, these conversations give an accurate picture of the imperatives driving decisions—especially during the fast-moving events described in this volume. Each section is introduced by a summary narrative, which is continued where there are gaps in the telephonic transcripts. Where necessary to achieve continuity, I included summaries of appropriate interdepartmental meetings.

This book deals with two crises that were handled importantly on the telephone: the Middle East War of October 1973 and the final withdrawal from Indochina in 1975. The Middle East War involved frequent use of the telephone because I was in New York when it broke out, attending the United Nations General Assembly, and afterward because time pressures complicated the use of more formal means of communication. The final extrication from Vietnam had to be accomplished under emergency conditions requiring frequent telephone contact.

The two crises covered in this volume were accompanied by domestic crises in the United States. The Middle East War occurred in the midst of the Watergate crisis; indeed, its two culminating events spanned the entire period of the war. During the opening of hostilities on October 6, President Nixon was obliged to deal with the resignation of Vice President Spiro Agnew. During the second week, Nixon was negotiating a procedure for releasing the White House tapes. This led to the resignation of Elliot Richardson as Attorney General and the dismissal of Archibald Cox as special prosecutor. The so-called Saturday Night Massacre occurred while I was in Moscow on October 20 negotiating a Middle East cease-fire. It led soon after to the start of impeachment proceedings against President Nixon in the House of Representatives. As a result, while these efforts were taking place, Alexander Haig was—as the conversations show—a principal contact to Nixon even for me.

The withdrawal from Vietnam was the end of one of the most bitter divisions in American history, and the position of all the key actors was shaped by the positions they had taken previously, even though by the time of the actual withdrawal these divisions had been overtaken by events. Nevertheless, the basic categories of the debate continued during the last month even as Indochina was engulfed by catastrophe.

The reader should keep in mind that the conversations reflect the mood of moments of crisis. Thus the congenital day-to-day differences between the Department of State and the Department of Defense appear more dramatic than their final outcome. On fundamental issues, Secretary of Defense James Schlesinger and I generally wound up on the same side even if we arrived there by circuitous routes influenced importantly by the bureaucracies we headed. A good illustration is the airlift to Israel, the evolution of which is traced in these pages.

The National Security Council has cleared these conversations for publication, and I want to thank Dr. Condoleezza Rice for the meticulous review by her staff. I have made the deletions they have requested and indicated their placement in the appropriate manner by ellipses enclosed by brackets, shown as: [. . .]. The conversations have been slightly edited to omit repetitions. These edits have been indicated by ellipses, shown as: . . . Conventional courtesies such as greetings and good-byes at the beginning and end of conversations have also been omitted.

All times shown are Eastern Time.

The Middle East War
of 1973

The Middle East crisis that erupted into war in 1973 had many components: the Arab-Israeli conflict; the ideological struggle between Arab moderates and radicals; and the rivalry of the superpowers, the United States and the Soviet Union. These ingredients had separate origins that had grown intertwined; a solution to one could not be accomplished without grappling with the others.

Creation of the state of Israel with American (and, at the time, Soviet) support in 1948 had inflamed Arab nationalism and led to a war at the end of which borders were based on the armistice lines. Established as a nation by force of arms, Israel lived thereafter unrecognized, ostracized, and bitterly resented by its neighbors. In 1956, Israel moved into the Sinai Peninsula as an adjunct to the Anglo-French Suez operation. Forced back by the United Nations to the 1947 border, Israel achieved a demilitarized Sinai and freedom of navigation to its Red Sea port at Eilat. In June 1967, Israel erupted across the armistice lines after Egypt, under President Gamal Abdel Nasser, spurred on by Soviet disinformation, declared a blockade of Eilat and ominously moved its army into the demilitarized Sinai toward Israel. The war ended in six days with Israel in possession of the Sinai Peninsula from Egypt, the West Bank of the Jordan River, and the Golan Heights from Syria, compounding Arab frustration with humiliation.

Israel, never having lived within accepted frontiers, saw no essential difference between locating its boundaries in one unaccepted place or another; condemned to Arab belligerency, it sought the widest possible security belt and held on to its conquests. The Arab nations, in the aftermath of that defeat, resumed a defiant posture under the leadership of Egyptian President Nasser. At an Arab summit in Khartoum they adopted the principle of "No peace, no negotiation, no recognition of Israel." A war of attrition started, as part of which the Soviet Union established an air defense system of surface-to-air missiles along the Suez Canal. In 1970, there was an upheaval by the Palestine Liberation Organization in Jordan. Syria invaded Jordan in support of the PLO, United States forces were placed on alert, and the crisis ended with the PLO's expulsion from Jordan.

Afterward, the Arab countries were torn between their ideological and religious objection to the existence of the Israeli state and the practical reality that they could not alter the status quo except through some form of diplomacy. Moderate Arab governments like Jordan and (under Nasser, ambivalently) Egypt felt their way toward a formula that accepted Israel on its prewar (1967) borders (that is, the armistice lines of 1947). But, pending a settlement of the status of the Arab Palestinians, they would grant no more than an end to the state of belligerency—another form of armistice—rather than the full peace that Israel demanded.

And the Palestinian issue was deadlocked further by the attitude of the Palestinian nationalists who refused to accept Israel's legitimacy on any terms. Syria refused to negotiate for *any* conditions; it objected to Israel's existence, not its borders. Iraq strenuously added its weight to that of the radicals, as did Libya and Algeria. The PLO, whose claim to represent all Palestinians was not yet recognized by the Arab states, called for the creation of a secular state in Palestine—that is to say, the disappearance of Israel. And Israel came more and more to identify its security with its presence on the West Bank. This impasse blocked Middle East diplomacy for all the years between the wars of 1967 and 1973.

The symbol of the deadlock was United Nations Security Council Resolution 242 of November 22, 1967. It spoke of a "just and lasting peace" within "secure and recognized boundaries" but did not define any of the adjectives. Rejected by some Arab states, interpreted by those that accepted it as well as by Israel to suit their preconceptions, it became more an expression of a stalemate than a means of its resolution. Those Arab leaders willing to negotiate at all construed it to require total Israeli withdrawal to the pre–June 1967 frontiers. Israel professed that none of its prewar borders was secure; it insisted on retaining some of the occupied territory of each of its neighbors. To make doubly sure that its interests were safeguarded, Israel put forward a demand as seemingly reasonable as it was unfulfillable: that the Arab states negotiate directly with it. In other words, Israel asked for recognition as a precondition of negotiation.

The Arab states, not to be outdone, demanded acceptance of their territorial demands before they would consider diplomacy. No Arab leader, however moderate, could accede to Israel's demands and survive in the climate of humiliation, radicalism, and Soviet influence of the period. No Israeli Prime Minister could stay in office if he relinquished the claim to some of the occupied territories as an entrance price to negotiations. Israel chased the illusion that it could both acquire substantial territory and achieve peace. Its Arab adversaries pursued the opposite illusion—that they could regain territory without offering peace.

Egypt became the key to Middle East diplomacy. Tactical necessity reinforced what Egypt had earned by its size, tradition, cultural influence, and sacrifice in a series of Arab-Israeli wars. Egypt was the most populous Arab country, the cultural hub of the area. Its teachers were the backbone of the educational system of the Arab world; its universities attracted students from all over the region. It had the longest continuing history of any nation, with the exception of China. And it had borne the brunt of the Arab-Israeli conflict. As both monarchy and republic, it had engaged itself in a struggle that went

beyond narrow Egyptian national interests. It had sacrificed its young
men to the cause of Arab unity and of Palestinian self-determination.
In the process, it had lost the Sinai Peninsula and repeatedly risked its
national cohesion. Egypt had earned the right to make peace.

But so long as Nasser was President, he paralyzed Egypt by am-
bivalence. On the one hand, he indicated a general willingness to
participate in the peace process—albeit in the name of an unfulfillable program. He demanded Israel's withdrawal to the 1967 borders
in return for Egyptian nonbelligerency; peace would depend on an
Israeli settlement with the Palestinians, then demanding the destruction of the Jewish state. Nor would Nasser negotiate directly with
Israel. Rather, America was asked to bring about the Israeli withdrawal, in return for which Nasser would confer on us the boon of
restored diplomatic relations. In the meantime Cairo radio remained
as the center of anti-American—indeed, anti-Western—propaganda
throughout the Middle East. In short, Nasser wanted to lead the
Arab world from an anti-American position, to present whatever
concessions he obtained as having been extorted by Arab militancy,
backed by Soviet arms and Soviet diplomatic support. The United
States had no interest in vindicating such a course.

In the resulting stalemate, the role of the Soviet Union oscillated
between the malign and the confused. Its supply of arms encouraged Arab intransigence. But this achieved no more than to increase
the dangers of the deadlock; it could not remove it. Moscow never
managed to choose among its dilemmas. So long as it one-sidedly
supported all the positions of its Arab clients, it could not advance either the negotiating process or its own role. For we had no motive to
support the program of the Arab radicals who were castigating us; in
the unlikely event that we would change our view, we did not need
the Soviet Union as an intermediary. In other words, Moscow could
contribute effectively to a solution only by dissociating itself to some
extent from Arab demands and thus jeopardizing some of its friend-
ships in the Arab world. But if it did not do so, it risked backing ob-

jectives it could not bring about and thus earning disdain as being impotent. Moscow could stoke the embers of crisis, but once they exploded into conflagration, it could use them for its own ends only by courting a great-power confrontation, something from which the Soviet Union had until then carefully shied away.

Like the other parties, the Soviet Union temporized. It acted as the Arabs' lawyer but could not advance their cause; it bought time through the supply of weapons, but this only escalated the level of possible violence without changing the underlying realities.

There was no American interest in imposing a settlement on Israel under radical pressure, for that would reinforce the conviction that America was best dealt with by extortion. Within the Arab world, we needed to strengthen the moderates as against the radicals, the governments associated with the West as against the clients of the Soviet Union. We therefore refused, as a matter of principle, any concessions to Egypt so long as Nasser (or his successor, Anwar Sadat, for that matter) relied on anti-Western rhetoric, buttressed by the presence of Soviet combat troops. And we saw no point in proceeding jointly with the Soviet Union so long as Moscow's position was identical with the radical Arab program. Sooner or later, we were convinced, either Egypt or some other state would recognize that reliance on Soviet support and radical rhetoric guaranteed the frustration of its aspirations. At that point, it might be willing to eliminate the Soviet military presence—"expel" was the word I used in a much criticized briefing on June 26, 1970—and to consider attainable goals. *Then* would come the moment for a major American initiative, if necessary urging new approaches on our Israeli friends.

In 1970, Nasser died, and Anwar Sadat began to move in that direction, though in an ambiguous way. He continued to rely on Soviet military equipment, while cautiously exploring diplomatic alternatives. In 1971, there was an attempt to bring about a disengagement agreement along the Suez Canal, under the auspices of a U.N. representative, Swedish diplomat Gunnar Jarring. It deadlocked because

Israel saw no benefit in making concessions in the aftermath of the deployment of up to twenty thousand Soviet military "technicians" along the Suez Canal; the United States had no incentive to use pressure, and the Soviets were not prepared to challenge the United States directly.

In 1972, Sadat expelled the Soviet military technicians, after the Soviet failure to achieve diplomatic progress on the Middle East during the Richard M. Nixon–Leonid Brezhnev summit in Moscow. But conditions were still not ripe for a breakthrough. A presidential election in the United States and the need to deal with the conclusion of the Vietnam war precluded progress in 1972. In 1973, there were Israeli elections, and Nixon had committed to Israeli Prime Minister Golda Meir to delay any diplomatic initiatives until after these were held on November 1. Nevertheless, he had made clear that the United States would undertake a major diplomatic effort afterward. In preparation, I met twice with Mohammed Hafiz Ismail, Sadat's security adviser, in 1973, and I also spoke in that vein to Egyptian Foreign Minister Mohamed el-Zayyat on October 5, 1973, the day before the war broke out.

Sadat nevertheless surprised all parties by going to war on October 6, 1973. The surprise was a failure of political analysis. Every American and Israeli assessment before October 1973 had agreed that Egypt and Syria lacked the military capability to regain territory by force of arms. What no one understood at first was that Sadat was aiming not for conquest but to change the equilibrium in negotiations he intended to start. The shock of war, he reasoned, would enable *both* sides, Israel as well as Egypt, to show a flexibility that was impossible while Israel considered itself militarily supreme and Egypt was paralyzed by national humiliation. Separately we reached the same conclusion.

Political assumptions color intelligence estimates. As late as noon on October 5, less than twenty-four hours before the attack, the CIA reported to the President:

It appears that both sides are becoming increasingly concerned about the activities of the other. Rumors and agent reports may be feeding the uneasiness that appears to be developing. The military preparations that have occurred do not indicate that any party intends to initiate hostilities.

Against this background the Middle East War erupted unexpectedly in October 1973.

Setting a Strategy

At 6:15 A.M. on October 6, 1973, I was asleep in my suite at the Waldorf Towers in New York City, my headquarters for the annual session of the United Nations General Assembly, when Joseph J. Sisco, the energetic and brilliant Assistant Secretary of State for Near Eastern and South Asian Affairs, barged into my bedroom. As I forced myself awake, I heard Sisco's gravelly voice insisting that Israel and two Arab countries, Egypt and Syria, were about to go to war. He was confident, however, that it was all a mistake; each side was really misreading the intentions of the other. If I set them right immediately and decisively, I could get matters under control before the shooting began. It was a flattering estimate of my capacities. Unfortunately, it turned out to be exaggerated.

What had triggered Sisco was an urgent message from the United States Ambassador in Israel, former Senator Kenneth Keating. Two hours earlier, Prime Minister Golda Meir had summoned Keating to her office in Tel Aviv. It was extraordinary for an Israeli leader to be at work that day—for it was Yom Kippur, the Day of Atonement, the holiest day of the year for Jews. It is a day spent in fasting, prayer, and reflection; it is supposed to remind man of his insignificance in relation to God and climaxes a High Holy Day season in which, according to tradition, God decides the destiny of all mortals for the coming year.

Golda's startling message was in effect that Israel's encounter with destiny had already begun: "We may be in trouble," she told Keating. Egyptian and Syrian troop movements, which both Israel and the United States had assumed to be simply military exercises, had suddenly taken a threatening turn. Keating reminded her that not twelve hours previously he had been assured by Israeli defense officials that the situation was not dangerous. This was no longer accurate, Mrs. Meir replied; the Israelis were now persuaded that a coordinated Egyptian and Syrian attack would be launched late that afternoon. Since the Arabs were certain to be defeated, she suggested, the crisis must result from their misunderstanding of Israeli intentions. Would the United States convey urgently to the Soviet Union as well as to Israel's Arab neighbors that Israel had no intention of attacking either Egypt or Syria? Israel was calling up "some" reserves, but as a proof of its peaceful intentions was stopping short of general mobilization. Keating asked whether Israel was planning a preemptive strike. Golda emphatically reiterated that Israel wished to avoid bloodshed; it would under no circumstances initiate hostilities.

When Sisco awakened me there were only ninety minutes of peace left for the Middle East. So skillfully had Egypt and Syria masked their war preparations that even at this stage the Israelis expected the attack to come four hours later than the time actually set. I knew that no diplomacy would work if an Arab attack was premeditated. But my view was still colored by the consistent Israeli reports, confirmed by U.S. intelligence dispatches, that such an attack was nearly impossible. I therefore plunged into a frenetic period of intense diplomacy to head off a clash, more than half convinced that Egyptian and Syrian actions grew out of a misunderstanding of Israeli intentions.

My first move was to call Soviet Ambassador Anatoly Dobrynin, as had been requested by the Israeli Prime Minister, obviously waking him up:

SOVIET AMBASSADOR ANATOLY DOBRYNIN–KISSINGER
Saturday, October 6, 1973
6:40 A.M.

K: Where did we get you?

D: At home.

K: Are you in Maryland?

D: I am in the Embassy.

K: We have information from the Israelis that the Arabs and Syrians are planning an attack within the next six hours and that your people are evacuating civilians from Damascus and Cairo.

D: Syrians and who?

K: And Egypt are planning an attack within the next six hours.

D: Yes.

K: And that your people are evacuating some civilians from Damascus and Cairo.

      . . .

D: They asked you to tell us this?

K: They asked us to tell this. I have just received this message from the Israelis.

D: This is what they said?

K: That is correct.

D: [Unable to hear]

K: The Israelis are telling us that Egypt and Syria are planning an attack very shortly and that your people are evacuating from Damascus and Cairo.

D: Yes.

K: If the reason for your evacuation—

D: For our—

K: Yes. The Soviet evacuation, is the fear of an Israeli attack, then the Israelis are asking us to tell you, as well as asking us to tell the Arabs.

D: The Israelis?

K: Yes. They have no plans whatever to attack.

D: Yes.

K: But if the Egyptians and Syrians do attack, the Israeli response will be extremely strong.

D: Yes.

K: But the Israelis will be prepared to cooperate in an easing of military tension.

D: What?

K: Cooperation in an easing of military tension.

D: Yes.

K: All right. From us to you. The President believes that you and we have a special responsibility to restrain our respective friends.

D: Yes.

K: We are urgently communicating to the Israelis.

D: You?

K: Yes.

D: Communicate to the Israelis?

K: If this keeps up, this is going—there is going to be a war before you understand my message.

D: I understand. You have communicated with the Arabs and Israelis.

K: Yes, and particularly to Israel, warning it against a precipitous move.

D: I understand.

K: And we hope you might do the same thing and use your influence to the greatest extent possible with your friends.

D: Just a minute. This is the end of the message?

K: That is right. I would like to tell you as you no doubt—that this is very important for our relationship, that we do not have an explosion in the Middle East right now.

D: What is our relationship?

K: Until an hour ago I did not take it seriously, but we have now received an urgent phone call from Jerusalem saying the Israelis believe it will happen within six hours and they are mobilizing.

D: Who? Israelis? Don't you think the Israelis are trying to do something on their own?

K: If it is, we are telling them not to do it. I cannot judge it. As of yesterday, our evaluation was that the Egyptians and Syrians were making military preparations but we thought [it was] another one of those bluffs. You understand?

D: I understand.

K: As of yesterday, Israelis had made no preparations that we had picked up but as you know they can move fast.

D: I understand and I will transmit this message. I will do it and take all measures necessary.

K: You can assure Moscow we are taking most urgent messages with Israel.

. . .

My next call was to Mordechai Shalev, the Deputy Chief of Mission at the Israeli Embassy in Washington (the Ambassador, Simcha Dinitz, was in Israel for the Jewish holiday).

ISRAELI DEPUTY CHIEF OF MISSION MORDECHAI
SHALEV–KISSINGER
Saturday, October 6, 1973
6:55 A.M.

K: We have a report from Keating [U.S. Ambassador to Israel] that you people are expecting military operations in about six hours.

S: Yes.

K: First of all I must tell you [you] should have come in with your message yesterday. You should not have relied on doing it in Washington when I am here. [The message asked the United States to reassure Egypt and Syria that Israel had no intentions to attack.]

S: I did not have it at that time. They told me you would not be able to see me anymore.

K: You must be kidding. Let's not worry about that.

S: Did you not get the message?

K: Yes, but very late at night.

S: We announced fifteen minutes ago that we have taken precautionary measures and [are] instituting alert of the army, which includes mobilization of some troops.

K: I want to say the following. We are in touch with the Soviets and the Egyptians, urging the utmost restraint. Dobrynin has said they will cooperate with us. We are setting up special communications. We would like to urge you not to take any preemptive action because the situation will get very serious if you move.

S: Yes.

K: If you could communicate this.

S: I will do this immediately.

K: We will keep you informed of any responses and of any conversations we have. You stand by your phone.

Five minutes later, I contacted the Egyptian Foreign Minister, who was in New York.

Egyptian Foreign Minister Mohamed
el-Zayyat–Kissinger
Saturday, October 6, 1973
7:00 A.M.

K: Mr. Foreign Minister, sorry to disturb you. We have had a report, which does seem very reliable, and an appeal from the Israelis to the effect that your forces and the Syrian forces are planning attacks within the next several hours.

Z: Several hours?

K: Yes. We have been in touch with the Israelis. The Israelis have asked us to tell you of the seriousness and that they have no intention of attacking, so that if your preparations are caused by fear of an Israeli attack, they are groundless.

Z: Yes.

K: And on the other hand, if you are going to attack, they will take extremely strong measures. This is a message I am passing to you from Israel. I want to tell you I have just called the Israeli Minister [Deputy Chief of Mission Shalev] and I have told him that if Israel attacks first we would take a very serious view of the situation and have told him on behalf of the United States that Israel must not attack, no matter what they think the provocation is. Now, I would like to ask you, Mr. Foreign Minister, to communicate this to your Government.

Z: I will do that.

K: Urgently. And to ask them on our behalf to show restraint at a time when we are at least beginning to—

Z: I will do this immediately, although I am very apprehensive that this is a pretext on the Israeli part.

K: If it is a pretext, we will take a strong measure against them.

The rest of the conversations, designed to find out what was going on, are self-explanatory. The next call was to my deputy, Brent Scowcroft.

DEPUTY SECURITY ADVISER GENERAL BRENT
SCOWCROFT–KISSINGER
Saturday, October 6, 1973
7:15 A.M.

K: Does Dobrynin have the message in front of him while he is talking [to Moscow]?

S: It is on the way out, but probably has not reached him yet.

K: Are they actually on the way?

S: Yes. I told them.

K: Okay.

OLEG YEDANOV, ASSISTANT TO AMBASSADOR
DOBRYNIN–KISSINGER

Saturday, October 6, 1973
7:25 A.M.

K: I know the Ambassador is talking to Moscow. I want him to have some information. Make sure he does not get off the line until we are through. We have just been given an assurance by Israel that at our request they would not launch a preemptive attack.

Y: Yes. I see.

K: And we would like Moscow to know this, and we would like Moscow to use their influence with Egypt and Syria in this same direction.

Y: Okay.

K: We have assurances behind which we stand.

Y: Yes.

ALFRED L. (ROY) ATHERTON, DEPUTY ASSISTANT
SECRETARY OF STATE FOR NEAR EASTERN AND SOUTH
ASIAN AFFAIRS–KISSINGER

Saturday, October 6, 1973
7:30 A.M.

A: Received a report from Ambassador Keating, speaking to Mrs. Meir a few hours ago. The central thing is she asked that we pass the following message to the Egyptians and to the Soviets: Israel is not planning to attack Syria and Egypt and is deploying its forces in case of foreign attack and on a contingency basis has called up some reserves. Israel is well aware of the militant feeling of the Egyptians and Syrians. If they attack, they will lose, although the attacker can cause damage, which Israel wishes to avoid. Israel will not—repeat not—launch an attack; noting that Israel would successfully defend itself if attacked, she emphasized that the Israeli government wishes to avoid bloodshed.

K: When did we get that?

A: It just arrived on the basis of a meeting the Ambassador had with her at a meeting earlier today.

K: That is the most important part of it. Get it over to Scowcroft right away. And, Roy, can you hush the thing up as tight as we can?

A: Yes, we will do that.

K: And I will get the piece shut up in my shop. Okay, thank you.

FOREIGN MINISTER ZAYYAT–KISSINGER
Saturday, October 6, 1973
7:35 A.M.

K: Sorry to bother you again. I want to keep you informed. I have had a reply from the Israelis to my request not to initiate any military operations. They have given formal assurance they will not launch [an] attack nor initiate military operations. I want to tell you if they break this promise to us we will take the most serious view.

Z: Thank you. This seems like what happened in 1967 [an Israeli preemptive attack on Egypt]. Because Russians were telling us there was a concentration on the frontier.

K: Are the Russians telling of this concentration?

Z: Yesterday someone from the delegation told us that there was concentration on the Syrian front.

K: That is why we should learn from 1967. We now have an Israeli promise they will not launch a preemptive attack and we are giving you all the information we have. We are doing the utmost to get restraint by them.

    . . .

Z: May I ask how you are contacting. Is [Israeli Foreign Minister Abba] Eban here?

K: The Israeli Ambassador in Washington. His communications are better. . . .

    . . .

MINISTER SHALEV–KISSINGER

Saturday, October 6, 1973
7:45 A.M.

K: We have passed the word to the Soviets that you are not planning any preemptive moves, and that we have your assurances. We have certain responsibilities if the Israelis cave.

S: Yes.

K: We are facilitating communications with the Egyptians to Cairo. The Soviets have talked to Moscow on some of our lines.

S: What about the Syrians?

K: We have no means of communicating with them. The Soviets will have to do that. I may send someone to the Syrian Embassy.

S: Good. I have passed on the other message. I am at your disposal.

K: Good. You can be certain you will be informed of all we do.

AMBASSADOR DOBRYNIN–KISSINGER

Saturday, October 6, 1973
7:47 A.M.

D: I have talked to [Soviet Foreign Minister Andrei] Gromyko and I sent your message.

K: Have you seen the messages we gave you?

D: Not yet.

K: Not in your hands?

D: No.

K: If I kill some people and get the bodies to you can you get them out of the city?

D: Ha ha ha.

K: You got the message we have Israeli assurance—no preemptive attack?

D: Yes. I already have passed that along.

K: The messages that are coming to you are overtaken by events.

D: I have already passed your message and Scowcroft's to Moscow.

K: So you are up-to-date. I have talked to the Egyptian Foreign Minister and passed on the Israeli message to him. I have also told him about the Israeli assurance that there would be no preemptive attack and that we will see to it that that is carried out. He told me he would communicate this urgently to Cairo. We have not been in touch with the Syrians. That is the weak point in this situation.

D: I understand.

K: Our influence in Syria is not as good as it is in Jerusalem.

D: I understand.

K: You can pass that on to Moscow in case they don't know it. That is about all we have done.

D: All has been done as you have directed me.

K: Except that we have talked to the Egyptian Foreign Minister about it.

D: You spoke with him on the telephone?

K: He is in New York. We had a good conversation in New York. Yesterday we had a friendly meeting, but inconclusive. As I told you, we are not going to play any games. You will be told what we do. You can reassure Moscow on that point.

COMMANDER JONATHAN HOWE, HANDLING COMMUNICATIONS IN THE SITUATION ROOM–KISSINGER

Saturday, October 6, 1973
7:51 A.M.

K: When I ask you to do something, it must be done that second. We have asked that two messages go to the Soviet Embassy and they have not gotten there yet.

H: I will look into it.

K: Get these people off their behinds. What conceivable reason [is there] not to have them sent there yet?

H: I don't know unless they have to be sanitized.

K: That is a Xerox problem, as I understand it.

H: I will take care of it.

K: I want them there and in their hands and a report back.

Foreign Minister Zayyat–Kissinger
Saturday, October 6, 1973
8:15 A.M.

Z: I could not get the President. He is in operations room. I got this following information: At 6:00 this morning there was some navy units and airplane units—Israelis took [i.e., instigated] some provocation on the Egyptian borders. We have actually tried to repel them and are doing so.

K: Did they try to cross the Canal?

Z: In the Gulf of Suez; a maritime action supported by planes. This is in our territory. It is far away from the Syrian borders and the Suez Canal. There is a first communiqué which has been published.

K: Are these Israeli naval units?

Z: He said naval action supported by planes. I don't know exactly. I have asked for more information. Apparently this military contact is happening in Egyptian waters in Zafara and Sukhna. Far from the Suez Canal. South of Canal.

K: Okay.

Z: I see from the Israelis here, [they] are calling a meeting of Foreign Ministers.

K: As I told you, we will oppose any Israeli offensive action [or] by anyone else.

Z: I got your message.

K: I will work on this immediately. I would urge [you] in the meantime to show restraint as much as possible and to confine any action to the place where it has started.

Z: Inside Egypt is a bit difficult.

K: If inside Egypt, of course, you will want to repel, and we are not urging not to defend your territory but to try to confine, and we will get to [the] Israelis immediately. We will set up, if you want to, we will arrange communications to Cairo if you want to get in touch immediately.

Z: I have told them. What kind of communications?

K: Commander Howe will call you or call one of your assistants and tell you how to have very quick communications.

Z: He should call our Ambassador Meguid [Ahmed Esmat Abdel Meguid, Egyptian permanent representative to the United Nations].

K: We will contact him and tell him how to get fast communications. Give my warm regards, and we will do what we can.

ISRAELI FOREIGN MINISTER ABBA EBAN–KISSINGER
Saturday, October 6, 1973
8:25 A.M.

K: . . . Are you aware of the message given to us last night?

E: Yes. I received a message to the effect of this and what we fear they may be up to, both in the North and South. Three hours ago, I was told to stand by and there would be further details.

K: I want to bring you up-to-date on what I have done this morning. I received a call at 6:00 this morning from Ambassador Keating that he had been told there were these authentic reports and urging us to use our influence. I called first the Russians and told them to use maximum restraint and we established communications for them to Moscow. I have called the Egyptian Foreign Minister and urged maximum restraint on him. We received a message from the [Israeli] Prime Minister through Ambassador Keating, in which she assured him the Israelis were taking [i.e., mounting] no preemptive attacks. I passed this along to the Egyptians, as well as to the Soviets, and told them this was our very urgent recommendation to the Israelis and we were happy to have these assurances and in these circumstances even greater restraint is needed. We set up communications for the Egyptians to Cairo. He [Foreign Minister Zayyat] has talked to Ismail [Mohammed Hafiz Ismail, Sadat's security adviser]. He tells me [about a] naval action in the Gulf of Suez. If that is the case, it would be very unfortunate; it is inside Egyptian waters.

E: What is the naval action?

K: Shooting. Israelis—air and naval attacks. Given the urgency of the situation, I thought I should talk to you about it. If your people are doing this, they will know where it is. I must urge you strongly not to have any Israeli operations in these circumstances.

E: That surprises me. We have assurances of no preemptive attacks. Where can I reach you?

K: You can reach me at the Waldorf. If those [lines] are busy, call the White House.

. . .

MINISTER SHALEV–KISSINGER
Saturday, October 6, 1973
8:29 A.M.

S: Just had a call from Jerusalem that while Cabinet was in session news was received that hostilities were opened by the Egyptians and by the Syrians. Apparently mainly by aerial bombardment along the borders.

K: I have had a call from the Egyptians saying you were undertaking naval actions on the Gulf of Suez on the Egyptian side.

S: Well, I don't know about that.

K: It has not in the past been your preferred method of operations.

S: No.

K: It is not how in the past you have started things. What are you doing?

S: I presume we are taking care about that.

K: Again I would like to urge the greatest possible restraint.

S: I think you have assurances from us that we are not going to open, but it looks that they have already opened.

K: Do you know what has happened?

S: No. This whole thing started only twenty minutes ago.

K: Will you please keep me informed?

S: I will do so.

I next spoke with General Alexander Haig, Nixon's Chief of Staff, who was with the President in Key Biscayne.

GENERAL ALEXANDER HAIG, WHITE HOUSE
CHIEF OF STAFF–KISSINGER

Saturday, October 6, 1973
8:35 A.M.

K: We may have a Middle East war going on today.

H: Really?

K: I want you to know what is happening. I am sending a report to the President and to you of the events this morning. We got a report at 6:00 this morning that Israelis were expecting Syrian and Egyptian attack within six hours.

H: Yes.

K: First I thought it was an Israeli trick for them to be able to launch an attack although this is the holiest day. I called the Israelis and warned them to restrain. I called the Egyptian Foreign Minister urging restraint. I called Dobrynin. I gave all of our communications to Dobrynin and he called Moscow. I got a return call from the Israelis giving us assurances that no preemptive Israeli [action] would be taken. The Egyptians called me back to say Israelis were launching a naval attack in the Gulf of Suez and fifteen minutes later a call came from the Israelis saying that the Egyptians and Syrians were bombarding all along the front and launching air attacks. Now, it is not conceivable that the Israelis would launch an attack with [a] single action in the Gulf of Suez. That has to be the prediction and all I want you to know is that we are on top of it here. You should say that the President was kept informed from 6:00 A.M. on and I will let you know what is going on.

H: Have there been any border crossings?

K: As of this moment I just know of a report from Jerusalem relayed to me by the Israeli minister—air attacks all along the Egyptian and Syrian fronts. I don't know what [the] Israeli counteraction is. I have a report from the Egyptians that Israeli naval units are shelling them in the Gulf of Suez and they will be driving them off.

H: What is your view of the Soviet attitude?

K: My view is that they are trying to keep it quiet and they are surprised.

H: Do you believe that?

K: Yes. I think it is too insane for them to have started it.

H: You never know. A lot of difficulties here [refers to imminent resignation of Vice President Spiro T. Agnew].

K: That is the one factor. I think our domestic situation [i.e., Watergate] has invited this. I think what may have happened is the Soviets told the Egyptians . . . that there will not be any progress unless there is stirring in the Middle East and those maniacs have stirred a little too much. It looks to me now that the Israelis are certainly going to hit back hard. They have already partially mobilized. Probably, I will be going back to Washington and will decide in a few hours. I am having Scowcroft call a WSAG [Washington Special Action Group] meeting. We are locating the Sixth Fleet. No two ships are in any one place. It will probably take us a week to round up the sailors. We will have to move it by tomorrow if something is going on.

H: Okay, Henry.

K: Don't let [presidential press secretary Ron] Ziegler shoot off at the mouth without our knowledge. Your position is that the President is on top of the situation and getting regular reports from the U.N. [New York] this morning. We have nothing further to say. If there are any announcements to be made I will check with you as to whether they should be made from here or the White House.

H: I will say the President received a report at 6:00.

K: Say 6:30. Say I have been in contact with all of these people, and we will give no comment. We have sent [a] message to Saudi Arabia and Jordan and urged them to restrain.

H: Okay.

K: You stay near the phone. If you are with the President, tell the switchboard to put me through.

UNITED NATIONS SECRETARY GENERAL
KURT WALDHEIM–KISSINGER

Saturday, October 6, 1973
8:40 A.M.

K: Mr. Secretary General, I wanted to report to you about some events that have happened this morning that may conceivably get out of control. I received a call at 6:00 this morning from our Ambassador in Jerusalem that the Israelis believed that an attack by Egypt and Syrian forces was imminent, and since then I have been on the phone with the Israeli Foreign Minister [and] with the Egyptian Foreign Minister several times to urge maximum restraint on all parties, and I have received word from the Israelis that they would not launch preemptive action. The Egyptians called back and said there was an Israeli naval attack taking place in the Gulf of Suez—which was not the usual method of Israeli attack. As soon as I hung up from that, I received a message from the Israelis that Egyptian and Syrian air attacks were going on all along the fronts. No troops had yet crossed, at least. This is what I know as of this moment and I just wanted to talk to you and express our cooperation that we are attempting to establish.

W: Thank you very much.

K: I don't know what action is called for yet. I think we should try to calm the situation as much as possible, but it may get out of hand. What would be helpful [would be] if you could contact the Syrians before you contact the Egyptians.

W: I was sitting next to the Syrian Executive Minister and the Foreign Minister yesterday, but they did not say anything about this.

K: I was sitting next to the Egyptian Foreign Minister yesterday, but he did not say anything.

. . .

FOREIGN MINISTER EBAN–KISSINGER

Saturday, October 6, 1973
8:50 A.M.

E: I got a message a quarter of an hour ago at least that the Syrians attacked at two o'clock with artillery and bombs in Golan and Schmona—from Syria then—and the next news was that the Egyptians also [mounted] an air attack at a place called [unclear] in Sinai, and [made] attempts to cross the Canal.

K: Do you have any reports on your reactions yet?

E: No, this was the first news I got.

K: I have a report from the Egyptians alleging that you started everything with a naval attack near Syria near some oil fields.

E: We have nothing on that.

K: I don't myself believe that you would start a general war with a naval attack in one place, but you always do surprising things. Could you get me the facts?

E: They said the first move was a naval attack?

K: They claim the first move—

E: South of the Suez?

K: South of the Canal. The Egyptian Foreign Minister called me and gave me a name but it was an Arabic name. If you were attacking some place, you presumably knew where it was.

E: Yes. That is not at all convincing. The news preceding this— there was a very wild exodus of Soviets from [Syria]. Do you have that?

K: I have my news and I have called it to the attention of the Soviets.

. . .

GENERAL SCOWCROFT–KISSINGER

Saturday, October 6, 1973
8:50[?] A.M.

. . .

S: Have you talked to the President?

K: Yes. Have you gotten the messages to Dobrynin?

S: Yes. The messages are with him. There is a WSAG meeting in two minutes.

K: Tell them to stay quiet. Any discussion will be from Key Biscayne or [State Department spokesman Robert] McCloskey. Put the fleet into position; if we want them to move, they can move; and find out how long to get them together. What reinforcements are available. Get a plan from [Chairman of the Joint Chiefs of Staff Admiral Thomas] Moorer by noon to see what we can move if this gets out of hand and tell DOD [Department of Defense] to shut up about military moves or anything. If they need a presidential order, I will get one for them in writing.

S: Right. I have told DOD and CIA that.

K: CIA is no problem but tell the Chiefs also. From Moorer find out what forces are available for movement throughout the Atlantic and how quickly it could be done.

S: These two carriers probably cannot get the troops back since this is a weekend.

K: Find out by noon how long it will take. Also what additional forces are available. No one is to move anything, but they should get ready to move. I would not call troops back until noon. They should get themselves in a position to do it if they get the order.

MINISTER SHALEV–KISSINGER

Saturday, October 6, 1973
9:00 A.M.

S: The latest I have is, there is a full-scale battle along the Canal with the Egyptians trying to cross in our direction. They have bombed various places in Sinai. The story about a naval battle is a cover-up for their action.

K: Right. I need as many facts as you can give me on the naval battle, even if it did not take place. I am quite persuaded, Mr. Minister. It is clear the dominant action is in the Canal and along the

Golan Heights. We would appreciate as much information as possible.

S: I am passing along all that I get. I will pass it directly to you.

K: Good. I have not decided whether to stay up here or go to Washington. I will probably go to Washington during the day. You will be kept informed.

S: Thank you.

FOREIGN MINISTER EBAN–KISSINGER
Saturday, October 6, 1973
9:07 A.M.

E: The P.M. asked me to tell you that the story of naval action by us at the Gulf of Suez is false. Her Hebrew vocabulary is very rich and she poured it out. I asked about our action so far. Our reaction so far has been defensive. I presume this means going on within our area.

K: Are you going to the Security Council?

E: She asked me to wait a little, but inform the Secretary General.

K: What is your view about going to the Security Council?

E: I will ask that. It is not unreasonable. If we did so, I think a point for us. I have recommended it and, if accepted, we should be the injured party.

K: You recommend that we do not do it.

E: So long as there is a possibility of our doing it quickly, I think it a more natural course.

K: Could you let me know? Find out about that.

E: Certainly.

SECRETARY GENERAL WALDHEIM–KISSINGER
Saturday, October 6, 1973
9:12 A.M.

W: I wanted to give you the latest information we got from our observer units. There is fighting in all sectors. The Egyptian ground forces have crossed the Canal in five places. The impression we have is, this is really a rather big-scale operation, and it goes on to say the Syrian forces have crossed lines near and south of Kanetra. This is about the cable we got a few minutes ago.

K: Thank you very much. I appreciate it and we will reciprocate by letting you know anything we learn.

By the time of my conversation with Waldheim, the Washington Special Action Group (WSAG) had met at 9:00 A.M. (This was the crisis management group of the Nixon administration, chaired by the National Security Adviser and comprising the Deputy Secretaries of State and Defense, the Director of the Central Intelligence Agency, and the Chairman of the Joint Chiefs of Staff. Brent Scowcroft acted for me while I was in New York.) Even with the information available at the time, the participants found it impossible to alter the preconceptions with which they entered the crisis:

> We [the intelligence agencies] can find no hard evidence of a major, coordinated Egyptian/Syrian offensive across the Canal and in the Golan Heights area. Rather, the weight of evidence indicates an action-reaction situation where a series of responses by each side to perceived threats created an increasingly dangerous potential for confrontation. The current hostilities are apparently a result of that situation, although we are not in a position to clarify the sequence of events. It is possible that the Egyptians or Syrians, particularly the latter, may have been preparing a raid or other small-scale action.

There was no dissent. There was also no explanation of how Syria and Egypt could have been triggered into a simultaneous attack on fronts over two hundred miles apart by the "action-reaction" cycle. CIA Director William Colby reported without disagreement that, according to Damascus radio, Israel had launched the attack. Defense Secretary James Schlesinger commented that while Syria's reputation for veracity was not high, it would be the first time in twenty years that Israel had *not* started a Mideast war: "I just don't see any motive on the Egyptian-Syrian side." Admiral Moorer thought that Israel might have attacked in order to preempt the introduction of more sophisticated air defense equipment in Egypt and Syria. Only Alfred L. (Roy) Atherton, Sisco's deputy, challenged the consensus: "This is the last day in the year when they [the Israelis] would have started something. And there were no signs of advance Israeli preparations."

I had resolved any doubts about what was happening, as is shown by the following telephone conversation with Dobrynin.

AMBASSADOR DOBRYNIN–KISSINGER
Saturday, October 6, 1973
9:20 A.M.

K: Our information is that the Egyptians and Syrians have attacked all along their fronts and also—

D: Is it the Canal?

K: The Canal and the Golan Heights. Zayyat is claiming the Israelis launched a naval attack on some isolated spot in the Gulf of Suez and that triggered the whole thing.

D: I saw on a ticker, they claim that Israel began [the] attack. Zayyat told you.

K: He told me not along the Canal but in the Gulf of Suez. We are all going to have to be taking formal positions. You and I know that is baloney; if they are going to attack, they will not launch an attack in the Gulf of Suez and not at the key points. Not their style.

D: I understand.

K: How is it that the Syrians and Egyptians are starting at the same minute—all along the front? If it started with an Israeli naval attack, you and I are having a problem in how to get this stopped. We are using our maximum influence with the Israelis to show restraint. So far they tell me they have kept their response to their side of the line and that they have not made any deep penetration of Arab territory. But you know them as well as I do, and it [Israeli restraint] will not last much longer.

D: Okay. I will send additional message to Moscow. Really madness.

K: Total madness. I will probably come back to Washington during the day and we should meet urgently. We should, I think, use this occasion to, first, not to have everything we have achieved destroyed by maniacs on either side and, after quieting it down, to see what can be done constructively.

D: All right. Thank you very much.

THE PRESIDENT, RICHARD M. NIXON–KISSINGER

Saturday, October 6, 1973
9:25 A.M.

N: Hello, Henry. I wanted you to know I am keeping on top of reports here. The Russians claim to be surprised.

K: The Russians claim to be surprised and my impression is that they were supposed to be surprised, because apparently there has been an airlift of dependents out of the area going on for the last two or three days.

N: I agree.

K: And so our impression is that they knew about it, or knew it was possible. They did not warn us.

N: What is happening now? What is the status?

K: Fighting has broken out on the Golan Heights and along the Sinai. The Egyptians claim that the Israelis had launched a naval attack in the Gulf of Suez which triggered the whole thing. That I just can't believe. Why a naval attack? The Israelis claim that so far the fighting is still mostly in Israeli territory and that they have confined themselves to defensive action. My own impression is that this one almost certainly was started by the Arabs. It is almost inconceivable that the Israelis would start on the holiest holiday for the Jews, when there is no need to, and there is no evidence that the Israelis launched air attacks, and they gave us an assurance—which we passed on this morning—that they would not launch a preemptive attack, and we told the Arabs that if the Israelis launch a preemptive attack we would oppose them and they should exercise restraint. My view is that the primary problem is to get the fighting stopped and then use the opportunity to see whether a settlement could be enforced.

N: You mean a diplomatic settlement of the bigger problem [the overall Middle East crisis]?

K: That is right. There is going to be a Security Council meeting almost certainly today and we are still debating whether we should call it or the Israelis should. Somebody has to call it in the next hour.

N: I think we should. We ought to take the initiative. Can't we get the Russians to? I think we ought to take the initiative and you ought to indicate you talked to me.

K: Let me call Dobrynin right away on that. In the debate there are going to be a lot of wild charges all over the place.

N: Don't take sides. Nobody ever knows who starts the wars out there.

K: There are two problems. . . . The long term, I think it is impossible now to keep maintaining the status quo ante. On the immediate thing, we have to avoid getting the Soviets drawn in on the side of the Arab group. If they join us in a neutral approach, in which both of us say we don't know who started it but that we want to stop it, that would be best—if they make a defense on the part of the Arabs. But first we ought to see if they will join us in a neutral approach—that will be the best.

N: Let me know what develops.

K: We have sent you a report an hour ago, but that is already overtaken. I may return to Washington today.

N: Okay, thank you.

AMBASSADOR DOBRYNIN–KISSINGER

Saturday, October 6, 1973
9:35 A.M.

K: I have just talked to the President and he asked me to make the following suggestion to you. There will be undoubtedly a Security Council meeting today, don't you think?

D: I think so. Because the situation is very dangerous.

K: We would be prepared to take a neutral position in the Council as to the facts of the matter asking that we don't know who started what but we are in favor of [the] status quo ante.

D: Your suggestion is restoration of [the 1967] cease-fire line [that is, the prewar line].

K: Restoration of the cease-fire line and restoration of cease-firing and then have a fact-finding commission. We are prepared to proceed with the discussions which [Soviet Foreign Minister Andrei] Gromyko and I and the President agreed on on the settlement.

D: Outside the Security Council?

K: Yes.

D: Just between us?

K: Right. We are willing to look at the whole situation. Now if you take the position that you will have to defend the Arabs, we will be forced into the position of defending what we believe—of making clear we believed the Arabs launched the attack and we are then in a hell of a mess. It will affect a lot of our relationships.

D: I understand.

K: Moscow's constructive approach would be if we both took the position of not [having] the time to discuss who started what. Let's get the fighting stopped and restore the cease-fire line and call on all parties to observe the cease-fire line.

D: I think it is a constructive way to start.

K: We will hold up anything until we hear from you. Can you get us a quick answer?

. . .

U.N. Minuet

A war had clearly broken out. But the United Nations organ designed to help maintain peace or to restore it was passive. The reluctance of its officials to be involved matched the reluctance of the parties to have the United Nations adopt a position. But as the war continued, the issue was bound to move to the United Nations, if only to ratify an outcome. This raised two issues: the appropriate forum, and the tactics within it. As to the forum, there were two choices: the General Assembly and the Security Council. We did not want the General Assembly as a forum because the Nonaligned (a group of some eighty nations) would support the Arab side, the Europeans would be at best ambivalent, and the Soviet bloc would have no choice but to go along with the majority of the developing nations even if the Soviet Union did not lead the charge. Thus, a balanced outcome would be next to impossible. The composition of the Security Council would produce a better opportunity and, in any case, we had the veto. Our strategy—as reflected in the 9:25 A.M. conversation with Nixon—was to use the then prevailing policy of détente to seek a joint approach with the Soviet Union. This was to prevent the Soviet Union from emerging as the spokesman for the Arab side, isolating us in the Islamic world, and dividing us from Europe. Above all, it would also gain time to permit the military situation to clarify, since we were still convinced that we would soon have to deal with the political consequences of a rapid Israeli victory.

Sir Laurence McIntyre, President of the United Nations Security Council–Kissinger

Saturday, October 6, 1973
10:08 A.M.

K: I wanted to talk to you about our general state of knowledge of the Middle East problem, as you undoubtedly know.

M: Yes.

K: We received an urgent call this morning from our Ambassador in Israel that they thought an attack might be imminent and they were asking us to use our influence and also to assure other interested parties they would not make a preemptive attack. We did that and I called the Egyptian Foreign Minister and the Soviet Ambassador, etc. Events seem to have overtaken us. Now we are consulting with various parties and seeing what time is best for a Security Council meeting. We will keep you informed about whatever conclusions we reach. We would be grateful for any conclusions you reach. We would like to get a sense of what would emerge in a Security Council meeting before we go into one. I am speaking to you very frankly about what we are doing.

M: Thank you very much indeed. I might mention to you that the Israeli permanent representative has called me not to ask for a meeting but to simply give me an outline of what happened as he understands it and, too, he told me he had been speaking to your mission here and that some consulting was going on and he promised to keep me informed likewise of anything that developed. That is where we stand. I have not heard anything from the Egyptians or other Arab representatives.

K: I had a brief talk with the Secretary General to bring him up to date on what we have done. Of course, we believe this is a Security Council matter and not a General Assembly matter.

M: Yes. Where are you speaking from?

K: From the Waldorf. Where I was preparing a speech devoted to peace on earth—if you would like to make some suggestions as to appropriate themes.

M: I shall think about it.

K: It does not have my undivided attention. One thing I did want to say is, if there is a meeting and when there is we will do our utmost and we would appreciate any help we could get to keep it at as high a level as obtainable and avoid any cheap shots. You appreciate this situation, which is fraught with exaggeration and we are trying to avoid that.

. . .

SECRETARY GENERAL WALDHEIM–KISSINGER
Saturday, October 6, 1973
10:22 A.M.

W: I wanted to tell you the following. We got confirmation from our observers in the Middle East saying about what you told me, that there is heavy fighting along the Egyptian and Syrian lines. There is no fighting along the Jordanian lines. They indicated they would send more detailed reports as soon as they get more information from our observers. I had a conversation with [Egyptian Foreign Minister] Zayyat and he is asking for a General Assembly meeting to be convened. I told him that I doubted if it could be—technically—done. I doubt if we could convene so quickly. I asked him about requesting a meeting of the Security Council. For the time being he has no instructions but will send a document to us and ask for circulating of these documents.

K: Our view is that it should go to the Security Council first.

W: Exactly. I don't think the General Assembly has a chance. It is not technically possible before Monday. I do feel it is a matter for the Security Council. I asked him [Zayyat] this question and he said he had no instructions with this regard. I expressed my deep concern and told him they should do everything to calm down the situation. He got rather angry and said, "We don't attack. The others do," and so on.

K: Our information—our impression—is the opposite. For your personal information, and do not share it with others, we are talking with the Soviets to see if we can develop a common approach in the Security Council. Until we have that, I think if there could be a slight delay if anyone pushes for a meeting which has not been the case yet, until we get the Soviet reaction if we are dragging our feet a little bit, it is to get the Soviet reaction. I understand no one has asked.

W: Nobody.

K: Our point is [the] peace and security issue and it belongs in the Security Council, and a General Assembly meeting would be frivolous and we would oppose it.

W: I rather discouraged Zayyat.

K: We would oppose it even on Monday. I want to make that clear.

W: I'm glad you are telling me.

K: We are trying to come up with a constructive Security Council meeting, and for your personal information, what we are trying to do is to see if a common approach could be developed with the Soviets for restoration of a cease-fire and the cease-fire lines. If that can be done, someone would call a Security Council meeting.

W: That would be the best approach. Hope it works. If there is any question, I will call you.

K: If you call me—and this would give the two governments a chance to concert their action.

W: Right. I think it important to keep in close contact. Don't you think the Soviets would be afraid to do that because of their relations with the Arabs?

K: They also have to worry if they are afraid of their relations with us.

W: I think the approach very good and I hope for the common approach.

K: Again, speaking privately, my estimate is the same as yours that they will not agree to it.

W: I know from my experience they are very much interested in not doing anything which would create the impression that they are working against the Arabs; or doing anything that would make their relations with the Arabs negative.

K: I think it is so important to try that we should give it a chance. So far no one has asked for a meeting, and we will not ask for one until we have the Soviet reply. If you can avoid it—I know your position. If you can delay a meeting until we have had a Soviet reply; if anyone should ask—

. . .

GENERAL HAIG–KISSINGER
Saturday, October 6, 1973
10:35 A.M.

K: I wanted to bring you up-to-date on where we stand and to tell you my strategy. You may have to calm some people down.

H: Good. I am sitting with the President.

K: Okay. The Egyptians have crossed the Canal at five places and the Syrians have penetrated in two places into the Golan Heights. This we get from the U.N. observers. Our assessment here is re the facts; it is inconceivable that the Israelis' attack [had there been one] would turn in two hours and have the Egyptians crossing the Canal.

H: No question about that.

K: Inconceivable. We have to assume an Arab attack.

H: I think the President feels that way.

K: The open question is, is it with Soviet collusion or against Soviet opposition. On that we have no answer yet. I have called, first, as far as our public position [is concerned], the Secretary General, who leaks like a sieve, to tell him about all of the efforts we have made and I have told him that I have been in touch with the Soviets. I have been in touch with Dobrynin and said we should jointly call a Security Council [meeting]. The Soviets and we. And we jointly offer a resolution calling for an end of the fighting and return to the cease-fire lines established in 1967. I have told them this would be a sign of good faith towards both of us and we would hold up calling for a Security Council [meeting] until we hear from them. I have informed the Secretary General of that.

The Soviets said they would get an answer from Moscow. This is designed in part to smoke them out. If they want the fighting stopped, this will stop it fast. If they refuse to do this, then we have to assume some collusion. Now, if they refuse to do it, we have two problems. The first is to get the fighting stopped and the second is the long-term policy. In order to get the fighting stopped we cannot give the Soviets and the Arabs the impression that we are separating too far from the Israelis. That will keep it going.

H: Right.

K: Therefore, as to the facts of the issue, if the Soviets could cooperate with us, we will take a neutral position. We will say we don't know the facts but they should stop fighting. You see what I mean?

H: Right.

K: If the Soviets do not cooperate with us and wholeheartedly back the Arabs on the immediate issue of the fighting we, in my judgment, have to lean toward the Israelis.

H: Right.

K: For these reasons: 1) In order to get the fighting stopped; 2) to prevent the Soviets from coming in at least with bluster and get a cheap shot; and 3) to put some money in the bank with the disassociation with the Israelis in subsequent efforts to get a settlement. All depends now on the Soviet reaction. Then after we get the fighting stopped, we should use this crisis as a vehicle to get the diplomacy started. Now there is no longer an excuse for a delay. The return to the cease-fire will have two aspects. If today the problem means the Arabs would have to give up a little territory—my estimate is that starting tomorrow evening the [Arabs] will have to give up territory [as a result of military defeat]. My view is if the Israelis make territorial acquisitions we have to come down hard on them to force them to give them up. You see.

H: Yes.

K: We have to do that in case of the Arabs but I think it is an embarrassment we won't have very long.

H: Yes. Unless we have had a terrible erosion there.

K: That is the strategy that I am proposing. I think we have no choice. I think the worst thing we could do is to now take a sort of neutral position while the fighting is going on, unless the Soviets take a neutral position with us. If they take one with us, we should take a neutral position. That is ideal. If they don't join us and go to the other side, we have to tilt.

. . .

K: If the Soviets are all out on the other side we have a mischievous case of collusion and then we have September 1970 [when the Soviet ally Syria invaded Jordan] all over again and we had better then be tough as nails.

H: The President is seriously considering going back to Washington.

K: I think that a grave mistake. There is nothing we can do right now. You should wait to see how it develops. Wait until at least this afternoon. So far not even a Security Council meeting has been called.

H: He agrees with that. His problem is if it is an all-out war for him to be sitting down here in this climate would be very, very bad.

K: Let's wait for the Soviet answer. If the Soviets refuse to cooperate with us, we will know we are in a confrontation and he should then take leadership.

. . .

K: You will make sure that the President is comfortable with this strategy. I think it is our only possible course and it has to be seen in the general context of his ability to act and of what follows afterwards.

H: Is there any effort to get the fleet in a decent posture? The President is concerned about that.

K: That is right. The fleet has been instructed into a position just short of calling them back to ship. They are to locate their people and move on several hours' notice.

H: He does want them assembled as soon as possible for appropriate action if needed.

K: That is being done but we wanted to wait until reports are confirmed and that will be issued within the hour. They need that much time to locate their people.

H: I will be back after discussing it with the President.

Several telephone calls implementing the strategy followed.

MINISTER SHALEV–KISSINGER
Saturday, October 6, 1973
10:55 A.M.

S: The Prime Minister wants to give you a personal assurance on the basis of the trust that exists between you and her that the attacks were initiated by others.

K: That is our assessment too and I have just said this to the President.

S: About the specific questions of a naval engagement the Egyptians talked about, there is no truth to that at all.

K: I cannot believe that you would start a naval engagement and have the Arabs cross the Suez Canal.

S: She will go on the radio in just a few minutes.

K: I want to inform you on a personal basis only for the Prime Minister that we have proposed to the Soviets that we jointly call—the U.S. and the Soviets—a Security Council meeting and [for a] return to the cease-fire lines. [This is] an attempt to smoke them out to see if they were behind it and give us a basis for leaning towards your position in the actual debate. This is only for the Prime Minister.

S: I will pass that on. You have had no reply on that?

K: No. I will call you the minute I get a reply.

S: One thing, I wish to raise—our military people have submitted a list of urgent items that they need very much in a hurry.

K: I am coming back tonight and we had better discuss that in person.

SENATOR JACOB JAVITS (R.-N.Y.)–KISSINGER
Saturday, October 6, 1973
11:01 A.M.

J: Quite a Yom Kippur. What is your report?

K: My personal estimate, which I don't want you to repeat—it is clearly an Arab attack. . . .

J: What do you think brought this to a boil this way?

K: What we have to determine now, Jack, is whether there was Soviet collusion or not. We have offered the Soviets joint action in the Security Council to restore the cease-fire and the cease-fire lines with approval of the Israelis. This should smoke them out.

J: All will be nullified if these fellows—if they make any effort.

K: The resolution is to return to the cease-fire line.

J: I know the diplomatic thing would work that way but all could be very, very sharply affected if the Arabs have any success. It will be very hard to deal with them.

K: Our estimate is that unless the Israelis were totally surprised, which is not impossible because of Yom Kippur, they would be in their lowest posture ever.

. . .

J: Has the President had any reaction?

K: I have talked with him and if he agrees that [if] it looks like Soviet collusion, we have to do September 1970 again [when the United States organized resistance to the Syrian invasion of Jordan]. If there is Soviet collusion, we will come down hard. If they pull away from the Arabs we will pull away and stay neutral from them. We are assuming that the Israelis can take care of themselves. If that is wrong, we have to go back to the drawing board.

J: What I have heard did not make me very happy.

K: We are keeping in closest touch with the Israelis. We are not making a move without discussing it with them.

Ambassador Dobrynin–Kissinger
Saturday, October 6, 1973
11:25 A.M.

K: I am checking about the Security Council. I was told that the Egyptians asked for the General Assembly meeting. But it is impossible to get the General Assembly until Monday and in any event it is a threat to the peace and security and we will not have it in the General Assembly.

D: I understand.

K: It is a grievous suggestion. We cannot accept it.

D: I understand.

K: I have talked to the President again and he wanted me to call you and to underline again his very grave concern that this not be used to destroy everything that it has taken us three years to build up.

D: By whom?

K: By any of us.

D: Who, really?

K: If you take the position of support all out for the Arabs, that would be in effect encouraging what seems clearly to us an Arab attack; no one in their right mind believes that the Egyptians could have crossed the Canal in five places. I would be glad to have your military analysis on that part. Since all of the fighting [is] on Israel territory, I think the facts are clear. We are prepared before the Security Council to take a neutral position if you do and we are prepared to make a joint resolution just calling for [a return to the] cease-fire line.

D: I understand and I have sent that.

K: Today the Arabs are on Israeli territory but we don't believe this will last seventy-two hours and after that the problem will be to get the Israelis back to the cease-fire line. If we agree on this course, no matter what the military operations, no matter how successful the Israelis may be, we will stick to this proposal and we will be prepared to oppose them.

D: As you say, back to the cease-fire line. I understand.

K: Right.

D: This is essentially what you mentioned.

K: We have not responded to an urgent Israeli request for additional military supplies. If it gets out of hand, we will be forced to do that. For all of these reasons it will be important to our own relationship that it be handled as much jointly as we can and you should say this to the Secretary General on behalf of the President—he just got through talking to me. I am coming back to Washington this afternoon and I will be in touch with you then.

D: Okay.

K: The reason I am hopeful we will settle it is that you did not leave town.

D: If I did not receive your call until 9:00, I would have gone today. We planned to take quite a nice dinner at our Maryland estate and we were leaving for vacation. You see how it happens. I hope we can handle it.

K: Your Arab friends were terribly deceitful. Zayyat told me there would be at least the three months of quiet and he would meet me again in November and he wanted to come to Washington next week and, since our conversations and the President's conversation with Gromyko, we thought we had this time period to make a reasonable approach.

D: My impression too.

K: We are taking this matter extremely seriously. If you will let your colleagues know, we would appreciate it—as quickly as possible.

SIR DONALD MAITLAND, BRITISH AMBASSADOR TO THE
UNITED NATIONS–KISSINGER

Saturday, October 6, 1973
11:35 A.M.

K: I just received your message about your views on the Security Council. I wanted you to know that we have approached the Soviets to take with us a joint position asking them [the combatants] to return to the cease-fire line and a cease-fire and to take a neutral position.

M: Absolutely.

K: We wonder if you would agree, until we have heard from the Soviets, that we try to defer a meeting.

M: I see the argument.

K: There is one problem in our mind. As we do establish the facts, it may be more difficult to get that kind of resolution. There seems to be no question in our mind that the Arabs started this one.

M: Quite likely. Our government without cutting across any consultations or any bilaterals outside—

K: Our proposal is to do it in the Security Council. Our feeling is while we are doing this, if we could show ourselves in business and call for a cease-fire and return to the original line and go into recess to allow our real work to go on.

M: I am not sure the Soviets will go along with that. But when were you thinking of doing this?

K: We felt we should not let today pass.

M: I agree on this.

K: We are not rushing into anything this morning. I was thinking about something in the course of the afternoon.

M: I am in agreement with you on that if you could say—

K: I am trying to get back to Washington and I am trying to get a quiet two hours in which to do it. As a general proposition if you felt inclined, say two or three o'clock, to call for a meeting, [that] would not sound unreasonable to us.

M: That is what we had in mind.

K: We wanted a couple more hours today.

M: I would not interfere with that. We felt it would be wrong for the world to know these large-scale operations do go on and we have not shown our heads.

K: No problem with us on that.

. . .

Minister Shalev–Kissinger

Saturday, October 6, 1973
11:55 A.M.

K: I have talked to the President again and to the Soviets. I want you to know what we are doing. We are getting our fleet together in the Mediterranean and [will] start moving it toward the eastern Mediterranean. This will take us about twelve hours. . . . We will almost certainly approve tomorrow the military equipment within reason that you may need, especially if the Soviets line up with the Arabs; then we will certainly do it.

S: You will do it.

K: If the Soviets line up in the U.N. with the Arabs, we will surely do it, and if not, we will probably do it, but we just want to see. But we would appreciate from you as much of the true military situation as you feel you can give us so we can make our evaluations, and also any plans you may have. We are going to propose when there is a Security Council meeting, whether or not the Soviets agree, that there should be a restoration of the cease-fire and a restoration of the cease-fire lines.

S: And you are doing that irrespective of their agreement or not.

K: We will wait a few hours to get their agreement. If not, we have concerted with the British and they will call a meeting and we will then propose this.

. . .

S: Good.

K: We are not going to do it until about 2:00 or 3:00 this afternoon for a meeting 5:00 or 6:00 this afternoon. And all we will do is ask for a cease-fire and we ask for a return to the cease-fire lines. The British are prepared to say they think the Arabs started this.

S: I think it is quite clear. The U.N. observers have also reported that from both fronts.

K: To all practical purposes there is no question.

[. . .]

GENERAL HAIG–KISSINGER
Saturday, October 6, 1973
12:45 P.M.

. . .

H: We are returning to Washington.

K: What is he going to do?

H: It is conceivable we will have an announcement about the Vice President. That is the first thing.

K: That is a slightly different problem.

H: You bet it is and what I am telling you is the two are going to be linked together. He cannot be sitting down here in the sun with what is going on in the V.P. thing. It is not firm yet but we will know very shortly.

K: If that other thing is happening then I can see a reason for coming back from the point of view of diplomacy. I would keep his return for later. Supposing the Soviets get tough and if he then returns that would be a good move. If he returns early it looks like an hysterical move. I am giving you my honest opinion. If the Soviets took a position of having kicked us in the teeth that would be a signal that [the President's] return is a signal that things are getting serious. We will not have heard by 3:00. We probably won't know until the first thing in the morning.

H: All right. I will try to hold this down here.

K: I would hold him until the first thing in the morning.

H: Okay.

K: We have put him into the involvement with all morning phone calls. Ron [Ziegler] can put that out too.

H: Right. Okay.

K: But don't you agree, speaking personally?

H: I know, except I know about the other problem.

K: You are a better judge of that. The problem I am handling in my judgment is if we played this as a crisis—say nothing, act tough, without stirring up the atmosphere.

H: Right. I will be in touch. I will go back to him on this thing.

K: Thank you.

SECRETARY GENERAL WALDHEIM–KISSINGER
Saturday, October 6, 1973
1:20 P.M.

W: I want to keep you informed of the developments here. Zayyat came to see the President [of the General Assembly] and saw him in my presence. He asked him to convene an urgent meeting of the General Assembly. I mentioned this to you, that he had already suggested that to me. . . . The President reacted as I did. He said it was not technically possible— He cannot do it so quickly. After a lengthy conversation el-Zayyat agreed to send him a letter which he had prepared and signed in the office of the President and instead of having a special meeting of the General Assembly he asked to circulate this letter. It is a two-page letter which accuses the Israelis to have started the aggression and that they had to react and they accused the Israelis for having launched this aggressing along the Egyptian-Syrian border and continues the Israelis' policy of occupation of the Arab territory and the increasing of the utilization of the Arab territories.

K: I guess we will see it eventually.

W: It is an accusation [against] Israel for not having accepted the U.N. resolution [242], etc. This is the situation and this letter will be circulated as a General Assembly document on request of el-Zayyat, and to speak on Monday morning in the General Assembly. He came to my office and told me that he had still no request for any Security Council debate. Is that right? I can imagine they don't want it.

K: We feel there should be a Security Council debate sometime later this afternoon and we will oppose any General Assembly debate of the subject.

W: It is a case for the Security Council.

K: We do not think the General Assembly competent.

W: It has been declined to have a General Assembly meeting. We don't have this problem, at least over the weekend. If el-Zayyat asks for the floor, the President has to give him the floor. When I asked him, he said he would ask for the floor only when he sees how things develop. I think he wants to see how the military operations develop.

. . .

By 2:10 P.M., we received a preliminary reply from the Soviet leadership. Its tone was friendly, keeping open the possibility of coordinated action, but it did not foreclose any options. Its treatment of Soviet foreknowledge was equally ambiguous. The Soviet leaders claimed to have learned of the opening of hostilities at about the same time we did. This may have been technically true. But they withdrew their civilians from Egypt and Syria two days before, clearly in anticipation of imminent war.

DICTATED BY AMBASSADOR DOBRYNIN TO
GENERAL SCOWCROFT
> *Saturday, October 6, 1973*
> *2:10 P.M.*

[Message to President Nixon and Secretary Kissinger from Soviet Government, dictated by Ambassador Dobrynin]

D: "The Soviet leadership got the information about the beginning of military actions in the Middle East at the same time as you got it. We take all possible measures to clarify real state of affairs in that region, since the information from there is of a contradictory nature. We fully share your concern about the conflagration of the situation in the Middle East. We repeatedly pointed in the past to the dangerous situation in that area.

"We are considering now as well as you do, possible steps to be taken. We hope soon to contact you again for possible coordination of positions."

U.S. AMBASSADOR TO THE UNITED NATIONS
JOHN SCALI–KISSINGER
Saturday, October 6, 1973
3:45 P.M.

K: I had a sort of nothing response [from the Soviets] saying we got the information at the same time we contacted them. They would like to coordinate action with them [the Arab side] and will contact us. I think we should hold off another hour or so until I can talk to Dobrynin.

S: That's just the opposite of the impression we are getting here. The information here is that Malik [Yakov Malik, Soviet Ambassador to the United Nations] [unclear] Security Council.

K: That may be the direction. They don't say coordinate action in the Security Council.

S: Right, and that we know definitely that Egypt doesn't want a Security Council meeting.

K: We are going to call them. I just want to have one more reading from Dobrynin.

   . . .

AMBASSADOR DOBRYNIN–KISSINGER

Saturday, October 6, 1973
3:50 P.M.

K: Anatol, I have your message. I can't say it is a model of solidity. It either means you are confused or you are cooperating with them.

D: With whom?

K: The Arabs.

D: Why?

K: What do you think it means? Will you explain it?

D: It was very clear that they [Soviet leaders] do not know exactly what is going on, but from their side they will compare it—we both will compare together—[but] as for their definite planning we will do that later.

K: How much later? We feel very strongly and let me have your reaction. The Egyptians want to put in the General Assembly and we consider this a frivolous act. We must say if it turns into a General Assembly debate, then we will let it take its course. We are certain it will turn out to be a military victory for the Israelis. Then everyone will come to us. If it turns nasty, we will shut off communications for a while [that is, let the Israelis run free]. We feel we should put it into the Security Council.

D: Yes.

K: But we have turned it off until we have heard from you. How much longer should we wait until we [have] heard from you?

D: One hour. They are having a meeting there.

K: I will wait until 5:00 to make a decision. Let me assure you, we want to cooperate with you.

D: That is our answer.

K: That is my impression from your answer. What I said to you is for the benefit of your friends. No one should think they can diddle us along.

D: No. No.

K: And have a great propaganda debate on Tuesday. What we are thinking is we'll call the Security Council. We will propose without condemnation of either side a cease-fire and a return to the cease-fire line.

D: That is it.

K: I will send over to you a draft resolution.

. . .

MINISTER SHALEV–KISSINGER

Saturday, October 6, 1973
4:00 P.M.

K: How are you?

S: Hungry [because Yom Kippur is a day of fasting].

K: Well, that I can appreciate. Can't you get dispensation to eat in a crisis?

S: I have passed it on and they are preparing something.

K: What about the pilots? I hope they are eating.

S: Don't you worry. Special rations for things of this sort.

K: Do you have anything more for me?

S: I hope I'll have it at some later point. I just have some information based on some phone conversations.

K: Since we talked?

S: Yes—they are slowly pulling them out—two bridgeheads—we are able to establish. I think the number of planes we downed is about twenty on the Egyptian side and half of that on the Syrian side.

K: Okay. In terms of strategy, please pass this on to Mrs. Meir—doesn't go any further, not the whole Cabinet.

S: It will—nobody here.

K: You know that the Egyptians have asked for a special meeting of the General Assembly. It will go into a debate on Monday. Our judgment is the General Assembly is a bad forum for you—extremely bad. . . . In order to make [our strategy] effective, we must call a Security Council meeting.

S: Yah.

K: We have had a response from the Soviets about the proposal—they are noncommittal at this point. Saying they are studying the matter and they are trying to find out. . . . I have already told the Soviets if the General Assembly turns nasty, into a propaganda battlefield, we will become very tough.

S: Yah.

K: I will be glad to have any—current information, but this is what we have decided to do.

S: I will pass [it] on to Mrs. Meir. I know from earlier conversation [that the] Soviet reply was not quite—

K: We don't know exactly what the Soviet reply is.

S: [unclear]

K: What I have told you is the Soviets' reply is friendly at this point but noncommittal. We would like some expression as to your strategy.

S: I will pass this on right away.

K: I know they have other things to do in Jerusalem, but if they could give us as frequent as possible a report as to—help us from looking foolish. When is Dinitz coming back?

S: Day after tomorrow, or tomorrow, not sure.

K: Keep us closely informed.

GENERAL HAIG–KISSINGER

Saturday, October 6, 1973
4:15 P.M.

K: Dobrynin says he will hear again in another couple of hours and, as far as where we stand in New York, Egyptians are against the Security Council meeting and the Soviets, who are without instructions, are supporting Egypt. The British, who wanted to call it, are getting cold feet. Tell the President we are still waiting for the Soviet reply. If we don't get it at 6:00, we will call a Security Council meeting.

H: Right.

   [. . .]

K: It is manageable here. He [the President] will want to know exactly what we will be doing. At 6:00 we will call a Security Council meeting. I will say the President has instructed me to go back to Washington. And I will say the President will have something to say at a later time.

   . . .

H: The President agrees with this approach. I think that's fine, Henry. The only worry we have here is about the Soviets.

K: —and for that, we have to be prepared to take them on. They will have to be prepared to help on this kind of thing . . . we cannot be the soft guys in this crisis.

H: No question about that. We can't take that.

With the overall strategy established, I turned to consultation with allies and Congress, beginning with the British Ambassador. Joe Sisco (Assistant Secretary of State for Near Eastern and South Asian Affairs) handled consultations with other allies.

BRITISH AMBASSADOR GEORGE ROWLAND STANLEY BARING,
EARL OF CROMER–KISSINGER

   Saturday, October 6, 1973
   4:25 P.M.

   . . .

K: I wanted to give you—and this is for the Prime Minister only—the general strategy. We hope to work as closely as we did in September 1970.

C: I'm sure we would wish to do that too.

K: . . . Let me give you our reading of the situation. We are quite confident that the Arabs started this and we in fact were given assurances, when we transmitted to the Egyptians and Soviets our request not to launch a preemptive attack. We told them that if Israel launched an attack, we would oppose them publicly.

C: Was this recently?

K: That was during the night, but it was too late to be—to affect decisions once we had the information. Now the—our assessment of the situation is this. We have approached the Soviets and proposed calling a Security Council meeting and that there be a simple resolution calling for a return to the cease-fire lines and a cease-fire. We are doing this because that is a neutral type of resolution which requires no condemnation and we suspect within a couple of days, unless our judgment is really off, the Arabs will be on their knees begging us to do this. We want to have a platform of having moved in this direction before that.

C: Before that, yes.

K: If the Soviets support us in this, we are home free. If they do not, we will have to move quite drastically to make it clear that the Arabs were the aggressors in this particular instance, and more or less side with the Israelis. The reasons for this—we are beginning, as you could see from the newspapers—and as I have told you—a series of diplomatic moves in an attempt to make at least some progress, and this action depends on being able to convince the Israelis, to make other security guarantees.

C: I discussed with—

K: If they are not [able] to see what we can do, then no guarantees by us will have the slightest significance. If the Soviets don't join us in quieting things down, you have to assume collusion beforehand. We are prepared to take them on. It is in the interest of everybody, including Western Europe, not to run across us in this particular instance.

C: When would the Security Council meet?

K: I have called Dobrynin. We have had already a reply from the Soviets—and I will not give anybody else the full flavor of this: if the General Assembly turns into a propaganda battle, we will be unreachable for the rest of the week. No matter what beautiful speeches are given in New York. We will not then be as easy to deal with as we are now. On the other hand, we are willing to co-operate now to proceed on a neutral line.

C: Sure.

K: We will wait. I have given him [Dobrynin] until 5:00 and we will wait an extra hour, until 6:00 this evening, to produce a reply from Moscow. If not, I have been asked by the President to ask Ambassador Scali to call for a Security Council meeting. We will not be condemnatory at the meeting unless the Soviets turn towards the Arabs. We will be very grateful, if your representative could be instructed to coordinate support.

C: I will get on this right away.

K: Let me know what your representative is instructed to do.

C: Was this completely out of the blue, as it is to me?

K: Oh, yes, the first time—and this is for your Prime Minister—we were requesting [. . .] reports, even called in the Israeli Ambassador [. . .], they predicted fully defensive preparations. I got a report this morning. They were still maintaining that last night. We received the first confirmation this morning. Then I got on the telephone, gave assurances to everybody—but three hours later it started.

C: You have got friends, like in North Vietnam and other parts of the world; they are a little unreliable.

K: In Moscow, you mean?

C: No, I mean among the Arabs. Don't you think they have been clever?

K: Oh, yes, very clever. Whether they have committed suicide depends—depends on how the military operation goes. Our information is, though we don't have the complete picture, is that they have crossed at five points, only two [bridgeheads] are left.

. . .

Late in the day we received the first substantive communication from Moscow.

AMBASSADOR DOBRYNIN–GENERAL SCOWCROFT
Saturday, October 6, 1973
5:45 P.M.

D: I have a reply from Moscow in connection with the two or three talks with the President on the convocation of the Security Council. Here is a summary:

We have a serious doubt about what kind of results could be achieved by a hasty convocation of the Security Council meeting right now. As far as we know not a single side asked for a convocation of the Security Council from the conflicting parties.

Secondly, the circumstances are not quite clear in a sense that there is not yet clear communications with the conflicting parties. We presume, both we and you, have no circumstance to have good communications with the parties of the conflict to find out what is going on. Under these circumstances, we feel it would be rather undesirable to have the meeting because this meeting would lead to open polemics between yours and ours as is well known our position in the Middle East is known. And our positions wouldn't change for this particular meeting of the Security Council. We would be forced to state our known position and open confrontation with you.

Our position in the Middle East for many years since '67— Israel who occupied Arab lands and victims of aggression, the Arab countries, whose territories are occupied. We don't think this will lead anywhere. We will be forced to say already there are good resolutions in the UN organization. The matter is to fulfill them. We feel it is undesirable to convene the Security Council. At the same time in the complicated and rather dangerous situation, the matter continues of close consultation between us and how to settle the Middle East problem. This is a summary of the telegram. I will be here. I am available.

FOREIGN MINISTER EBAN–KISSINGER

Saturday, October 6, 1973
6:00 P.M.

E: Detailed report—

K: If you could get it to me as soon as possible. If you give it to our people in—they will make—copies and they will have it in Damascus before I see it.

E: The Syrian advance fell because of nightfall. A garrison surrounded at Mount Harmon. No communication with the people in it. We have destroyed sixty tanks. A number of ours are out of action. Syrians have fired three missiles of the Frog type, that's—

K: I know what that is.

E: They didn't fall where intended. Fell in a small valley [Mikal]. Bombarded the kibbutz—ten killed in the north and thirty wounded.

K: How many planes were shot down?

E: I don't know that. On the Egyptian front our position is difficult. Secure a foothold on the eastern bank. Have a bridgehead and during the night will try to pass forces over them. They shot one air-to-ground missile toward Tel Aviv. One of our aircraft shot it down—brought it down—while still in the air. Brought down about fifteen of their helicopters. Lost three aircraft on the Egyptian front. Fifty killed and 140 wounded.

K: This is the sort of information—you have no idea of any plans— offensive—

E: Our Defense Minister said it will take some days but we will restore our position. I have confidence we will restore it.

K: You think we should not be precipitate—what is your personal view—

E: That is my personal view.

K: —of not being precipitate? The ability of our government not to be precipitate is well tested.

E: There are all degrees of precipitation even when the debate is beginning.

K: I'm considering whether to go tonight or tomorrow.

E: I would say tomorrow—

GENERAL HAIG–KISSINGER
Saturday, October 6, 1973
6:05 P.M.

K: We are considering possible steps we are taking. Dobrynin says we'll hear again in another hour. In New York the Egyptians are against the Security Council meeting. The Soviets are without instructions. The British are getting cold feet. I'll wait till 6:00 for the Soviets. If we don't get it, we call the Security Council. By tomorrow if we haven't got them to stop it, we will be accused of collusion. [Then] a wild propaganda battle in the General Assembly; we will shut off our phones. They had better come to us now—Defense wants to turn against the Israelis. . . .

H: Sounds like [Deputy Secretary of Defense William] Clements.

K: It's manageable here. Around 6:00 I'll call the Security Council meeting. In New York as I was leaving a microphone was pushed in front of me. I told them the President has instructed me to return to Washington. As a former deputy of mine—do you agree with this approach?

H: I think that's fine. The only assessment we need to worry [about] is how the Soviets read us.

K: We cannot be soft guys in this case. . . .

H: No, we can't be soft.

AMBASSADOR DOBRYNIN–KISSINGER
Saturday, October 6, 1973
6:20 P.M.

K: I haven't seen the text of your message yet. Give me your interpretation. What do you think? [What are you] really saying? It will be polemical.

D: My impression is that we don't have information from the Arabs. Tomorrow will be all right. They find it will be polemical session—a small unit and on first line you and we will be. They don't like this idea.

K: What are you saying?

D: None of the participants are asking for the Security Council, so what's really for us to do?—then this forced you to say old story about our position.

K: What we have is a case of a military attack. A difficult position— a question of negotiation. It is one thing for the Soviet Union to take a stand in preliminary negotiation; it is another to take a stand after hostilities have started. In three days you'll be begging us for it [the Security Council meeting].

D: I understand—our position. In Moscow [they] don't want to become involved immediately. They will try to get territory back—

K: What are you telling them privately?

D: We don't like this idea.

K: Yet—if you knew of it, why didn't you consult with us?

D: Not a question of that.

K: We told Gromyko what we intended to do. We told—

D: The question is how far do we go or not go? The situation could be some discussion on our—

K: If there was evacuation on your part.

D: I don't have that information—

K: Two conclusions.

D: Just saying we don't like this idea.

K: I would have . . . three points: first, public opinion, secondly Congress, and then the special relationship we thought existed between us. If you tell us in debate on Monday—we understand—you tell us to wait, we will have a real donnybrook—do you know what that means? We will have a brawl in the General Assembly and will then make it insoluble. We've been holding up the Israelis on bombing. I don't know if we can keep this up.

D: That's clear to me.

K: Zayyat has asked for the floor on Monday.

D: All I can tell you is that I will talk to Moscow.

K: I'll talk to Key Biscayne and tell you what we are going to do. I'll call you back, so don't go to Maryland.

AMBASSADOR SCALI–KISSINGER

Saturday, October 6, 1973
6:40 P.M.

S: Security Council now holding meeting—shall we stay where we are?

K: I heard they are not going to call a formal meeting, but have informal consultations. Same position—to be for a cease-fire and return to the status quo ante, and you should call attention to—[the] following points:

If we call only for a cease-fire, we would be using the U.N. to sanctify aggression—can grab territory, ask the U.N. to call a cease-fire and then if the victim—creates a dangerous precedent.

If the military situation takes a turn and Israel starts beating up on the Arabs, it should be kept in mind that we are prepared to stick, even if—with the resolution for a status quo ante.

It would be unbecoming for the U.N. to turn itself into a— that is our position and we will maintain it throughout the crises. As Popper [David Popper, Assistant Secretary of State for International Organization Affairs] pointed out we did not follow it in '67 but in '73 we will. [In 1967, there was a cease-fire in place.]

S: We are following it in '73 is the main point.

K: Yes, the main point, but I think we should stay calm and not go around discussing it too much. I will let you know whether we decide to go directly for a Security Council [meeting] tonight, when we've got more information.

GENERAL HAIG–KISSINGER

Saturday, October 6, 1973
7:10 P.M.

H: Just talked to the President. He feels that we possibly should not wait too much longer for the Soviet answer before moving with the resolution [for a cease-fire and return to the status quo ante].

K: Exactly right. First, though, a Soviet answer is coming in now. Second, my recommendation is to move tonight; whatever is the answer, we move into the Security Council as soon— We will put forward a call for a cease-fire and return to the status quo ante before the fighting started. . . . [Otherwise] we will be rewarding the attacker— Once the Israelis start beating up on the Arabs—Israelis grab Arab territory—I feel we must recommend a cease-fire and return to status quo ante [even] if it gets voted down—best position with the Chinese. Can't have precedents set in which—can grab territory and then call for a cease-fire.

H: Henry, what do you think about our announcing here, first on that thing?

K: That's fine. Just say that the President has instructed Dr. Kissinger to move immediately— Wait for the Soviet answer. It's coming in now, but I will let you make the announcement down there. I'll call you as soon as I have got the answer.

Immediately thereafter, I reviewed the state of play with Dobrynin, pointing out the threat to U.S.-Soviet relations. The strategy was to induce Soviet restraint to create conditions for an outcome that would, in the end, reduce Soviet influence by creating Arab doubts about Soviet consistency.

AMBASSADOR DOBRYNIN–KISSINGER

Saturday, October 6, 1973
7:20 P.M.

K: Here is what we will do. In deference to the message which you have sent us we will not go to the Security Council tonight, though it [our intention] originally was to go at six o'clock. We will wait for a decision on how to proceed until 9:00 tomorrow.

D: In the morning?

K: Yes. Give you a chance to go to church. If you could get me an answer from Moscow which is a little more specific than this.

D: On what?

K: What exactly are your intentions? My impression is—I understand you don't want to get into a public disassociation.

D: I will put it quite friendly. We are rather in a difficult position publicly.

K: If you can give us some indication what you are doing privately. You and I have handled these things [in] private. We are interested in the results. We want a cease-fire and status quo ante. I repeat: by Tuesday you will be asking us. It is not a question in which we are asking for a favor. We are trying to prevent an exacerbation of our relationship—a situation where in this country and the Congress will have very serious consequences. If you tell us you are working with the Egyptians and the Syrians and by Monday morning this will be over and no further debate is necessary.

If you will tell us that you believe that by Monday morning there will be in effect a cease-fire and return to the status quo ante. We don't want this to become a public affair. Tell us something we can understand. It will be kept confidential, as everything has been kept between us. I am not asking for you to agree for concerted public action. I am asking you tomorrow morning for a concerted practical action, [one] that will lead to the result we want. I genuinely believe and you will tell Gromyko and Brezhnev by Tuesday at the latest the situation will be a different show. Right? No?

D: I understand.

K: Our reading of the situation is that the Arab attack has been totally contained, that now they are going to be pushed back, and this process will accelerate as the [Israeli] mobilization is completed, which will be no later than Monday morning, and after that we will see what we have seen before. This is our military reading of the situation. We think the matter could be wound up tomorrow. The Arabs have proved their point. They have attacked across the Canal. They can withdraw on their own and return to the status quo. We can both enjoy a good Security Council debate.

D: I don't understand in a political sense what do you think? What do you want from our point of view, our position—which is a principle from the beginning of '67 [return of Israel to 1967 borders].

K: I know your position.

D: It is not a public debate that I am telling you. For us to tell the Arabs is very difficult. I had rather hear from Moscow but as I understand our position the difficulties we are now facing is that the Arabs are trying to regain the lands occupied by Israel. They have been using that argument to us, and for us to tell them you cannot free your land, it is ridiculous.

K: I recognize the situation. I am not saying it is all easy. We have a different situation. There have not been any raids on Damascus and Cairo, but I would not bet anything on tomorrow.

D: I understand.

K: Is it possible for the Politburo to imagine a complete course of action which we agree on privately?

D: What course of action do you propose besides Security Council?

K: A de facto return to the status quo ante, a de facto return of the cease-fire. I have already told the Egyptians that I would make an effort after the Israeli election. I have told Gromyko I would talk to him in January. None of this we will do if these pressures continue—

D: I understand.

K: We have a framework out of which we could crystallize [progress]. The Arabs have now proved their point.

D: Henry, how could they?

K: You see they are going to lose. It is not a case where we are asking. . . .

D: I understand. The military point of view. I cannot argue with
you. You know the situation better. I am trying to understand the
situation better politically.

K: They have next to nothing [territorial gains].

D: What is the question—asking them to return somewhere if they
have nothing?

K: We have two choices: we can let this war continue until the exact
calibrated moment when the Israelis have pushed [the Arabs] out
of every territory but before they start heading for Damascus. If
we are lucky and hit that moment exactly right we can hit the
cease-fire then. Probability is that the Arabs can hold on another
twenty-four hours and [are] then going to retreat to their capitals and wait for winter.

D: I understand what the situation really is. But for us to go to the
Arabs and say, look here, I don't know how many you have—one
or two miles but you have to go back. They say you invite us to
give back territory that belongs to us?

K: Can you not say that it was your understanding that an effort was
going to be made for negotiations? They have proved their
point, of the urgency in which they see this, and this is a good
psychological moment for them to make a generous gesture,
rather than wait until the outcome of these hostilities. By Monday evening they will be thrown out of there anyway.

D: I understand.

K: This is a new strategy—of using the threat of one's own defeat.

D: I know. There are many [things] that could be said. The question
is, from the practical way. From a practical point of view because
they put on us all the cats and dogs. On the Russians because we
asked them to give back land which we have already said—

K: I understand your dilemma.

D: They will say you are in collusion with the U.S. and Israel.

K: Who will be the first?

D: Cairo. From a man you met [means Zayyat]. The Russians were in collusion with the U.S. and [unclear].

K: If you and we could find a way of settling this now, then it would be an overwhelming argument in all of the things we have been going through [regarding détente] as to what the practical consequences have been of our relationship.

D: I understand.

K: I think it would overwhelm in one blow all of these things we have been facing. If it goes the other way, and Monday you and we are going to be up at the rostrum calling each other names, it will be a disaster.

D: I can assure you we will not be calling the U.S. names. I am not sure what the Israelis will be calling.

K: You know some of the local people cannot always distinguish those two.

D: We will try to put them out of the country on this particular American line. You understand?

K: I understand.

D: This we could take care of.

K: It still would not change the objective condition. The various people who are harassing you will be more inflamed.

D: I know. That is why I keep returning to the practical thing. You understand?

K: I understand it.

D: They would say you have spoken of liberating [after the 1967 cease-fire]. It is impossible for us.

. . .

K: Anatol, with all due respect, we will face this problem somewhere in the next forty-eight hours. Suppose you do nothing and we do nothing. By Tuesday, or Wednesday at the latest, the Arabs will be defeated unless our estimates are wrong. At that point what are we going to do?

D: Did you approach once more the Egyptians?

K: No. You think I should?

D: I think you should. Tell them your estimate. Otherwise it would be such an invitation. You are [unclear] and we their friends are saying, go back from your own land.

K: I will approach them tonight and I will call you after I have talked to them.

D: I think it would be much better. From us, it would look like we are trying to sell them out.

K: We have to leave it at this. We will not go to the Security Council tonight—to give ourselves a chance to think. You think and we will think. Try to get me an expression from Moscow by 9:00 in the morning.

D: Ask for 9:00? That is 5:00 [Moscow time].

K: Tell them they will have to go to early mass.

D: They would find it strange to have these kinds of discussions going on over the weekend.

K: I can imagine what kind of discussion is going on there. I understand the [unclear]—are very happy today.

D: This is a basic problem. I also understand your ingenuity.

K: If I have any ideas I will call you.

D: Not at night. I go to sleep quite early.

K: You are not going to bed now, are you?

D: No.

K: What you have to understand is, if it turns into a propaganda battle on Monday in the General Assembly, then our only protection is to be extremely tough and to teach the facts of life to people who like to make great speeches and we will see what is more important—a speech or reality. I will be very brutal. That will be our strategy. We want to get it settled before then, at least with an understanding.

. . .

GENERAL HAIG–KISSINGER
Saturday, October 6, 1973
7:30 P.M.

K: —and claimed that the Russians alluded to the Israelis. I told them [the Russians] in three days they [the Israelis] would throw them [the Egyptians] out and be coming to us.

H: Sure.

K: I told them [the Russians] the General Assembly debate on Monday which will start if we don't start on the Security Council—my recommendation unless you feel strongly to the contrary. I have told him [Dobrynin] unless he hears from me to the contrary, I will give him until tomorrow to avoid this dilemma.

H: Yes.

K: If not, we will have to go to the Council. If we don't do that we will get creamed in the General Assembly on Monday.

H: I think they have understood the position; tonight is fine.

K: I told Dobrynin if it goes to the General Assembly and if the U.S. is taken over the coals I want them to know we are taking the position that words are words and deeds are deeds and people who can commit deeds will be let [to] run loose for a couple of days. You make sure the President is fully informed.

H: I will. I know he is anxious to do something in the morning.

K: By 10:00 you will be able to announce he has asked that it be moved to the Security Council.

H: I don't understand what the Soviets think they are going to gain.

K: Actually, they [the Egyptians] seem to have gotten across in larger force than they [the Israelis] thought possible.

H: Really?

K: The Israelis say there is a real bridgehead across the Canal. Sixty dead and 110 wounded. You have to multiply that by a hundred to get the equivalent American casualties. If we suffered six thousand dead and fifteen thousand wounded in one day. No joke.

The Israelis say they have shot down six helicopters with troops. [The discrepancy between information here and in my 6:00 P.M. conversation with Foreign Minister Eban can only be explained by later intelligence.]

H: There are generally ten to fifteen in a helicopter.

K: Okay. We will proceed on that basis.

H: If you feel you need to change.

K: I am comfortable with this.

H: I take it you had rather do it tomorrow?

K: Yes.

H: You will get much better news play tomorrow. From a political point of view, it is better to have given the Russians a few more hours and lean over backwards.

K: We had better keep book on that. If they play it the hard way we know what we are up against. There are two things: Number one is I think as long as we know that the Soviets have been capricious and that way it proves to be there will be no limits on what we can do. If they play soft and spongy it would be very hard to be tough.

H: With the President.

K: That's right.

H: He will be making a mistake.

K: You have to figure as you go down this thing if the Soviets are using us we have to call a spade a spade and not play with them whatever the price.

H: That is my view.

K: We are in good shape.

H: That is totally my view. I don't think we can play it spongy.

K: As long as you play it that way.

H: They will be playing it spongy and we will still have to call a spade a spade.

K: That is all right too. That has a time limit on it. I have given them until 9:00 tomorrow morning. I think it would be a mistake [to go earlier] because we have no one else lined up [votes in the Security Council].

H: Precisely. I told him that.

K: Would he [Nixon] rather go tonight?

H: Instinctively, he would. I told him the British fell off the status quo ante aspect and you felt we ought to be very careful not to go against the others until they had thought about it. If you go back to Dobrynin and tell them this is what we are going to do.

K: I have already told them that.

H: As much as you can.

K: I told them I would try to sell this in Key Biscayne.

H: All right, Henry.

GENERAL HAIG–KISSINGER

Saturday, October 6, 1973
8:00 P.M.

K: . . . British will support resolution for simple cease-fire but not cease-fire ante. This faces us with a problem. Next move—sanction against Israel for refusing a cease-fire. By Tuesday or Wednesday Israel may be in Arab territory and then they will accept it. Third point—anyone who can grab territory and then submit to a cease-fire— Number one, do we go to Security Council tonight, Number two, with what sort of resolution.

H: My instincts are today up there.

K: We can give the Soviets till tomorrow morning at 9:00. If they are surprised they are confused—if not surprised then stalling for time.

H: I don't know how the battle is going.

K: They are aggressive. The Israelis are being excessively timid.

H: They are not surrounded—Syria.

K: Do—but not any missile attacks on other line.

H: Don't want a missile attack. I think the Egyptians want them to come in there against their missiles—and the Israelis didn't nibble. We could probably wait till morning—not overly hungry as long as we aren't snockered.

K: By 9:00 in the morning we should go.

H: That's what I think.

AMBASSADOR W. TAPLEY BENNETT, U.S. DEPUTY
REPRESENTATIVE TO THE UNITED NATIONS–KISSINGER
Saturday, October 6, 1973
8:45 P.M.

K: Were you with Scali at the—

B: Yes, I was, sir.

K: What happened?

B: We were successful in preventing any statement tonight.

K: Well, did anyone want to make a statement?

B: Yes. The Australian President had a statement already prepared which would have said that tomorrow—that we were consulting for meetings that— I have it right here in front. I can read it to you if you like.

K: Yes.

B: "The President of the Security Council announced on 6 October that he had consulted urgently the members of Council on the fighting which had broken out in the Middle East that day. Paragraph. On the basis of information so far available, the members of the Council had expressed serious concern with the situation which has developed and deplored the fact that hostilities had been resumed in breach of the cease-fire. Paragraph. The President had been authorized by members of the Council as a first step to ask the Secretary General to call on all sides for an immediate cessation of all military activities and to report promptly to Council members on their response. Paragraph. The members of the Council had authorized these provisional measures in accordance with [unclear] of the agenda without prejudice to the rights and claims or positions of the parties con-

cerned." John Scali pointed out that this would be quite unacceptable from our side without a withdrawal at the same time
that was coequal with the cease-fire from our point of view.

K: Very good.

B: And the final upshot of it was consultation with the British,
French, Austrians, and the Australians and the upshot was they
agreed on no statement at all and John said that he would hope to
have instructions by 10:00 in the morning.

K: Good. Perfect.

B: The Chinese have taken the position that they will not agree to
any statement because neither Syria or Egypt has asked for Security Council action.

K: Would they agree to a meeting tomorrow?

B: I suspect they will oppose it, but every member has the right to
call for it.

K: But that means they'll veto any action?

B: That may well be the result.

K: Okay. Bye.

B: We'll be here, and John is making his Columbus Day speech at
the Waldorf.

K: No, you tell him he's doing a great job.

FOREIGN MINISTER ZAYYAT–KISSINGER

Saturday, October 6, 1973
8:48 P.M.

K: I just wanted to touch base with you at the end of a rather hectic
and I'm sure rather trying day for you and for all of us. Let me
tell you candidly what our evaluation is and I'll speak to you in
the candor that we always have. First, I thought we had done
rather well in our discussions yesterday [about the peace process
to start in January] in establishing a basis of some mutual confidence, and I look forward to seeing you down here and resuming
our discussions in November. Now, we are in the difficult situa-

tion that if the fighting doesn't get stopped in a reasonable time, events may again get out of control. Now, our evaluation is that if the fighting goes on, the Israelis will probably gain the upper hand. You know, you can disagree with this but this is our estimate and therefore when we suggest that we would prefer a cease-fire plus a restoration of the status quo ante, I—

Z: Anti what, Mr. Kissinger?

K: No ante, before this last round started.

Z: Very strange.

K: I understand your point and we talked about that on Friday, but then that will in time work to the advantage of the Arab side if the evolution is the way it may be. I just wanted you to know on a personal basis that if the fortunes of war should go the other way, we would not look with favor on any further Israeli territorial gains. And we would like to have this thing wound up in a way that does not make it more difficult to resume what I thought was a beginning of a better possibility for discussion. I don't have a very concrete proposal, and we have tried to be restrained today in the hope that perhaps something could be developed.

Z: Of course, the question of, you know when you think about five thousand Egyptians killed and then going back to where we were, is something out of the question, in Cairo. If I were in Cairo, I would think madness.

K: How many Egyptians killed?

Z: I don't know how many people, but I don't know how many killed but could be thousands killed.

K: Of course, our impression is that the action was initiated probably by your side this time, but we may be wrong.

Z: Even so, but how can you advise anyone after doing this [suffering five thousand killed] to go back where he was? I mean this is completely unreasonable. And just remember that you were speaking what can we give them since they cease-fire. Everything was so good that they started the cease-fire the fact of their occupation for seven years, six years, was quite all right because of the cease-fire. I think it better for them and the evolution to find there is a war really, and therefore find a solution for it.

K: That I agree with you on completely.

Z: They were so pleased and didn't want to do something because there was a cease-fire. And the cease-fire, which was costing us every day that which I spoke to you about. I don't know who began this or how it began, but we should move with the best [unclear] which we have now.

K: Which is what?

Z: I don't know but a position of going back to where we were—of course, nobody can suggest this to the government, but me anyhow, but I don't know what other positions are up. I didn't go to the Council because really I . . . I didn't know what to do in the Council, the Council can have votes with me, but with one veto.

K: What is your view?

Z: I don't know. Do you have any suggestions? You have been studying this for some time and you know the other people; we don't have relation with them.

K: You see, our theory is that the other side is going to launch a very strong attack within the next day or two, and then we will have another major problem to contend with and we would like to keep the fighting contained as much as possible to give diplomacy an opportunity. I mean, you have certainly made your point, which you had already made to me eloquently, about the intolerable nature of the situation.

Z: The situation is really impossible for us. It has been repeatedly said, this is Egyptian land. Nobody can [unclear]. Security was assured for Israel by the water canal, and therefore how can they leave the security?

K: No, I think it was a very effective operation in many ways.

Z: There is no security there. Security is possible only at the acceptance of coexistence.

K: I unfortunately don't have a concrete plan, Mr. Foreign Minister, but I do believe you have made a very [good point]. The events of today have made a very strong point and now the question is how to go from here to some positive result rather than to an expansion of the war, which then could reverse many of the things that have happened.

Z: I would like Cairo—I would do anything. I don't care very much for war, or for all this kind of thing.

K: Look, I really—you convinced me yesterday, very much, of your serious intent and goodwill.

Z: In any world, how to get peace is the most important thing.

K: I couldn't agree more.

Z: The question now, what can I suggest? To go back to establish the [line] of yesterday? I don't think I can even whisper it.

K: Supposing it happens in a day or two anyway.

    . . .

Z: Yes. So I think if there is no extra help from anywhere we can defend what we have to the best of our abilities, but there is a point now that this question of security was over-rated and perhaps no protection. We can tell that now, and begin asking something, doing something perhaps.

K: That I understand and from that point of view if we now show statesmanship, something positive could emerge out of all of this. If it's done in some concrete and practical way. That's why I called, you know; I don't really know. I just wanted you to know that I'm open for discussion, and that we are not lined up in order to create difficulty.

Z: Well, I should hope not, because it is not good for anyone.

K: But you see this now goes to the General Assembly?

Z: I'm not going to the General Assembly. There is a mistake about that. What I wanted to do is give the General Assembly the note I gave them today. On Monday I am going to give the [note] again and that's all. We don't want a debate in General Assembly.

K: You do not want a debate?

Z: No.

K: Well, that is a misunderstanding. I thought that you wanted it.

Z: No. I don't want it until November, to give you a chance. What I am expected to do is to read the letter which I gave to the President [of the General Assembly] today to read it as a statement of what had happened and sit down and hear other speakers . . . as they wish. Because there was no meeting today I [delayed] any demand or request for a debate. I know the radio says different but I hope you look [unclear]. But I didn't ask for a debate and did not even raise the question. If this would help. But this is something [unclear]. Ask them what is going to happen in the spot, this is more important.

K: Now supposing you know we said we were going to give this opportunity. How can we get the fighting stopped now?

Z: I don't really know. You are far away. You can have more cool head, you can tell me what to think and I plan to take a plane tomorrow morning to see the President [Sadat] and then come back. I will do anything because I sincerely believe until the end all wars are going to end by some sort of peace and the peace that we want. For this I think there is understanding, you have said it repeatedly.

K: You explained that to me on Friday.

Z: Yes, and it has been said before you can say clearly, perhaps you cannot say it but this [is] a fact. So if we can have any encouragement of any endorsement of this by America for example you can [unclear] think clearly that the [unclear] of all states to preserve rewards for rewards. Something like this. I'm not speaking for myself. I don't know, can you think about it until tomorrow and we will call you again and see what can be done.

K: Let me think about it tonight and I will call you tomorrow.

. . .

The key issue with respect to U.N. strategy was not to pass a particular resolution; it was to prevent the isolation of the United States, the further inflaming of the Arab world, and a coalition of Europe and the Soviet Union with the Arab world. Specifically: (1) We opposed a cease-fire in place because it would have set a precedent for using the United Nations to legitimize gains through military attack. (2) We sought a basis for U.S. policy and U.N. action when what all intelligence services predicted as the inevitable Israeli victory occurred. (3) We sought to keep the Soviet Union from leading an ideological and geopolitical crusade against the United States and Israel. (4) We sought to control the option of dominating the diplomatic peace process after the end of hostilities. Therefore, we stayed in close contact with the Egyptian Foreign Minister and with Sadat. This would prove a line that never broke, even during the most intense period of conflict.

To prevent confusing signals that might come to Moscow from Cairo, I informed Dobrynin of my conversations with Zayyat. It also served as a warning that we were developing our own communications with what was still a Soviet ally with which we had no diplomatic relations.

AMBASSADOR DOBRYNIN–KISSINGER
Saturday, October 6, 1973
9:10 P.M.

K: Hello, I called your ally, el Zayyat.

D: Yes, what was his reaction?

. . .

K: He said he doesn't insist on the debate himself, on Monday, and if we tell him not to have it, he won't have one.

D: If we tell him?

K: If I—

D: If you tell him.

K: Yeh.

D: But you tell him. But you mentioned to him that [unclear] to have it, I'm sure.

K: I told him I'd call back tomorrow.

D: Why didn't you tell him from the very beginning?

K: I told him I'm against it.

D: But you said that he will do it if you talk to him, so what is he waiting?

K: I want him to think a little bit. I told him I'm against the debate.

D: Why is he waiting then?

K: If you would let me finish, what he wants also is another thing. I told him our assessment was that they would be driven back at least to where they were; he said he cannot propose withdrawal to Cairo, they'd fire him. But he said if I propose anything at all to him, they would be receptive.

D: This I think is what I really—what I tried to tell you in the sense not to just propose withdrawal but to provide them with something.

K: Can you give some thought to some formula overnight?

D: About what kind of things we could propose?

K: Yeh, I don't know myself. If I have an idea, I'll mention it to you.

D: Okay, I will put it this way, Henry, because this is really up to [unclear], but I would rather if you have a chance by 9:00 to get in touch with Cairo (?) but I will try to do it.

K: Well, or maybe to us.

D: I understand in this case, but either your proposal would like to consult Cairo—not a proposal they wouldn't accept—what really they had in mind—to mention indications outlining their thinking.

K: Yeh.

D: So this kind of thing would be whether he would like some kind of statement from both of us, or mention to them in order to get them set up to say look here, I was then, but I was asked to do on with—I don't know—oil consultations or something along this line, you see.

K: Exactly.

   . . .

LORD CROMER–KISSINGER

Saturday, October 6, 1973
9:38 P.M.

K: . . . Our thinking is that we probably won't be able to avoid calling for the Security Council meeting tomorrow sometime.

C: No. That is okay.

K: But we really feel very strongly that a simple cease-fire is (a) short-sighted in the present circumstances and I will tell you why. Our judgment is that within seventy-two hours the Israelis will be pushing deep into Syria. They may not go into—beyond the Suez Canal but they will wipe out what is there. And we may then find such a resolution extremely handy on getting them back. Oh, well—

C: Oh, well, I think—

K: In addition to the general principles which I stated earlier. Now we are quite determined that if the Israelis go beyond the present cease-fire lines that we will push them back.

C: Yes, that is the point I was trying to make. If they do do that, then I think we are going to have a new situation.

K: Yes, but if we don't position ourselves now. Let me tell you, Eban is not eager to have a Security Council meeting.

C: I am sure he is not.

K: And . . . if there is one, he wants a return to the status quo ante [. . .]

C: Yes. . . .

. . .

C: I think it is a very difficult one.

K: Now what we will do—it will go to the Security Council tomorrow and I am just telling it to you people so that they can think about it. We do not intend to fall on our swords to get a vote tomorrow.

C: No.

K: What we will do is to introduce our resolution. And then we don't mind going at a stately pace.

C: No. I think that is probably very sensible, don't you?

K: But what we need is to have it in front of the Security Council so that [if] the [unclear] go crazy at the General Assembly, we can stonewall on the ground that it is before the Security Council and we won't participate in the General Assembly debate.

C: No. What General Assembly debate is really the worst of everything.

K: Exactly, but we need to have a [unclear] position because if isn't to anything else we have to speak before the Assembly.

C: Yes, I am with you. I absolutely see that point.

. . .

October 7, 1973

The day began with a discussion with Haig, who was with Nixon in Key Biscayne and acting on his behalf because Nixon was preoccupied with the resignation of Vice President Spiro Agnew, in the process of being negotiated. The issue of military supplies for Israel was emerging more insistently. I recommended continuing delivery of items already promised or in the pipeline. Now that I had returned to Washington from New York, interdepartmental exchanges took place generally at the National Security Council or WSAG level. Most of the day was spent in marking time. The Security Council, the institution specifically designed to deal with breaches of the peace, was paralyzed by obstruction from all sides. The Soviets were stalling; Egypt, depending on which ambassador one believed, was either stalling or preparing for a cease-fire in place; Israel wanted time to complete its mobilization; Syria had not been heard from. Only the United States was prepared to go to the Security Council, but our preferred resolution amounted only to a sophisticated delaying tactic because no other Council member was likely to support us. Since everyone wanted time and we wanted to keep the issue out of the General Assembly, we had decided to call for a formal Security Council meeting toward evening, to postpone the debate until the next day, and to aim for a vote by Tuesday or Wednesday. By then, if our intelligence estimates were to be believed, Israel would have restored at least the original lines. Everyone might then be prepared to accept a cease-fire in place.

GENERAL HAIG–KISSINGER
Sunday, October 7, 1973
9:35 A.M.

K: Where are you?

H: In my room, about to go to see the boss.

K: We haven't heard from the Soviets. I think around noon [press secretary Ron] Ziegler ought to say we are going to the Security Council. Before it's done, check again. We have next to no support. On the other hand, the Arabs are doing better than anyone thought possible. I have just talked to the Israelis. They will need until Wednesday or Thursday. They are not all that eager for a Security Council meeting. In fact, nobody is—the Israelis, the Soviets, the Egyptians, the British. On the other hand, I think we can have a low-key meeting. For the Security Council to do nothing while fighting goes on is absolutely intolerable and I think we have to go ahead. We should seek return to the status quo ante.

H: Yes.

K: If we go, we must ask for return [to the status quo ante]—the Israelis will never forgive us for a straight cease-fire, and they'd never observe it anyway.

H: It's going to be tough if we are all alone.

K: On the other hand, a simple cease-fire request would make it seem that we have turned against the Israelis and this would have incalculable domestic consequences—and international ones too, and we would have changed our position of yesterday.

H: Are the Israelis panicking?

K: They are almost. They are anxious to get some equipment which has been approved and which some SOB in Defense held up, which I didn't know about. I think, myself, we should release some of it.

H: I think so too.

K: I think if the Arabs win, they will be impossible and there will be no negotiations. A change would be ascribed to our own domestic crisis [Watergate].

H: Right, I agree. I think we have got to stand by principle. We'll have to provide the stuff we have been committed to unless they can stabilize this thing quickly—two or three days.

K: That's what they think. If we don't move today somebody will move with a simple cease-fire resolution.

    . . .

H: Anything else the boss should know, Henry?

K: No, those are the main things.

H: Interesting report. The Israelis are shocked by the confidence of the Arabs.

K: Yes, that's right.

H: This might make easier negotiations.

K: Depends on how we conduct ourselves. We must be on their [the Israeli] side now so that they have something to lose afterwards. Therefore I think we have to give the equipment.

H: What are we talking about, ammunition and spares?

K: Let me see, I have it here. [Reads from list.] What we can do is send those which have already been approved.

H: Do we airlift them?

K: We don't have to do anything. They are sending a plane over and we could do it on the ground—that they were picking up things they had already ordered. My profound conviction is that if we play this the hard way, it's the last time they [the Israelis] are going to listen. If we kick them in the teeth, they have nothing to lose. Later if we support them they would be willing to help with Jewish emigration or MFN [Most Favored Nation] or other stuff. [Most Favored Nation status for Soviet trade was being blocked by an amendment put forward by Senator Henry Jackson (D.-Wash.) and Representative Charles Vanik (D.-Ohio), making it conditional on Jewish emigration from the Soviet Union.]

H: Will be in touch before noon.

K: Have Ziegler read the announcement to me.

FOREIGN MINISTER EBAN–KISSINGER

Sunday, October 7, 1973
10:00 A.M.

E: I have two things to add to what Shalev told you. You will be getting a military roundup very soon. I have had some telephone talks—the night was not particularly good. More forces were sent over.

K: You're talking about Sinai?

E: I'm talking about Sinai but even in the north there was further penetration there, in the Harmon area. Our garrison fell at Mount Harmon. We're not at full capability because of the special circumstances of yesterday. You'll get the military reports and I think they will reinforce the conclusions in the message.

K: I have just discussed it with my colleagues—not the message but the general strategy.

E: I understand you're asking for a special Security Council meeting tonight to preempt—

K: Yes, to preempt somebody else introducing a straight cease-fire resolution.

E: You could ask for a meeting and table a resolution tonight. Then ask for discussion tomorrow.

K: Well, if that can be done. Our judgment is that we need a platform on which to stand.

E: I have just been given a radio report that Britain had received instructions to call for a meeting. Perhaps you can have a word
with them telling them not to hurry. If you could ask your Ambassador to be in touch, we could go over it.

K: We haven't given him instructions. Let me check with the
British about whether they are going to proceed. I can't believe
they are going to proceed without checking with us.

E: You could make two points: (a) you will ask for a meeting, (b) it's
your opinion that is all it requires. That will have [a] preemptive
effect and gain time. The full military report will reach you and
will reinforce the conclusions in the message. The Ambassador
will return this afternoon and will want to see you.

K: I will see him as soon as he arrives and we will check with the
British.

THE PRESIDENT–KISSINGER

Sunday, October 7, 1973
10:18 A.M.

K: I just wanted to tell you we have had a call from Dobrynin that a
message from Brezhnev to you is coming through in the next
two hours, so I think we should hold this thing up until we get
this message. I know this might be impatient-making—

N: It what?

K: I know that these delays are difficult, but the problem is we may
end up with no support at all.

N: We can't do that.

K: I think we should make a record that we have been very active
before we go to the Security Council and not get totally isolated.
It is best to know where the cards lie. I think we can wait, even if
we take some flak. If we can see this through, we have a major
platform.

N: We'll have to do that. With Brezhnev I don't think we will learn
anything.

K: —Somebody on the Arab side will put in a simple cease-fire resolution. . . . We're going to be in a hell of a position in vetoing or
voting against a simple cease-fire. We had a message saying they
will have their equipment by Wednesday or Thursday, but they
will not accept a cease-fire before they have thrown them out.
My view is that if we cannot break ranks during this crisis, we can
really do it afterwards because then they will have something to
lose.

N: One thing that we have to have in the back of our minds is, we
don't want to be so pro-Israel that the oil states—the Arabs that
are not involved in the fighting—will break ranks.

K: So far we haven't done anything.

N: You are keeping Scali informed?

K: Yes.

N: PR is terribly important. Even if we don't do anything— Let
Scali go out—he can do a lot and prattle and cause no problem.

K: We held a meeting of four perm reps and some others to—

N: You keep one step removed—we can use you for the power
punch.

K: I recommend that you announce that you have asked for a meeting of the Security Council as soon as we have the Soviet message. I have told Dobrynin that we are not hell-bent on a
Security Council meeting—that if the Soviets made a proposal
where we could settle outside the Security Council, we would
consider it. I called the Egyptian Foreign Minister last night.
Some of our oil people in this country are [end of transcript].

GENERAL HAIG–KISSINGER
Sunday, October 7, 1973
12:35 P.M.

K: Let me tell you where matters now stand. The Egyptians have
told the British—he [they] didn't want a Security Council meeting but if one were held we will be totally alone— My suggestion

is, we hold our announcement till 4:00 this afternoon. No sense forcing a vote and getting all stirred up. No sense rushing in and getting nothing out of it. By Wednesday or Thursday, it is my thinking it will be over—so [the] U.N. can contribute to [the] situation as it exists. With the Israelis and the Arabs not yet wanting a meeting, I think we should hold off till about 4:00 this afternoon.

H: Yeah, I think that's fine.

K: We'll say we're prepared—tomorrow morning or tonight. Might be better to have informal consultations tonight. We haven't heard from the Soviets yet but will soon.

H: I agree with you. He [Nixon] is comfortable. Knows it [the war] will be short and he doesn't want to go up there and get licked.

K: Right. Now all we will get is [a] cease-fire, but should—get a position to handle the after period. The Arabs want to get me into this.

H: Good, Henry. I think this is all right. We'll hold till around 4:00. I'll get back to you on the Soviet thing.

K: You're reachable within the next hour?

H: Oh, yes, I'm right here.

Ambassador Dobrynin–Kissinger

Sunday, October 7, 1973
12:40 P.M.

D: I'm really nailed down. I'm still waiting for a message.

K: I think you should tell Gromyko that I'm so used to his customary precision that this worries me.

D: I will.

K: We've been holding up doing anything till we've heard from you. I've talked to Key Biscayne but that can be managed. I want to say as a friend of yours, if you make a unilateral move—we've made no move. I am trying to protect ourselves against moves that may not take factors into account.

D: I am waiting for this message. I don't know what it involves.

K: Now it's 10:00 [P.M.] in Moscow.

D: They are in [unclear].

K: Are they still there in [unclear]. Is this good for the boys with a Middle East crisis?

D: [Laughter] Good for them. I am sitting and waiting.

K: We'll wait a little longer. You let me know. Call me by telephone and tell me it's coming. I have no reason—if in your judgment there is any chance this could put my considerations to my contacts.

D: I will advise Gromyko and tell him.

K: Okay. We'll be in touch.

D: There is nothing specific.

K: We are waiting for your message. We are holding off the British until we hear from you. We don't want to talk with them till we hear from you.

D: Okay, I will call you even before the translation.

K: Good.

SECRETARY GENERAL WALDHEIM–KISSINGER

Sunday, October 7, 1973
12:55 P.M.

W: Good morning.

K: How are you?

W: Worried and busy. I wonder if you can tell me about your affairs and decisions?

K: I was going to call you. We have been exchanging thought with the Soviets to see what could be done. The Soviets are not willing to do very much.

W: My impression too. Most of the members are—not having a Security Council today.

K: What worries me is, here is a major military conflict and if the Security Council can't meet what is it for?

W: This is why I thought I should ring you up. We can explain it to our experts but what do we say to the public?

K: We are expecting a communication from the Soviets. I would like to call you around 4:00 and see about moving the Security Council.

W: Good.

K: We could ask for it tomorrow morning.

W: Then we could avoid debate on the General Assembly—under the rules of procedure the General Assembly can't meet on it if the Security Council is meeting.

K: Zayyat told me he wasn't that insistent.

W: If there is a meeting of the Security Council, easier to avoid debate in the General Assembly, especially if Zayyat doesn't want to speak.

K: If you can use your influence with the President [of the General Assembly] to keep Middle East debate from breaking open into an inflammatory— [They were disconnected, and the call was placed again.]

K: You haven't had any request from anyone else to do anything?

W: I just got a report that West Germany and Britain have called immediately for a Security Council meeting. By chance I had the British Ambassador here when it came in. I am trying to verify the matter.

K: We should stay in touch. We are prepared as soon as . . . we get the other communication. It will be helpful if you use your influence to keep the debate out of the General Assembly. We will call for a Security Council meeting tomorrow.

W: We'll be able to clarify the West German and British move. I don't know if this is true. Thank you very much. I'll keep you informed.

K: Are you reachable? I will call you no later than 4:00.

FOREIGN MINISTER EBAN–KISSINGER

Sunday, October 7, 1973
1:15 P.M.

E: The best way to proceed is the way you suggested yesterday.

K: We will probably proceed later this afternoon.

E: I had a report that [British Prime Minister Edward] Heath and [German Chancellor Willy] Brandt will convene—

K: I just talked to Waldheim, who gave me the same report. We are thinking we should table the resolution today and ask for a meeting in the morning. I have to wait a few hours till I can get to the President. We—proceeding on [the] discussion we had earlier today.

E: I think the urgent thing is a public decision by the U.S. to convene the Council. Trouble about tabling the resolution is, you don't get in, you won't have priority.

K: But if we call a meeting we will have priority.

E: Yes. I get the impression that in the last few hours the military situation has improved. Attacks on bridgeheads have succeeded.

K: Yes.

SECRETARY OF DEFENSE JAMES SCHLESINGER–KISSINGER

Sunday, October 7, 1973
1:30 P.M.

K: I have been talking to the President all morning on where we stand. We have had another very urgent request from the Israelis for some ammunition and various items from that list, including forty Phantoms, which of course is out of the question, but the President's inclination is that if the Israelis will be able to pick it up, to give them some other stuff, laying claim for diplomatic—

S: They are most interested in Sidewinders at the moment, Henry.

K: Do you think you could handle it at Defense so that it doesn't leak?

S: I think we can do it.

K: We did it in '67.

S: They have indicated they would pick it up, and not have to get our transport involved.

K: Could you let me know by the time of the WSAG?

S: Yes, sir.

K: Perhaps you could go through the list of things you think we could give them.

S: Sidewinders are what they are most interested in now; in fact, they are sort of quietly desperate about that.

K: They have made three separate appeals to the President now. They say their losses have been very heavy.

S: Well, their aircraft losses have been substantial because of the SAMs [surface-to-air missiles]. There is something very peculiar about the Egyptian front. They [the Israelis] seem to want Egypt to come in—[the] Egyptians didn't move their forces heavily across the Canal last night. The Israelis seem to be lying back. The forces they moved across were relatively small. The Syrian front is much more problematical. In both cases they may be— subtle game of attempting this time to show they really are vulnerable in view of the feeling around the world that they are just bullies.

. . .

THE PRESIDENT–KISSINGER

Sunday, October 7, 1973
2:07 P.M.

K: I talked to Dobrynin this morning. He hasn't gotten a message yet. I think if we don't hear by 4:00, we should go ahead anyway and call for a Council meeting for tomorrow. I have talked to Waldheim, Eban—oh, I have talked to everybody and it's a sort of a kaleidoscope. Nobody knows what's—

N: At least calling for a Council meeting shows some action and we still might decide to do nothing tomorrow. . . . We don't have to hear from Brezhnev. If we want to change our views, we can change our views.

K: That's right. But it's almost inexplicable how a war can go on for two days without the U.N. even meeting. I think Ziegler should say something like that, that war has been going on for two days; we think there ought to be a Council meeting.

N: Absolutely right.

K: And the U.S. will—

N: Whatever you work out with Ron is fine with me. The war's going on about as it was?

K: Actually the Arabs are fighting much better than expected—

N: Which, the Egyptians or Syrians, or both?

K: Both, actually the Syrians are advancing, the Egyptians are across the Canal—you know yesterday was a Jewish holiday. The Egyptians caught the Israelis unprepared—

N: Like Pearl Harbor, isn't it?

K: Right—until tomorrow and then introduce the idea of return to pre-cease-fire line. By tomorrow the Israelis will be reversing the tide.

N: Do you think they will?

K: By tomorrow they could turn the tide—work against Israel. If we introduce the idea today, the Arabs will claim we are trying to push them back. By Wednesday morning at the latest Israel will be in Arab territory.

N: Do you think they have the stuff to do it? Israel is convinced they can do it despite—

K: I am seeing the Israeli Ambassador, who has just returned from Israel; promised to come in about 6:30 to give me the latest—

N: Boy, don't you wish Rabin [Yitzhak Rabin, recently retired as Israeli Ambassador to Washington and who later became Prime Minister] were there now?

K: Oh, gosh—

N: He won't know what's— Can't you get a message from some-body out there, Moshe Dayan [Israel's Defense Minister] or—?

K: We are in contact with Dayan—more tractable—and that's why we have a difficult tightrope. Not dissociating in a crisis.

N: I understand, right.

. . .

N: Are you working well together over there?

K: Working well—you have noticed—newspapers, that as a team, rather than playing State against the White House.

N: Right. You go ahead and tell Ziegler whatever you want.

K: If there is any message, I will get it to you immediately.

N: You think you will get one from Brezhnev?

K: Yes. I'll let you know if there is anything.

GENERAL HAIG–KISSINGER

Sunday, October 7, 1973
3:10 P.M.

K: I am beginning to think those sons of bitches in Moscow are schnookering us. I think we should go at 5:00.

H: Yes, we can do it at 5:00. We're not going to be leaving until 7:30, so they can do it.

K: I have to make some phone calls. Get Ziegler positioned for it.

H: I told him to get in touch with McCloskey [Robert McCloskey, responsible for public affairs at the State Department].

K: No, get in touch with me. Has to call me for the language—McCloskey doesn't know beans about the substance.

H: I told him to make a simple statement. I will have him call, though.

K: We are getting frantic appeals for Sidewinders from the Israelis and the Defense Department is giving them the run-around.

H: You can tell them the President said to do it.

K: The idea was to have the stuff delivered to an air base and have them come out in El Al and pick them up. This is money in the bank. Now whatever happens in negotiations, if the Arabs come out ahead, they will be totally unmanageable. This way, if we don't help them [the Israelis], they won't come out ahead and we will wind up with nothing.

H: I've discussed it with the President and he is in full agreement.

AMBASSADOR DOBRYNIN–KISSINGER
Sunday, October 7, 1973
3:25 P.M.

D: Received the text. I could read it to you but then I could give to you oral, however you like.

K: What's the essence?

D: This say[s]—it is a letter from boss to boss [Brezhnev to Nixon]— it is saying about that recollection how [the] question was discussed between them, minister to minister, saying we are always in favor here to do something but nothing [was] done. We regret very much it bothers you. And then after—these things, then it goes like this. It would be possible to say a lot more to this but the main thing now is to take urgent effective measures to get rid of the cause of the conflict. With the situation in the Middle East— will continue to remain a source of constant danger. It would be very important if there came on the part of the Israelis a statement of its readiness to negotiate. Keeping in mind at the same time the security of the Israelis [and other] countries, so that area would be guaranteed—what is acceptable for Israel, to the interest of the Israeli people themselves. And if at all possible, to seek security of states in a seizure of foreign territories. As you know, Mr. President, we have always exercised restraint.

In effect the effectiveness of such a [guarantee] for the Israelis—claim of the Arabs' lands which ensures turning point in the dangerous situation in the Middle East, could be the beginning of the process of settlement on the basis of U.N. decisions [Security Council Resolution 242]. We would like to hope that now when the situation is especially urgent, demands this will use its possibilities for a necessary—of Israel in this direction. It goes without saying that we are ready to continue American confidential consultations on the whole Middle East problem, along the lines we have talked about during meeting with you, Mr. President. I would like to underline specifically, we firmly proceed from the premise that the current activities in the Middle East should not [impair] all the things that have developed—in [Soviet-]American relations. We do not allow even thought to the contrary.

Then there is an oral thing: that in our recommendation to the Arabs, to the Arab leadership, I wish to say that—I do not have that—will come in further communication.

K: You recognize as nonpractical possibility in the present situation. You know as well as I do it doesn't say anything.

D: Explain to you that we—from Israel not only Egyptians and Syrians take into consideration, U.N. and Chile, where you do the same thing. Decided to make this move without preliminary consultation with Egypt and Syrian government. Without asking their agreement.

K: Well, Anatoly, we will have a critical period this week; it is obvious to me.

D: I hope it will not be [a] crisis.

K: You know yourself we are perfectly prepared to ask Israel after it is over to make accelerated diplomatic moves.

D: Have you seen the statement made by el Zayyat?

K: That doesn't mean anything either.

D: Saw it on the ticker—

K: Okay, Anatoly. Could you get it typed up and sent to General Scowcroft?

D: Translate it too?

K: Yes and translated; send it to General Scowcroft.

. . .

SECRETARY SCHLESINGER–KISSINGER

Sunday, October 7, 1973
3:45 P.M.

K: Talked to the President again on this supply thing. He's decided to go ahead.

S: Can't guarantee we can do it without exciting attention.

K: We did it in '67. We would like them to pick it up.

S: Are you willing to use U.S. aircraft?

K: No; they are coming here.

S: I've got a scheme. Tell you about it later at the meeting.

K: We would like them to pick it up.

S: Well, I want to talk to you about that, when we get over there.

K: I have had to shift the meeting to 6:00. I had an effective turn-down from the Soviets. Only way now to get resolution is to let Israel get back to the cease-fire line with our help and then get negotiations going afterwards. If we force them back to the cease-fire line [then] we will make points with the Arabs, rescue them from the Israelis. Can you have a separate meeting, you, Brent, and I?

S: Sure. We have some alternatives to present to you.

LORD CROMER–KISSINGER

Sunday, October 7, 1973
4:25 P.M.

K: I've been talking to the President and we are going to ask for a Security Council meeting.

C: For today?

K: No. We'll propose it for tomorrow and we'll not break our backs getting a resolution quickly. We will lean towards a resolution along the lines I described to you.

C: Yes, something about stately pace.

K: Stately pace is right. I think by Tuesday a de facto situation may have resumed.

C: Very likely.

K: We will be glad to drop that part of what we disagree on. We will keep it if the de facto situation turns against the Arabs— Perhaps not oppose it too violently—greater use to obfuscate—

C: I see.

K: If I could figure out something we could table and if your man could cooperate with us in keeping discussion going—on the next day we could go over to your side of de facto situation—or you go to our side of it, against the Arabs. By Thursday, [it] can be a totally new situation.

C: Right.

K: All this, of course, is only for the Prime Minister or Foreign Minister.

C: Yes. I'll have to talk to Maitland [Sir Donald Maitland, British U.N. Ambassador]. We are motivated that it's ethically more correct and the Arab world will take offense the other way.

K: I understand your points very well. Problem is that the Arabs will take a licking.

C: Yes.

K: If that's the case, then the problem of our representative cooperating so he doesn't draw the issue—that quickly, that gives both the greater possibility.

C: Do you think the other members of the Security Council will come along?

K: How can they refuse?—a messy debate. A dangerous precedent to have a war going on for forty-eight hours and for the Security Council not to be seized with it.

C: Quite. I agree with you. Have the Russians expressed a point of view?

K: They have promised to concentrate criticism on Israel and not on us.

C: Won't they try to stir up the debate?

K: I don't object if they draw it out. That doesn't bother us right now. Isn't that what I understood you to say yesterday?

C: Oh, yes—

K: A discussion going—and a framework. The idea of stopping the Arabs is not going to be our problem on Wednesday— This is really—

C: I agree entirely.

K: If we wait until Israel has won and then come out, we're in trouble.

C: I agree. I'll get on to London, then.

K: We can count on [our] tactics being supported?

C: Yes.

K: Good. Thank you.

AMBASSADOR DOBRYNIN–KISSINGER
Sunday, October 7, 1973
4:40 P.M.

. . .

K: Anatoly, I wanted you to know what the President has decided to do. We'll announce at 5:00 we are asking for a Security Council meeting.

D: When are you announcing?

K: In about forty-five minutes, it shouldn't be on the TASS tickers before that. We haven't yet decided whether we will propose a resolution or what it will be. It may be just a discussion. But we don't see how we can avoid asking for a session. I think it's use-ful—keep the principle we discussed yesterday and we keep calm with each other. If your Ambassador conducts himself the same way, we will get through the day. I'll let you know in the morn-ing—we're not going to table a resolution tonight, even if we table one tomorrow—we can discuss. I will let you know a cou-ple of hours before we do it.

D: All right.

K: The President comes back tonight and I will have a chance to talk with him. I understand your view—a certain lapse in events that may overtake our discussion.

D: All right.

K: That's why we're not tabling anything. That gives us several hours to decide what to do.

   . . .

AMBASSADOR SCALI–KISSINGER
Sunday, October 7, 1973
4:45 P.M.

K: John, how are you? Where are you?

S: I'm fine. I'm in my office.

K: Where we now stand is the President is going to announce that we are asking for a meeting of the Security Council. We are going to ask for it tomorrow morning. I have explained the strategy to Popper [David Popper, Assistant Secretary of State for International Organization Affairs] and he will call you—but the main thing is to delay as long as possible to obfuscate the situation. I have told the British what our general line is and they have sworn they will cooperate without question and keep it open. If the situation is restored the second part of our thinking—becomes moot. You are not to indicate that we're to table a resolution. Just ask for the meeting.

S: All right.

K: Let them guess. Our primary purpose is to beat the Assembly. David [Popper] will call you and give you the details.

S: All right.

K: Major thing is to not do too much too fast.

S: Very good, Henry.

FOREIGN MINISTER ZAYYAT–KISSINGER
Sunday, October 7, 1973
4:55 P.M.

K: Television star here. I can't retaliate. If you put me on Egyptian radio, no one would understand me, what I was saying.

Z: Of course, of course, but if you came to my country—

K: I hope to be able to come.

Z: Have you got—[the] letter [to me from Sadat's security adviser Hafiz Ismail]?

K: Was it substantive or personal?

Z: I think it's important. It speaks about our continual searching for peace.

K: Oh, that's very constructive and I am delighted. You can be sure we will respond in a positive way. I want to tell you what we are planning to do—way you have handled the situation. As I understand, you will make a statement but not ask for debate—very much in the spirit of our conversation.

Z: Of course. Well, I promised you that—

K: We are going to ask in the next hour for a Security Council meeting tomorrow. We have not really made up our mind whether we will come forward with a resolution—thought it not possible not to have key discussion in the U.N. Our—will be the same, as it will be low-key and decided to permit constructive— conditions of our relationship. Only reason I wanted to explain to you that we are doing it as a matter of principle of not having a war go on which isn't even discussed in the U.N. We will conduct the debate on our side without criticism of any country. We haven't yet decided whether we will put forward a resolution. If we do, I will let you know.

Z: This would be very embarrassing.

K: I understand that, and—we will take a new look at the situation.

Z: Of course, our reaction would be to—object— You understand we cannot—

K: We are not asking for support. I assure you, though, that whatever happens tactically in the next week, our strategy will be the one I discussed with you—continuing the atmosphere from our side—

Z: —get the letter—

K: Certainly, when I get the letter, I may call you after I have seen it.

SENATOR J. WILLIAM FULBRIGHT (D.-ARK.), CHAIRMAN OF
THE SENATE FOREIGN RELATIONS COMMITTEE–KISSINGER

Sunday, October 7, 1973
5:00 P.M.

K: I wanted to tell you that we will be asking in the next half hour for a meeting of the Security Council, probably in the morning.

F: Umhum.

K: And that this will then seize the U.N. with it. We have also talked with the Secretary General and others this afternoon. I think we have it worked out so we won't have debate in the General Assembly.

F: Good. And is the Secretary General agreeable?

K: Well, that isn't so clear yet. I think there will be in particular, a noncontentious spirit toward the U.S.

F: I think that sounds hopeful. Any new developments on the war front?

K: It's night now.

. . .

SENATOR GEORGE AIKEN (R.-VT.), RANKING MEMBER OF THE
SENATE FOREIGN RELATIONS COMMITTEE–KISSINGER

Sunday, October 7, 1973
5:05 P.M.

A: Things any better?

K: I think that by the end of this week this will be behind us. We are going to ask for a meeting of the Security Council tomorrow.

A: You'll ask for one tomorrow?

K: Yes and to have informal consultations tonight.

A: I see. You say the Russians were tolerant.

K: [The] Russians are confused and wasting time. Maybe they don't know what they are going to do.

A: That's possible that they don't. Too bad we had this three-day holiday all at once and Yom Kippur on top of it all. These things always happen, like the seventh of December.

K: Yes, that's right, always on a weekend.

A: I have had a feeling that you are going to do all right.

K: I think we'll calm it down.

A: One of the press called me last night and said you said you called Mike [Senate Majority Leader Mike Mansfield (D.-Mont.)] and me. If you said you had, of course you had. I have got a feeling, though, you are going to come out of this, maybe looking better than you did before.

K: I think in the long term we can use this.

A: Russians withdraw from Egypt?

K: They pulled out all their advisers. They expected something was coming but they didn't want to get involved.

A: I think you're doing it just right.

FOREIGN MINISTER EBAN–KISSINGER
Sunday, October 7, 1973
5:08 P.M.

K: Good afternoon. We have now decided to go ahead along the lines we discussed earlier. Therefore, you mustn't do anything. The President—not the President himself but Key Biscayne—is going to announce that we will ask for a meeting of the Security Council. We will then, around 5:30, ask the President of the Security Council for a meeting tomorrow. We will let it go at that for tonight. We will not indicate today whether we will table a resolution or what it will be. Don't want to get too much—generated. We will table a resolution along—this is for your private information—lines we discussed. I understand you will have to speak before the Council.

E: I will have to speak very early.

K: At the Council—we will count on your eloquence—and in this case wouldn't mind if you sacrificed eloquence to length.

E: Oh, yes, I agree; it often happens in inverse relation. I'll just say we want—cease-fire in full.

K: Not necessary for you to make any proposal as long as you discuss the situation in great detail.

E: —saying Egypt and Syria encroached on us and not us on them. I assure you we are keeping an eye on other Western Europeans; presume you are doing so as well.

FOREIGN MINISTER ZAYYAT–KISSINGER

Sunday, October 7, 1973
6:20 P.M.

K: Mr. Foreign Minister.

Z: Yes, Mr. Kissinger. Sorry to call you on such a small matter.

K: Not at all.

Z: But we have demonstrations here in front of our mission, breaking all the windows and it is not important if it is only our lives, but we have all the Foreign Ministers of other countries and they will be—

K: No, no, no, it is inexcusable. On behalf of the U.S. Government, let me apologize to you.

Z: Well, it's not a question of apologies, it's a question of—

K: It is under the jurisdiction of the New York police. We will take immediate steps.

Z: I know, but we don't care if it is under the New York jurisdiction or the San Francisco jurisdiction—

K: No, no, Mr. Foreign Minister; we will take immediate steps.

Z: All right. Thank you very much.

K: Immediately.

NEW YORK CITY MAYOR JOHN LINDSAY–KISSINGER

Sunday, October 7, 1973
7:10 P.M.

K: Hello, John.

L: Mayor Lindsay calling.

K: Yes, how are you?

L: I think that the Arab Ambassador here is hysterical.

K: [laughs] Not the Ambassador; it's the Foreign Minister.

L: Whoever it is that was calling.

K: He told me he didn't care about his life but the lives of so many innocent people.

L: Well, there's six thousand people demonstrating. It is well under control. The action is all moved down to the courts because our police arrested a whole mess of people, both JDLs [Jewish Defense League] and Arabs. So the crowd has moved down to the courthouse where they're all in the can at the moment. They're arrested anyway.

K: Okay.

L: We believe it is well under control. We've got about a thousand cops on. I'll be glad to send the bill for overtime to the State Department.

K: Oh, control your enthusiasm.

L: I think it's all right. If there's any developments that change, I'll of course call you.

K: Many thanks.

L: I've been in touch with Scali and I've just got off the phone with Waldheim. So I think they're reasonably calm at the moment.

K: Many thanks.

L: And we'll be alert through the night and all day tomorrow.

K: Good.

SENATOR MIKE MANSFIELD (D.-MONT.), SENATE MAJORITY
LEADER–KISSINGER

Sunday, October 7, 1973
8:15 P.M.

K: I just called you earlier in the day to tell you what we had decided to do. Now, we have already taken it to the Security Council. We have been in consultation all day with the British, Israelis, Arabs and we think conditions are right now to start discussions in—

M: What's the attitude of the Russians?

K: . . . My impression, quite honestly, is that they were taken aback by what the Arabs did this time. This is confidential information, but they have informed us they pulled out all advisers against the wishes of the countries before the fighting began.

M: Since the fighting broke out?

K: Before the fighting broke out, they knew about it about two days in advance. So, there are no Russians involved.

M: That's good. The position we are going to take tomorrow is to request a return to the situation to what it was before the fighting started. Our estimate is with the Israelis succeeding, now that will look increasingly attractive—

. . .

THE PRESIDENT–KISSINGER
Sunday, October 7, 1973
10:30 P.M.

K: Hello.

N: Hello, Henry. What's new?

K: We have got the thing pretty well orchestrated, Mr. President. The Security Council meeting is set for 3:30 tomorrow afternoon.

N: At our request.

K: Yes, at our request.

N: I mean is anybody joining us?

K: In calling it? No, but we don't need anyone to join us— I've got us well positioned. I think we should not, Mr. President, propose a resolution which will only be defeated, but develop our philosophy—how it should end.

N: [. . .] are you going up there or is Scali going to?

K: No, Scali can do it.

N: If the U.N. is going to fail, let it fail without us.

K: By Thursday evening everyone will be pleading with us to introduce that resolution. I told the Russians we were not introducing a resolution—have consultations.

N: No message from Brezhnev?

K: Oh, yes. We heard from him.

N: What did he say?

K: It was a friendly message, but it didn't say anything. One thing it did say was that the Russians pulled out all their advisers against the wishes of the Arab governments, and we have confirmed that through our sources. Also they have withdrawn their fleet in the Mediterranean.

N: Where's our fleet?

K: Well, actually our two fleets are very close together. Ours went east and theirs went west. They have moved back and we have moved up— Military situation sufficiently clear. Everybody wants a settlement. Also arrangement for Israelis to stick to—if they go beyond the [previous lines]. If you appeal to them to return, they must return. I have checked this with Mrs. Meir and she agrees.

N: I see. With regard to the report I was reading coming up on the plane, possibly out-of-date by now, but the doggoned Syrians surprised me. They're doing better than I ever thought.

K: The Israelis haven't thrown in the reserves yet. They're doing damned well. They've taken [unclear], penetrated two points and that mountain. You must have seen it when you were there.

N: Yes, I remember.

K: They have done pretty well. Implacement won't be complete until tomorrow. Then Ismail [Sadat's security adviser] sent me a message suggesting [a] possible framework for negotiations. Not yet adequate. It's where North Vietnam was four months before the breakthrough. The same message was sent through the Shah [of Iran], but it's not yet adequate and it's not quite time to do [it]. We have to get the war stopped first. Then—diplomacy.

N: The thing to do now is to get the war stopped. That would be [a]

great achievement. One of the greatest achievements of all. People in this country would think—really tough.

[. . .]

K: It's a little premature. One usually smells a point when one can
say they see it come together. Wednesday or Thursday perhaps.
I've been calling a lot of senators in your behalf, after you decided to go to the U.N.

N: I will be in the morning. Will you be at the White House tomorrow?

K: I'll be in around 8:00, 8:30.

N: Good. Why don't you come over and we'll have a talk, publi-
cize it.

The reference to a letter from Egypt's National Security Adviser,
Hafiz Ismail, on behalf of Sadat—which Zayyat had also mentioned
earlier in the day—was one reason we believed we were in a position
to control the pace of diplomacy. On the first day of the war, Sadat
had taken the extraordinary step of contacting us. In a message addressed to me through intelligence channels, Ismail informed us of
Egypt's terms for ending the war. The terms were not acceptable, requiring the withdrawal of Israel to the 1967 borders. But they were
clearly an opening position. Communicating with us was risky
enough. Sadat could not compound the risk of alienating Syria and
perhaps the Soviet Union—whose support was essential for the conduct of the war—by immediately offering concessions that might
drive Syria to abandon the common struggle or the Soviet Union to
reduce its supplies.

What was significant was the fact of the message, not its content.
Sadat was inviting the United States to take charge of the peace
process, despite the fact that at the United Nations we were advocat-
ing that he give up territory that his armies had just captured. The
message included an avowal that showed Sadat knew very well the
limits of what was attainable: "We do not intend to deepen the en-

gagements or widen the confrontation." If that phrase had any meaning, it was that Egypt did not propose to pursue offensive operations beyond the territory already gained nor to use America as a whipping boy—as Nasser had done in 1967. But if we understood Sadat correctly, a gap would inevitably develop between Egypt's military dispositions and its political objectives; this must sooner or later lead to a political negotiation.

At the end of the day, I summed up our strategy at a WSAG meeting:

> Egypt doesn't want a confrontation with us at the UN and the Soviets don't want a confrontation with us period. Our general position will be a restoration of the cease-fire lines. The Arabs will scream that they are being deprived of their birthright, but by Thursday [October 11] they will be on their knees begging us for a cease-fire. . . . We're trying to get this over with a limited amount of damage to our relations with the Arabs and the Soviets. If we can also put some money in the bank with the Israelis to draw on in later negotiations, well and good.*

As this day progressed, our strategy seemed to be vindicated.

---

* The following exchange reflects, however, the beginning of my doubt about our intelligence appraisals of an early Israeli victory:

KISSINGER: Euphoria has set in.

COLBY [CIA DIRECTOR WILLIAM COLBY]: The Syrians think they're doing well. They're not looking at the long term. Egypt may have intended to make only a limited move across the Canal.

KISSINGER: Why aren't they clinching their gain? Every foreign ambassador who saw Sadat today was told that Egypt didn't want a cease-fire until they were at the Israeli border.

SCHLESINGER: You're being logical. You can't ascribe that kind of logic to them.

RUSH [DEPUTY SECRETARY OF STATE KEN RUSH]: It's difficult to think Sadat would cross the Suez and just sit there.

KISSINGER: My judgment is that he *will* cross the Suez and just *sit* there. I don't think he will penetrate further.

October 8, 1973

A joint estimate by the CIA and DIA [Defense Intelligence Agency] held that the Israelis should turn the tide on the Golan Heights by Tuesday night: "pressing the offensive against the Syrians might take another day or two"—presumably to complete the destruction of the Syrian army. On the Egyptian front it was predicted that the outcome would be clear by Wednesday at the latest. This relatively neutral statement was amplified in a manner indicating little doubt about the prospect: "Several more days of heavy fighting might follow as the Israelis work to destroy as much as possible of Egypt's army."

In these circumstances, diplomatic delay seemed to fit our needs. With every passing hour, the difference that divided us from the rest of the Security Council—whether there should be a cease-fire in place or a return to the status quo ante, as we sought—would be overtaken by events. Once the Israeli army reached the lines at which the war had started, we could accept a simple cease-fire. If Israel advanced beyond these lines, a Security Council majority could be counted on to adopt our original position of restoring the status quo ante, and we would go along with it. It was in our interest, or so it seemed, to keep everything as calm as possible lest the impending Israeli victory inflame friendly Arab nations or tempt the Soviets into seeking to or reversing the course of events by military threats. The Soviet Union, for its own reasons, was also playing for time. The outcome would therefore depend on which assessment of the situation proved to be the better one.

To further these prospects, I sent a reply to Hafiz Ismail designed to induce restraint by Sadat. It said in essence that Egypt had made its point; no more could be gained militarily; the United States was engaged diplomatically:

> I would like to reiterate that the United States will do everything possible to assist the contending parties to bring the fighting to a

halt. The United States, and I personally, will also actively participate in assisting the parties to reach a just resolution of the problems
which have for so long plagued the Middle East.

The rest of the day was spent briefing congressional leaders,
keeping the Soviet Union diplomatically involved to prevent it from
leading a charge against us at the United Nations and in the Arab
world, and keeping open the prospects of an American leadership of
the peace process in the Middle East.

REPRESENTATIVE THOMAS "DOC" MORGAN (D.-W.VA.),
CHAIRMAN OF THE HOUSE FOREIGN RELATIONS
COMMITTEE–KISSINGER
Monday, October 8, 1973
9:46 A.M.

K: Mr. Chairman, we've had a difficult time getting together.

M: Yeah, I've been moving around.

K: And I was at a meeting. Just wanted to give you a brief rundown
on where we stand.

M: Right.

K: Mr. Chairman, ever since we got word of impending conflict,
what we have been trying to do is to get—first to try to prevent it
and that failed, and then we tried to get it stopped— Now we are
in touch with all the permanent members of the Security Council and constantly in touch with the Egyptian and Israeli Foreign
Ministers, and very much [in] contact with the Soviet Union.
We tried on Saturday to get a Security Council meeting started
asking for an end of hostilities and we couldn't generate any support for it from anybody and therefore a call for it would simply
have meant that there would be no resolution and we would have
been worse off. So we spent all our time trying to generate a consensus on some resolution that people might agree on, we also
asked the President of the Security Council to have informal

consultations and he couldn't get any support, so we went through that process all day yesterday and then finally late in the afternoon we decided to call for a meeting ourselves when no one else would do it with us. We are now going to have a meeting this afternoon and we will try to get the fighting stopped, but I wanted you to know that—

M: The resolution now—just—

K: We want to see what the situation is, we don't think it is a good idea to have a resolution that doesn't have support, because then we're worse off, and we don't want if we can avoid [it] to be in a confrontation with the Soviets and Egyptians and so we are now positioned that we are the only country that's in touch with all the parties—and we will put in a resolution just as soon as we think it has enough support to pass.

M: Yes, ah huh.

K: But I wanted you to know that we are very active, and that as soon as we see anything jelling that can work, we'll propose it but I think you'll agree what we don't want is a yelling match that makes the situation worse.

M: I agree with that.

AMBASSADOR DOBRYNIN–KISSINGER

Monday, October 8, 1973
9:54 A.M.

D: I just received an oral message—a very short one, but I think it is fairly urgent. An oral message from Brezhnev to the President and he asked me to tell you personally about it. The message is very short and I will just read it: "We have contacted the leaders of the Arab states on the question of of cease-fire. We hope to get a reply shortly. We feel that we should act in cooperation with you, being guided by the broad interests of maintaining peace and developing the Soviet-American relations. We hope that President Nixon will act likewise."

K: I can answer that for you right away because I have just come from the President. This reflects our spirit and we will also—we are eager to cooperate in bringing peace. I was going to call you. Just for your guidance—with reference to the discussions we have had, we were not going to put in a resolution at the Security Council this afternoon.

D: Not going to?

K: No, we are just going to have a general discussion. But we would appreciate it since we are doing that, that you don't confront us with one without discussion.

D: I don't know—I have a telegram from—which will sent to our Ambassador to the delegation to the United Nations—with instructions—I don't know yet.

K: Will you let me know what you are going to do?

D: But I will right now mention to them that you are not going to put any—you are not going to today, yes?

K: We have no intention to put one in today unless there is a drastic change.

D: Of the situation.

K: We thought that since you wouldn't agree with us on our proposal and since we wouldn't agree with you, it would be best to have a general discussion.

D: I think so. Maybe there will be some reply and then we will be in touch with you, of course. But as of now my personal feeling is that the best thing to do is a general discussion without—

K: Why don't you inform Moscow of this?

D: I will do that right away.

K: Also, we will take a conciliatory—you know not a conciliatory but—

D: I understand—under the circumstances.

K: We will follow your line of not attacking you.

D: I understand.

      . . .

SENATOR JOHN STENNIS (D.-MISS.), CHAIRMAN OF THE
SENATE ARMED SERVICES COMMITTEE–KISSINGER

Monday, October 8, 1973
10:20 A.M.

K: Never any lack of excitement, Mr. Chairman.

S: You're at the right place though. You'll find a way.

K: Mr. Chairman, I just wanted to call you to bring you up-to-date on what's going on.

S: That's mighty nice of you.

K: What we are doing is, we're not making any grandstand plays. We could have called a Security Council meeting on Saturday but we first told the Russians we wanted to stay in step with them and have them act responsibly. We then went to the Egyptians and Israelis and to the British and French and it turned out that there was no consensus for anything.

S: No what.

K: No agreement to do anything, so rather than force a confrontation in which we would get outvoted we stayed in contact with them and kept offering our good [offices]. Then yesterday afternoon we went ahead and unilaterally called a Security Council meeting for today and now this morning we had a message from the Russians saying they want to stay in step with us and they would do their utmost to keep the situation from getting out of control. So even though you may not see much visible action, I think we've contained the crisis and we think that in another couple of days we'll have it quieted down.

S: That's fine.

K: So, we think the Israelis will rectify the military situation and just for your information we will be in favor of the restoration of the cease-fire lines as they were when the fighting started. That was our position Saturday afternoon when the Arabs were gaining territory. This will be our position tomorrow when the Israelis will be gaining territory. We'll apply it totally evenhandedly.

. . .

LORD CROMER–KISSINGER

Monday, October 8, 1973
11:00 A.M.

K: I wanted to bring you up-to-date on what we are doing.

C: Thank you.

K: We have decided not to introduce a resolution this afternoon. We will state our general objective along the lines of a cease-fire and a return to the positions prior to October 6 but not in the form of a resolution but in a form of a philosophical statement. We thought this would give you an opportunity to—we will then not have votes and competing views. Our instinct is that by to-morrow this whole question will be moot.

C: As quickly as that?

K: Say Wednesday. My personal instinct is tomorrow. My recommendation to you is not to push for a straight-out cease-fire because you may be ratifying Israeli territory again. I think our Saturday position will look better to you tomorrow night.

C: I have long thought this might be the case.

K: I would urge—we will put ours forward constructively and ambiguously. If you could get your demon draftsmen in London to do the same thing—

C: Fine. Thank you for letting me know. Incidentally, I gather something is on the AP tape that says Fulbright and the British Ambassador are reluctant about what is going on. I am not reluctant. We are hand in hand with what is going on.

K: I have not seen that and I would think Fulbright is going along. I think you and I are in good standing.

C: Right.

K: We don't mind a shade of difference that would permit us to move to another position. Let's play it that way through the rest of the day and tomorrow we will see what will have crystallized.

C: Have you decided whether to do anything concerning the Lebanon plea to you to intercede on their behalf with the Israelis?

K: I am not aware of that.

C: I think they made an appeal formally.

K: To us?

C: That is my understanding. That is what he [Lebanon's President] told us he is doing.

K: If so, we either have not received it or my associates are not keeping me informed about countries with less than ten million population. If the Lebanese made such an appeal we would intercede on their behalf.

C: I will ask my people at a lower level to get in touch with yours.

K: Tell your people to get in touch with Sisco.

C: All right, Henry.

SENATOR MANSFIELD–KISSINGER
Monday, October 8, 1973
11:25 A.M.

K: How are you, Senator? I wanted to give you a brief word on the state of play. We have now had information from the Russians saying they are using their influence to restrain and they hope we are doing the same thing. Of course, we are already doing this. Also, very confidentially, I have made this exchange with the Egyptians and I have concerted with the British for the Security Council meeting this afternoon and with the Russians to keep it from degenerating into a shouting match. The reason we are not formally putting forward a resolution is because it does not do any good to have a lot of competing resolutions, all of which will fail. We are trying to crystallize a consensus and I wanted you to understand our strategy. As soon as a consensus exists we will support it, as we were ready to do from Saturday on. For your own private information, we took the position that everyone should return to their position when the fighting started. The Arabs told us this would be very unsatisfactory to them. We took that position because we assume the Israeli position would change.

M: You mean last Friday.

K: I want you to know that whoever is ahead at the time of the resolution, we are going to be urging a return to the positions of Friday. My judgment is this will be working against the Arabs soon. You may be catching some flak on this. I don't see how we can have another territorial grab.

M: Aiken [senator from Vermont] called me. He got wind of a resolution and he was much opposed to it. He wanted to support your position and not have something contrary to what you were trying to do. Minority Leader Scott [Senator Hugh Scott (R.-Penn.)] came in later and agreed. We said we would take that position. It is impossible to have any resolution here until you get a chance to make your position known and make these contacts.

K: We don't object to a resolution that calls for a return to a position of Friday for the reason that we think that position will be reached certainly by tomorrow and after that the Israelis are going to be advancing into the Arab country.

M: I see. Okay. You can talk to Scott on that basis and I wish you would too.

K: I don't want to have it said that I urged it.

M: I will talk to Scott and say that I asked you. And if he wants to call you.

K: And that I would be happy to talk to him.

M: Good, Henry.

SENATOR HUGH SCOTT (R.-PENN.), SENATE MINORITY LEADER–KISSINGER

Monday, October 8, 1973
11:35 A.M.

K: You are a mind reader. I was going to call you.

S: Mike and I were talking and of course to Aiken and, as Mike told you, both of us are taking the position that you need all the elbow room you can get.

K: Right.

S: There will be God knows any number of senators coming in

with any number of resolutions and the major question—the reason Mike is here with me now is, shall we continue to say no resolution, as far as we are concerned, or should we give some thought to a resolution which supports you.

K: If you think you could get a Senate resolution supporting the course we have taken and expressing our view that the Senate favors a cease-fire and return to the positions the parties occupied Friday—

S: That is our position.

K: —before the outbreak of hostilities. We have not said that publicly but it will be the position we will take. If we could point to strong Senate support that would be helpful.

S: All right. Mike is right here. Suppose we do that. Most of the resolutions are being sent in to me and they are very fiery and partisan.

K: I think the best thing, from our selfish point of view and from the national point of view, is if the Senate could express support for the way the crisis has been handled and expresses the hope that the administration will seek an early cease-fire and return to the positions occupied when the fighting started.

S: All right. I think that is all right with Mike. We will work out a joint resolution. We will do that.

K: That would be very helpful.

THE PRESIDENT–KISSINGER

Monday, October 8, 1973
11:50 A.M.

N: Regarding Scott and Mansfield, did you in effect tell them—are they going to put out that we support such a resolution?

K: Yes. They are saying this—they are not saying this is a resolution. They are saying this should be our objective.

N: They will indicate that the administration favors that objective.

K: That we should favor that objective. I said this would not run afoul of anything we are trying to do. I did not tell them to do it. Otherwise they were going to do something much stronger.

N: Yes. Would it be helpful if I were to lean on them and to tell them not to go too far?

K: No. Mr. President, this is not going too far.

N: On their part.

K: No. No. Not going too far on their part. Scali will have spoken before they can get any resolution like this passed. This is essentially our position. They are supporting you.

N: If I had to be in touch with them, I could say we appreciate that support.

K: I think that would be appreciated. That would be a nice gesture.

N: Fine. Fine. Okay.

SENATOR JAVITS–KISSINGER
Monday, October 8, 1973
12:55 P.M.

J: Has Hugh Scott talked to you about this resolution?

K: Yes.

J: Have you worked anything out with him?

K: I talked to him and to Dinitz too to make sure it did not bother them. We would welcome a resolution along the following lines. An expression of approval and recommendation that supported a restoration of the cease-fire at the line prior to the hostilities.

J: They have one in here that exercises it full diplomatic—and elsewhere to achieve a defensible border. Whatever the words of the 242 are. Does that bother you?

K: No.

J: We have two parts. Approving the way the crisis is being handled and supporting restoration of the agreed-upon cease-fire line.

K: I would not use cease-fire line—that creates confusion like in '67.

J: Support restoration.

K: Of the positions the two sides occupied before the outbreak of hostilities.

J: Last is the pragmatory phrase. Okay?

K: Good.

J: Is that all right today?

K: That would be fine.

There were periodic briefings from the Israeli Ambassador, who rarely forewent an opportunity to remind me that, in addition to armies in the field, he disposed of legions in Congress.

ISRAELI AMBASSADOR SIMCHA DINITZ–KISSINGER
Monday, October 8, 1973
1:14 P.M.

D: With your permission I will give you the latest information I have and the special thing from the Prime Minister. The situation on the front looks considerably better. We have gone over from containment to attack, both on the Sinai and Golan Heights. Our military people think that a good possibility we will push the Syrians all the way across the cease-fire line and we are also moving out the Egyptian forces in the Sinai.

K: I have seen a report that you have crossed the Canal.

D: I have seen this too and I talked to the Prime Minister's office an hour ago and I could not get any confirmation. I was waiting confirmation on that. I will read to you this subsequent message [when I get it]. Continuing with the military review: it is all the more important for us to gain time to complete the job. We will not only reject—I am waiting instructions from the Prime Minister—we not only reject that which freezes the cease-fire but which calls for return, which is unrealistic because there is no guarantee they will withdraw their forces. I want to tell you we suffered very heavy casualties both in human and equipment—from the SAM-6s, which were very effective against our planes. I don't have an additional figure against the thirty-five planes I told you about yesterday. The human casualties I think are over one hundred or maybe hundreds. We have no confirmation.

K: Hundreds?

D: Yes. Hundreds. It is quite possible that we will take some military positions on the other side of the Canal. I am saying this without confirmation. The earlier message from the Prime Minister is that it is possible that we will take military positions on the other side of the Canal and on the former cease-fire line of the Golan Heights in hot pursuit and to insure ourselves against new attacks and to have some new political cards to play as we talked yesterday. I don't have confirmation of any action such as this because the fighting is still, to the best of my knowledge, still on our side of the cease-fire line. Now, I have a special message from the Prime Minister to you, which I will read, and when we see each other I will take it to Peter [Rodman, a key staff aide]. "The Prime Minister wishes to convey to you her profound appreciation not only for your help but for your wise counsel. She says in the cable that you understand exactly the situation that goes on in our minds as if you were sitting with us here. The aims of our fighting are absolutely clear to you. It is our objective that the heavy blows we will strike at the invaders will deprive them of any appetite they will have for any future assault. Our extraordinary military efforts extolled [sic] a heavy price, especially planes. We are faced with a tremendous gap in quantity. Our planes are hit and being worn out. The Prime Minister urgently appeals to you that there is an immediate start of delivery of at least some of the new Phantom planes." End of message.

K: I will do my best and tell her for her information I have talked to the President this morning and to General Haig about the replacing of aircraft losses which, as you know, met some opposition yesterday and he has agreed in principle.

D: I see. How do we proceed? Shall I wait to hear from you?

K: You had better wait to hear from me. It might affect your own calculations.

D: That is very important. I will send a message right away.

K: I don't want to mislead you. We will maintain our position on the cease-fire line—we discussed this yesterday—without prejudice to the immediate military operations. That is the position we will take at the Security Council. We will not introduce a resolution, just a philosophical talk.

D: Of course.

K: One other thing. We have had a much more conciliatory Soviet message this morning, urging us to urge restraint, but we have answered that we are urging restraint. At any rate, we are warning them against any action and I am giving a speech tonight in the *Pacem in Terris* conference and I am making two pointed references that détente cannot survive irresponsible actions. In one context I mention specifically the Middle East. I am going also in this speech to mention our MFN [Most Favored Nation] position and I hope to God this is not a week when every Jewish league will start attacking me on this position.

D: To a degree I can speak in the name, that I don't think that it will happen this week in any way.

K: I don't think it would be very wise. That is not my major problem. The final question I have, Mr. Ambassador, is, the Lebanese have asked us to appeal to you that you should not violate their sovereignty and rather than send you a message through the ambassadorial channel I thought it easier to tell you directly and not have too much paperwork.

D: I am sure we have no designs to violate their sovereignty.

K: If you have no such designs and you could pass such a message to me that I could pass to them and to the British, it would help establish the climate we all need.

D: I will confirm it to you. We will keep the British out.

K: Confirm it to me and if you could do it soon it would be helpful.

D: I have one item for you—an additional item. I have received many calls during the morning from senators of all sorts. All with sympathy and request for help. I assured them all that [the] American government is urging peace, stability and seeing things eye-to-eye and that we have no problem. Some wanted to sponsor a resolution and instead of this I think what they are doing at this stage is coming out with a statement. Scott will be contacting you shortly.

K: He has done so and I have told him that I have no objection to the sort of resolution and I discussed it yesterday with him. I am not pushing it.

D: I am not either, by the way. Senator Bayh [Birch Bayh (D.-Ind.)] and Senator [Alan Cranston (D.-Calif.)] from California and Kennedy [Senator Ted Kennedy (D.-Mass.)] came out with a statement. They are all lining up. I am not asking any initiative on their part. Just briefing them and many are asking whether they can help materially. I say to them, I am in close touch with the government and we have no outstanding problems.

K: Right.

D: Yesterday I gave you information from our intelligence re the Russians and the Syrians. I have a correction. They are not sure about it and ask me to tell you not to use it unless we have further confirmation.

K: Okay.

D: Whatever can be done on the planes and other equipment we would be grateful and it would be helpful.

K: The other equipment I will do something about today.

D: I will wait to hear from you and I will tell the Prime Minister what you have told me.

K: I will try to get the antitank and electronic stuff today.

D: Perhaps we should schedule to see each other—you are going to—

K: We might be able to do it later this afternoon.

SENATOR SCOTT–KISSINGER

Monday, October 8, 1973
1:15 P.M.

K: When you hung up, it occurred to me there might be some slight ambiguity. The return to the cease-fire line is the one that existed on Friday night, October 6, not in 1967.

S: In the legislative history we have covered the fact we were acting in support of what you had already done as well as what you were trying to do in the future. Javits has been in the meeting. I am with the Vietnam legislators now [on Vietnam appropriations]. He will make more of a point of that. Resolution reads— "deploring of outbreak of hostilities in the Middle East. Resolved that it is the sense of the Senate that we deplore the outbreak of hostilities in the Middle East and we support the good offices of the United States President and the Secretary of State to urge the participants to bring about a cease-fire and the return of the parties involved to lines and positions occupied prior to the outbreak of current hostilities and, further, that the Senate expresses the hope for a more stable condition leading to peace in that region."

K: Excellent.

S: We did not say more peaceful—more stable position leading to peace.

K: Could not be better, from my point of view.

S: We have made legislation history by saying we support what you have done as well as what you are trying to do. Javits, I think, wants to be in on the act. But he is going to say on the floor what a great guy you are.

K: I cannot object to that. Tell him I agree with it.

S: Sure. A pleasure.

K: Good-bye and thanks.

Senator Ted Kennedy (D.-Mass.)–Kissinger
Monday, October 8, 1973
1:40 P.M.

HAK: I just wanted to bring you up-to-date. On Saturday, first our efforts were to prevent the outbreak of the war and, after that, to get it ended. The difficulty we faced was that the Arabs were opposed to a Security Council meeting and, for their own reasons, so were the Israelis. We tried to stay in touch with the Soviets, the British and not one member of the Security Council was ready to have a meeting. Therefore, no resolution could have passed, and we thought it a mistake to try to force a resolution which would just have exacerbated everybody. Curiously enough, the Arabs, Israelis, British, and Soviets were pleading with us to take that course.

TK: You mean not to have a Security Council meeting.

HAK: Not to have a formal one. We held informal ones all day Saturday night, and it enabled the Soviets not to be in opposition with us, and it enabled us to stay in close touch with the Egyptians as well as the Israelis. We decided yesterday afternoon just not to go to the U.N. It would leave the U.N. totally discredited, so we asked for a Security Council meeting, and we are going to present not a formal resolution but our view, which is the outbreak of hostilities should be ended and a return to the positions held by the parties before the fighting started. That is going to look more attractive to the Arabs today than it did Saturday because the Israelis are gaining the upper hand, and it will look more attractive to them tomorrow. We are prepared to turn this into a resolution if it gets any support. In the meantime, we have had active exchanges with the Soviets. We are trying to keep them out of this, and it now looks as if we are in a pretty good position.

TK: What do you think—I don't know what that beep is—

HAK: Are you recording?

TK: No. I did not know what the possibilities were that it might continue. What are the pressures going to be on the Israelis to slow down? Is that real?

HAK: We have already told the Israelis we cannot support them beyond the present positions for mopping up, etc. But our judgment is by the end of this week it will be over. Both sides are suffering very heavy losses.

TK: I guess it is all going for the Israelis?

HAK: This afternoon it looks as though the Israelis are gaining the upper hand.

TK: You saw the resolution by Mansfield?

HAK: Yes. It looked all right to me. I understand that Eagleburger [Lawrence Eagleburger, Undersecretary of State for Administration, and a top aide] and your assistant are setting up a lunch or a meeting.

TK: Yes.

HAK: I will support that.

TK: Thanks, Henry. Appreciate that.

FOREIGN MINISTER ZAYYAT–KISSINGER
Monday, October 8, 1973
1:45 P.M.

K: Mr. Foreign Minister, two things. I have softened the statement we are making to an almost unrecognizable point and I have added another point that peace in the Middle East requires observance of all the U.N. resolutions, which I am sure you will recognize the Israelis will not be enthusiastic about.

Z: Thank you. I will hear it.

K: You will find that it is a minimum statement given our conditions here that we can make.

Z: I will have to hear it.

K: I just want to tell you and assure you, as you will see from my communication to Ismail, that we are trying to maintain.

Z: I am now very disappointed.

K: Mr. Foreign Minister, you should think back to previous meetings. You will find that this is the least that has ever been done.

Z: I was looking at *Life* magazine and I was reading something from you that we must see how much physical security is necessary to get—

K: That is right.

Z: Now you are really helping them to stay on this false issue of security.

K: My position is the one I explained to you on Friday and that position will be maintained. Secondly, the principles we are announcing will be maintained even if the Israelis are gaining territories.

Z: As I said, we would not allow it.

K: I understand. There would be no one who would understand it.

Z: No one would understand it?

K: I have no question about that. I understand you. Where shall I send that message to Ismail?

Z: I am here at the Waldorf Towers, 37F.

K: Okay. What time would be a good time to deliver it?

Z: Anytime. My wife is always here.

K: We can give it to her?

Z: Yes.

K: We will deliver it to the Waldorf at 37F and we have instructed our delegate—are you planning a reply?

Z: Of course. I was going to reply if they want to stay on our land.

K: I think you will find that not the case. You will find enough reference to other resolutions that it will say exactly the opposite. I have done my very best and you will see that we are facing enormous congressional pressure here but we are doing our best. You and I should maintain a contact because we want to move in the direction you and I discussed. Your statement today, I have read, and it is a very constructive one.

Z: Thank you.

K: You have behaved throughout in a most statesmanlike manner.

Z: This I hope so.

K: We will do our best.

Z: All right.

K: You and I should talk every day while this is going on.

FOREIGN MINISTER EBAN–KISSINGER

Monday, October 8, 1973
2:40 P.M.

K: Mr. Foreign Minister, I have been told by the Secretary General that he has agreement of the Egyptians not to speak at the Security Council if you will not.

E: I have given my agreement.

K: I think this would work well.

E: It works well in what we are trying to achieve.

K: This is what will happen at the Security Council unless something unexpected occurs. Scali will put forward our position and then it will adjourn.

E: I have spoken to the Australian Prime Minister and he is willing to cooperate too.

K: The only items before the Security Council will be something we are phrasing generally. We are saying [the] Egyptians and Syrians started it. We are not here to assess blame. Our principle is that the governments should set a cease-fire and a lot of words ending up with "the governments should return to the original positions." I think it would be helpful if you would not urge this for a while, so it does not look like American collusion.

E: I think so. We have made our point. I don't think we have to say anything to anybody today or to the press.

K: We are getting a congressional resolution passed down here.

E: I have heard from the Ambassador about that.

K: Which urges this.

E: Yes.

K: I don't think there is any need for you to make that point again. We don't want to make it easy for the Egyptians to claim collusion.

E: I want to know whenever silence will be helpful.

K: Are you prepared for a six-hour speech or silence?

E: Right. And your advice is always one of those extremes.

K: I do tend to go to extremes. You are quite right.

E: Unless I hear from you to the contrary, I will not speak. I will be there as a courtesy but will not ask for the floor.

AMBASSADOR DOBRYNIN–KISSINGER

Monday, October 8, 1973
3:00 P.M.

K: ... I want to tell you we are sticking with what I told you this morning. We are making a statement saying we don't want to assess blame and we are saying some principles of a settlement in a very general way—which includes the ideas I gave you, but stated so vaguely they are just there to invoke later on. If your representative can restrain himself, I think we can have a quiet session. I understand the Egyptian may not speak and we have urged the Israelis not to speak unless the Egyptian speaks. And I understand the Egyptian said he would not speak. If we can get these two quieted down, we could have a brief session.

D: You will not propose a resolution.

K: No. We are making a philosophical statement. Just translated from the German.*

D: Good.

K: I am counting on you to not come in with a resolution.

D: For all of my information there is none.

K: As I understand it Malik [Yakov Malik, Soviet Ambassador to the

---

* Joke about my accent.

United Nations] is not a member of the Central Committee and
he would not dare overrule you.

D: Definitely.

K: In all seriousness, I wanted to know your instructions [so as] to
avoid any confrontation with Malik. Our statement is phrased in
such a way that it should provoke no reaction by even the Arabs.
We have just one sentence referring to [a] return to previous positions. It is not as a proposal but will facilitate a good atmosphere. In our judgment by tomorrow evening it will be greatly
welcomed by your friends.

D: By tomorrow evening?

K: Or Wednesday.

D: You mean the cease-fire.

K: I don't know whether they will want a cease-fire but the military
will be such they will not be occupying much of Israeli territory
by tomorrow evening. It does not make any difference then; we
can drop it. We are not putting in any resolution. After this
speech, we will do nothing. I assure you we will not do one other
thing today. We do not now plan to put in a resolution.

D: This is the point.

K: As I understand Brezhnev's message this morning, it was: we
should stay in concert with this. Our answer to that is yes. We
will do nothing until we hear from you.

D: Have you had a chance to speak to Zayyat?

K: I have talked twice to him.

D: Today?

K: Yes.

D: Is he going to win the war?

. . .

K: My impression is, their assessment is they think they may be
winning.

D: He thinks one way publicly and the other way privately. It is difficult to say.

K: He did not make a specific proposal. He was not nasty. He just did not have a specific proposal. It is a new theory of warfare. I don't know if they learned it at your staff college or not. I am convinced that if you start a war, you know where you are going.

D: Okay. Be in touch.

   . . .

AMBASSADOR SCALI–KISSINGER
Monday, October 8, 1973
3:15 P.M.

K: You got the statement. It will not shake the world. Our information here is that there is a chance that no one else will speak but in any event if the Egyptian speaks and you feel obliged to reply, be very gentle with them. I don't insist that you reply but be very gentle and refer to the fact that the spirit of my conversation about peace is maintained. We don't want a confrontation with the Egyptians. It is my understanding that the Soviets are instructed to lay off us.

S: I was at a lunch with the Foreign Minister of Sudan and the permanent representative, Malik, left early because he has inscribed himself to speak.

K: When did he do that?

S: About forty minutes ago when he left this lunch.

K: To inscribe himself?

S: Yes. My understanding from the Security Council President.

K: You will have to judge the situation. We don't want a donnybrook with the Soviets this afternoon. If he gets offensive, we will have to. If anything, my understanding is, he will work over the Israelis. We will say we have deliberately avoided putting blame in our statement and we regret that he has concentrated on the past in such an erroneous way and we urge him to concentrate on the future. Okay?

S: Right. We know the Syrians and Israelis have asked to participate, but with no sign that they will speak today.

K: My information from the Israelis is that if the Egyptians do not
speak, even if the Syrians do, Eban may not speak. Eban is con-
fining himself to saying simply what he said this morning.

S: Very well. I have the text of this thing before me. I thought it essential for me to be there at the lunch.

K: You had to do that.

S: I will follow the instructions implicitly.

K: You are doing a great job. I think tomorrow this thing will get
lively. I think the Arabs have not yet understood what the military risks are.

S: If I can detect the atmosphere, the feeling is they were winning
and held the upper hand.

K: That has to be lack of communications. That is not our information.

S: This is the very definite feeling I picked up at the lunch.

K: By Tuesday or Wednesday it will be changed.

SECRETARY GENERAL WALDHEIM–KISSINGER
Monday, October 8, 1973
4:55 P.M.

. . .

W: I have talked to Ambassador Meguid [Egyptian permanent
representative to the United Nations]. There are two developments I want to bring to your attention on this occasion.
As far as the military situation is concerned, I got this call
from Ambassador Meguid telling me that Port Said has been
attacked by Israeli airplanes and he is quite upset about this
and instructed by his government to bring that to my attention
and to the attention of the [General] Assembly and Security
Council.

K: By what reasoning?

W: I think they still don't understand that war is war. If one has a war, one cannot avoid civilian targets.

K: It is the civilian targets.

W: The civilian population of Port Said.

K: They object to the bombing of civilians.

W: That is correct.

K: And they have every right to.

W: I don't know whether they will ask the Ambassador to talk: saying attacked by Israeli aircraft and wanted to bring to my attention and to the attention of the President of the [Security] Council. Zayyat will make a statement on that this afternoon. He wants to interrupt the general debate in the plenary. I asked him if he would make this statement in the Security Council. He said no, they would not speak in the Security Council. You would speak in this procedure, as originally planned.

K: I have never seen a diplomacy like this. Have you any idea of what they think they are doing? All our information is that they are going to get beaten in battle. I have never known why a side that is losing a war insists on time. We will maintain our position no matter who is winning.

W: For your information, the Ambassador told me sort of confidentially—I don't know why he stressed it—but he said the military was in good position as far as the two bridges along the Suez Canal [are concerned]. He said the military situation was not bad for them. I got different information, but I think it is in the light of this opinion that the Security Council debate is not good for them.

K: I think by tomorrow the debate will pick up.

W: Exactly. My opinion is the situation will be different and they will be happy to—

K: My view too.

W: The other important information I want to give you is, yesterday evening I got a report from our observers saying the Egyptian high command requested withdrawal of all of our observers along the Suez Canal. Request to be made by your government or the Secretary General. It was a consensus of the Security Council on the 10th of July 1967, after the Six Day War that these observers were sent to the Canal Zone.

K: Exactly right.

W: I waited during the night for a request and did not get it. I rang up this morning and asked him and he said he did not know about it and he would check with Cairo and shortly after that he contacted [unclear] and came to see me. He said he had gotten instructions of withdrawal along the Canal for their own security. They are now behind our lines and cannot serve any purpose anymore and thanking us for the good services done in the past and they are not needed anymore and we ask your withdrawal. I sent around 10:00 this morning a letter to the President [of the Security Council] informing of this request and informed McIntyre about this. In the meantime, which is also important, we got the report that some of them—two–three of them—have been escorted to Cairo by the Egyptian forces. The rest apparently still there. We are waiting for a final report. This is the situation that is rather awkward.

K: There is nothing you can do about it.

. . .

AMBASSADOR DINITZ–KISSINGER

Monday, October 8, 1973
5:05 P.M.

D: We have received a full account of today's battle for delivery to you. I will do that later. I am telling you now, in answer to the specific question, that our ground forces are not—repeat not— operating on the western side of the Canal.

K: Good. I don't know why I am saying good. That is up to you.

D: I am calling your attention to what our chief of staff said in answer to that question: he said not yet. The cable I have said not operating yet. I presume we are now busy mopping up the remainder of the Egyptian forces on our side of the Canal.

K: May I make one other suggestion? It would help if your Foreign Minister in New York would not make a proposal.

D: I want to make that point. He told me you talked to him.

K: It puts us in the position of having aligned ourselves with you, which we don't object to, but it is in our common interest to keep [from] precipitating [charges of collusion].

. . .

D: I will tell Eban we are of the opinion that no one will talk. If the Syrians talk and he feels it necessary to say something he will say something about this morning.

K: No concrete proposals. You will find our statement extremely mild but our major point is to prevent the Russians from replying. The less we do now to precipitate the better.

D: The exercise is to be very conservative.

K: Yes.

D: I can call later with news of the battles.

K: Call Scowcroft and tell him you have talked to me. Discuss with him about the movement of some of the ammunition and electronics.

D: I will call him now.

AMBASSADOR DOBRYNIN–KISSINGER
Monday, October 8, 1973
5:40 P.M.

[Transcript missing first sentences.]

D: . . . We are not going to do anything at the Council—no kind of resolution in the Security Council. Our representative in the Security Council has instructions not to have any polemics with the American representative. Meanwhile we continue to consult urgently with the Arab side. In this connection, we would like, and hope, that you will do everything not to force the Security Council to accept any resolutions—

K: You can count on that.

D: —until we have finished our consultations with our allies.

K: May I make a suggestion to you. Your Arab friends are going around New York saying I am giving them an ultimatum.

D: In New York?

K: Yes. I thought we had an agreement specifically.

D: They are trying to delay the Security Council meeting.

K: It is not going on yet.

D: No?

K: It has been delayed. My own recommendation is, we don't care whether it take place or not much. Let's have it, get it over and adjourn it. I promise you we will not introduce a resolution.

D: I can give instructions along those lines. . . .

K: Let's see what happens. You can promise Moscow flatly there will not be a resolution in the near future. There will not be a resolution. We are making a very mild statement.

D: I understand.

. . .

K: Let's have an understanding that neither one of us will introduce a resolution without giving the other one notice.

D: Exactly my instructions from Moscow.

K: We will not do it, I promise you, without giving you time to consult with Moscow. You do the same for us.

THE PRESIDENT–KISSINGER

Monday, October 8, 1973
7:08 P.M.

N: Hi, Henry. What's the latest news? I got the military news.

K: Yeah. Well, on the diplomatic front we had another message from Brezhnev asking us not to table a resolution and promising us he would not table a resolution without consulting with us, telling us they are using a great effort on the Arabs.

N: Yeah.

K: First of all, if this turns out to be true— Well, first of all, we're in no hurry to table anything.

N: No.

K: We're making our record. We're the only ones that are pushing for anything.

N: Yeah, yeah.

K: But if we bring it off—by Thursday it will be over, in my view.

N: Oh, sure.

K: If we bring it off, Mr. President, if this thing ends without a blowup, without either the Arabs or the Soviets, it will be a miracle and a triumph.

N: Right. The one thing we have to be concerned about, which you and I know looking down the road, is that the Israelis, when they finish clobbering the Egyptians and the Syrians, which they will do, will be even more impossible to deal with than before and you and I have got to determine in our own minds, we must have a diplomatic settlement there.

K: I agree with you.

N: We must have. We must not tell them that now, but we have got to do it. You see, they could feel so strong as a result of this, they'd say: Well, why do we have to settle? Understand? We must not, we must not under any circumstances allow them because of the victory that they're going to win—and they'll win it, thank God, they should—but we must not get away with just having this thing hang over for another four years and have us at odds with the Arab world. We're not going to do it anymore.

K: I agree with that completely, Mr. President. But what we are doing this week is putting us in a position to do—

N: To do something, that's right.

K: To do something.

N: And to do something with the Russians too.

K: Exactly.

N: I'm not tough on the Israelis. Fortunately, the Israelis will beat these guys so badly I hope that we can make sort of a reasonable [proposal]— You and I both know they can't go back to the other [1967] borders. But we must not, on the other hand, say that because the Israelis win this war, as they won the '67 war, that we just go on with status quo. It can't be done.

K: I couldn't agree more. I think what we are doing this week will help us next month.

N: Maybe. I hope so. But in any event, on Brezhnev, he may be wanting— Of course, the other thing that Brezhnev may be thinking of: his clients are going to get clobbered. You know, that's the only reason [Soviet Premier Alexei] Kosygin came to see [President Lyndon] Johnson [after the 1967 war].

K: Yeah, but in '67 they were moving their fleet around, threatening war, castigating us at the Security Council—breaking diplomatic relations with Israel, threatening our oil installations. And no one has made a peep against us yet.

N: That's great.

K: And that's a major triumph for our policy, and we can use it in the MFN fight [Jackson-Vanik that prevented MFN status for the Soviet Union unless it removed obstacles to Jewish emigration].

N: Thank God, yeah. You've got the Congress in good shape and you've got—

K: I had a good talk with Stennis [Senator John Stennis, chairman of the Senate Armed Services Committee].

N: How good? Does he think we're doing the right thing?

K: Oh, he says he's marking it down on this calendar. He said it's a great day.

N: Because why?

K: Because he thinks we're in control and we're handling it well.

N: Right. Good, good, good. That's good. Actually, though, the Israelis are really moving now, aren't they?

K: Well, they will be by tomorrow morning. I mean, they're in a position now from which they will—

N: They'll cut the Egyptians off. Poor dumb Egyptians, getting across the Canal and all the bridges will be blown up. They'll cut them all off—thirty or forty thousand of them. Go over and destroy the SAM sites. The Syrians will probably go rushing back across now.

K: No, the Syrians—that will turn into a turkey shoot by Wednesday.

N: Yeah, yeah—surrender.

K: Either surrender or a terrific shellacking.

N: Just so the Israelis don't get to the point where they say to us: We will not settle except on the basis of everything we got. They can't do that, Henry. They can't do that to us again. They've done it to us for four years but no more.

K: The first thing we've got to do is to get them back to their lines prior to the cease-fire.

N: I agree.

K: Which this they've promised us. But no one else knows we're going to manage it. And the next step then will be to start the diplomatic offensive.

N: Right.

K: Right after the [Israeli] election, which is two weeks from now.

N: That's right. Oh, I know, you've got to wait until after that. The first of November.

K: Right.

N: Good. Let me know if anything comes along.

JOSEPH SISCO, ASSISTANT SECRETARY OF STATE FOR NEAR
EASTERN AND SOUTH ASIAN AFFAIRS–KISSINGER

Monday, October 8, 1973
7:20 P.M.

K: Joe, did that [Security] Council meeting ever get off?

S: Yes it did. Scali spoke and it went that way. Zayyat is speaking right now and I have not been able to catch it and is still rolling on.

K: Oh, Zayyat is replying?

S: Well, I don't know that it is a reply. He really is going—as little as I heard—is that he is going into the history of the efforts to achieve a peace, which was pretty much the line that he took in the General Assembly as well. So he is speaking.

K: Okay. That is fine. Then they'll adjourn, you think?

S: I think so. It will roll on a little bit longer. Now, one other development. What has occurred since you and I read that little message from Hussein.[. . .] So what I've done for you—

K: Now, look, I've got to get off to my speech. Can you give me a one-minute summary?

S: Sure. Thirty-second summary. The message you will be getting suggested to you will be fuller than the one you and I talked about because there are a couple of questions that have to be answered and the message seeks to answer them. So therefore—

K: What are the questions?

S: Well, one, he feels that this is a good time to strike while the iron is hot and see if you can't get a negotiating process started and I make the right kinds of noises in the reply without, you know, making—

K: Just say that I have offered that to the Egyptians already.

S: All right, I'll add that. I also reminded him that you started explorations in New York and his Foreign Minister you hope really reported that you see.

K: Yeah.

S: But glean through the message when you come back tonight is the point I'm making. I'll just position it in the White House for you.

K: Okay.

S: Good.

K: Right, thank you.

S: Thank you very much. And have a good speech.

K: Wait a minute! The Israelis have formally replied on Lebanon.

S: Oh, good.

K: You can get a message off. They promised to guarantee its sovereignty and independence.

S: Guarantee sovereignty and independence.

K: The only thing they ask, provided that Lebanon undertakes no military actions of its own against Israel.

S: Provided that it does not undertake any military action of its own against Israel. Okay.

K: And they authorize us to communicate that to the Lebanese.

S: Good. I'll send that out.

October 9, 1973: A New Situation: The Israeli Crisis, the Airlift, and Cease-fire Diplomacy

The gods are offended by hubris. They resent the presumption that events can be totally predicted and managed. Our strategy had been based on the assumption of an overwhelming and rapid Israeli victory—an assumption at every point supported by intelligence sources and Israeli communications. This caused our diplomacy without urgency, since time, we thought, was improving our negotiating position. That assumption was exploded by a telephone call from Dinitz at 1:45 A.M. Tuesday, October 9.

Ambassador Dinitz–Kissinger (at home)

Tuesday, October 9, 1973
1:45 A.M.

D: I hope I didn't wake you.

K: It's all right.

D: I didn't want to wake you up but your secretary said— The reason I am disturbing you, we have an evaluation of the situation up to midnight. I am sitting here with the military attaché, who was the commander of our [unclear]. The situation really is placing us [in] a number of difficult situations, which to make a long story short, whether we will be able to get the parts we need as well as the planes. But I thought if it is not possible now, maybe very early in the morning I would like to bring the military attaché with the material to you for you to get a complete picture and together we can then cable the Prime Minister the situation we are facing.

K: All right. Let me see, let's aim for about 8:00—shortly after 8:00 in the Map Room of the White House.

D: Fine, I will be there.

K: Is it a difficult situation?

D: Difficult in the choices that we are facing. To make it simple, in the Canal we have—five divisions of infantry, which means about fifty thousand people [Egyptians] and seven hundred tanks. Although the bridges are destroyed behind them, the choice is then to press forward with the Canal behind them. The question that we are facing is how to handle the situation and that depends on what we will be able to get—planes and etc.

K: Antitanks is easier than planes in the short time.

D: I suggest that we wait until the morning. If you think it is advisable that Haig participate too because I will bring my general.

K: Let me see what I find in the morning.

D: Thank you very much. I will see you in the morning.

At 8:20 A.M., Dinitz was accompanied to the White House by his Israeli armed forces attaché, Mordechai Gur. General Scowcroft accompanied me. Dinitz and Gur grimly explained that Israel's losses to date had been staggering and totally unexpected. Forty-nine airplanes, including fourteen Phantoms, had been destroyed. This figure was high but not completely surprising, since both Syria and Egypt possessed large quantities of Soviet surface-to-air missiles. The real shocker was the loss of five hundred tanks, four hundred on the Egyptian front alone. Dinitz implored me to keep the numbers secret from everyone except the President. If they were known, the Arab countries now standing aloof might join for a knockout blow. Many puzzles cleared up instantly. "So that's why the Egyptians are so cocky," I exclaimed. "How did it happen?" Gur explained that a significant number of Israeli tanks were lost on the way to the battle by being run too fast in the desert after having been inadequately maintained in reserve depots. I indelicately reminded Dinitz of his prediction two nights before of victory by Wednesday. He admitted that "obviously something went wrong."

What Dinitz was reporting would require a fundamental reassessment of our strategy. The Syrian army, though suffering serious casualties, had not broken. Israel would therefore find it difficult to shift its forces from the Golan to the Sinai. And Israel's equipment losses on the Egyptian front were about equal to Egypt's. Israel stood on the threshold of a war of attrition that it could not possibly win, given the disparity of manpower. Gur suggested that Israel's best chance was against Syria. Unless the Egyptian armor ventured beyond the belt of surface-to-air missiles, an Israeli offensive in the Sinai would be too costly.

Two conclusions followed: An Israeli victory based on its existing inventory, supplemented by a limited amount of special high-tech equipment from the United States, was no longer possible. A major resupply effort of Israel would be necessary if the war were to be brought to a rapid conclusion. And a different diplomacy would soon be necessary. For in a protracted war of uncertain outcome, diplomacy might have to supply the impetus to break a military stalemate.

The most immediate issue was resupply.

Such was Israeli consternation that Dinitz and Gur did not know exactly what Israel's priorities were, except planes. Tanks, which Israel desperately needed, were in short supply and difficult to transport quickly. Gur suggested shipping some from Europe, but even that would take several weeks. It was agreed that El Al planes could begin to pick up more consumables and electronic equipment immediately. But clearly Israel's small fleet of seven civilian aircraft would not be able to handle heavy equipment. As for the larger items, I promised to assemble a special meeting of the WSAG and give Dinitz our answer before the end of the day.

Gur asked for intelligence information. I instructed Scowcroft "to give them every bit of intelligence we have." I never doubted that a defeat of Israel by Soviet arms would be a geopolitical disaster for the United States. I urged a quick victory on one front before U.N. diplomacy ratified Arab territorial gains everywhere. "We are concentrating now on a fast Syrian victory," replied Dinitz. "With the Egyptians, it will take longer."

At the end Dinitz asked to see me alone for five minutes. Prime Minister Meir, he told me, wanted to come to the United States personally for an hour to plead with President Nixon for urgent arms aid. It could be a secret visit. I rejected the visit out of hand and without checking with Nixon. Such a proposal could reflect only either hysteria or blackmail. A visit would take Golda away from Israel for a minimum of thirty-six hours. Leaving while a major battle was going on would be a sign of panic that might bring in all the Arab states still on the sidelines. It would leave Israel leaderless when Golda's dauntless courage was most needed and major decisions might have to be made. (I learned after the war that Defense Minister Moshe Dayan was recommending at that very moment a withdrawal deep into the Sinai.) And because her visit could not be kept secret, we would be forced into taking public political positions which might destroy any possibility of mediation after the war. The Arab world would be inflamed against us. The Soviet Union would have a clear field.

At 9:40 A.M. that Tuesday, I convened a special meeting of the WSAG confined to the most senior departmental representatives. Staff was barred to enhance security. I reported the conversation with Dinitz and Gur, omitting the figures for tank losses. My colleagues were skeptical. CIA Director William Colby reported that Israel was doing well on the Syrian front and holding its own in the Sinai; Israel was simply trying to obtain the maximum military aid from us before victory, as a sign of unrestricted support not so much for the war as for the period afterward. Since I chaired the meeting as Presidential Assistant, Deputy Secretary of State Kenneth Rush spoke for the State Department. There had been no time to give any instructions; Rush supported Colby. Schlesinger saw no problem with sending auxiliary equipment not requiring American technicians. But his concern was that meeting Israel's requests and thus turning around a battle that the Arabs were winning might blight our relations with the Arabs for a long time. Schlesinger stressed the distinction between defending Israel's survival within its pre-1967 borders and helping Israel maintain its conquests from the 1967 war. Other participants concurred.

My own view was that events had gone beyond such fine-tuning. There was agreement that a defeat of Israel with Soviet arms would skewer the political as well as the strategic equilibrium in the Middle East. Avoidance of an Israeli defeat was therefore in America's strategic interest. It was at that point, not during the war, that we could appeal to the Arab nations by the way we conducted the postwar diplomacy. Six options would be prepared for presidential decision after the completion of a state visit by President Félix Houphouët-Boigny of the Ivory Coast later in the day.

DEPUTY SECRETARY OF STATE KENNETH RUSH–KISSINGER

Tuesday, October 9, 1973
9:20 A.M.

R: Hello.

K: Ken, I have just had some very personal information to the President from the Israelis which isn't too good but which I want to share with you and which I don't want to repeat on the telephone.

R: All right.

K: But I'm holding a meeting of the principals only of WSAG and therefore none of you. Maybe we could treat you as a principal for this purpose. Why don't you get over here.

R: What time is it?

K: Immediately. And without any debriefing in State. Say you're coming over to see me.

At the same time we received reports that Soviet diplomats were urging heretofore uninvolved Arab states to enter the fray.

AMBASSADOR DOBRYNIN–KISSINGER

Tuesday, October 9, 1973
11:29 A.M.

. . .

K: . . . Anatol, I just got a message from Amman.

D: Yes, saying what? What's happening there?

K: Well, saying that your Chargé—Let me read it to you.

D: Okay.

K: "The Soviet Chargé asked to see King and was received this morning. Chargé said Soviets fully support Arabs in conflict with Israel. He said Soviet Union thought all Arab States should enter battle now."

D: Soviet, what?

K: "Soviet Union thought all Arab—"

D: Soviet Union?

K: Yes.

D: Thought or fought?

K: Recommending to the King.

D: Un-huh.

K: "King considers this a Soviet request for him to send his army into action."

D: We asked King to go into action?

K: Yeah.

D: Unbelievable story. Was it ours—? I don't have any information at all. I could quite [readily accept] that we discuss with them and saying that we [unclear] our support of Arab countries is nothing new. But as you said we asked King to send—yes?

K: That's right.

D: I will check with Moscow right now. It was our initiative or it was—

K: No, it was your initiative.

D: It's an unbelievable story, I should say.

K: You know, I'm not drawing any conclusions but we really urge you to keep people calm.

D: No, no. May I have a second try once again? Soviet Union thought—

K: "Soviet Union thought all Arab States should enter the battle now."

D: Enter the battle?

K: Yes.

D: He actually mentioned to the King?

K: Yes.

D: Okay, I will check this with Moscow right away. It's an unbelievable story.

K: Okay.

D: I'm sure on this country I should know. (laughs) I think this is really unbelievable, that he asked him to do this. He may just say in

general. Well, I will check with Moscow, then I will be back with
you, all right?

K: Okay, good.

   . . .

In the course of the morning, we received additional information that Moscow had advised President Boumedienne of Algeria in
the same sense.

AMBASSADOR DINITZ–KISSINGER
   Tuesday, October 9, 1973
   11:37 A.M.

K: Hello.

D: Dr. Kissinger?

K: Yes, Mr. Ambassador. We have to meet with the President. That
won't be possible because of the visit of the Ivory Coast President until 4:00 this afternoon. You will hear from me sometime
afterwards.

D: After 4:00.

K: Yes.

D: Fine.

K: The most accurate information you can give me about the real
military situation before then would be very important.

D: Fine. At 4:00 you will get it.

K: Well, get it for me by 3:00 if you can.

D: Fine. I will do this and then you will get back to me after the
meeting.

K: I'll get back to you after the meeting. I don't [know] whether you
have a correct assessment about [the] domestic situation here. If
you do, I don't think they have in Jerusalem.

D: About what?

K: About what is possible in our government.

   . . .

D: ... I wanted to ask you, Tuesday morning I had a stream of calls from the Senate and the House—individuals, asking what they can do and what the situation is.

K: Well, I can't discuss that with you on the telephone.

D: I see. So we will discuss it when I see you?

K: Right. You know, we don't object to senators and congressmen asking for support, as long as they don't get specific.

D: Right.

　　. . .

SENATOR FRANK CHURCH (D.-IDAHO)–KISSINGER
Tuesday, October 9, 1973
11:48 A.M.

K: Hello, Frank, how are you?

C: Well, I'm fine. I know you're a very busy man, Henry, and I won't take much of your time.

K: Not at all, always happy to hear from you.

C: More on the Middle East. Now that it has broken out and you're right in the midst of it, I think the only good that might come of it is that these Egyptian and Syrian forces are broken sufficiently to eliminate the threat for a long time to come. I was wondering about the losses that the Israeli government has sustained in the air and what we can do about helping replace those losses.

K: Well, of course, we have two problems, Frank. One is to help and the other to start a massive influx of equipment while the battle is going on is a rather serious matter.

C: But the Phantoms, is there a way that they can be slipped in? Because I understand the Egyptian and Syrian forces are getting rapid replacement from their Arab allies.

K: Well, frankly, we are looking into it today. And we are, incidentally, on other equipment not inactive.

C: Uh-huh.

K: And it's a difficult thing to discuss on the telephone.

C: I understand.

K: But I understand what you are saying.

C: Well, I just wanted to express my concern about it and I think it's a tragedy that this thing has broken out again but that's it. If we act more decisive, the victory I think the better under the circumstances.

K: I agree.

C: All right.

K: I think on the strategy we are in substantial agreement.

C: All right, Henry. I just wanted to express my feeling and I won't—

K: No, I'm glad. You know, I won't suffer any pain if you say anything publicly as long as you don't mention the type of thing that should be done.

AMBASSADOR DINITZ–KISSINGER

Tuesday, October 9, 1973
3:45 P.M.

K: Hello.

D: Dr. Kissinger?

K: Yes.

D: I explained to Eagleburger a few lines on the current situation in—

K: Yeah, come on, I'm in a great hurry. What is it?

D: There are no basic changes on the ground. The major thing is we have destroyed a hundred Syrian tanks today. Only thirty Syrian tanks remain in the Golan Heights.

K: You destroyed a hundred today?

D: We destroyed a hundred today. Only thirty Syrian tanks remained within our area of the Golan Heights. There are more outside. Our losses in planes increased to forty-nine from the beginning of the war. We lost eleven today. All of them six [unclear] Syria. The rest can—not meaningful, the rest of the changes.

The Egyptian front remains steady. They lost several dozens of tanks when they tried to cross the bridges today. On the ground there was no change.

K: We have a report here that you hit the Soviet Embassy in Damascus.

D: Somebody just heard it on the radio, but we have no report of this whatsoever. I would inquire of course in Israel.

K: Okay. Well, I have to run to see the President.

D: Fine. I'll expect to hear from you. Thank you.

After meeting with the President, I conveyed his decision to Dinitz at 6:10 P.M. Nixon ordered to speed the delivery of consumables and aircraft, which would be sent at the rate of two a day, starting immediately. Heavy equipment—like tanks—would not reach Israel before the end of the fighting. We would guarantee to replace Israel's losses of heavy equipment; thus Israel would be freed of the need to maintain reserve stocks during the battle. Schlesinger was given discretion to determine the degree of Israel's need while the war was still going on. If he judged that Israel needed tanks during the battle, he should ship them immediately. Dinitz volunteered that Israel would pick up everything possible in unmarked El Al planes. There was no talk of an American airlift—except if tanks were urgently needed in an emergency.

The rest of the day was devoted to a technical implementation of these decisions. At 7:25 P.M., I advised Dinitz to deal with Schlesinger on resupply. I also warned him that the new military situation might require a new diplomacy.

AMBASSADOR DINITZ–KISSINGER
Tuesday, October 9, 1973
7:25 P.M.

K: Mr. Ambassador. I have talked to Schlesinger. You can now go ahead. The only other thing I would like to point out to you is a situation now developing in which it is very hard for us to resist a cease-fire in place proposal. Therefore in designing your strategy you should keep that in mind.

D: Cease-fire in place; you mean back to the lines—?

K: Cease-fire to whatever line they are at—Eban and I discussed. You might be ready to accept Tuesday night.

D: Next week?

K: It depends on the tactical position. It's a hell of a position for the United States to take— Our tactical assessment is that we may be in a position where we [are obliged to] veto a resolution urging you to go back to '67 borders.

D: Yes, but nobody takes that seriously.

K: Maybe not, but we can get a majority vote [against us]. May not be serious but it will pass unless we veto it—going back to the line, also their staying where they are after weeks of fighting it will be a hell of a thing to defend in public opinion. There is no reason to suppose that will develop. If I were an Egyptian with some sense of balance, I might at some point tell the Russians—

D: When I last talked to Eban he was under the notion that such a resolution would be vetoed by you.

K: That was on Sunday. He told me he—Tuesday. Here it is Tuesday—until Thursday or Friday. Going to be extremely tough at that point.

D: Naturally we will do our best.

K: I am referring to one particular comment you made.

D: About letting—

K: —letting the situation develop slowly.

D: We would not, on our own initiative, want it to be slowly. We would just take necessary time, no more than the necessary—

K: Don't think we should discuss it on the telephone but I think they should be aware in Jerusalem how the tactical situation is developing. We can drag it out but there is a limit to what can be done. We, of course, would not specifically introduce it; you have no worries on that score.

D: Of course not. I will make them aware of the situation, both Eban in New York and in Jerusalem.

SECRETARY SCHLESINGER–KISSINGER

Tuesday, October 9, 1973
7:30 P.M.

K: I have talked to Dinitz in the sense that you and I talked and they will be getting in touch with your people. He also said that at some point somebody on your staff should suggest that he see you and I strongly favor that.

S: —I'm for it.

K: —might institute what might have to take on an emergency basis on the heavy stuff.

S: That's right. You understand we'll have to take over the equipment of the [unclear] for the M28s [tanks]. We'll have to stand down a division.

K: Give them some M48s [a new type of tank].

S: We're pretty well clean of that.

K: They seem to have enough airplanes—they are willing.

S: With this kind of movement we won't be able to keep it quiet. With all the Israeli planes flying around it will be impossible for the Arabs not to find out.

K: It's extremely important to keep it [as] low-key as we possibly can.

S: Right.

K: If we can get through this crisis without antagonizing the Arabs.

S: The Russians are acting up.

K: Yes, I'm going to scare the bejesus out of Dobrynin in about five minutes.

Late at night, I received a telephone call from the British Ambassador, who had not yet caught up with the new military situation and was afraid lest the Israelis advance too rapidly and then stay at a line beyond where hostilities had started. He was looking for ways to receive credit for inducing Israel to stay at the prewar line. But the strategy of returning to the status quo ante which we had pursued at the beginning of the war—and had been rejected by Britain then—was no longer relevant in light of the information we had been receiving all day. I thought it best to let the United Kingdom discover the new facts for themselves.

LORD CROMER–KISSINGER
Tuesday, October 9, 1973
11:38 P.M.

. . .

C: . . . You and I talked about this thing between the cease-fire lines one way or the other. Eban made some remarks in New York which would point that if the politicians in Israel have their way they'll stop on the line and if they do that and this is an entirely a [personal] remark. It's not HMG [Her Majesty's Government] at all. I think it's very important that the U.S. and/or the West get its credit for them stopping on that line. I think we want to think about some wording for that.

K: Let me understand it.

C: If the Israelis can push the Arabs back to the line and stop there and don't go beyond it (which is what we were talking about before). We want to get some *credit* if we can for the U.S. and all of us for having started them to do just that.

K: I agree. That's been our strategy all along.

C: But have we worked on any wording on this? Because it could happen suddenly.

K: Is that what you think?

C: Well, it's my personal thought. It's not my government's thought. It could happen quite suddenly, and very soon, that they get to the cease-fire lines, the Israelis, and they stay put. And then this sort of strategy we were talking about before really doesn't work very well. Do you see what I mean?

K: Yes. I see what you mean.

C: If it was either one way or the other way, we have the problem that you and I discussed—that if the Israelis push them back to the line and then the Israelis stay on that line and don't push further, then we've got a new situation in a kind of way which we need diplomatically before we review our situation with the Arabs. I mean to take credit for, if we can contrive to do so.

K: I couldn't agree more.

C: Our minds work the same way.

K: And I can tell you that if the Israelis cross the line, they'll move against us.

C: If they do that.

K: I see, but if they don't, you want us to take credit for it [maintaining the status quo ante].

C: That's my suggestion. It's not my [government's] view.

K: But how would we do it?

C: I don't know. That's why I think why we want to apply our minds to wording, which is directly what we hoped would happen.

K: What is your view—well it's happening now.

C: Well, Eban's remarks in New York that implied they might do that. He made that today—

K: That they might stop at the line?

C: Yes.

K: Oh, yes, that I think is possible and that we strongly urged him to do.

C: Oh you have done.

K: Yes.

C: Then you can take credit for it.

K: Oh yes we can take credit for it.

C: Well, that's fine.

K: I thought you wanted some public statement.

C: Yes. If it does happen, because I think they'll have political problems in Israel. I think the military will want to go further.

K: Well, what do you think is going to happen in the Security Council? Are you people planning to put forward some resolutions?

C: No, not at all.

K: Because you think it would be vetoed.

C: I don't think we have any particular proposition to put forward.

K: You mean like the straight cease-fire.

C: Well, we could do that but I think you felt, and I think we say in
view of that was rather too simple. But I think if the Israelis stop
on the line, the sort of statutes that you and I were discussing a
couple days ago are slightly overtaken by events. Because we
were thinking either it would swing one way or the other.

K: Right.

C: But if they do, I mean, it saves self-restraint that they do do that
and in a way makes the Western diplomacy more difficult. With
the Arabs, I mean.

K: That I agree with.

C: It's still a question of just trying our minds of that contingency
and if we have any ideas. I haven't gone to London, mind you. If
we have any ideas on that it could happen quite abrupt see and
we ought to take advantage of it from the relations with the Arab
world and everyone else.

K: Are you people surprised at the course of hostilities?

C: No. They are going rather slower than I think we anticipated.

K: Us too.

C: That's the only element of surprise in it.

K: But that makes a lot of difference.

C: Yes, but it also gives us a little bit of opportunity to think out
what we're going to do.

    . . .

Since all decision-makers were in Washington and there was no
time pressure, most discussions were at face-to-face meetings and
not on the telephone.

The resupply decision involved three issues: (a) mode of delivery; (b) relations with the Arab world; (c) the political framework in light of the changed military situation.

On October 9, no issue regarding mode of delivery had yet arisen. The assumption was that the Israeli commercial airlines could pick up the consumables and that the rest could be delivered after a cease-fire, as the President had promised.

As for the Arab reaction, a difference in perspective developed between Israel and the United States. Israel favored the most ostentatious means of delivery; all American policymakers were agreed that we should do our utmost to prevent a confrontation with the Arab world—especially the moderates among them—though not to the point of impairing American strategic interests. We sought to give Israel the confidence and the means to face the next few crucial days when the outcome hung as much on Israel's self-assurance as on its arms. But we also strove for a low profile in the method of resupply; we were conscious of the need to preserve the American position in the Arab world.

To this end, I responded to another message from Ismail on behalf of Sadat, which had arrived in the morning of October 9 and expressed appreciation for the U.S. government's "good intentions." I stressed that the United States "now understands clearly the Egyptian position with respect to a peace settlement." In that spirit the United States

> wishes to reiterate its willingness to consult urgently with the parties concerned in order to achieve a just peace settlement in the Middle East. In these difficulties, it is important to keep this long-term perspective in mind and to avoid confrontations and bitter debate as we seek to resolve the present crisis. . . .

The most complex problem was that of diplomatic strategy, which evolved around the issue of the cease-fire. The previous Arab-Israeli wars in 1948 and 1967 had ended with cease-fires in place,

supported by the United States. No such move had yet been proposed by the fourth day of the war. Indeed, the United Nations Security Council was seized of the issue in a most desultory way. The
United States had urged the meeting for symbolic reasons but had
not pushed for a resolution in order to give Israel a chance to restore
the status quo ante. We were prepared—in the early days of the
war—to veto a resolution calling for a cease-fire in place. But as the
war turned to attrition, that position would not be sustainable indefinitely.

The Arab states, in the flush of early successes, did not ask for a
cease-fire in order to extend their gains. Israel sought no resolution
to preserve the option of a decisive victory. The Soviet Union stood
on the sidelines, reluctant to separate from its Arab allies but uneasy
because of the warnings of imminent Israeli victory received from
the United States, and also careful not to jeopardize their relationship with the United States.

We considered a defeat of Israel—a de facto ally—by Soviet arms
as undermining Middle East stability and guaranteeing continued
warfare aimed at Western interests and sustained by Soviet arms. We
saw an opportunity to start a peace process by convincing the Arab
states that the Soviets could provoke a war but not achieve diplomatic progress; hence American diplomacy was indispensable.
Diplomatic progress required an Israeli military success but not in a
manner that united the Arab world against America. We needed to
restrain the Soviet Union during the war to enable America to dom-
inate the postwar diplomacy and thereby to reduce Soviet influence.
But as the war turned into a stalemate, this position of procrastina-
tion would not be sustainable. Once all the parties understood the
new strategic situation, some cease-fire proposal was probable. If we
accepted it while Israel had lost territory on both fronts, the war
would end with a clear-cut setback of America's ally. The United
States' position in the postwar diplomacy would be severely im-
paired. The proposition that America alone among the superpowers

could produce progress would be discredited. Soviet arms would have achieved success; Soviet diplomacy would have protected it. The probability of another war would be high, since Israel would want to regain its previous supremacy; the Arabs would become convinced that their arms could break every negotiating deadlock. It was therefore imperative that Israel make progress on some front before cease-fire diplomacy gained momentum. This meant the need for progress in the north against Syria. So long as Egyptian forces remained in the belt along the Suez Canal, which was protected by Soviet-made SAM batteries against air attacks, the southern front was likely to remain stalemated.

October 10, 1973

By October 10, Moscow had awakened to opportunity. Israel could not sustain a war of attrition; a cease-fire in place would ratify Arab gains. Fortunately for Israel, Sadat was not yet ready for such an outcome, believing he could extract further concessions from prolonging the war. Therefore Dobrynin brought a message that Moscow would not oppose a cease-fire if it were put forward by a third party. He suggested a joint abstention by the United States and the Soviet Union. The Soviet Union was not prepared to move such a proposal because Sadat was not yet ready. But Dobrynin suggested that this might simply be a question of face: Sadat might accept a cease-fire if advanced by someone else.

In this atmosphere, we decided to stall the Soviet cease-fire initiative to give Israel an opportunity to make gains against Syria that it could balance in any negotiation against its losses in the South. Our situation was complicated because Dobrynin's overture coincided with the resignation of Vice President Spiro Agnew.

AMBASSADOR DOBRYNIN–KISSINGER

Wednesday, October 10, 1973
8:13 A.M.

D: ... Henry, I received a message for the President and to you from the Secretary General. I have not translated it yet but I will translate from the telegram as I read it.

K: But you'll send over the substance a little later?

D: OK. "Acting in the spirit of mutual understanding reached with the President on this score, we during the last days were having consultations with the leaders of Egypt and Syria on the correction of ceasefire. Frankly speaking these conversations with the Arabs were difficult and prolonged but we have now the opportunity to say to the President that the Soviet Union is ready not to oppose the resolution of the Security Council in favor of ceasefire. The President of course understands that in the present situation to work in the Security Council for the resolution of ceasefire the Soviet Union could not do it but the main thing is that we will not oppose. We will not vote against. Our representative will abstain during their voting. To come to this decision was not really easy. A decisive factor was that we took into consideration this particular case, the pro-interest of supporting this and other developments, preserving and developing all those positives which have taken place during the last years of the Soviet/American relations and in the international situation in general. We would like to draw attention, President, to one more circumstance. It is necessary to limit for the first time being the decision to ceasefire and either we will broaden the resolutions with more additional conditions on this matter for instance about their creating certain kinds of conditions or withdrawing troops on a condition [idea of returning to the status quo ante]. This very clearly will lead to the failure(?) that would really matter. This would have the ability to act combined. We are mentioning about this only because there were some hints on this kind of decision which were heard in a speech made by the representative of the U.S. during the last Security Council meeting. If that kind of position were put forward it would put us in a very difficult situation and the Soviet representative would be sure in this circumstance to object and vote against. We hope that this will refrain from happening and the combined action of the Soviet Union and the United States will facilitate or help to establish this line on the Middle East and the resumption of actual efforts to reach a political settlement. This business about a revelation or perhaps allegation of your sending supplies to Israel. This was really a very important step and of course could ruin the whole national situation and we got rather hot on this matter. We are giving the whole Security Council, and we hope that they will try, a chance to act in conjunction with us."

K: We need a few hours to consider this and we will let you know later today.

D: I will wait to hear from you.

K: Wait till you hear from me but you can say it's a constructive message.

D: OK.

K: You will hear from me. I have to meet with the President. If you could get me the text of this sent over.

D: All right. It will take an hour or so.

AMBASSADOR DOBRYNIN–KISSINGER

Wednesday, October 10, 1973
8:39 A.M.

K: I just wanted to tell you we won't really have a chance for a systematic examination until after Mobutu has left around 11:30.

D: 11:30?

K: Yes. So we'll get an answer sometime in the afternoon.

D: All right.

K: And we would urge you—because we have to do a lot of talking now also.

D: I understand. No, no. If I understand correctly, you do just not want to do anything to discuss—

K: We would appreciate it if you now didn't do anything until we've had a chance to discuss it here. And then during the course of the afternoon I'll let you know what our reaction is.

D: Okay.

K: Now, may I say another thing—we notice there is a very substantial airlift of Soviet supplies going into Egypt and Syria.

D: Airlift?

K: Airlift. I can give you the numbers and types of aircraft, but I'm sure Grechko knows it.

D: He should know as well as you do. Sometimes he knows better, maybe, no?

K: But we really don't think that is very helpful, because that's going to force us to do at least the same.

D: Okay, I will flash to Moscow—I'll get back to Moscow.

K: And we—it really, Anatol.

D: You say heavy?

K: Heavy—about 22 airplanes, I consider that pretty heavy.

K: Coming through Budapest, just in case they are looking for the last airport—

D: I see.

K: It will make it easier to find them.

D: I understand.

K: It really is important Anatol, that our actions can't be latter represented as our having been maneuvered or tricked—

D: No, I understand. On this around a half-a-day—

K: I would expect it by the middle of the afternoon.

   . . .

AMBASSADOR DOBRYNIN–KISSINGER

Wednesday, October 10, 1973
11:45 A.M.

K: Anatol, I just wanted to tell you the following. We are having a major domestic problem, which as you will see, even you will recognize it's major, which is coming to a head early this afternoon.

D: Yeah.

K: And so there will be decisional delay until I can get you—But you will get your formal answer.

D: You mean it happens today or tomorrow?

K: By the end of the day I will give you an answer.

D: By the end of the day.

K: I just want you to know. You will see that this is not a delaying tactic.

D: Yeah. But what is the crisis? Could you tell me that?

K: Well, it concerns the Vice President.

D: Oh, I see.

K: So I wanted you to know that and I'll be in touch with you around 4:00 or 5:00 o'clock this afternoon.

D: 4:00 or 5:00.

K: Right.

D: Okay.

K: We are thinking very seriously about what you said.

D: No, I think this is really a chance for both of us.

K: No, no, I recognize it. Now, may I urge you, however, really both you and your friends, not to force us into anything prematurely.

    . . .

K: . . . The only people who know up to now are the President.

D: I understand.

K: And, as you will see very soon, the President cannot possibly address this question for a couple of hours.

D: I understand.

K: But what I've told you about this domestic situation, Anatol, is a sign of my great confidence in you.

D: No, no, no. I understand. But does this coming affect in any way—

K: It affects nothing.

D: Nothing. I mean, from the point of view of foreign policy.

K: In terms of foreign policy, it, if anything, strengthens our abilities.

D: I speak in a sense of ability not a public relations because sometimes—

K: In terms of our foreign policy, it either affects it not at all or strengthens it.

D: Okay.

K: But in terms of making a decision and in terms of getting time with the President, that is now very difficult until into the afternoon.

D: I understand. Okay. Well, until the end of the day.

K: And, therefore, we don't want to get anything started with a lot of other countries.

D: Yeah, I understand.

K: Good.

D: Thank you very much. I will await your call.

K: And we have not yet discussed it with the Israelis.

D: I understand.

K: Because we do not want their lobby to start working here.

D: Yeah, I think this is the wise thing.

K: Before we have a chance to—

D: To make your own decision.

K: To make our own decisions on how to handle it.

    . . .

Ambassador Dobrynin–Kissinger

Wednesday, October 10, 1973
5:40 P.M.

. . .

K: Tell Malik nobody in New York knows anything, tell him not to say anything to anybody.

D: Yes, Henry. OK.

K: Yes, I will be in touch a little later.

D: You can call me.

K: I will call you. Presents significant problems for us. As well as for you. Would not push you. I understand, privately, waiting for a couple—problems. We consider it a serious proposal and we have to think this thing through to think how to answer.

D: Henry, I see in the news media—build-up.

K: For your information, we are doing next to nothing.

D: It says build-up going on in news media, suspect beginning of new . . . check with Malik doing something or not?

K: Anatoly, you have gone through too many crises with me. We are trying to get this thing settled. You are going to hear from us during the course of the evening.

. . .

Ambassador Dobrynin–Kissinger

Wednesday, October 10, 1973
9:45 P.M.

K: Anatoly, given all the events of today and that we have to talk to some other people, we won't be able to give you an answer till tomorrow.

D: OK, you will call tomorrow.

K: Yes. I will call and I must say from all reports I have heard, your people are much more disciplined than mine. We may have a lousy foreign policy in the next months that I am here but there will be discipline.

D: I understand. You are playing it quite well. Don't overplay the theme of Russian irresponsibility.

K: Who has said anything about Russian irresponsibility?

D: From your speech, as you know.

K: That was just a little warning. I did not say you had as yet been irresponsible.

D: I am just telling you—that I not argue with you—they use expression you usually use.

K: What was that, look, if it was Marvin Kalb—I did not talk to him.

D: Well, I don't know—the theme on the radio is the State Department wants—

K: I will keep things quiet tomorrow. I promise you there will be no comment from the State Department about Russian irresponsibility or else.

D: But this then goes on—in the briefing—some off the record and some on the record.

K: By whom? what do you think—no one has been authorized—just a minute Anatoly, before you go into one of your wild charges.

D: You understand that—

K: You're engaged in a massive airlift in the Middle East and that is not helpful because we have been very restrained.

D: I don't know.

K: I'll be glad to send you the figures. I spend all day at the White House but tomorrow I promise you.

D: Even McCloskey [Robert McCloskey, responsible for public affairs at the State Department] made some comment on and off the record. I like him—he is very nice—but he too makes comments.

K: What did he say?

D: I don't recall but on the record he said, he was asked what Russians were restrained—He said he couldn't report.

K: You have to—that the message the General Secretary sent to Algeria did not fill us with ecstasy [urging Algerian participation in the war].

. . .

Simultaneously we became aware of a Soviet airlift of twenty planes to Syria. And a Saudi brigade was also being moved to Syria. These events produced a suggestion from Schlesinger to abandon our existing approach in favor of a more far-reaching step, the occupation of part of Saudi Arabia or perhaps of the Trucial States.

SECRETARY SCHLESINGER–KISSINGER

Wednesday, October 10, 1973
8:27 A.M.

[First minute not transcribed.]

S: —the Soviet resupply operations.

K: Yeah.

S: That's gone overt now, and in particular the movement of the Saudi forces up to Syria—

K: Are they moving?

S: Yeah, you remember the original brigade which the Jordanians would not permit to move.

K: Yeah.

S: They have now requested rights to move other brigades from Saudi proper through Jordan and Jordan can't really resist it.

K: Yeah.

S: So I think that we are going to get into a position in which all of our interests in Saudi Arabia are at risk and it might be desirable to examine the fundamentals of our position.

K: Well, what are the fundamentals of our position, as you see it?

S: Well, the fundamentals are that we may be faced with the choice that lies, cruelly, between support of Israel and loss of Saudi Arabia, and if interests in the Middle East are at risk, the choice between occupation or watching them go down the drain.

K: Occupation of whom?

S: That would remain to be seen—it can be partial.

K: But which country are we occupying?

S: That's one of the things we'd like to talk about.

K: Who's we?

S: Me.

K: Okay, I have heard an urgent message, which I've got to take up with the President and I'll be back to you later this morning and we'll get together this morning.

S: Okay.

K: Wait a minute, how are our supply things going?

S: Okay. Fairly well, given the limitation on aircraft.

K: Right.

S: If they are able to get contract aircraft, of course they can move the stuff more rapidly.

K: Okay, well, I'll be back to you.

AMBASSADOR SCALI–KISSINGER
Wednesday, October 10, 1973
12:15 P.M.

. . .

S: —I want to tell you something new. . . . Hoveyda, the Iranian Ambassador [to the United Nations] still manages to be on friendly terms with el-Zayyat and he said to el-Zayyat, it seems to me you already have a victory. You should now be thinking of the next step. El-Zayyat said, "We are open to a move towards peace and will study it."

K: That's all right. Just sit tight, John. We've got to get all the pieces together. But you must give me this kind of information.

S: Could you give me some guidance for my own personal information?

K: I don't know yet—expecting to hear something later on today. I will be in touch with you as soon as we have confirmed it.

S: Larry McIntyre, the President of the Security Council, now feels under some pressure to show the manhood of the Security Council. He is quite willing to do nothing today, but I don't think I can keep him from resuming tomorrow.

K: Exactly what I am counting on.

S: Avoid today if we can?

K: Try to avoid it today. Try to make sure to get all the pieces in place and be ready to move tomorrow. Going to do some more cross checking today.

S: All right.

K: —all the principal parties—we are being in touch with—to not to get any eager beavers up there, jumping the gun.

S: Nobody's going to jump the gun—

K: I don't mean you—other people up there who may be getting some sense of things.

S: Just a moment ago the Syrians urgently went to Malik [Soviet U.N. Ambassador] saying they needed to discuss something of great importance.

K: Well, I think the Israelis are bombing in Syria again.

S: They put it in very urgent terms.

K: Okay, John, as soon as I know something—

S: Just remember, on the other end I can't do what I'm supposed to do—

K: Actually, John, you probably know a tiny bit more than I do. But I don't want to move until I have all the pieces in place. As soon as I have more information, I will call you.

S: I know that. I understand and approve of that.

GENERAL SCOWCROFT–KISSINGER

Wednesday, October 10, 1973
12:25 P.M.

K: You talked to Dobrynin. Were you firm?

S: I was firm. He said he would call off Malik right away and tell him to shut up.

. . .

S: That's what I told him.

K: Then there's no need for me to call him.

S: I don't think so. No.

Foreign Minister Eban–Kissinger
Wednesday, October 10, 1973
12:35 p.m.

E: I would like to share a few thoughts with you. I talked with the President of Security Council and others. Before that I would like to thank you and your government warmly for response to certain requests we have been making. Everybody in Israel very moved by that. The second matter, very strange situation indicates deadlock likely to be prolonged. Third, Soviet-Arab position of asking for a cease-fire with return to the situation of seven years ago [1967 borders]. Not put forward. No consensus. Know it wouldn't be adopted.

K: We would veto that.

E: Sufficiently assumed that deter anybody from making proposal. Secondly, your Ambassador suggested—

K: I understand, I have several people waiting for me—and thirdly it is the straight cease-fire in place, right?

E: . . . Sadat told European Ambassadors that even if they lost one million men there—they wouldn't have a cease-fire [in place]. We must get used to the idea that we won't have a cease-fire unless the Soviets change.

    . . .

K: You have to understand what I have told our Ambassador. We will not put anything forward. Will become very tough for us if somebody else puts something forward.

E: I agree; we have seen no signs of it here. Did not wish—

K: I have just instructed Scali to do nothing today, which is against his temperament.

E: While I was in McIntyre's office, Waldheim called saying there has to be a meeting. Press is talking about lack of a meeting. Australian very dry about—

K: Good, Mr. Foreign Minister. I'll call you later this afternoon when we are able to see things here more clearly.

    . . .

GENERAL SCOWCROFT–KISSINGER

Wednesday, October 10, 1973
4:50 P.M.

. . .

K: You can call [Dinitz] and say we have definitely decided not to have any meeting today and we have authorized the charter service. We favor chartering planes to Israel.

S: No indication of the trend of your thinking?

K: Say—no joint U.S.-Soviet resolution. We will try to stay away from— Did you tell him not to do anything?

S: I said keep fighting hard but it would be disastrous to do anything to preempt the President—anything foolish like bombing downtown Cairo. He said the Prime Minister has said we will not rest till we have punished them severely for their aggression. I said we were aware of what the Prime Minister said. I'll call him back and tell him.

K: You think we're doing the right thing?

S: I do. I tried—if they have any idea of their timetable it would be helpful— We're not the only factor. He didn't respond. He said he had another forty aircraft grounded for the rest of the week— that means one third of the air force is out of action. He said had delivered two and in addition there would be five more. I said no, there would be three more for a total of five.

K: You call Schlesinger and say if we have to sweeten the pot, how many aircraft can we spare to do it? But call him on the secure line.

S: Yes.

SECRETARY SCHLESINGER–KISSINGER

Wednesday, October 10, 1973
7:15 P.M.

S: I indicated that I have talked to you about the two Phantoms before we sent them off. There is no other practical way to do it than to send along a U.S. tanker [aircraft].

K: When do you do that?

S: Let it go at 6:00 A.M. tomorrow. It has already hit the newspapers. Some spokesman indicated that we were continuing to supply.

K: Well, you might as well let them go.

S: Secondly, we were preparing to send some Marines to the Mediterranean—normal transfer—ready at Norfolk.

K: I would do that for a week.

S: You would do that?

K: Yes, I mean I would not send them for a week. Well, you're keeping a—there.

S: Well, it takes ten days to get to Gibraltar.

K: Well, hell, in ten days it will be over.

S: You're confident about that?

K: Well, if not, we'll need them. Is that all of your business?

S: And I have noticed that forty USAF have been—

K: Jim, you have my word that we'll make no move in that direction without letting you know—option one plus five plus replacements [Phantoms] for losses and you handle replacements of heavy equipment.

S: Yes.

K: I don't know if you heard from Scowcroft?

S: No.

K: Well, if I want to sweeten the pot for the Israelis—what planes can you scrape together?

S: I just don't know.

K: Look, this is based on the assumption of no combat.

S: Only Phantoms—

K: The Israelis told me this afternoon that in addition to the planes they have lost, forty others are out of action.

S: We're scraping spare parts for them to try and fix that up—the Soviet resupply operation.

K: Good, it is much more massive than ours. Dobrynin called me and he said, Henry, I know you too well. When I read about our resupply, I know you're doing it too.

S: You know him too well.

K: That's right and maybe that will get us out of this. I think we may
be able to gin something up here.

S: Good. You know what the problems are.

. . .

SECRETARY GENERAL WALDHEIM–KISSINGER

Wednesday, October 10, 1973
8:27 P.M.

W: I am sorry to disturb you but I thought I should inform you
about the situation here. The meeting was not satisfactory. As
you know—the controversy with Malik. Zayyat informed the
Nonaligned countries not to do—to avoid any resolution in the
Security Council because they wanted to continue fighting and
any resolution would prevent this. That is why the Nonaligned
did not insist on working out a draft resolution. As you know, the
Israelis are not interested in having a resolution. I talked to Eban
and he told me that the Council debate cannot continue—on a
resolution—they intend to hold—tomorrow afternoon—have
three speakers.

K: Who?

W: Peru, Kenya, and Guinea.

K: Who?

W: Guinea.

K: I didn't know Guinea was in the Security Council.

W: It is not definite yet. The situation here is that both sides don't
want a resolution. Both sides don't want a cease-fire because
both think they will gain—

K: I have asked John Scali to come back here and give me a full
story and we'll be in touch with you.

W: I hope to give a brief statement to all parties about stopping the
fighting.

K: Let's see what the situation is and I will give you my judgment.

W: I would appreciate it if you could let me know what you are
feeling.

K: You're not bound by my views but why don't we talk in the
morning?

W: More and more people in the government are asking me what is
the Secretary [Secretary General of the United Nations Wald-
heim] doing to stop the fighting—why is the Secretary not trying to stop the fighting and get them back to the negotiating
table. That's the psychological background.

K: I understand and I am not objecting. I thought if I could give you
my view and then you could do what you want.

W: I am very grateful and I understand. My impression is that they
are not interested in doing anything against [the] wish of [the]
Arab countries. And I am very worried about the message from
Brezhnev to [unclear] and the airlift to Syria is very dangerous—
dangerous developments.

K: We agree and we're saying something about this tomorrow.

W: Thank you very much.

K: Please stay in touch and I will take the liberty of contacting you
in the morning.

During the course of the afternoon, I informed Dinitz of the Soviet offer of a cease-fire brought about by U.S.–Soviet abstention
from a resolution to that effect. Our decision as to timing depended
in large part on the military prospects about which it was difficult to
obtain a clear judgment. Whatever the decision, resupply of Israel
was essential.

GENERAL SCOWCROFT–KISSINGER
Wednesday, October 10, 1973
8:59 P.M.

K: Brent, look, the Defense people are just going to have to stop
dragging their feet. First, the Israelis are going wild. They think
we are stabbing them in the back.

S: They are really uptight.

K: Yes, why shouldn't they be? What is your personal judgment?

S: I wish we could get some feeling about what is going to happen over the next forty-eight hours. If we settle into a stalemate, we will have big trouble. If they break out, we can move ahead, but if not, there will be a strong pressure for a cease-fire. We either have to go for a cease-fire or a massive reequipment. Did he [Dinitz] give you any idea of what may happen [regarding Israeli attitude toward a cease-fire]?

K: No. He asked for a chance for Golda Meir to reply. Dobrynin can wait.

S: You still have an excuse.

K: I don't need an excuse; just tell him I can't get a decision.

S: I think you can get by tonight.

K: But in forty-eight hours we face the same problem. If there is no resolution in forty-eight hours, can we get through the weekend?

S: I don't think we can.

K: The only thing that is holding us up is that they are all afraid of our veto.

S: I don't think we can get through the weekend [without a U.N. vote on cease-fire], do you?

K: No.

S: Without knowing—their prospects—anything decisive happens, we can get through to Friday. You can build on maybe forty-eight hours but we can't stall forty-eight hours because I think somebody will do something.

K: Right, and we cannot veto it.

S: I think that would be disastrous.

K: Okay, fine. Thank you.

GENERAL HAIG–KISSINGER

Wednesday, October 10, 1973
9:14 P.M.

. . .

K: I have just had a bloody session with the Israeli Ambassador and he says he cannot acquiesce to this without giving Mrs. Meir a chance to get to the President, so we have to wait till tomorrow morning. My judgment is that we have to give them the twelve hours [regarding the cease-fire proposal by a third party which Dobrynin had proposed and which I had stalled].

H: Absolutely, absolutely.

K: I'll just call Dobrynin and tell him we can't give them an answer. Another thing, what happens if—

H: They have to understand if the thing [the cease-fire proposal] is gonna go, that's it. Do you think there is any way—

K: They are also saying the end result will be a victory achieved with Soviet arms and both sides of the Canal in Egyptian hands.

H: What will be the outcome?

K: They [the Egyptians] think they are going to win.

. . .

AMBASSADOR DINITZ–KISSINGER

Wednesday, October 10, 1973
10:00 P.M.

K: Sometime during the course of tomorrow. You have to understand when I said—Monday or Tuesday that my nightmare is that the Egyptians will come with a resolution which we might have to veto and that would be regrettable—if [it] were [the] Egyptians asking for a cease-fire—so this is the reality I want you to know. I am not asking you to accept it.

D: I understand. I am now in the process of receiving some cables from Israel that might shed some light on this.

K: I must have an idea of how much time you will need. If you want to pass this on to Eagleburger—

D: I can't because it is of an operational nature.

K: Can I call you?

D: Anytime, anytime. I will be in the office all night. I have talked to my staff about the charter—I hear from my air force that the Phantoms that were to leave tomorrow will be delayed because of a hurricane.

K: Well, I can't help that.

D: I know. This is something that I just learned and—

K: That means five will go on Friday.

D: So, maybe all five can go on Friday. I am just telling you this— But it may get out. So, I'll expect a call from you.

K: Yes, I'll call you and thank you.

October 11, 1973

By Wednesday afternoon, October 10, it was clear that the seven El Al planes could not pick up all the required consumable equipment. After consultation among the WSAG principals, it was therefore decided that Israel should be given U.S. government permission and support to employ private air charter companies to carry the additional equipment.

The resort to air charters turned out to be a fiasco. No charter company was willing to risk an Arab boycott or its planes in a war zone. The Defense Department could have brought pressure on the charter companies, which rely on Pentagon business, but it felt no urgency because it estimated that Israel still had stocks for two weeks—longer than any projection of military operations. The Department of Transportation (which was the other option) wanted to stay out of a military confrontation. For a day, the two departments adeptly pushed the ball back and forth into each other's court.

Neither the State Department nor the Defense Department bureaucracy was enthusiastic about the President's decision and especially about an airlift, fearing the consequences in the Arab world. The Defense Department was, in addition, concerned that immediate shipments of heavy equipment had to be taken away from American combat units. I was pressing for resupply as, indeed, the strategy outlined above required. But I wanted to do so in the most unobtrusive manner possible. Schlesinger never rejected these urgings. The problem developed on the technical level, if indeed a forty-eight-hour delay before the entire U.S. airlift was put at Israel's disposal can reasonably be called a delay. Brent Scowcroft and Joe Sisco, who tirelessly worked to organize the charters, were in effect given the runaround. But fundamentally the problem was that all alternatives were explored before we faced the reality that since no private company would assume charters to Israel, the United States government would have to run the risk either by undertaking the airlift itself or by chartering the planes in its own name.

But on October 10, whatever our perception of the resupply problem, we had to delay the cease-fire diplomacy until there was a change on the war front. We thought the optimal military circumstance for the postwar diplomacy we were planning was if Israel could restore the prewar situation or perhaps go beyond it. This would demonstrate that the military option backed by Soviet arms was an illusion; that diplomatic progress depended on American support. Failing that, it might be possible to negotiate on the basis of an Israeli military advance on one front, even with a setback on the other—though this would be a much more complicated state of affairs.

On October 10, however, neither of these conditions yet existed. Israel had barely recaptured the Golan except for some Syrian outposts in the Mount Hermon area. Two Egyptian armies were firmly established across the Suez Canal. There was no prospect of an offensive in the Sinai so long as the Egyptian armor had stayed behind the missile defense shield along the Suez Canal, which prevented Israel from using its air force as artillery. Based on its experience in the 1967 war, Israel had neglected building up its ground-based artillery and relied on airpower to fulfill that role. The only Israeli option was an offensive against Syria scheduled for the next morning (Friday). We would stall the Soviet overture until the results of this operation became clearer. (It must be remembered we had been told by Ismail that very day—October 10—that Egypt insisted on its demand for total Israeli withdrawal from the Sinai. And we had heard nothing from Syria.)

THE PRESIDENT–KISSINGER
> *Thursday, October 11, 1973*
> *11:00 A.M.*

N: Are you back at State?

K: Yes.

N: The thing I wanted to say was this. In following this strategy, I want you to lean very hard on the Israeli Ambassador [and say] that I am very distressed about these stories and I have information—I am talking to the press people. It is not coming from him but from lower-level people who are putting out the line that we are not supporting Israel. I will not tolerate this, and if I hear any more of this, I will hold him responsible. Will you tell him?

K: Yes.

N: You and I know that Israel is not going to lose this war but we cannot fight both sides. If we hear any more stuff like this, I will have no choice domestically except to turn on them. I can get the names of these people.

K: These fellows that are writing—

N: I know, but these people go over there. They think it helps the

Israelis but it does not. The Embassy people should have them cool it.

K: I will have them do it immediately.

N: We are helping them; he knows that, doesn't he?

K: Yes.

N: It is like the Agnew thing. He talked all right but his lower-level people did not. The Israelis have to trust us or there is no game.

K: I will call him immediately.

GENERAL SCOWCROFT–KISSINGER

Thursday, October 11, 1973
11:00 A.M. [as recorded]

S: Did you see the UPI ticker? It says war tanks and carriers have crossed over the border—

K: No.

S: It has been described by Moshe Dayan as a drive all the way toward Damascus. The CIA says the sortie level is high.

K: Let me call Dinitz.

S: Okay.

MINISTER SHALEV–KISSINGER

Thursday, October 11, 1973
11:10 A.M.

K: What is the Ambassador [Dinitz] doing in a synagogue on Thursday?

S: It is the first day of [Sukkot] and a bar mitzvah and for morale he went for a few minutes.

K: For my morale, it is not very good for you on the one hand to ask me to slow down the U.N. and you get Dayan to say on radio and TV that you are heading for Damascus. How can we get the U.N. to slow down when you make this kind of announcement by your Defense Minister?

S: You have a point.

K: With the greatest difficulty I got the President to slow things down, and now I am confronted with that news item. What will I tell the Soviets now?

S: I will get on to Israel.

K: Point two. The President is beside himself with what he considers inspired newspaper articles and I urge you to keep your people under control in what they say to the press. If it gets back to the White House that someone has talked to Israeli personnel, there will be hell to pay.

S: Do you have anything specific?

K: I have nothing, but he said he has. I was going to wait and call you about this after I had something else to talk to you about. If you want to cooperate with us diplomatically you must cooperate with us on this. We cannot ask the U.N. to slow down [on the cease-fire] with this announcement [Dayan's] that is out. I am sitting here with my associates now working on this thirty-six-hour delay when we get this ticker. Second, what in the hell am I now going to tell the Russians. This looks like the most extreme form of collusion and bad faith. You would have had the eight hours for the reality of this to become apparent if you had kept quiet. See what you can do to quiet things down in Israel and for God's sake stay off the radio and TV. Will you let me know?

S: I will.

Assistant Secretary Sisco–Kissinger
Thursday, October 11, 1973
2:40 P.M.

K: The Israelis are running amuck on this charter thing.

S: I know. Let me tell you where we are. This is the point where you had better intervene. The charter people have been very cooperative in the sense they are scouting around trying to find them [transport planes]. The problem is there does not seem to be a great deal available. Whether this is in any way politically motivated on the part of these people, I do not know. What has been done before is when this came up in the context of other emergencies—I think related to VN [Vietnam]—what we threatened to do is, the Secretary of Defense has the authority in coordination with the Secretary of Transport to mobilize up to two hundred aircraft for DOD operations in support of this kind of an emergency. This would be civilian type. When the Defense Department threatened to do this, then the civilian carriers got off their dime and did something. The situation, of course, is not necessarily comparable in the sense that they were talking about VN rather than Israel. We have been having a problem on the Pentagon side. They are dragging their feet. That is our impression. I would suggest if you could take a minute with Schlesinger and ask him what he thinks of this notion. The civilian carriers are not falling in line.

K: Could you call them and find them and tell them this is what we will have to do?

S: I will call you back.

K: And I will call Schlesinger.

ASSISTANT SECRETARY SISCO–KISSINGER

Thursday, October 11, 1973
3:00 P.M.

S: I am on the other phone with Schlesinger now.

K: I have promised you tomorrow morning to give a briefing before the House.

S: Yes. I want to talk to you about the Russian angle and the supply angle. Other than that, I can handle it.

K: Good.

S: I have laid this out to Jim [Schlesinger]. He tells me that the

White House had promised to nudge this National Air Association. Who in the White House can I talk to. Brent [Scowcroft]?

K: Yes.

S: I will get back to Jim on the phone now.

AMBASSADOR DINITZ–KISSINGER

Thursday, October 11, 1973
3:05 P.M.

D: I just got a cable from Golda. She says she is doing everything in her power to restrain.

K: Not in action but in words.

D: I said in your remark was to the words and not the action. She understands the situation and, well, I'll let you talk now.

K: Two things: First, I have just ordered the military to charter twenty aircraft and then you'll have them. They will be civilian aircraft chartered by us.

D: Good.

K: Secondly, I can delay the Security Council meeting through tonight. But I can't avoid doing something with the Russians. I have been avoiding Dobrynin all morning, though he has called every half hour. I think by tomorrow night we'll have to move in that direction. You should develop a "yes/but" strategy.

D: A standstill resolution—is that what you have in mind?

K: That's what I have in mind.

D: You think the Russians will want a standstill resolution by tomorrow night—the Russians want to—the resolution now.

K: Well, they are driving me crazy since early this morning.

D: Could you tell me what he has in mind?

K: Of course. The President is getting furious because he thinks you are churning up the press.

D: We are caught in a real dilemma. We are not telling them that the resolution is not all right. When we say the President is as usual, we can't tell them anything. All this situation—one contradictory after the other and everybody is speculating, but you can assure the President—

K: Look, you know what the problem is. Jackson [Senator Henry Jackson (D.-Wash.)] called me about my lack of attention to the problem.

D: He called you after he talked to—I told him we have a logistical problem—that is what he called about and he said that Dr. Kissinger—but Schlesinger is scared—

K: He is.

D: Damn right. We are appreciative of the charter. Can you do something about the planes?

K: They will move tomorrow.

D: The five.

K: Yes.

D: Can we get a large-scale—should I talk to Schlesinger?

K: Let me talk to him.

Ambassador Dinitz–Kissinger
Thursday, October 11, 1973
4:30 P.M.

D: I want to bring you up-to-date on the situation, up to 5:00 (six hours ago in Israel). We have penetrated in a front which is twelve kilometers wide and ten kilometers inside the road to Damascus.

K: Right.

D: I have another cable.

K: You are going to wind up like Paul on the road to Damascus.

D: As long as we don't wind up like Peter. Another cable says we have advanced twenty kilometers. Probably some places twenty kilometers.

K: You understand that I was not telling you—

D: I understood you completely, but I don't think my boss did. Even before I talked to you. We have since that time, the Syrian troops are dismantling. The Syrian troops and armor are in disarray.

K: Good.

D: I don't want to bother you with the airports we have bombed. It is important that the Syrian air force is not particularly active and seven were shot down. We observed five to twelve airplanes from the Soviet were on the way to Damascus. They returned to their base in Europe because of our tanks at the airport. They came again in the afternoon and this time they landed. Twelve landed in Syria with equipment. Until 5:00 our losses on the two fronts were ten aircraft—three Phantoms, six Skyhawks, and one Super [unclear].

K: How many?

D: Ten aircraft—three Phantoms, six Skyhawks, and one Super [unclear].

K: How did you lose them?

D: All to missiles. We have information that on the Egyptian front there has been no change. Our air force was active there. We estimated seven hundred to eight hundred tanks on the east bank of the Canal. Their attempt to go to Adaz was not successful. We have information that the A [unclear] are concentrating some forces at the northern airport. We don't know their intention. I think that is all. Do you have any reply from your talk on the heavy stuff from Schlesinger?

K: I mentioned it to him and he said he would look at the schedule again.

. . .

GENERAL SCOWCROFT–KISSINGER

Thursday, October 11, 1973
4:40 P.M.

. . .

S: I have talked to Brinegar [Claude Brinegar, Secretary of Transportation] and he will get right on it and call me back.

K: That would be the best solution. Call off the WSAG for 6:00— What is my schedule for in the morning? They don't seem to share it with me.

. . .

ASSISTANT SECRETARY SISCO–KISSINGER

Thursday, October 11, 1973
5:35 P.M.

K: Can't reach Scali for possible instructions. I have reliable information that the Security Council is meeting tonight. It was called by the Kenyans, who want to make a speech. Zayyat feels he has to express something and will express his outrage about the bombing and about the call for—

S: Sure, right.

K: Now, under no circumstances is Scali to say anything.

S: If the press ask—No press. Scali called and said he would like to see Malik. I told him not to see him until I get to talk to Henry.

. . .

GENERAL SCOWCROFT–KISSINGER

Thursday, October 11, 1973
7:55 P.M.

. . .

S: Are you coming over here at all this evening?

K: No, first thing in the morning.

S: Did you talk to Schlesinger about the F-4s scheduled for tomorrow?

K: I think two a day is fine.

S: Two a day can—

K: Throw in another one and make it six.

S: They have in mind keeping a two-a-day schedule. Send two from here and two from Europe and then two from here again.

K: For an indefinite period?

S: At least through six.

K: Then tell Dinitz he is getting at least six but that we may keep it going.

S: Right, okay. . . .

. . .

The discussions of resupply and cease-fire were briefly interrupted by a side problem: the desire of Jordan to respond to Syrian calls for help in a way that did not trigger an Israeli response.

BRITISH PRIME MINISTER EDWARD HEATH–KISSINGER
Thursday, October 11, 1973
8:00 P.M.

K: Hello.

H: Henry?

K: How nice to hear from you.

H: We have had from our channels a message from Hussein and he is under considerable pressure. He is trying to see what he can do to move a brigade into—

K: I think I know the content of that message. Your Ambassador talked with our Ambassador there. I take it you want us to talk to the Israelis.

H: If you could do that and say to let him do this as a minimum and not put in an attack. Then I think he could beat the pressure.

K: Yes, I understand. I think it will be possible. If you don't hear from me to the contrary. Well, you will hear from me in any event. I don't think we should leave this in the negative. I will call the Israeli Ambassador immediately.

H: I think that is the best arrangement really. Let him appear to be doing something when he really isn't.

K: Exactly right. We may want to talk to Rowley [British Ambassador, Lord Cromer] tomorrow with some ideas we are developing. We want to be able to do it before noon, that is about 6:00 P.M. your time. Will you be available? I will have an answer for you on the other matter well before then.

H: Yes, see you next week. Thank you so much.

AMBASSADOR DINITZ–KISSINGER

Thursday, October 11, 1973
8:10 P.M.

K: ... The Jordanians, in order to avoid the pressures, want to move a brigade to Syria which is out of harm's way. They don't care what you do, but they want to make sure you don't attack them.

D: Is it an infantry brigade?

K: An armor brigade.

D: Will they fight us or will they just stand there?

K: They will just stand there.

D: I will have to pass it on to my government.

K: We will get you the name of the area.

D: This is called, Dr. Kissinger, to fight war with all of the conveniences.

K: He said it is a wooded area and not agreeable. Eagleburger will call you. Call me through the White House board. I promised the British an answer tonight. They have to promote the cease-fire and they are getting extremely restive. I told them to wait until tomorrow. My present plan is to tell the British Ambassador around one that they should start exploring it, which should delay it into Saturday to give us another forty-eight hours.

D: When you said cease-fire, both in regard to Britain and Russia, is that cease-fire and standstill?

K: —But you should be in a good position.

D: My judgment is that you should be better off— With the situation in the far north after tonight I have an inkling that the Russians will not be interested in a standstill tomorrow.

K: Well, that is their problem. I can only deal with one thing at a time.

D: I wouldn't wish that on the Russians, Mr. Secretary, that they should have your mind.

K: If they now do have a new proposal I will have to think it over and we should have another forty-eight hours. I think I should get it going underway.

D: I think the important thing now is to gain time. I have another several things I would like to discuss.

K: I was told by Scowcroft only a half an hour ago that the planes will be on their way.

D: I was told this afternoon to call the Secretary of Transportation, who was out. I talked to the undersecretary, who said he would help me and get back. Scowcroft said he would get back to me.

K: I was told half an hour ago they are forthcoming. I can't actually handle it at this moment. Ignatius and [Secretary of Transportation] Claude Brinegar were meeting to work it out. Where are the El Al planes?

D: They sent two yesterday and one or two flew today.

K: I am moving heaven and earth here—I want to tell you another thing. We are sending two tomorrow, two the following day, and two the next day. That is better than one a day because it gets a pipeline going.

D: If I see it that is six in three days—I got another message from the

Prime Minister and she cannot understand the delay. Is there any movement on the tanks?

K: Let's get the present stuff moving before we get too frantic on something else. Can I call you around midnight? Will let you know about Britain.

D: All right.

AMBASSADOR DOBRYNIN–KISSINGER

Thursday, October 11, 1973
8:25 P.M.

K: We think we should move with the British and we have had a call from the Prime Minister to that effect. I told him we will talk first thing in the morning.

D: The Security Council will meet in the morning.

K: In the morning? Just let me set it up first.

D: As to now, what exactly can I say about the British?

K: I do not have a—now but I have started my discussions with them.

D: The first impression was all right?

K: The first impression was positive.

D: As of now, the first reaction was favorable, but the final reply will be given tomorrow.

K: That is right but I have not told them about your involvement. I don't want an overzealous man in your Embassy staff in London to go running— Let me handle it. I will be back to you tomorrow around noon at the latest. I will tell you by 1:00. Nothing will happen at the Security Council meeting that isn't fully coordinated with you. We are arranging that only after you approve will we proceed, so there will be no call to meeting unless you approve. We will try to work out some resolution and if you approve it we will get someone to call a meeting. We will get the British to call the meeting.

D: That is all right. I think it is maybe good to tell our people.

K: I can't let Scali into this until I have the British lined up.

D: Tomorrow you will call. In the meanwhile I will explain to Moscow that they need to think it over.

GENERAL SCOWCROFT–KISSINGER

Thursday, October 11, 1973
11:37 P.M.

K: What do you have—just the three-line UPI item?

S: Yes, that and I was just handed an item from the Israeli Consul. It reports that 1,600 Israeli tankers and infantry have broken through the Syrian line. The armored battalions are four kilometers east of—

K: I don't care about that.

S: The other item is that Dayan made the statement in a news conference in Tel Aviv, that—

[. . .]

K: Okay. He made the statement at a news conference.

S: Yes.

K: Okay.

October 11 saw as well the by now regular exchange of messages with Sadat. Ismail, on behalf of Sadat, urged us to restrain Israeli aerial attacks on Egyptian civilian targets. Agreeing to transmit the request, I made two other points. I warned against permitting Soviet military participation in any form. Such an action was certain to involve the United States directly and in opposition to Egypt. And I once more reminded Sadat through Ismail of what he had—unknown to me—already concluded, that Egypt would need the United States if there were to be successful postwar negotiations:

No United States forces are involved in military operations. No United States forces will be involved in any way unless other powers intervene from outside the area with direct military action. . . . The

United States stands ready to consider any Egyptian proposal for ending hostilities with understanding and good will. It will attempt to be helpful when hostilities are ended. Whatever the inevitable pressures of the moment, the U.S. hopes that both sides will not lose sight of this objective.

October 12, 1973

The Soviet airlift was continuing while we were having difficulty getting ours started. Nixon was preoccupied with selecting a new Vice President, the first time a President in office was able to appoint his own successor. I told him where we stood with respect to the air charters and our stalling on the Soviet cease-fire proposal, now forty-eight hours old.

At a testy luncheon, Dobrynin objected to the eastward deployment of the American Sixth Fleet, now located near Crete in close proximity to the Soviet fleet. He emphasized that the Soviet Union could not be indifferent to threats to Damascus. If Israel continued its advance, matters might get out of hand. I warned that any Soviet military intervention would be resisted and wreck the entire fabric of U.S.-Soviet relations.

That morning, Dinitz informed us of Israel's readiness to have a cease-fire in place resolution introduced by Britain the next day.

AMBASSADOR DINITZ–KISSINGER
Friday, October 12, 1973
8:35 A.M.

. . .

D: On the Jordanian thing. Unfortunately, the answer is no. He is also field director to the Prime Minister, and he will get the same answer [unclear] the situation there where there is so many forces in battle. The difficulty to prevent Jordanian troops there from escalating into involvement of the fighting.

K: But does that mean you'll attack Jordan?

D: No, no. It just means that we are advising them not to take the unit. The answer is we are absolutely against the [movement] of the Jordanian regiment, or the Jordanian division into Syria.

K: Yeah, but of course will you attack Jordan if it moves?

D: Well, there is no answer to this and I'm, you know, the thing is that the Prime Minister has been asked the same question by the King and asked indirectly not to do this. But I don't think that it means that we are to warn Jordan, no. I will clarify this further. The answer is that we are against the concept—

K: Well, that's obvious. The question is are you going to attack Jordan if he transfers the unit?

D: Okay. I'll get this cleared within—

K: Now, secondly, we just had an appeal from Sadat, and he says that you're bombing civilian populations.

D: I have no information on this.

K: Well, could I urge you not to bomb—

D: In Egypt?

K: Yeah.

D: All right. I'll check on this too.

K: Not to bomb civilian targets.

D: I'm pretty sure—

K: I don't believe you are, but I want to make sure that we have transferred the request.

. . .

THE PRESIDENT–KISSINGER

Friday, October 12, 1973
8:38 A.M.

K: Mr. President.

N: The morning report.

K: Mr. President, I was just checking ours and just talking to the Israelis to find out what was going on. The Israelis are still advancing into Syria, although they are now getting heavy counterattacks and the Iraqi armored division is beginning to fight them.

N: The thing we have here from CIA indicates that it was pretty tough up there in the Golan Heights and that sort of thing. So apparently they are having a pretty good fight up there.

K: That's right. But they [the Israelis] claim to be advancing and they claim to be reaching their objective. Of course it is obvious that all the fighting is tougher for the Israelis than it has ever been before.

N: Of course.

K: We had a call from Heath [British Prime Minister Edward Heath] yesterday, transferring a request from Jordan which we received already directly that if he is forced to move an armored unit into Syria, whether he could get an assurance from the Israelis that they wouldn't attack him.

N: From Jordan?

K: That was a hell of a question to ask.

N: Of course they'll attack.

K: Well, I asked, I put it to the Israelis and they said they are not trying to add to the divisions facing them from Syria, but they're not looking for an excuse to attack Jordan.

N: No, they don't want to fight another country. Well, it's really going on, isn't it?

K: Oh yeah, we've had an appeal from Sadat to prevent Israeli attacks on civilian targets and we're sending a reply back saying we've made that appeal to the Israelis. Then we've had an appeal from King Hussein. Today diplomacy is going to begin moving. I'm seeing the British at noon, to see whether they can put up a simple cease-fire.

N: With the idea that the Soviets really would abstain?

K: That's right. That would still pass it.

N: The Soviets certainly wouldn't, unless the Chinese— But the Soviets, why would they abstain from such a thing? I mean—

K: Well, they just, because right now there's a sort of a balance in the sense that the Israelis gained in Syria and lost in Egypt.

N: Although they haven't gained in Syria quite as much as we'd hoped apparently.

K: I can't get a clear report of that.

N: Now what about our own activities with regard to resupply, etc. Has anything gone forward in that respect?

K: Well, last night we finally told Schlesinger just to charter some of these civilian airlines, airplanes from civilian airlines for the Defense Department and then turn them over to the Israelis.

N: Good.

K: We've tried everything else and these civilian airlines just wouldn't charter to the Israelis directly.

N: That's all right.

K: So that's going to start moving later today.

N: But they have not yet actually run short of equipment?

K: No. And of course the most important assurance you gave them was that you'd replace the equipment.

N: The planes and tanks, right?

K: Right. So that they can expend what they've got, knowing they'll get more.

N: The lines that be, it seems to me, if you're—simply that we're not going to discuss what's going to be done, but the President has always said that it is essential to maintain the balance of power in that area.

K: I'm giving a press conference today.

N: But maintaining the balance of power, do you think that's too provocative?

K: No, we've always said that we—

N: That's what I mean. That's a signal to the Israelis, etc.

K: I'm giving a press conference today. I've got to navigate that one.

N: Yeah. Well, there's no more to be done. Of course I don't know anybody that's got a better idea as to what we're doing.

K: There's nothing else to be done, Mr. President. After all—

N: In terms of intervention, that's out of the question.

K: Impossible.

N: In terms of massive open support for Israel, that will just bring massive open support by the Russians.

K: And it wouldn't change the situation in the next two or three days, which is what we're talking about.

N: —the Israelis are not looking at two or three days. That's our problem, isn't it? They may be looking at two or three weeks before they can really start clobbering these people.

K: In two or three weeks the international pressures will become unmanageable.

N: I see. Well, then, if it's two or three days then, the Israelis have just got to win something on the Syrian front. Right?

K: That's right.

. . .

STATE DEPARTMENT SPOKESMAN ROBERT MCCLOSKEY–
ASSISTANT SECRETARY SISCO–KISSINGER

Friday, October 12, 1973
8:46 A.M.

M: Good morning, sir.

K: How are you?

M: Fine. Joe Sisco is on the line with me.

S: Good morning, Mr. Secretary.

M: We're calling to get Joe a little advice on his session this morning, particularly on the arms-to-Israel question. Joe, go ahead.

S: Mr. Secretary, with all these articles that came out this morning—they seem to be Pentagon sources to me. I'm assuming that this has not been deliberate on our part. Is that correct?

K: I haven't seen any but—

S: Yeah, well, there's a Getler article in the *Washington Post*.

K: Oh, those sons of bitches.

S: Yeah. The burden of the articles is that we are getting close to a decision. What I'd like a little guidance on is this: I was going to play it in the lowest possible key.

K: That is correct.

S: Even though it's a secret session, it isn't going to be a secret session with that many congressmen on hand. Will the United States supply military equipment losses of Israel? I was just going to say what you would normally say on it publicly. I'm really not going to get in this thing and that the focus of our efforts is to get the fighting stopped and that's where we really want to keep it. Now, of course, there's a lot of heat there on the Hill on this one, as you well know. Do you want me to go a little shade further or not?

K: How would you go a shade further, Joe?

S: Well, let me try it out. You know what our policy is—

K: Because I have a press conference too and I don't want—

S: That's why I'm checking. Because if I say one thing and then you and I are different, it will— I was going to say something like this: Well, you know what our policy has been and I am not aware of any change in our policy.

K: Of military supply.

S: We're just talking about that. How does that sound to you?

K: That's good and I'll say the same thing.

M: I think you have to say that much.

S: Now on the Russians, can I stick basically low-key with what Bob [McCloskey] said?

K: Yeah. But say we have warned them and it is too early to make a judgment whether they have in fact acted irresponsibly.

S: Yeah. Too early and could I add the sentence that Bob said that of course, if it were to become massive—that is, if they press me, I'm not going to say any more than I have to—why obviously, this puts a new face on the thing.

K: That's right.

. . .

AMBASSADOR DINITZ–KISSINGER

Friday, October 12, 1973
11:04 A.M.

K: I am on my way to a press conference.

D: Okay, I just wanted to tell you, we are thirty kilometers from Damascus. We are shelling the airport of Damascus which is a military airport, not of the city.

K: Okay.

D: Something, other things I want to tell you, but I will tell you when you come back.

. . .

GENERAL HAIG–KISSINGER

Friday, October 12, 1973
12:55 P.M.

K: How are things going?

H: Good, good. How about you, how did the press conference go?

K: I sort of was very evenhanded, so the Jewish community—they might be mad. I think my task is to keep the Arabs quiet and the Soviets quiet while slowing [the U.N. process]—

H: You know the Soviets have alerted three airborne divisions.

K: Well, I am seeing Dobrynin for lunch. If they did that, that's it.

H: They are going to force us to counter. We can't ignore that.

K: How did you learn about it?

H: Latest SitRep.

K: Absolutely. If they do that, we are going in. I will tell that to Dobrynin at lunch, but we better alert some of ours.

. . .

SENATOR HUBERT HUMPHREY (D.-MINN.)–KISSINGER

Friday, October 12, 1973
2:30 P.M.
(in eighth-floor dining room with Ambassador Dobrynin present)

H: I know you are very busy, Henry, but I felt it necessary to call you since I can't make it to the Senate Foreign Relations Committee meeting this afternoon. I feel very strongly that we should insure prompt delivery of the necessary planes for Israel. I understand we are making deliveries right now, but that they are rather slow and may be strung out over several months. I would like to see a number of planes made available promptly.

K: Hubert, that is not exactly what is being done. You understand, keep in mind that whatever we do give them, they come back the next day asking for five times as much.

H: But I understand the Russians are replenishing the Arab stocks. Some senators up here on the Hill have heard that they are taking delivery on SAM-6 missiles and that several Antonov planes are landing daily.

K: From what we can tell, most of these [Soviet] deliveries are consumables. If we are wrong, that is something we will have to look at.

H: I just don't think we can let that little country that we have so much invested in get clobbered.

K: Hubert, let me say something as a friend: we have to navigate carefully.

H: How do we know the Russians aren't fooling us?

K: If the Russians are fooling us, we know what we will have to do. Anytime you have any suggestions, feel perfectly free to call me.

MINISTER SHALEV–KISSINGER

Friday, October 12, 1973
3:15 P.M.

K: I wanted to check your message to Eagleburger.

S: Yes.

K: Does that mean we can move anytime? Because so far we have been delaying.

S: That means that the latest proposal you made us, about timetable, which would sort of bring us up to tomorrow evening, I thought—

K: Is that what you accept?

S: We accept that. We are not urging you for any further [delay]—

K: Good. That is the course on which I will stay. Thank you. I have some information for you.

S: Yes.

K: We have information that the Soviets have mobilized three airborne divisions and when I called this to the attention of the Soviet Ambassador, he made some extremely threatening noises. I told him we would not tolerate it.

S: Yes, sir.

K: I wanted you to be aware of this development. If they intervene we will be forced to do something drastic. But you should know it. He also wants you to know they are against your getting close to Damascus. I am just passing this on to you for information. If you want to pass anything on to me for them [Soviets], I will do it. I told him it would lead to severe deterioration of relations with us, and we would take action if they put in combat units.

S: Let me get that.

. . .

SECRETARY SCHLESINGER–KISSINGER

Friday, October 12, 1973
5:40 P.M.

. . .

S: We have a package of replacements worth about $500 million, along the lines of—meeting. Jackson wants fifty Phantoms within twenty-four hours.

K: Tell him to go screw himself. I don't mind you making a commitment to whatever package seems reasonable. I still think we ought to get something moving, but not in quantities that would get this blown sky-high.

S: We are moving in the Azores. I will call you back after I check with him. Did you have anything else?

K: I just returned your call.

S: Good. We will go ahead with the package, which consists of thirty Skyhawk A-4s, sixteen Phantoms, 125 tanks, including sixty-five M60s, and a whole range of other things, three Hawk fighters and so on.

K: If you could tell him this was White House orders, this will help us enormously.

S: I'll do that. Delighted to talk with you.

AMBASSADOR SCALI–KISSINGER

Friday, October 12, 1973
5:50 P.M.

K: Hi, John. How are you?

S: Fine. What was it you called about?

K: You called me.

S: You just called me off the Council floor. Malik just said there will be grave consequences if the Israelis continue to hit civilian targets in Syria, Egypt and things like Soviet ships and targets.

K: We don't reply.

S: No, I don't intend to reply.

K: If they make an overt threat of any reaction by them, you better warn them.

S: I will—They just said there will be grave consequences, to which I will not reply. If this meeting ends, I may be in town tonight for the Vice President thing.

K: I thought you would be the one.

S: Maybe I am. I have been told to come.

K: So have I. See you soon, John.

S: I will be in touch.

FOREIGN MINISTER EBAN–KISSINGER

Friday, October 12, 1973
5:53 P.M.

E: I know you have a great variety of problems at this moment.

K: That's right.

E: I refer to the message I asked Minister Shalev to send you this morning, about what ought to ensue in the Security Council [cease-fire proposal].

K: Right.

E: I would very much like—before anything is done—a chance to consult with you, perhaps—

K: My understanding on this, is not to happen until tomorrow.

E: Yes, there is still a round of speeches—low-profile on which—if I could come in tomorrow morning.

K: Not before tomorrow late afternoon.

E: Couldn't come in in the morning, anyway you would like to arrange—

K: I don't mind you coming in openly.

E: Perhaps I could do that. There are one or two things Mrs. Meir asked me to put to you—

K: All I need is the time to do it. How about 9:00?

E: Later would be better.

K: Unfortunately have Bourguiba Jr. [Habib Bourguiba, Jr., son of the President of Tunisia] coming at 10:00, and I have changed him twice already.

E: All right, at 9:00 then.

LORD CROMER–KISSINGER

Friday, October 12, 1973
6:50 P.M.

C: Heard nothing from London. Will you be at hand—

K: I can be reached through the White House board.

C: Okay. Just as soon as I get anything I'll let you know. I passed on the second thing you gave me [cease-fire timing]—

K: Not necessary to do it tonight, but it would be helpful to get a preliminary reaction. What is your personal reaction?

C: My personal reaction is in favor. It seems a sensible thing to do. I think it is a role we could usefully play.

K: If they give us any trouble, you and I, why don't we just go ahead on our own.

C: Right. Get set up with our own office in the U.N. One of the problems—slowing at home logistically is damned party conference at Blackpool but the communications are quite good and I hope to hear this evening.

K: Good, because we need to design our strategy.

C: I think the options for the future are extremely difficult. Not looked at the—paper we gave you in New York on guarantees.

K: Oh yes, it's a lot more relevant now than then.

C: That's what I mean.

K: In fact I want to talk to you about that. I was looking forward to talking to Alec [Sir Alec Douglas-Home, British Foreign Secretary] about it.

C: I am at your disposition whenever you want to talk—

K: Let me get this operation underway first, then turn energetically to that aspect—

At 7:00 P.M., the Soviet Deputy Chief of Mission, Yuli Vorontsov, requested an immediate appointment for Dobrynin, who was said to have an "urgent" message to deliver to me. Since I had to be at the White House for the announcement of Nixon's choice of Gerald Ford for Vice President, I asked that the message be delivered to me there at 8:00 P.M. In the event, Dobrynin lodged a protest that Soviet ships had been hit and expressed Soviet readiness "to defend its ships and other means of transportation." I rejected the protest, warning that any Soviet military intervention—regardless of pretext—would be resisted.

SOVIET DEPUTY CHIEF OF MISSION
YURI VORONTSOV–KISSINGER

Friday, October 12, 1973
7:00 P.M.

V: What are you doing in town?

K: Only leave time—get damned Middle East thing—

V: I decided to stay and shoot it out.

K: One of the worst threats ever made against me.

V: I am a secret weapon and they use me—

K: Where is the Ambassador?

V: He's opening a youth exposition, but he plans to visit you this evening. Wants to talk to you urgently. Will it be possible to reach you—in an hour's time?

K: Look, I have to be at the White House at 8:30. Tell him if he can arrange for me to be a member of the Politburo, I can make him Vice President.

V: He only has an hour to make a decision.

K: Tell him to come to the State Department at 8:00.

V: And you have to be at the White House at 8:30?

K: And I can't be reached there. Have you got the message?

V: Yes, we have got the message and it is being translated now. By 8:00 he will have it—it the State Department.

. . .

AMBASSADOR DINITZ–KISSINGER

Friday, October 12, 1973
7:45 P.M.

D: Dr. Kissinger. I just came back from Clements [William Clements, Deputy Secretary of Defense]. I mean Schlesinger and Clements was there, and I also had a talk with the Prime Minister. When can you see me?

K: We have a few other problems tonight [appointment of Gerald Ford as Vice President].

D: I understand this. I am not trying to—I thought I had some important things on the political situation.

K: I have Dobrynin coming in a few minutes with a very important message.

D: It might be related.

K: Can you tell me about it now?

D: We regard the message that your people sent us as very serious—about the threat [mobilizing three Soviet divisions]—and the Prime Minister hopes that you are reacting to it very strongly.

K: There is no question of that. I was very upset about the harassment from the pro-Jewish senators this afternoon. As if we had not done enough.

D: The committee [Senate Foreign Relations Committee], or two or three members, knew exactly what you had done. They were concerned with two Phantoms a day and that shipment did not get out even today. That was [Stuart] Symington (D.-Missouri) and [Jacob] Javits (R.-N.Y.). I felt I had to tell them—and also emphasized what you had done to help.

K: We will not heed to Soviet threats and we are staying on the schedule we discussed with you.

D: The Prime Minister said we could start the schedule [for the cease-fire] today.

K: It is now too late for that. Especially after the threat we should show no nervousness.

D: You can start anytime [the cease-fire proposal].

K: Once you have been threatened, it is better to stick to your course. One thing that Javits said was that we would make you pay for your diplomatic gains. We got the Soviet message [regarding a cease-fire] Wednesday morning and here we are in Friday.

D: I did not enter into the political arena at all.

. . .

AMBASSADOR DINITZ–KISSINGER

Friday, October 12, 1973
8:25 P.M.

K: I have to be very brief again because I have to run off to the White House.

D: I know.

K: I had a talk with Dobrynin. He had two messages. One, to protest against our resupply and the second, extremely threatening, about your bombing of civilian targets and threatening that Tel Aviv will not be spared if this continues. I said that if any Soviet planes are seen over the area—there will be direct American involvement.

D: Let me get this down.

K: We are moving an aircraft carrier from Gibraltar to the— If any Soviet personnel, planes or ground personnel appear in the area, the U.S. will intervene. I have no authority to say this. I would not want to have Dayan hold a press conference.

D: What Dayan says never relates to our cables. That is the problem.

K: You can believe this is true. I have discussed it with the President this afternoon, but I would not like [it] to get out, especially on the day the Congress passed the War Powers Bill.

D: What?

K: A bill that limits the President's power to make war. A second problem on the scenario, I have discussed with you [the cease-fire]. We are not triggering it tonight under any circumstances. . . .

[. . .]

. . .

LORD CROMER–KISSINGER

Friday, October 12, 1973
9:33 P.M.

C: Ah, look, have you got anything from Dobrynin?

K: Yes, I've had a word with Dobrynin. And he says this: he said your information is correct, but irrelevant.

C: What does he mean by that?

K: He means that, he asked me to say that they had no right to say flatly that the Egyptians will accept it, but they do say that if you put it forward on the assumption that the Egyptians will accept it, it would be a very good gamble.

C: A very good gamble?

K: Yeah. But what he was really trying to tell me is, now I know the Israeli attitude, which will be yes, but. They may raise one or two—

C: Well, yes, we've been explaining this to our Ambassador in Tel Aviv. I certainly didn't tell him what was going on, but he'd seen the Director General of the Ministry of Foreign Affairs, [Avraham] Kidron, earlier in the day. And they were just playing hard to get. They said, of course, they were under great pressure from the military as they were expected to be. They should go through with it.

K: What you people have to assume is that we wouldn't ask you to do this if we didn't think there was a reasonable possibility.

C: No, no, no, that I take 100 percent. I mean there's no problem with that at all. We have to check a little bit. I don't mean this with any mistrust of your information.

K: No, no, it's entirely up to you. I'm just giving you the answers I receive.

C: Yes, sure. When you say the information is correct but irrelevant, I'm a little bit perplexed by that.

K: They seemed to be convinced that the Egyptians do not want to be in the position of, they do not want to—

C: They do not want to be—

K: They do not want to be in the position of having asked for it. But they apparently would accept it if the Security Council passed it without their indicating that they wanted it.

C: Yes. Imposed by the Security Council. I mean, without their asking for it.

K: That is correct.

C: I get the sense of that, and they wouldn't come out in refutation of it in other words, obviously. I mean they might make a bad public demonstration but in reality they wouldn't.

K: Eventually they will accept it.

C: You still feel this is right, Henry, don't you?

    . . .

K: My own judgment is that it is the right thing to do. I believe it is the way to peace, or at least a good gamble on it, and I think it would be a useful role to play and the reason we have asked you is because we thought you were the most trustworthy of the members of the Security Council.

C: I thank you, sir.

    . . .

LORD CROMER–KISSINGER
    Friday, October 12, 1973
    9:43 P.M.

K: Let me read you from what is called an oral note which Dobrynin handed me. "Acting in the spirit of understanding which is characteristic of our relations with the President (don't throw up please) we were consulting during the last several days with the leaders of Egypt and Syria on the question of termination of hostilities. Frankly speaking, the conversations were protracted and not easy but nevertheless we are now able to say to the President that the Soviet Union is ready not to block adoption of the cease-fire resolution in the Security Council. The President, of course, understands that in the present situation the Soviet Union cannot vote in the Security Council in favor of the cease-fire resolution, but the main thing is that we will not vote against it. Our representative will abstain during the vote." Now this, of course, is in total strictest confidence.

C: Of course. Now, as far as the participants in the event of consent, we obviously have to get our lines fairly straight.

K: I think after you have decided to proceed, we will then instruct Scali to talk to Maitland [Sir Donald Maitland, British Ambassador to the U.N.].

C: That's fine. It's what is on the ground that worries me.

K: What happens on the ground is that they will probably continue fighting until it is adopted.

C: I'm sure they will. There is no doubt about that. The question is, will they go on afterwards and repudiate any of this. But I don't believe they will, personally.

K: My smell, Rollie, is that this is going to do it.

C: I think it's well worth the effort.

K: I don't see what we have to lose.

. . .

As we waited for London's decision on whether to sponsor a cease-fire, Dinitz came to my White House office at 11:20 P.M. and began a process that was to end with the decision to undertake an airlift. He reviewed the military dispositions and reiterated Israel's willingness to move toward a cease-fire in place. At the same time it became clear that Israel's armed forces had not advanced significantly during the day. This led to the following exchange:

KISSINGER: Do you want us to start it [the diplomacy] tonight? Did you make the offensive today? I have the impression no.
DINITZ: No.
KISSINGER: If we could synchronize your moves better—I think the

urgency will disappear if there are no military moves tomorrow. If I knew there was no offensive today, I would have started earlier.

DINITZ: I must tell you: Our decision whether to start a new offensive or not depends on our power. We thought we would have by now in Israel the implements to do it—the bombs, the missiles, etc.

The seeming inability to synchronize diplomatic and military means provided the impetus for the airlift.

SECRETARY SCHLESINGER–KISSINGER
Friday, October 12, 1973
11:45 P.M.

K: I've just been meeting on an urgent basis with Dinitz, who says they are running out substantially of ammunition. They based their strategy on the assumption that they would get the ammunition replaced this week, as the President had promised them on Tuesday, and that they are stopping their offensive in Syria because they can't move because of lack of supplies. And the Egyptians have transferred artillery over and now they are saying there is a problem of a major thrust into the Sinai. And it is true we gave them our assurances.

S: Well, what do you want to do?

K: Well, I don't know what I want to do. I just feel that we did make some undertaking—you know it would help us. I was raising hell with them for not keeping their offensive going for a day while we were setting up the scenario on diplomacy. And now they have got to stop it.

S: Well, we can—

K: Are you sure that your people . . .

S: Well—

K: I just don't find the initiative. If they wanted something to happen, then it would happen.

S: You mean on the obtaining of charter flights?

K: Well, on just getting—you know, some way in four days could have been found. I don't know what it is; it isn't my job. I just don't see—except for you, I don't know anyone over there who has any intention of making this happen. . . .

   . . .

S: Well, we have the possibility of just telling the U.S. aircraft to go on whatever they need.

K: I just find it hard to believe that every company would refuse to charter unless somebody sort of told them in a half-assed way.

S: Well, the problem with that is that they have good business outside. Unlike other circumstances, back during the Vietnamese war when they agreed to charter, they were going around—equivalent half empty on the charter flights.

K: For example, did anyone talk to—the fella I had—who is head of Continental Airlines? Six?

S: Six, right.

K: Bob Six. Now I know goddamn well he is a great patriot, and if somebody told him we needed airplanes, I just can't believe that he wouldn't do it, unless you winked at him and said but if it doesn't happen until next week my heart won't be broken.

S: Well, it is—what is—when are they going to start running out of reserves?

K: They are out now. They have stopped their offensive. And they are now in deep trouble in the Sinai. I am basing this on a message from the Prime Minister to the President. And you know maybe it is not true, but it is a hell of a responsibility to take.

S: Well, if we started now and really turned the screws on these guys, I suspect that we can collect a few aircraft for tomorrow. But I think if you want to do something about it, you better let a U.S. aircraft fly all the way in.

K: That I would have to discuss with the President.

S: Or another thing we could do—

K: But can't we turn the screws on these charter companies? I am just convinced that if the screws were turned, they would have produced.

S: I think that that may be right. We never went back at them again because of the decision to go with the Military Airlift Command to—

K: Well then [unclear]. They could then pick it up in the Azores if they wanted to. It is already there.

S: The stuff's in the Azores? What do you mean they? Are you talking about the charters?

K: Well, if the charters picked it up here and the Israelis picked up what is already in the Azores, that would at least put some steam behind it.

S: Well, how much do they need?

K: I have no estimates of that.

S: Okay. Let me see what I can do. One thing we could do, we could take these ten or twelve C-130s that we are planning to give them and load them up and let them go all the way.

K: Well, let's do that. Well, I will call Dinitz and tell him to have his military guy get in touch with you.

S: Okay.

K: But will you tell [General Gordon] Sumner [Department of Defense officer in charge of resupply] for Christ sakes to get off his ass, because if a catastrophe happens there is going to be some accounting. From our point of view, we needed the Israeli offensive moving. If the Israelis are on their knees tomorrow night, we are not going to—

S: Well, Henry, it would have been desirable for them to tell us that they were going to run out of ammunition.

K: Well, on the other hand, I must tell you, we told them every day that this stuff was coming. There wasn't a day that we didn't tell them that they would have twenty aircraft in the morning and then they didn't have them in the evening.

S: I really can't say that that was the case until the night before last;

it was assumed that these guys were going to be able to haul them themselves along with the aircraft that they would round up. It wasn't until yesterday that we—the night before—that we started this search for aircraft on their behalf. So, ah, the situation—

K: We can reconstruct what went wrong later. Let's see what we can get going here.

S: Okay.

K: Because this whole diplomacy is going to come apart if they look impotent. It can only work if they look as if they were gaining, not if they look as if they were losing.

S: Okay. The first thing to do is to have those C-130s that we turn over carrying ammo. Do you want U.S. pilots to fly in those C-130s? I don't see any reason why not.

K: I've never thought this thing through from that point of view. Why don't you work that out with their military attaché?

S: Okay, very good.

October 13, 1973

SECRETARY SCHLESINGER–KISSINGER
Saturday, October 13, 1973
12:49 A.M.

. . .

S: . . . Henry, it's only five hours ago we talked to these people. We've been asking them what their daily supply is; they have exhibited no uneasiness about it at all.

K: Because they don't trust the people in the room.

S: You mean to say that when General Gur is alone [with] General Sumner, that he doesn't trust him?

K: No, with Gur with Sumner, he should trust him.

S: Sumner has been trying to get it out of Gur for five days and Gur has been perfectly relaxed about the day supply.

K: Because Gur claims that—I mean Dinitz—I don't know Gur—Dinitz claims that was because every day we told them, which is true, that they were going to get twenty planes moving. And every day it didn't happen. If it had been moved, they would have been all right. So they say.

S: Every day goes back one night.

K: Now, I told them Tuesday night, based on an assurance of Sisco, with which you have nothing to do—said they were going to get twenty charters the next day. And we told them Wednesday night, if everything else failed we were going to requisition it through MAC [Military Airlift Command]. Then we told them Thursday night, it would now be requisitioned through MAC and then we told them Friday morning that this wasn't working.

S: That's right. It's two days—

K: It's about forty-eight hours, but you're responsible for twenty-four hours; I'm responsible for—be that as it may, let's not worry about what happens. It seems to me we have these options. We've got the ten C-130s, which we could load.

S: Right. We've got ammo in the [unclear] now.

K: Yeah, but we don't know when that's going to be released.

S: How about your negotiations with the Portuguese [for transit through the Azores]?

K: We just sent a telegram two hours ago.

S: Okay. Well, they simply cannot be that short of ammo, Henry. It is impossible that they didn't know what their supply was—and suddenly they've run out of it.

K: Look, they have obviously screwed up every offensive they've conducted. And they are not about to take the responsibility themselves. I have no doubt whatever that they are blaming us for their own failures.

S: Right.

K: But you try to make that case here. And, above all, I really think we have this thing 90 percent licked . . . And you tell the [Deputy

Secretary] who is spreading the word that I'm driving the Saudis crazy that I have a promise from the Foreign Minister [of] Saudi Arabia—

S: I told them at about 6:00 this evening—he seems to be somewhat relieved. You mentioned this to me earlier—to tell him. He said he hoped it worked out that way.

K: It may not work out that way, but the only way it is going to work out [is] if we are going to get a quick end of the war—of which we nearly have all pieces in place. But we need an Israeli offensive.

S: Okay. Now, Henry, if they have enough ammo to carry him to-morrow, we can get the ammo in by tomorrow evening. But first of all, we have to find out what their supply situation is.

K: I would give a hell of a lot if I could keep them going through to-morrow, so that they are not sitting there when this goes into the Security Council.

S: The only way to do that is to move ammunition in tonight. And it's almost—it must be damn near dawn there.

K: It is dawn in Israel. It's 8:00 in the morning.

S: Are they out of ammo or aren't they?

K: How the hell would I know. They said they were stopping their offensive. I was meeting with them tonight to synchronize the diplomacy for tomorrow. And I said, where are you going to be tomorrow night? I was getting leery when they called me after having pleaded with me to give them another day; they called me at 4:00 this afternoon and said you can trigger everything [the cease-fire proposal] tonight. And I couldn't do it because I didn't have—I had geared my timing in such a way that I could recover all the pieces. I could have done it yesterday—I need twenty-four hours to get it going.

S: It's amazing to me—I sat with them from 5:30 to 6:30 and they simply did not mention ammunition problems—they didn't in-dicate any issue in that area. All they talked about was the reequipment and to get it in within two days.

K: They are so terrified now—or claim to be terrified of Israeli thrust into the Sinai—I mean Egyptian thrust.

S: That's incredible planning on their part.

K: Look, they fucked it up.

S: Hm huh. Okay, let me try to find out what the hell their status of supplies situation is. We had the impression that they had fifteen days of supply.

K: I bet you they counted their supply on the experience of the Six Day War.

S: Could well be.

K: I bet you they didn't expend as much in the whole Six Day War as they do in one day of this offensive.

S: That might very well be, Henry. I think that is very likely. Sooner or later they could have come back and told us what their problem was.

K: Well, because they would have had to face themselves, and I must say in their defense—not on the airplanes on which they and we never agreed—but on the other one, we told them time and again that they were getting all the consumables and they should fight as if they were coming.

S: Right. But they never told us they were running short.

K: Because you know what happened—as well as I do. These guys got the whole thing screwed up—every time. They are living in 1967. All day long yesterday they were telling me they were heading for Damascus and they were going to stop on the outskirts. This morning they told me they would use public transportations if they can. Now they obviously can't make it.

S: Okay.

K: No question in mind that 80 percent of the blame is theirs. But that doesn't help me tomorrow night. And you know, I just have to have them going as a fierce force while this is going on.

S: If they are out of ammo now, there is nothing we can do to get it there for today's offensive. The nearest step is in the Azores, and you know that's kind of screwed up unless we take the U.S. air-craft off and fly it in. It won't be in for five hours—

K: How about at least C-130s. I think what we have to do is to get them the ten C-130s. We have to twist the arm of the charters by telling them they will never get another defense contract—that's going to produce.

S: That's right, but we can get that stuff out all right, but we are not going to get it out there for Saturday.

K: No, but that, at least, will get it moving. So let's do it—a combination of the Azores [unclear], the ten C-130s, and forced charters. . . .

. . .

Ambassador Dinitz–Kissinger
Saturday, October 13, 1973
1:03 A.M.

D: My military attaché is just standing next to me. He just came into my office and said that General Sumner called him and General Sumner told him that because we cannot [unclear] the Golan Heights tonight or tomorrow he has an order to send some ammunition immediately that we need badly just now.

K: That's what you wanted, isn't it?

D: Yeah, we wanted ammunition but we want Sumner to [unclear]. So what is exactly—you have any idea how many planes or anything?

K: We are going to do three separate things. We are going to give you the ten C-130s immediately.

D: Ten C-130s. Directly.

K: Immediately. Now, you have to work out with Defense—we would prefer it if you place Israeli pilots in the Azores.

D: We understand.

K: If at all possible.

D: I would like to find out.

K: Well, you find that out. Second, we are going to force some char-
     ters out of the airlines. And, thirdly, we are going to use the
     Azores with your El Al, so you have three different operational—

D: Just to be sure I understand: the ten C-130s, which will approach
     either directly to Israel or through the Azores, depends on the
     availability of the Israeli pilots to continue to take—

K: Yeah, but make a big effort to put Israeli pilots—

D: Of course, we will; we will need Israeli pilots for—the charter
     will go all the way to Israel?

K: Yes.

D: You have any idea how many?

K: No; but we are going to force them out—we will try to force
     twenty of them.

D: I see. And now we'll have to fly from the Azores. So what we have
     to see is—

K: You will have all three of them going simultaneously.

D: We'll have to try and see whether we have enough pilots for El Al
     and for the ten C-130s—we'll check on it and will tell the De-
     fense. We have to deal with Defense, right?

K: Right, because—but if there's any problem call General Scow-
     croft.

D: Okay, at this point I'll call Scowcroft. All right; thank you,
     Doctor.

K: Now, wait a minute; since I'm interested in the diplomacy of
     this, I can't tell you how to conduct military operations, but I
     think it would be a disaster for you just to stop tomorrow.

D: Right. I will pass this information immediately to the Prime
     Minister, including these items you just told me.

K: Because if you are seen to be weak, there's no telling what will
     happen.

     . . .

The day became the turning point of the war. It was found that
the pressures the United States would have to exercise to produce

charters were indistinguishable from a direct airlift. Schlesinger and I had ordered the C-130s to fly directly to Israel. During the day, Nixon ordered giant C-5As to fly directly to Israel, and by the next morning, the entire airlift was American.

At the same time, we sought to implement the cease-fire-in-place diplomacy Dobrynin had proposed on October 10 and we had stalled to permit the military situation to evolve. But when we sought to implement the Soviet proposal, the strategy of a British cease-fire resolution adopted with Soviet and American abstentions began to fall apart. London would not proceed without Sadat; Sadat had changed his mind (if he had ever been willing to go along) and was planning an offensive into the Sinai for the next day—partly to relieve pressure on Syria—and Moscow was ambiguous, either because it had misjudged the situation or because it had never intended to follow through. Much of this initiative was carried out on the telephone.

AMBASSADOR DOBRYNIN–KISSINGER
Saturday, October 13, 1973
9:37 A.M.

K: I still haven't heard from the British. I am having a call placed to Home [Sir Alec Douglas-Home] to see what's going on.

D: You have talked on the telephone with him—placing a call—?

K: We agreed it should happen today. If they don't do it maybe we should try the Australians.

D: All right.

K: The second thing; we just received information that the Egyptians are planning airborne landings in the Sinai.

D: I don't know the significance of this—

K: We all have to realize that if anything looks like trickery we will have to—it will affect things.

D: Better to practice something on which we both agree. I didn't know anything about Sinai really—

. . .

K: We have not heard anything from the Israelis.

D: Nothing from the Israelis? I can pass this information to Moscow, do you think?

K: If we don't hear from the British by noon, we will go to the Australians.

D: Is this decided?

K: I will check with you after I have talked with Home.

D: I should check with Moscow but I don't really see that there is any difference.

K: No, I don't think you should check with them. We have to see what the British will do.

D: I expect to hear from you by noon. I will wait for your call.

SIR ALEC DOUGLAS-HOME, BRITISH FOREIGN
SECRETARY–KISSINGER

Saturday, October 13, 1973
9:38 A.M.

K: I am so sorry we will not be able to meet tomorrow. I was just talking with the President about the matter discussed with Rowley [Lord Cromer, British Ambassador] yesterday. We were hoping that you might see your way clear to doing that matter which we discussed.

DH: Yes. Have you seen or have the Israelis told you what Sadat said last night? Sadat said that a ceasefire *in situ* might be possible but they would have to have the agreement that Israel go back to the '67 line. They have repeated their one condition. I have sent our Ambassador in Cairo back to see him. I said, suppose we were to propose a cease-fire *in situ* immediately, followed by the introduction of an international force, immediately followed by a conference or some international initiative by the Secretary General. Would this appeal to him?

K: We just can't cooperate in that. We are not ready for that. We think he will accept, unless we have totally been misled. We believe the other thing will work as long as they claim they are yielding to somebody.

DH: Suppose Sadat turns us down?

K: Then we are in a stalemate.

DH: Then we will be in a worse position than before. We will have lost any ability to make a move. It looks like they will turn this down.

K: That is what you think. I have been told by the others that they will accept.

DH: You have been told by the Russians?—

K: I don't see any reason for them to say this and not mean it. What are they to get from it? It was repeated no more than an hour ago.

DH: Sadat says no, according to our sources.

K: When you speak of an international force, you mean total withdrawal?

DH: What I think is this. Suppose Sadat agrees to a cease-fire *in situ*. The international force is introduced while an international conference or Secretary General or some international machine goes in— Won't that be possible without a full withdrawal?

K: It won't be that— I think we have agreement on this, from the Russians and [we] might from the Israelis.

DH: All you have is Dobrynin's word that the Russians believe that Sadat would agree, and our information is that they could not agree to this. It would be an almost direct conflict of report unless the Russians were willing to pressure Sadat. Would they agree to this?

K: My impression is that if they have tricked us on this, they will pay the price of our entire relationship. They have all to lose.

DH: I will have another talk with Ted [Prime Minister Edward Heath] and give you a ring back but I think our credibility will be completely lost if we were to make the public initiative and he would not have it. He himself has given us the conditions to which he would agree to a cease-fire and it includes all the old things.

K: And the Israelis have given us the other position. The Israelis said it has to go back to the Canal. We can probably get them to go along and the Soviets can get the Egyptians to go along. Maybe we should try.

DH: The decision doesn't have to be made by Sunday night.

K: I thought by tonight. We can also ask the Australians to do it.

DH: My impression is, I can't see how the Russians can do this unless they are willing to say they will cut off their arms.

K: Maybe that is what they are willing to do. They didn't ask for you to do it, and since we can't propose the resolution, it can't be a maneuver directed against you. They would have preferred France to introduce the resolution.

DH: I see. What time is it in the U.S.? About 10:00 in the morning? I am traveling to London tonight with Ted in his plane and I will have another talk with him. We can't really risk being turned down by Sadat, and on our present information from him, he will be.

K: Unless they are committing a treachery, the Russians assure me they will go along with it. Where would they be to put it forward and we abstain and Sadat refuses and they back him up? I don't understand what they have to gain. Especially when they wanted us to ask France.

DH: What do you think the Israelis' response will be? Yes?

K: Yes, but it will not be accepted unconditionally. Let them put forth their conditions and then we might be able to go— It is just having these maniacs in some sort of balance—

DH: We have to try something.

K: Therefore, the Russians said any complicated cease-fire will be refused. The only thing they are willing to abstain from is a simple cease-fire.

DH: Let me think about it again and say in another three hours I will have another report in from our Ambassador, who is meeting with Sadat again.

K: You will not get a prior agreement from Sadat.

DH: No, but then I can't say. Suppose Russia pressures him into saying yes. That is not going to be a happy situation. Let me think about it and if it is to be worthwhile.

K: If this goes on, we will have to send a massive airlift in there. I just know—

DH: What is the state of the battle?

K: The Israelis claim that they have beaten the Iraqis [forces in Syria] and I would expect them to turn on Sinai. Today we start flying into Israel, which is very dangerous.

DH: Let me ring you back in three hours. Thanks for ringing.

AMBASSADOR DOBRYNIN–KISSINGER
Saturday, October 13, 1973
9:50 A.M.

K: I just talked to Home. They have been talking to Sadat, and Sadat says they will never accept a straight cease-fire.

D: They discussed directly with Sadat? I must send a telegram to Moscow right away—

K: I am pressing them and they will call me back in three hours.

D: Both our countries will abstain. Even in this case it is my firm decision—

K: We will still press the British to—

D: If Sadat even told them so, we will definitely abstain and will keep our word in this case. If we both abstain, it will be of political significance. What is now the problem? The British are not decided?

K: The British are reluctant because they think that Sadat will not agree to it. If Moscow could talk to him.

D: In three hours I will not get an answer unless I go by ordinary telephone.

K: No, that is too dangerous.

D: I think so. Really, even if he said so—

K: Because the British are afraid of Sadat saying no and going ahead—

D: Maybe we should go with Australia.

K: That is what we will do. Australia has nothing to lose in Egypt. I will be in touch with you in three hours. I will try to do something by tonight.

GENERAL SCOWCROFT–KISSINGER
Saturday, October 13, 1973
10:15 A.M.

K: Do we have to get permission to refuel American planes in the Azores?

S: I will have to check. I don't believe so.

K: If the answer is yes, then why do we have a base there?

S: The U.S. military does not need permission.

K: I want to know the name of the person who is inventing obstacles and have him removed from this operation immediately.

S: Did you hear this from the Israelis?

K: Yes. The Israelis are here now and were told the planes could not leave because of refueling. Whoever told them that will have to be removed from this operation now. Can you do that immediately?

S: I can do that.

LORD CROMER–KISSINGER
Saturday, October 13, 1973
10:26 A.M.

C: How did your talk go?

K: Very unsatisfactorily, because you are now negotiating separately with the Egyptians.

C: Don't know about negotiating exactly—

K: Well, trying to sign [a] separate resolution with the Egyptians. Both sides will accept— Thought you might get word to him [Douglas-Home] while he is thinking.

C: Take your point entirely.

K: After talking to Alec [Douglas-Home], I talked to Dobrynin. Dobrynin claims you have [a] misconception of the situation.

C: —that Egypt will agree.

K: Misconception about some kind of Soviet trick, but they didn't even know with whom we were going to set up the resolution. Alec said Dobrynin's word against Sadat's; why take Dobrynin's?

C: I see what's happening and, of course, I take your point.

K: What we have decided to do, if you are still dancing around we will not go along with any resolution other than what we have proposed. You are trying to come up with an idea of a peacekeeping force or peace conference, we will veto it. Too complicated.

C: Yes, well what I said yesterday—simplicity—

K: If you can press—to participate in the maneuver, which could not have had you as an object, we will move to Australia or France.

C: Quite. I don't think that will make a whole lot of difference. Don't think it will work any better.

K: Well, it probably won't with France, but it might with the Australians.

C: I don't think they will do it; still—

K: I will tell you honestly, if I can't get—to introduce the resolution, we will pour in supplies and see when the battle breaks. . . .

The threat of massive resupply was somewhat disingenuous since the airlift was already going full blast. The purpose was to prevent it as a response to provocation to moderate Arab, Soviet, and European reactions.

AMBASSADOR DINITZ–KISSINGER

Saturday, October 13, 1973
12:32 P.M.

K: Hello, Mr. Ambassador.

D: Yes, Dr. Kissinger.

K: A number of things. We are going to fly three C-5As today.

D: The Cs—the big ones with sixty tons.

K: Right. And we are just going to fly them through the Portuguese base [. . .] And we are going to fly at least three of the C-141s that are in the Azores to Israel and we have increased the number of Phantoms to fourteen.

D: Fourteen.

K: They will be there by Monday night.

D: Monday night.

K: Now, in the meantime, however, I must ask something of you, Mr. Ambassador. I just again have been called by Jackson [Senator Henry Jackson (D.-Wash.)] threatened with a congressional investigation, being told this is a lousy example of crisis management and he is going to demand an overall review of the national security system. I must say this—if I get one more threatening call by anybody I am going out of the supply business. And with all my friendship I am not going to stand for it.

D: Dr. Kissinger, I really want you to believe me that I have not talked not—yesterday I didn't even see him. I talked to Symington and to Javits yesterday and I haven't seen him yesterday or today—haven't spoken one word to him.

K: Well that may be, but someone has to get the word to him as to what is going on.

D: I am willing to call him and explain to him exactly what the situation is and when I talked to him three days ago the one thing I said was that we never had a better friend than Dr. Kissinger. And I can repeat it in his eyes. So I am willing to call him right now and say to him exactly what the situation is but I am not calling any [other] senators.

K: Well, the major point is we cannot hold still for a situation in which a massive attack is launched on our handling of this crisis. First of all I think it has been handled rather well. Even with some delays of delivery.

D: Exceptional [unclear] yes.

K: Well—but this item has been recovered now by flying in C-5s.

D: Right.

K: And ah—

D: Can I ask you on this supply thing, sir, so that I will be completely clear. The three C-5s will fly today? You don't have an estimate—morning—night—or something.

K: By this evening I am certain.

D: By evening. The three C-141s—this is an additional element, right?

K: Yes.

D: And that will also go out today from the Azores?

K: Yes.

D: Where will they pick up the supplies?

K: They brought the supplies to the Azores for you to pick up yesterday.

D: They have got the supplies?

K: And they are just going on with the supplies they brought to the Azores.

D: I see. Going on. I see. I don't know this. Frankly you— On the charters?

K: And we are going to get twenty charters. This time I am sure we will get them.

D: All right. Do I have to tell you our [unclear] people anything?

K: Well you just tell all of this to General Gerher. If there is any problem you let me know.

D: Fine.

K: You know I have to tell you this. Our whole foreign policy position depends on our not being represented as having screwed up a crisis, and with all affection for Israel, if it turns out that we are going to be under attack for mismanagement in a crisis, we will have to turn on you. I don't care who does it, if that happens, we will defend ourselves.

D: I understand this but there is no one—not only me—there is no one from our Embassy, I can assure you. I beg of you to believe me—I know you do what—

. . .

SECRETARY GENERAL WALDHEIM–KISSINGER
Saturday, October 13, 1973
1:13 P.M.

W: . . . What I wanted to tell you is the following. I had a long talk yesterday with el-Zayyat after the Security Council meeting— and they decided the following, which I wanted to let you know. Apparently they feel very strong militarily, whether it is justified or not. At any rate, he put to me the following points. He said they are ready to accept a cease-fire, if the Israelis give a commitment to withdraw to the 1967 lines.

K: Yeah, well, that's out of the question.

W: I told them this. I said I don't think there is any chance to get this. But I thought I should tell you because he mentioned quite a number of points: point one, commitment to withdraw to the 6th-of-June lines, point two, this commitment—the help could be done indeed by the United States. Then three, he would give an Egyptian commitment to international forces in Sharm ash Shaykh and also to international buffer zones. These international troops in the Golan Heights—not in the whole area but in an area along [the] Syrian border, and then he said we would accept an international conference to negotiate details, etc. But some sort of arrangement for the Palestinians would be found and the Palestinians would have—participate in such a conference. I thought I should let you know this. I am, of course, fully aware that especially the first point is not acceptable to Israel, because I have spoken to Abba Eban the day before. And I told him this first point is, as far as I can judge, definitely not acceptable to Israel. He said, but why should we not be more flexible since we have military advantages before?

K: Right.

W: They apparently feel militarily strong now and believe they are able to keep what they got on [the] east bank [of the Suez Canal] and don't want to be more flexible.

K: Right. Well, I appreciate this very much, Mr. Secretary General, and if I have anything to report to you, I will take the liberty of calling you.

W: Well, thank you very much. Do you have the impression that it sounds a major progress in your talks with the Russians?

K: I'll have a little better judgment of that later this afternoon and I'll call you if there is anything to report.

. . .

At this point the Soviet Union abandoned the effort for a cease-fire either because it had been a ruse all along or, more likely, because Sadat proved more obdurate than the Soviets had expected. Its method was to reject Australia as the country to introduce the resolution.

AMBASSADOR DOBRYNIN–KISSINGER

Saturday, October 13, 1973
1:40 P.M.

D: I have had [a] telegram from Moscow which says the Australian variation is not really a good one.

K: Isn't?

D: That's all I received—is the telegram and it says further explanation will come. I would like simply to tell you what I have, as of now.

K: Maybe the British are trying to become a world power as a result of this.

D: Could be. Anyway, the telegram says we will send you further instructions on this point. I simply am trying to tell you: I don't know why they are objecting; I only wish you to know what I have just received.

K: You have seen the press coverage of my press conference? It was very moderate with respect to our relations. I think it achieved the objective. Don't you?

D: To a certain extent, yes.

K: On the other hand, really, I hope, I see the massive airlift is continuing today [referring to the Soviet airlift].

D: On the same scale.

K: Now 105 planes flown in.

D: Altogether, from the very beginning, you mean?

K: And that's a terrific amount.

D: I know; I don't know the figures but it is—

K: —beyond a certain point, and we are approaching a point where we will have to do something, not done fully yet. I mean we are besieged by senators yelling and screaming. I hope Moscow understands. I am saying this as a friend; if we are played with, we will have to do something, with all reluctance. You should not try to pick up some easy victories—well, you know there are no easy victories.

D: No, that's very clear.

   . . .

Sir Alec Douglas-Home–Kissinger

Saturday, October 13, 1973
3:35 P.M.

DH: We have been over and over your suggestion with the Prime Minister. We don't think that the time is right for this initiative and we don't think we could take it now, although for the next few days we will try to wrack our brains to see if we have other suggestions. Our contact with Sadat has gone so far as to say that he feels so strongly he would invoke a Chinese veto if anybody proposed something of this sort. Therefore, the Russians would, in our view, have no chance whatever of looking on Sadat and forcing him to do so. This, at least at present. If you really want to do this, if you and the Soviet Union were to abstain, of course we would do our best, if you wanted to get the Australians to try this line.

K: Let me get back to you if we want to revive it. If we have any other ideas, we will be in touch with you.

DH: If we have any other ideas I will give you a ring tomorrow. At the moment, haven't got any idea. Didn't think we could take initiative of a simple resolution of cease-fire, as you ask, because we think Sadat really would reject it—what's more, he would reject it vehemently. I have talked to the Russians and told them this. It doesn't look really to be a starter. [The] Australians, of course, might be willing to do it. McIntyre is in a particularly good position to do it—if you want to launch it. Having gone over it again and again, don't think you can get the support in the Security Council. Anyway are you very worried about the effect generally about détente with the Russians?

K: —massive resupply for Israel on our side—

DH: Two other things. The French have exactly the same impression as us of Sadat. We think relations being what they are with Sadat, if there had been a glimmer of hope in a move like this, he would have said so; on the contrary, he gave us a totally, worse than negative signal.

K: I understand this. As to your question about whether détente is our motivating consideration—Détente is not an end in itself. I think developments now are going to drive us towards a confrontation.

DH: I know, this is a great worry. Couldn't you fix this with the Russians? Can't you get them to lay off?

K: We can attempt it.

DH: I don't want to discourage you from trying with the Australians if you—

K: Don't really think we will do it; not sure Russians would accept the Australians.

The American diplomacy had been proceeding on two tracks: resupply of Israel, and U.N. diplomacy for a cease-fire. We had with

Israel's agreement been prepared to abstain from a cease-fire-in-place resolution as long as Israeli gains in the Golan balanced Egyptian gains in the Sinai so that the subsequent negotiations would concentrate on the status quo ante, which we had recommended from the beginning. We had started the airlift before the cease-fire negotiations to improve our bargaining position and strengthen our hand in a continued confrontation if the negotiations failed—though we used the failure of the cease-fire initiative as a pretext to ease possile reactions in the Arab world and the Soviet Union.

The Soviet strategy is more difficult to explain. Abstaining from a cease-fire resolution if Sadat wanted to continue fighting would mortgage relations with Egypt. And if Sadat agreed, why would Moscow abstain? Perhaps expecting Sadat to refuse, Moscow put down a marker on which it might later settle if my prediction proved accurate and the Egyptian situation began to deteriorate.

Whatever the cause of Moscow's diplomacy, it enabled us to present the airlift as having resulted from a provocation and to accelerate it to speed a military outcome.

AMBASSADOR DOBRYNIN–KISSINGER
Saturday, October 13, 1973
4:00 P.M.

K: Anatoly, I have just heard from the British and they do not feel they can proceed. They were told by Sadat 1) he did not want a resolution and 2) if such a resolution were put in, he would call the Chinese to veto it. He would consider any— That leaves two possibilities. Either you tricked us—

D: It was always easy to check with us. After all, it was very clear—all the day before yesterday, when our answer came. It was very easy to be approved two days ago when we came to the General Assembly but—

K: First, we had to get somebody to put it in.

D: I understand that—if it came to the floor, we would abstain.

K: I don't doubt that you would abstain. What is the sense of such a maneuver if you thought the Egyptians wouldn't accept it? You encouraged our discussions with the Israelis— At any rate, the British won't introduce it and you don't want the Australians to introduce it.

D: —give our instruction. I am now waiting for instructions—

K: We are not going to do anything. We are now going to wash our hands of it and let nature take its course.

D: I will be in touch.

K: . . . It looks as if you want this war to continue and let us go through three days of meetings with the Israelis and British in the meantime.

D: Before then how could we know that the British would wait to give a firm decision? I am sure that the British would tell you we were not in touch with them at all.

K: You might have known what Sadat would do—

D: I am just telling you that it is a very wrong assumption.

K: We operated on the assumption when you told us you had discussed with Egypt that they would accept it. There is no reason—

D: At this very moment—would held under the pressure so to speak.

K: Now, when they say they are going to ask the Chinese to veto—

D: Maybe Sadat changed his mind and—

K: And they told the British they had said the same thing to you. That is—

D: No.

K: To gain time.

D: For whom, for them?

K: That's right.

D: For Israel to—the Syrians. It was a very interesting presumption.

K: There is no sense discussing it—

    . . .

GENERAL SCOWCROFT–KISSINGER

Saturday, October 13, 1973
4:05 P.M.

K: . . . As I understand, there are now fifteen C-41 and three C-5s underway. The Portuguese have—now [agreed to the use of bases in the Azores]. You start the charters. Since we are going to be in a confrontation, we should go all out. I am going to call—I want to warn him in the event you might get— Ask how long it will take the 82nd Airborne to get ready.

S: Of course.

K: Not to do anything—I think those bastards [the Soviets] understand only brutality.

S: I was just talking to Dinitz and they are very pleased with the report that things are on their way.

K: Are you getting the two ships loaded?

S: There is one in Boston at the present time and it is almost loaded.

K: Get that on the way.

S: The other is to be in on the 15th.

K: If they want to play, we will play.

S: I think under the circumstances we have no other choice.

K: It could be that the Egyptians were willing to do it. I told Dobrynin that they were diddling us along to gain time. He told me he thought we were diddling them along for the Syrian offensive.

S: That is possible too. I will call you back on the 82nd.

SECRETARY SCHLESINGER–KISSINGER

Saturday, October 13, 1973
4:15 P.M.

K: [The] Portuguese have agreed to use of the airfield.

S: For charters?

K: For anything.

S: Jesus Christ, that's a surprise. What did you tell them?

K: I just told them we wouldn't bargain. If they reject, we will re-member. When the crisis against which they want to protect themselves occurs— This is for your own personal information.

S: That means we can go over to charter by Monday—continue to fly the stuff into the Azores.

K: One problem you have to remember—looks like our diplomatic initiative is coming apart. The British won't play—because Egypt won't play, according to the British. We may be getting into a confrontation posture with the Soviets. [The] Soviets may just figure that if they have the whole Arab world against us— You know the 21st Armored Division [Egyptian] crossed the Canal; we just got the word from the Israelis.

S: —leave them alone in the—part of the Sinai. When they get out, the Israelis will look better.

K: [The] Israelis lined it up. [The] Russians assured me Egypt was lined up.

S: I don't get the Brits. Why not tell them we are not going to give them any Poseidons or Polaris [missiles for British nuclear sub-marines]?

K: No, they're going to get them anyway; these things have to be done in cold blood. No, don't share your information yet; do it tomorrow morning.

S: Well, I'm going to tell [Deputy Secretary of Defense Wiilliam] Clements about the Portuguese. Can I tell you something funny. One hell of a lot of stuff ready to move. We've got it on the planes in case we got the word to fly it direct to Israel. Then we found out the stuff was still sitting right here in the United States. We didn't get a clearance from the State Department. We've moved the stuff off to the Azores now; fifteen C141s and three C58s will be airborne at noon.

K: Moving into to Tel Aviv?

S: Yes, Henry.

Ambassador Dobrynin–Kissinger

Saturday, October 13, 1973
4:25 P.M.

K: Anatoly, I just talked to the President and he asked me to tell you that under these circumstances he can no longer observe any restrictions that I gave you yesterday on flying American planes.

D: Under what circumstances?

K: The plan we worked out is not being implemented because we didn't know the Egyptians' real feelings. We are prepared to stop when you are.

D: What?

K: We are prepared to stop our aerial supplies when you are willing to stop.

D: I will send that right now.

K: So what I told you yesterday as of an hour from now will not be accurate.

D: You don't want to wait even an hour?

K: We can always stop it. It will not be that massive that quickly.

Lord Cromer–Kissinger

Saturday, October 13, 1973
4:35 P.M.

C: Henry, I still haven't heard anything.

K: I talked to Alec and your people won't do it. They have talked to the Egyptians and they say they are violently opposed to it.

C: They won't give any—? Maybe the Egyptians have changed their minds in the delusion that they may win.

K: At any rate, I have just talked to the President, who is taking it extremely ill. When we look over the crises of the last three years we just don't seem to be able to get together.

C: Our clients are quite different, but our objectives are the same.

K: . . . We wanted to tell you we are starting an airlift into Israel. There will probably be a confrontation.

C: That was inevitable. I told our people in London that you would have no alternative. It is very disturbing.

K: Especially since what we asked you to do is what you proposed last week.

C: I think what has changed since then is that the Egyptians obviously got all above themselves.

K: The one consolation one has is, whatever the tactical—the West has—we will all go down together; at least we are doing it with the worst possible grace.

C: What will be your posture vis-à-vis when the Arabs start screaming oil at you?

K: Defiance.

C: Just defiance? It is going to be rough, won't it?

K: We have no choice.

C: Well, we tried.

K: You can transmit this to London.

AMBASSADOR DOBRYNIN–KISSINGER

Saturday, October 13, 1973
7:40 P.M.

K: I am going to see the President, wanted to check with you to see if you had an explanation yet.

D: In five or ten minutes I will get it. Could you wait.

K: Sadat informed the British that he informed your Ambassador under no circumstances would he accept such a proposal.

D: I will call you in ten minutes. Right?

K: OK.

Lord Cromer–Kissinger

Saturday, October 13, 1973
5:25 P.M.

K: Rowley. I hope you understood what I was telling you before was under instructions. That was not my own although I am not saying I disagreed with it.

C: I took it that way.

K: I have an intelligence report I don't want to read over the phone. It substantiates that we were not lied to. Would you like to come by for about five minutes?

C: Where are you? The State Department? Why don't I come in twenty minutes or so. I have some things I would like to talk to you about.

General Scowcroft–Kissinger

Saturday, October 13, 1973
6:45 P.M.

S: . . . The helicopter carrier will be leaving on Monday. The one that is going to release the one in the Mediterranean. That will be some movement in that direction. I just think that the news about the 82nd shouldn't break at the same time resupplies does. It may be—

K: I don't want that to happen. Now the dirt is going to start flowing.

S: That is too bad.

K: I had to use the British refusal with Russia to justify the airlift, which you knew we were going to do anyway.

S: That's right. Let's see, the first airplane will not get to Israel the earliest before 6:00 in the morning our time. I think the meeting is about right.

K: Okay. Thanks.

FOREIGN MINISTER EBAN–KISSINGER

Saturday, October 13, 1973
7:35 P.M.

E: I have thought about the political action we discussed today.

K: You understand it is not possible today. Hasn't Dinitz told you about the British?

E: He told me about the British refusal on—and the Soviets' refusal of the Australians. I only wonder whether the Soviet refusal is so strong that there is no chance they will change their minds—and if they want it, it seems to indicate—

K: I am no longer so sure they want it and I am assuming you don't want us to present it.

E: I gave Mrs. Meir a negative answer and she endorsed that— The other proposal is that the privilege of appearing in the Council is not limited to the Council. I thought vaguely about Denmark, Brazil, but I don't think they would be any more reasonable to the Soviets than Australia. The British refusal you think is quite final. It either does not happen at all unless the U.S. presents it and even then the Chinese veto is a possibility. If you think their objection to Australia is as firm as that all I ask is confirmation from him. The only possibility is that you— I am also trying to find out from home what the urgency is. We have managed to overcome the trouble this morning. I will find out if there is any— . . .

AMBASSADOR DOBRYNIN–KISSINGER

Saturday, October 13, 1973
7:55 P.M.

D: Oral message— First Brezhnev refers to discussion I had yesterday with your boss during reception.

K: Told me about that.

D: Expresses great satisfaction—about things that were said by the President to the Ambassador. Sure—shared his view and he would like me to tell to Dr. Kissinger he adheres exactly to the same points of view. Hope, no matter what difficulties—many good things done and will—to keep it.

K: Good. Hope—going to prove that [affirmation of goodwill].

D: Situation in Middle East and Security Council—for days, [the] U.S. and some countries with which they consulted don't come to the conclusion of immediate convocation of the Security Council. We don't know exactly reason of that. Question, reply—military situation in Middle East how it develops, it develops different, only through last days. In one day don't have time. Don't think try to follow us—our part. We are concerned on position about cease-fire. Same time tells—use bombardment of civilian targets in territories by Israel [Dobrynin's justification for abandoning the Soviet cease-fire proposal]. Make it more difficult [in] Arab capitals and peoples. That's why difficult to discuss on this, questions specifically—now Arabs are objecting—to accept Security Council resolution which deals only with cease-fire. They insist it should be accompanied by simultaneous cease-fire and should be another additional part of solution which should be staged withdrawals of Israeli troops from Arab territories, which was occupied in 1967. Isn't finished yet, finally consultation with Arab countries about [cease-fire]—don't have text yet.

K: We have worked for three days on the assumption you are now canceling [of a cease-fire achieved by joint abstention of the superpowers].

D: For two days we might have been quite prepared to do, but now the Arabs are objecting to this. We would like to decide the situation on a big scale—which means remove cause of all conflict. This will be a really major decision which will have to decide things—

K: Well, where does this leave us? Nowhere.

D: —now [to the matter of the] Security Council.

K: Now we are right back to where we were last Monday.

D: Looks so—

K: —took forty-eight hours to make possible.

D: For two days, the day before yesterday and yesterday and in the morning yesteday, I give you a reply—even I was shaken up with you—you know I was shaken up— The telegram from Gromyko wasn't received for some days. For two days our positions were very close, we were prepared to abstain—no other interpretation. Very firmly. We don't want to have complications for two days. Then the Arabs changed their position. The telegram from Gromyko says check with Kissinger, reply or not. We are complaining you don't—really waiting until you get the British or something. For two days we are on record not to vote at all—abstain with you—the Arabs categorically objected.

K: In the meantime, you sent in 140 airplanes. May be why the Arabs are so tough now.

D: Not really. The Security Council resolution two days ago—no connection with airlift. Holding [up] from your side. Maybe you relied too much on the British. Maybe the Australians—prepared yesterday. [The Australian option might have been acceptable twenty-four hours earlier.]

K: Yesterday the British talked to Sadat—what caused the delay? Sadat never would have accepted—

D: Yesterday morning—sent telegram yesterday—I was shaken last time I talked to you. . . . Very clear [regarding the] Security Council yesterday morning, I know up until today Malik had instructions very clear—abstain. [I] sent very strong telegram to Malik, when you have complained. Immediately called Scali, [said we were] going to abstain.

K: The point is, now objective military [situation is that]—despite very friendly words of Brezhnev that you are trying to avoid a collision, you have 140 airplanes [in the Soviet airlift to the Middle East]. Still much—we cannot not supply our friends while you are supplying yours.

D: Well, you had made your decision.

K: You waited for five days. Tonight Egypt is launching an attack in the Sinai— Tomorrow when some American airplanes reach Israel the Arabs are going to start yelling. We will not under any circumstances let détente be used for unilateral advantage. [You must have] no illusions about that. I have—airlift for four days— way of getting political settlement. Friends [Great Britain] have refused to participate in something took you two days to get Arabs—they change their minds. I think once we were in it with you, the Arabs, if the President had given the word to Brezhnev—believe at last moment on day it was supposed to be implemented say they wouldn't do it. We made agreement this summer, friends objected to it, we went ahead with it—it was important to us. You can tell Moscow to save itself the effort, we are not going to accept the Egyptian position. You will only exacerbate the situation by proposing it to us.

D: All right, fair enough.

K: —want to accept the Egyptian position, deal directly with it. I have had the Egyptian position since Wednesday.

D: Did they propose this to you before or on Wednesday?

K: On Wednesday the Egyptians sent us a proposal, of which they said they gave you a copy, and which is totally inconsistent with your proposal. [The proposal is that] Israel return to its '67 borders, [there be a peace] conference of great powers, Palestinians, and Arabs, to discuss only international [borders, that is, 1967 border]—and security and the future of Palestine.

D: On Wednesday, quite prepared to support—

K: I told the President, despite this message from Ismail, I relied on your word. This is quite inconsistent with what the Arabs told us. I assume the Arabs—you knew Egypt would agree in no sense, how you could support this, if Egypt wouldn't agree.

D: I understand this point of view. Change—few days ago.

K: Fine with us and we just have to see what happens now.

D: Is completely unacceptable, two-part resolution.

K: Well, what's the second part?

D: Stages, back to borders.

K: —secure and recognized borders.

D: '67.

K: No, unacceptable. May be in—in Moscow not to—add obligation not to exacerbate situation. Until this afternoon I believed—had possibility of pressing for a settlement, pressing for a cease-fire. Now that hasn't happened, you are unable or unwilling to produce a cease-fire—[U.S. and Soviets] are obviously on collision course no matter how many [protestations]— What do you think we can say to the people on Monday, had them quieted down on the weekend—so the utility of détente—to both of us [is called into doubt]. You don't think we will accept a military setback in the Middle East. You can't believe it.

D: Wouldn't believe it.

K: I recognize you have problems. [There are things you] have to— But there's no law that says you have to send in 140 airplanes.

D: I understand, it is a problem.

K: Until this minute not one American airplane has landed in Israel. Not one— My whole strategy has been based on reliance on you. I can tell you, in addition to whatever else is achieved, my own credibility with respect to what—is not exactly high at this moment. But not from you personally. Yesterday afternoon [we were] getting contrary report from Sadat than I was from you. I said I had absolute confidence—you never lied to us before.

D: Could you imagine the situation. You are taking a position proposed to other countries. Circumstances to be changed. This is the situation—exactly I should put it on really stake much while people involved have two . . . [unclear].

K: Why do we have to deal with you [on matters] that depend on Sadat, why not deal with Sadat directly?

D: It's up to you and the President to decide, [but there could be] disastrous results. . . .

K: We'll work this out when it's finished—we'll be able to demonstrate that special relationship. Developed would have concrete results, if you read the press conference, this was line I took.

D: I did.

K: On Monday this will be done to—

D: —public relations.

K: Monday you will have sent in fifty to a hundred airplanes.

D: You are now free—

K: Only inflame Arab leaders—victory for you. Only strategy is to make [clear] Arabs don't feel they can [win]—so three or four days from now we'll see what the situation is. Proposals like '67 borders, make the situation worse.

D: All right, send back the telegram.

K: The President is extremely agitated. . . .

D: In my telegram, I will quote, unquote you. I can assure you— otherwise, [situation] is dangerous.

K: We had an understanding to work on the basic issue in January. This has been completely disregarded now. We will not let ourselves be pressured into it. . . .

SECRETARY SCHLESINGER–KISSINGER
Saturday, October 13, 1973
[*no time indicated*]

K: We are going to have an NSC meeting on Monday morning.

S: Okay.

K: We don't know yet at what time. Will let you know.

S: Okay.

K: It would be helpful if we could get an accurate report of the Israeli military situation from somebody. Can your defense attaché handle it? Or should we send somebody out there?

S: Our attaché is pretty good, as a matter of fact we are about to reward him for his reporting—

K: Could we get a comprehensive report by tomorrow evening?

S: Supply situation—up to his ears in stuff. Did you hear the comment General G[unclear] made to our people? "Stop worrying about ammunition, don't want to jam up airports with that. Much more interested in other things." —wise to send it in. Once trade fields—tied down in the Azores—

K: We could represent the American airlift as a legitimate temporary thing.

S: This charter thing was no use to us until the Portuguese cracked.

K: Monday morning.

S: May be able to use publicly or—privately. Announce publicly willing to turn off military airlift. Charters will not work for government of Israel. Only work for Department of Defense . . .

K: What do we achieve by charters?

S: Not a hell of a lot. Thin cover at this stage—permitted Government of Israel to hire them—our government disengaged. Supply less effective cover in which we were going to hire them on behalf of Israelis, requested to do so by Department of Transportation—shifting to charters, public announcement.

K: Yes, but somebody will ask who chartered what. [It's still the] Defense Department, it's still American military planes, what do we achieve?

S: We achieve the ability to reduce the uniformed military role in this operation.

K: Okay, that's worth something.

S: It's not worth a hell of a lot. Worth something to use it to get something more—the Soviets are in there with military people and—

K: Trouble is facing Soviets alone. Don't give a goddamned—

S: It's the Arabs.

K: The Arabs worry me on airlift—

S: I think you can turn it into a virtue.

K: Keep in mind tomorrow at the WSAG how to handle that. What we achieve with charters. [We need to find] a better cover for it.

S: They would permit more effective use of Israel air fleet. What we would do is to have charters fly the stuff to the Azores.

K: I would prefer that.

S: We have a number of options—for charters to fly into Tel Aviv, rather than U.S. military personnel. Likelihood of government taking—with U.S. government or private chartered by U.S. government.

K: Chartered by U.S. Government. Don't know what to gain from it.

S: . . . Israel has no support—everyone treats them as—or pariahs.

K: This thing continue to point out what a—what I wanted to avoid. [This is what the] Arabs wanted to achieve.

S: Couldn't agree more.

K: How could we have avoided it?

S: Don't think you could.

K: Okay, we'll discuss the charter principle tomorrow.

October 14, 1973

With the cease-fire initiative thwarted and an airlift underway, a great deal now depended on the military situation and preventing or moderating a reaction from the Arab countries, as well as on avoiding a confrontation with the Soviet Union in the midst of the Watergate crisis. I therefore sent a message to Sadat via Ismail:

> The U.S. side wishes to inform the Egyptian side that it is prepared to cease its own airlift resupply efforts immediately after a cease-fire is reached.
>
> The United States wishes to emphasize again that it recognizes the unacceptability to the Egyptian side of the conditions which existed prior to the outbreak of recent hostilities. The U.S. side will make a major effort as soon as hostilities are terminated to assist in bringing a just and lasting peace to the Middle East. It continues to

hope that the channel to Egypt established with so much difficulty
will be maintained even under the pressure of events.

The U.S. will do all it can in this sense.

Messages in this vein were also sent to King Faisal of Saudi Arabia
and the Shah of Iran.

Nixon was between domestic crises. The issue of Agnew's resignation had been resolved by the appointment of Gerald Ford as Vice
President. The crisis over release of the Watergate tapes and the
start of impeachment proceedings was but a few days away.

THE PRESIDENT–KISSINGER
Sunday, October 14, 1973
9:04 A.M.

N: Hi, Henry, how are you?

K: Okay.

N: Anything new this morning?

K: Yes, the Egyptians have launched a big offensive and it's hard
to know exactly what is going on in an early stage of an offensive.

N: Of course.

K: The Israelis have claimed that they've knocked out 150 tanks and
that they've lost about fifteen of their own. But that in itself
would not prove anything—it depends where they [the Egyp-
tians] get to. The last information we have that is not absolutely
firm is that they may have reached close to the Mitla Pass, which
is about thirty kilometers from the Canal, and which would be
the key Israeli defensive position—it's about one third of the way
into Sinai and it would be a rather—
[. . .]

K: . . . The Israelis—there are two possibilities, one that the Israelis
are trying to draw them beyond the SAM belt in order to knock
out a lot of their forces and, in that case, the battle could be fairly

decisive. The other is that the Israelis are really in trouble and we should know that by tonight in any event. I think that makes clear why that peace move wouldn't work yesterday. I don't think the Egyptians were ready until they launched an attack.

N: That's right. And basically they told—the Russians might have wanted—we haven't heard anything more from the Russians?

K: No, but that's a little early. I'm certain we will before the end of the day.

N: What then? We have in effect told the Russians to—

K: The issue now is this, Mr. President. As of yesterday, we started out with the idea of a cease-fire and a return to the pre-hostilities lines. Incidentally, should the Israelis clobber the Egyptians that will turn out to be a pretty good position. Then we moved to a simple cease-fire. The Egyptians may have been ready to accept that before the Israelis got into Syria. The Egyptians are demanding a return to '67 borders; now that's absolutely out of the question, short of a huge [Israeli] defeat as a result of the war. That has to come as a result of the subsequent negotiations that follow the war. So now what we are trying to do is—I've talked to Dobrynin about that last night after you and I talked—is to see whether we can find a formula that links the cease-fire to the peace settlement.

N: I think we've got to get some way. Look we've got to face this—that as far as the Russians are concerned, they have a pretty good beef insofar as everything we have offered on the Mideast, you know what I mean, that meeting in San Clemente [between Brezhnev and Nixon in June 1973], we were stringing them along and they know it. We've got to come off with something on the diplomatic front, because if we go the cease-fire [route], they'll figure that we get the cease-fire and then the Israelis will dig in and we'll back them, as we always have. That's putting it quite bluntly, but it's quite true, Henry, isn't it?

K: There's a lot in that.

N: They can't be in that position, so we have got to be in a position to offer something.

K: Well I—

N: Because we've got to squeeze the Israelis when this is over and the Russians have got to know it. We've got to squeeze them goddamn hard. And that's the way it is going to be done. But I don't know how we can get across now; we told them before we'd squeeze them and we didn't.

K: Well we were going to squeeze them; we were going to start a diplomacy in November right after the Israeli—

N: I know we were, but—

K: And we have made all the preparations for that but that's now water over the dam. I think what we need now—if we can find a resolution that doesn't flatly say the '67 borders, but leaves it open—something that invokes the Security Council Resolution 242 that speaks of withdrawals and that's something everybody has already agreed to once. Plus a conference or something like that. Then perhaps by tomorrow we can move it to a vote in the Security Council.

N: Yeah, yeah. Certainly a conference would be fine.

K: And I know the British are working on something like that and I'm going to be meeting with Cromer later.

N: The British, then, are not just standing aside—that'd be terrible.

K: There are two things, Mr. President. The British basic attitude is lousy because they are trying—I put it to Cromer yesterday. I said what have you got to lose in Egypt that's compared to what you will lose in Saudi Arabia if this thing gets worse and worse. On the immediate specific issue, where the British are behaving badly, they are just passively sitting there picking up the pieces; they are not shaping anything. But on the very immediate one, Sadat did take a negative attitude, but they made no attempt to persuade him, nor did they want to run any risks. We might have done what you suggested yesterday, offering a cease-fire, if we could have gotten Britain and France to go along with it. But to go into the Security Council with a resolution that has only two members supporting it, one other member possibly supporting it, is suicidal.

N: Yeah, I understand.

K: But by the end of the day, this thing will become a lot clearer because the battle now in Sinai, whatever happens in Syria and Sinai, the battles just cannot be extremely protracted because supplies from both sides have to come a fairly long distance.

N: Desert battles are not protracted, we know that—that they move quickly. The other point I was going to make—what are we doing on the supply side?

K: If I could call you in an hour; I have a meeting which is going to start now.

N: All right.

K: In which I can give you an accurate report. Basically what we are trying to do is stop the military planes after today and put commercial charters in.

N: Yes, yes. As I say though, it's got to be the works. What I meant is—we are going to get blamed just as much for three planes as for three hundred—not going to let the Russians come in there for—with a free hand. On the other hand, this is a deadly course, I know, but what I meant is, Henry, I have no patience with the view that we send in a couple of planes, even though they carry sixty some—

. . .

N: My point is if—when we are going to make a move, it's going to cost us—out there. I don't think it's going to cost us a damn bit more to send in more and—I have to emphasize to you that I think the way it's been handled in terms of our things—I want in any future statements out of McCloskey—we are sending supplies, but only for the purpose of maintaining the balance, so that we can create the conditions that will lead to an equitable settlement. The point is, if you don't say it that way, it looks as though we are sending in supplies to have the war go on indefinitely, and that is not a tenable position.

K: Right. Right. If it hasn't been said before, we'll say it certainly today.

N: The thought is basically: the purpose of supplies is not simply to fuel the war; the purpose [is] to maintain the balance, which is quite accurate, incidentally, and then—because only with the balance in that area, can there be an equitable settlement that doesn't do in one side or other. That's really what we are talking about.

K: Right, Mr. President.

N: But now on the Russians—

K: I expect formally to hear from the Russians. I didn't get through talking to the Russians till 10:00 last night. And I gave them really a terrific—

N: We can't have this business of defending them all over the place—

K: If they don't do anything.

N: If they don't do anything. Now, basically, that's what they said. I think that they like the condominium business [imposing U.S.-Soviet solutions]. The British have stood aside, what ought to happen is that even though the Israelis will squeal like stuck pigs—we ought to tell Dobrynin—we ought to say that the Russians—that Brezhnev and Nixon will settle this damn thing. That ought to be done. You know that.

K: Exactly. Exactly right.

N: If he gets that through, I think maybe he'd like it. I'll call you in an hour—you call me in an hour.

K: As soon as the WSAG is over. Right, Mr. President.

N: Bye. Right.

THE PRESIDENT–KISSINGER
Sunday, October 14, 1973
11:10 A.M.

K: Hello, Mr. President.

N: Hi, Henry. I talked to Al [Haig] and got a little fill-in because I had to go over some other things with him.

K: Right.

N: And I am glad to hear that we are going all out on this.

K: Oh, it is a massive airlift, Mr. President. The planes are going to land every fifteen minutes.

N: That right. Get them in there. And the only addition that I said—I told them to check the European theater to see if there were some of those smaller planes that they need and fly them down there so that they can replace their aircraft losses. And the other thing is that these big planes, you can put some of those good tanks, those M60 tanks, on if necessary if that would have some good effect and put a few of them in there too.

K: Right, Mr. President.

N: So, in other words, don't—if we are going to do it—don't spare the horses, just let—

K: Actually, with the big planes, Mr. President, we have also flexibility. We can fly the Skyhawks in.

N: Put them on the plane, you mean?

K: Yes. I don't think there is a[nother] way—no country will let them overfly.

N: All right. How many can a big plane take?

K: It can take five or six.

N: All right—put some Skyhawks in; do that too. You understand what I mean. If we are going to take heat for this, well, let's go.

K: I think that is right. And I think, Mr. President, we discussed this in the group—I think after Al left. We can offer to stop the airlift if the Russians do after a cease-fire is signed.

N: Exactly. I think we should say—I think a personal message now should go. I mean you have been sending messages, but one should go from me to Brezhnev.

K: Everything I am sending goes in your name.

N: Good. But I think he should know—now, look here. The peace of not only this area but the whole future relationship is at stake here and we are prepared to stop if you are and we are prepared—you know what I mean. I don't know—have you got anything developed along those lines so that we just don't have—?

K: I have. I am developing it now and I think I could call Dobrynin and point it out to him.

N: Right, right. Put it in a very conciliatory but very tough way that I do this with great regret because—great reluctance—but that we cannot have a situation that has now developed and we are prepared to give tit for tat. The situation with regard to— nothing on the battle so far?

K: On the battle, it is the Israelis— No, that hasn't been announced yet—that they have knocked out 150 [tanks].

N: And lost fifteen. Yes, I heard that this morning.

K: Something like at 10:30 this morning.

N: The Egyptians—

K: —again seem to be heading more south than east and are not really trying to break into the Sinai at this point. So they are just keeping their defensive position down the coast. And they may be going for [garbled]. But, ah—

N: Nothing new in Syria?

K: In Syria the Israelis have told us this morning they have stopped their advance on Damascus. They stopped about twenty kilometers short. And they are now heading south for Syrian infantry divisions. There is a report from some foreign correspondents that went up to the front from Damascus on the Syrian side and indicated the Syrian army now was getting to be demoralized and were abandoning equipment. But still, Mr. President, they are the reason why the Egyptians are holding. Much of the Israeli army is still tied up down there. The estimate of our group was that it would take the Israelis three more days to knock out the Syrians and that they couldn't really turn to the Egyptians for another four days to five days.

N: What do we plan then?

K: Well what we plan is to try to get it wound up this week.

N: [garbled]

K: Yes.

N: Well, I know you are going to get it until someone is knocked out. That is the problem. Well, at least I feel better. The airlift thing is—as I told Al, if I contribute anything to [the] discussion it is the business that don't fool around with three planes. By golly, no matter how big they are, just go gung ho.

K: One of the lessons I have learned from you is that if you do something, you might as well do it completely.

. . .

The purpose of the assurances to the Soviet Union was to restrain Soviet escalation while stepping up our own resupply, which soon saw a plane land in Israel every fifteen minutes.

AMBASSADOR DOBRYNIN–KISSINGER

Sunday, October 14, 1973
12:36 P.M.

K: I just talked to the President.

D: Yes.

K: And he wanted me, for the benefit of your leadership, to know two things—to tell you two things. One, we are now engaged in an airlift, as you know, of equipment to Israel.

D: Is it heavy equipment or consumables?

K: It is mostly at this point consumables and we are keeping some restraints at the moment on heavy equipment. Considerable restraints on heavy equipment and a little but very little. We are prepared to stop the airlift immediately after a cease-fire if you are prepared to stop your airlift. But if not, we can first of all increase it considerably and include heavy equipment. I mean, we are not going at our maximum capacity or anywhere near.

D: No, I understand. It is not that you will continue intermittently.

K: Well, if it goes on, we will be forced into it sooner or later. As you know, we are already, as you know, under massive pressure on the Phantoms. We are sending a few but not anything like what we are asked to do.

D: Yes, I understand. Yes.

K: You know those were the major items he wanted me to—

D: At the beginning you said you begin an airlift, yes?

K: Beginning—it is in process. It is beginning now. Yes.

D: Well, that is a matter of information.

K: Well, it is a matter of information [coupled with a] proposal. If you are prepared to stop your airlift after a cease-fire, we are prepared to stop ours immediately.

D: All right, but it is connected with the cease-fire you mentioned, yes?

K: In connection with the cease-fire, yes.

D: Okay. I'll pass it on right away.

K: You know, Anatol, we all know now what is at stake, because if this goes on much longer—

D: Well, [unclear] if you had a chance to read my telegram, what I sent yesterday, it was exactly what I am told.

K: No, no I—

D: I make my own reservations, of course, but it was a direct quotation, everything you said. It is not only fair, but it is important for them to know the mood. At a certain point of our usual thing, I don't do direct quotations, but a summary, I make it. But yesterday I was rather in a detail of what you said because this is what I feel and—

K: But also I give you advice. I have kept press guidance for today to an absolute minimum and we will say nothing but—

D: For press, you mean.

K: Well, we will just say we are doing something but starting tomorrow, as I have already explained to you, we'll be forced to say something.

D: Yes, I understand. I am already make it clear for tomorrow: after this you might say something unless maybe there are some other things.

K: Well, unless we know where we are going.

D: Yes, I understand. I will telephone tomorrow.

   . . .

SECRETARY SCHLESINGER–KISSINGER
Sunday, October 14, 1973
Evening

S: How are you proceeding in relation to plans for resupply? We've got four more Phantoms to augment the ten we discussed this morning. Shall we send them in tomorrow?

K: I would send them in tomorrow, then have a day's pause, or a day's pause tomorrow and send them Tuesday.

S: That would bring the total up to twenty, if we should want to do it. On another item, the TOWs. As you know, they have never appeared out there before so there will be a certain dramatic effect. We are prepared to strip down our inventory a bit and—

K: What are they exactly?

S: It's an antitank missile, guided missile—much better, longer range and far more accurate.

K: Longer range than, oh—

S: Two–three thousand meters range.

K: But your question is not numbers; your question is wisdom of sending them. What's your instinct?

S: My instinct is yes.

K: My instinct is now we have started, we had better win.

S: Well, I just want to be in line with the diplomatic timing.

K: The diplomatic timing is: I told the Russians that if they want to affect anything here—by tomorrow morning, it doesn't hurt to teach them that when they cross us, something violent happens.

S: Your inclination, then, is to drag out some and send them off on an early flight.

K: Anything else, Jim?

S: No, Henry. Thanks.

October 15–16, 1973

Diplomacy was now following the momentum of military operations. Sadat's decision to attempt an offensive into the Sinai, probably to relieve the pressure on his Syrian allies, took Egyptian forces beyond the range of the air defense system along the Suez Canal. This enabled the Israeli armed forces to destroy over three hundred Soviet tanks and to reverse the military setback of the prior week. It was now only a matter of time until an Israeli offensive would push the Egyptian forces at least across the Suez Canal. The conditions for what had been our original position, the restoration of the status quo ante, were approaching. The Arab position that a cease-fire should depend on Israeli agreement to return to the 1967 borders was being made irrelevant by the pace of military operations.

We began to work for a cease-fire to be followed by negotiations on the basis of Security Council Resolution 242, which had been accepted by all parties in 1967 largely because its ambiguity lent itself to different interpretations.

Late on October 15, Sadat's security adviser, Ismail, replied to my message informing him of the airlift. He reaffirmed Egypt's "determination" to keep open "this special channel of contact." No other party spoke in Egypt's name; in other words, we should pay no attention to interpretations from Moscow that differed from what Cairo told us directly. Ismail denied any intention to humiliate Israel "because Egypt tasted what humiliation means." He expressed his "appreciation" for our efforts to achieve a cease-fire as a *preliminary* to a political settlement—contrary as they were to Egypt's views. However, experience caused Egypt to doubt that such a separation would work in practice. In short, Ismail spoke to the principal armorer of Egypt's enemy as would one urbane man of affairs to another. His objection to our approach was its impracticality; presumably if we could demonstrate how our diplomacy might succeed, Egypt might change its attitude.

Only then did Ismail refer to the airlift, dismissing it as "unacceptable," as he had previous arms sales to Israel. But he did not linger over it, nor did he threaten any consequences. Instead, he urged me to redouble my efforts to link a political to a military solution. And then—amazingly—he invited me to visit Egypt:

> Egypt will welcome Dr. Kissinger in appreciation for his efforts. The Egyptian side will be prepared to discuss any subject, proposal or project, within the framework of two principles—which, it is believed, Dr. Kissinger does not reject, neither does any one—that Egypt cannot make any concessions of land or sovereignty.
>
> With warmest regards. Hafiz Ismail

Early on October 16, we replied in a message designed to use the premise of future diplomacy to restrain Egyptian reaction to the airlift in the coming week:

> ...What can the U.S. do in these circumstances? Dr. Kissinger has often said that he would promise only what he could deliver but deliver everything he promised. With its five-point proposal contained in Mr. Ismail's message of October 10, the Egyptian side is asking, in effect, for Israeli agreement, as part of a cease-fire,

to Egyptian terms for a total settlement. In Dr. Kissinger's judgment, this is not achievable except by protracted war. No U.S. influence can bring this goal about in [the] present circumstances.

What the U.S. side can promise and will fulfill is to make every effort to assist in achieving a final, just settlement once a cease-fire is reached. Dr. Kissinger believes that recent events may well serve to make it less difficult for the U.S. side in the future to exercise its influence constructively and effectively on behalf of such a settlement. . . .

The Egyptian side therefore has an important decision to make. To insist on its maximum program means continuation of the war and the possible jeopardy of all that has been achieved. The outcome will then be decided by military measures. The U.S. side will not speculate on this outcome but doubts whether it will be clear-cut. In any event, circumstances for a U.S. diplomatic effort would not be propitious.

If diplomacy is to be given a full opportunity, a cease-fire must precede it. Only in these circumstances can the promised U.S. diplomatic effort be developed. Egypt will find the guarantee for the seriousness of this effort in the formal promise of the U.S. side to engage itself fully as well as in the objective situation. . . .

Dr. Kissinger greatly appreciates the thoughtful invitation of the Egyptian side to visit Egypt. Once a cease-fire has been achieved, he would be glad to give that invitation the most serious and sympathetic consideration as part of a serious effort to bring a lasting peace to the Middle East.

With warmest regards. . . .

The WSAG convened shortly after 10:00 A.M. Since the decision to resort to the airlift, its mood had been transformed. Gone were the hesitations of the previous week, the attempts to shift the potential blame for dangerous consequences. I stated the principle that should govern our resupply effort: "Our only interest in this semi-confrontation situation is to run the Soviets into the ground fast. Give them the maximum incentive for a quick settlement. Bring in more each day than they do." And as a rough guideline I suggested that we keep our resupply at least 25 percent ahead of the Soviets'. We decided to supplement the airlift with a strengthened sealift, for in the Black Sea the Soviets had been loading ships with enormous quantities of matériel, including their most modern equipment.

Among superpowers the winner in a crisis must carefully judge when to rub in this fact to his opponent. I stressed this theme to my WSAG colleagues:

> We must keep this whole thing low key today no matter what happens. There should be no backgrounders. If we can finish this off without a confrontation with the Soviets and without ripping our relations with the Arabs we will have earned our money. Everything else is grandstanding. We will take a very hard line on substance and keep the stuff going into Israel.

News continued to be favorable. We learned that a Soviet VIP plane was en route to Cairo; we guessed it carried Premier Alexei Kosygin, who had unexpectedly canceled an appointment with the visiting Danish Prime Minister. This had to mean that the Soviets would urge Sadat to accept our approach to the cease-fire; he needed no persuasion to persist in his proclaimed course. And Soviet pressure was likely to sour Soviet-Egyptian relations.

Almost concurrently we were informed that a small force of twenty-five Israeli tanks had crossed to the west side of the Suez Canal at Great Bitter Lake and was beginning to tear up the surface-to-air missile fields. If it continued, this guaranteed an Israeli victory because it exposed the Egyptian forces across the Canal to the full fury of Israeli airpower. But it was too early to tell whether the Israelis could sustain themselves on the west side of the Canal. The WSAG considered the move as only a raid, as indeed the Israelis first presented it.

At the end of Tuesday, October 16, I reported to Nixon that the odds were two out of three in favor of a rapid conclusion of the war.

In these conditions, of waiting for events likely to be favorable, there were few decisions to be made—hence the telephone records are sparse, focusing mostly on briefing newsmen and some senators. The key conversations on October 15 were:

SECRETARY SCHLESINGER–KISSINGER
Monday, October 15, 1973
9:08 A.M.

K: Hello.

S: Hi, Henry.

K: Just for your information, but not—I won't use it at the WSAG—the Soviets came in around three o'clock this morning with a proposal for a new move which we are now exploring.

S: Very good.

K: Which would go back to the cease-fire idea of Saturday and just link it to Resolution 242, which we can live with.

S: Good.

K: You know—but that we want to keep very quiet yet. I think we— the thing obviously they are sweating out is the—I think we should just keep going all out now on the supplies.

S: Okay. You want to move in those additional six?

K: I would move them tomorrow.

S: Okay. Now there is one little worry I am worrying about and that is the resupply of 175mm ammo. As you know, they have got their self-propelled 175 [artillery] threatening Damascus and we ought to think very carefully about supplying ammo for the destruction of Damascus. I don't want an answer from you now but I, ah—

K: Okay. Well, let me see whether I can make sure that they won't shell Damascus.

S: Okay. They are also pressing for bridging equipment and the bridges equipment, in view of the dearth of rivers, obviously is directed towards the move crossing this canal. Well, think about those and—

K: Let me think about that.

. . .

SECRETARY SCHLESINGER–KISSINGER
Monday, October 15, 1973
9:40 A.M.

K: Jim, one thing I promised Dobrynin while this thing is still in train is that we would make no provocative statements about the Soviets.

S: Right. Okay, I will be very careful to get that across.

K: Right, so you know we can whisper numbers but we shouldn't say anything else.

S: Well that is splendid. . . .

. . .

The reason for this was that events were running in our direction, and a confrontation, including a possible oil cutoff, would only complicate matters.

SENATOR JAVITS–KISSINGER
Monday, October 15, 1973
9:45 A.M.

K: I didn't have the chance to call you over the weekend. I just wanted to tell you what is going on. We launched on Saturday afternoon a massive airlift for Israel which planes land there every fifteen minutes, and tomorrow morning we will equal the percentage of what the Soviets have put in in five previous days.

J: Good.

K: And we are flying in F-4s at the average rate of about six a day.

J: That's terrific.

K: So there will be twenty in tomorrow.

J: That's great. Henry, what do you say about this political battle that is shaping up? They called me yesterday about a resolution that Jackson and the group want to put in tomorrow. I told them to read it to Marshall Wright [State Department Assistant Secretary for Congressional Affairs].

K: What is their resolution?

J: A resolution—you know—urging accelerated efforts, etc., exactly what you are doing. And you should ask Wright about that. He has got the text of this. And I have to pass on it this morning.

K: Well I haven't seen—I have got to look at the text. I don't mind it if it isn't critical of the administration.

J: No, it is not.

K: We had two problems in this respect, Jack. One is, the President has really gone all out.

J: I am sure of it and—

K: And for him to get lambasted then—

J: He won't be if I can avoid it. And I can.

K: And, in fact, if somebody could say something kind about it—

J: I am going to.

K: It would be rather important.

J: I am going to do it in the morning. You know when this [unclear] resolution is okay, when it goes in, I will make that the occasion.

. . .

SENATOR STUART SYMINGTON (D.-MISSOURI)–KISSINGER
Monday, October 15, 1973
3:15 P.M.

S: I was very reassured by what you said last night and I was a bit upset about what I read this morning.

K: About Jackson?

S: Scoop's [Senator Jackson] observation. The headline. I wanted you to know I talked with Dinitz and I told him and thought it was wrong. He said he knew it was wrong. I have been talking with him pretty much every day.

K: Aren't you nice.

S: I wanted to tell you that, if at any time—because, you see, I have felt there is no one more important than that little country and I mean it literally.

K: I know that.

S: On the other hand, in order to—why I am not quite sure—but I remember when Brezhnev, he was pushed pretty hard and I know it makes it more difficult.

K: Now when I tell Dobrynin we will lose détente, he will say what else can I lose except MFN [Most Favored Nation]?

S: Sometime I want you to meet a friend of mine, Abe Fineberg.

K: I would love to meet him. Does he come down here?

S: Yes. Could you see him?

K: I would love to. Could you arrange it?

S: Okay. They are pushing me pretty hard. You nor Schlesinger were available. I talked to his man but they cannot say that the Phantoms are going there.

K: For your information, they are going in about six to eight a day.

S: I know that, but they are built in my town. Can I say that?

K: Not yet.

S: That is what I wanted to know.

. . .

FOREIGN MINISTER ZAYYAT–KISSINGER

Monday, October 15, 1973
7:29 P.M.

Z: Mr. Secretary.

K: Yes, Mr. Foreign Minister. How are you?

Z: I'm sorry to disturb you this late.

K: Not at all, Mr. Foreign Minister. It's always a pleasure to hear from you.

Z: I got a cable from Ismail this morning. I think he sends you a message and he sent me this message. Don't you think it is better to postpone our meeting tomorrow for the time being?

K: It's entirely up to you.

Z: I think it would be better to leave it until we see what has come out of this.

K: All right. I will reply to him tomorrow.

Z: I was reading the President's remarks in the—I was reading them several times. I don't know what they really mean.

K: He was just explaining what our basic policy is and it didn't indicate any particular message.

Z: It didn't indicate any action or anything?

K: Not at this point, no.

Z: All right. Thank you very much.

Most of the calls on October 16 concerned the awarding of the Nobel Peace Prize to Le Duc Tho and me for negotiating an end to the Vietnam War.

AMBASSADOR DOBRYNIN–KISSINGER

Tuesday, October 16, 1973
11:42 A.M.

D: I hope I will be invited to the party.

K: What party?

D: Which you are going to give in connection with the award of the Nobel Prize.

K: I figure it like Groucho Marx said, "Any club that took him in, he does not want to join." I would say anything that Le Duc Tho is eligible for, there must be something wrong with it.

D: I congratulate you. You really deserve it. It will be something to remember. This call is really my best wishes.

K: I appreciate it very much.

D: Henry, probably I am among the few that can say with judgment what actions you have done.

  . . .

THE PRESIDENT–KISSINGER

Tuesday, October 16, 1973
11:46 A.M.

N: I wanted to congratulate you.

K: I know who deserves it.

N: Yes. Yes. I was going to make two suggestions. It occurred to me that you should make a little statement.

K: I have told everyone that I wanted to say that I would like to thank you for giving me the opportunity and, above all, for the leadership that created the conditions.

N: Fine. Fine. I was going to suggest that it might be well for you to drop over here and have a picture taken with me congratulating you. How about 12:30?

K: Absolutely.

N: That will give us some time. Come after you make your statement.

K: I will be there at 12:30.

N: Make your statement before you come, so they will not ask you to do it here.

  . . .

SENATOR BARRY GOLDWATER (R.-ARIZ.)–KISSINGER

Tuesday, October 16, 1973
3:57 P.M.

G: I hate to bother you with this. When the Shah of Iran was here, he asked Peggy [Senator Goldwater's wife] and me if we would come over. We are looking at December 1, but in view of the situation—

K: You mean in the Middle East, it will be all over before then unless we screw it up in the next few days.

G: I am sure glad to hear that. Are we working with the Soviets? No, you don't have to answer over the phone.

K: We are working with the Soviets and also with the Egyptians. It's a tough situation and could blow up.

G: Then it's all right for us to go over.

K: You will have a tremendous reception.

G: For a boy who is half Jewish that's not too bad.

K: Yeah.

G: Everything else all right with you.

K: Okay. I would like to meet in the next week with some of my conservative friends and tell them—I think they have some problems.

G: I hadn't heard a thing.

K: I want you to know the State Department is not a hostile party.

G: I know that. I am going to be here tomorrow but will leave—

K: When will you come back?

G: I will be here—and in November.

K: In November?

G: I have a lot of speaking engagements the early part of November.

K: I will get in touch with your office and we will work something out.

. . .

On October 16, in order to relieve tensions with the Arab countries, the President agreed to see a delegation of Arab Foreign Ministers—from Kuwait, Saudi Arabia, Morocco, and Algeria.

ASSISTANT SECRETARY SISCO–KISSINGER
Tuesday, October 16, 1973
4:10 P.M.

. . .

S: I am in the Operations Center. The task force takes no press calls. My point is, they have strict instructions. No one here has talked.

K: All right, it must be INR [the State Department Office of Intelligence]. I need talking points for the President for his meeting with the Arabs.

S: They will be in to you in about thirty minutes.

K: They ought to be along the lines we discussed. Should I see them first? Didn't they want to see me too?

S: He did say both you and the President—would you rather see them first or afterwards?

K: I would rather see them when—but the President—at 10:15 in my WH office and then from there to the President. And you'll be there too.

S: I'll be there. I will arrange that and unless you hear from me everything will be set up.

K: The only thing is if the President wants to see me—we should do it tentatively.

S: If the President wants to see you at 10:15, you'll meet them after the 11:00. I understand—limit the meeting with the Foreign Ministers to the President and you. One thing, you might want to include the Ambassadors.

K: No.

S: My question is do you want to include the Ambassador in your meeting? My recommendation is you include both the Foreign Ministers and the Ambassadors. Of course, it is a moot point and—

K: Well, I don't—I haven't got a clear idea yet. I hate those mass meetings.

S: This is not important. It is not essential. Why don't you decide tomorrow morning? The Ambassadors know they are not going into the President's meeting—

K: That's right.

. . .

SAUDI FOREIGN MINISTER OMAR SAQQAF–KISSINGER

Tuesday, October 16, 1973
4:35 P.M.

K: Mr. Foreign Minister. I look forward to seeing you tomorrow.

S: Thank you. Congratulations.

K: Thank you. I am calling on behalf of the President to tell you that after the end of hostilities, the President would be very pleased if His Majesty would accept an invitation to visit the United States.

S: Can we discuss this tomorrow?

K: There will be others present. Perhaps you and I can discuss it.

S: Is there a time for this?

K: We can find a time mutually convenient as soon as possible.

S: Thank you very much. See you tomorrow.

THE PRESIDENT–KISSINGER

Tuesday, October 16, 1973
End of day

K: Mr. President.

N: Any other developments on the diplomatic front?

K: I saw the Sudanese Foreign Minister.

N: Good.

K: And he has the impression things may be breaking. He's close to the other Arabs, you know.

N: I wouldn't include him in tomorrow—

K: No, they selected themselves— Let them go.

N: Think we have Sadat's position: we are not going to get a resolution of this thing until we get some kind of diplomatic offer they can save face with. The one you made was pretty good—

K: Wouldn't float that with those three [actually four—the Foreign Ministers from Saudi Arabia, Morocco, Kuwait, and Algeria] tomorrow, though—

N: No, no. I don't intend to float anything tomorrow.

K: I don't think we will get anything until Kosygin has returned from Cairo.

N: What tell him—?

K: He's got the offer.

N: What if he returns and says they won't do it?

K: I think there's a good chance they will do it.

N: Or some variation of it. Do you think he will return tomorrow. Kosygin visit, how long will it be?

K: I'll bet he will be back by tomorrow night. Or he may stay until Thursday.

N: You see Mansfield's [Mike Mansfield, Senate Majority Leader] brilliant suggestion—urging summit conference with the British, French, Japanese, U.S., and Russians? What in the name of heaven would be decided?—

K: Mr. President, it would kill us. It would be the Israelis and—us against six other nations. Insane.

N: It's just as it was in Vietnam, our friends on the Democratic side are petrified it will end, and they want to be out there suggesting and urging.

K: Makes no difference—unless somebody loses his cool.

N: Could happen.

K: Don't think it will, though.

N: Hope we've got that airstrip in Tel Aviv damned well protected.

K: They're not going to attack it.

N: Why not?

K: Because they're afraid we'll start attacking the Soviet airlift. Chances are two out of three—now moving towards resolution. Last week was too easy, done too much with mirrors—better solution this week, when we have shown our muscle.

N: If the airlift continues— How many—fifty planes? They'll have more planes in the end than at the beginning.

K: Well, they're going in at a rate of six a day, depends now on when it ends, is settled.

N: Well, the Israelis ought to be awfully grateful after this. . . .

K: There have been statements on Senate floor; Javits made one today— Diplomatically, it helps us that you are not way out in front until we get it done.

N: I understand, but we will—it ought to happen when we get through.

October 17, 1973

The American policy was to continue to wait for the evolution of military operations while simultaneously accelerating the airlift and seeking to calm Arab reactions to it. On the diplomatic front, we began to move toward a standstill cease-fire, to be followed by negotiations to implement Security Council Resolution 242. Resolution 242 had been passed in 1967 in the aftermath of the Six Day War. It provided for Israeli withdrawal from "territories occupied in a recent conflict" to secure and recognized borders. It did not specify "all" territories, and it did not define the adjectives. What it lacked in precision, it made up for in flexibility. It was well suited for beginning a negotiation in which reconnecting the different interpretations of the parties would be one of the objectives.

THE PRESIDENT–KISSINGER
Wednesday, October 17, 1973
8:44 A.M.

N: What's new on the diplomatic and military front this morning?

K: On the military front, it looks still like a stalemate. On the diplomatic front—all the intelligence analysts, who don't know what is going on, are now analyzing that something is going on simply because of the Russian visit, the low-key comments from Arab countries, and so forth. I don't think anything will go off until Kosygin has left Cairo.

N: Yeah, yeah.

K: And that's the big—

N: The question is whether—what he is there for—whether to gin it up or cool it down?

K: It's inconceivable. Well, either way, Mr. President, we are not slowing anything down just because he is there. We are pouring in arms at a rate about 30 percent greater than they do. Our total tonnage today should start exceeding theirs. We are not—as I said—we are not slowing anything down, but it's inconceivable to me that he is going to gin it up.

N: Yeah, yeah, yeah.

K: And there is still—

N: You haven't received any message from him?

K: We won't until he gets back, I am sure. But their press is still mute and I think they are trying to work something out. Now whether that is possible with the Egyptians, I don't know. All the information we have is that the Egyptians have been taking a tougher line than they have.

N: This Israeli raid [across the Suez Canal] was not that big, huh?

K: Apparently not.

N: I gathered that.

K: There is a tank battle going on now in the Sinai and we don't have any report of its outcome yet. Now, with these four Foreign Ministers, Mr. President, I—

N: I have read the talking points.

K: You have?

N: Yeah.

K: The major point, remember, is that [the] meeting was set before we did anything [the airlift]. They are not coming here to protest.

N: Yes.

K: And I would not float any particular idea on them because they are not the ones that are going to be able to negotiate it and the particular ideas are already before the Egyptians and Russians.

N: Yeah. Well, when they come down to say Israel must withdraw to the '67 border, what do you say?

K: You say that should be negotiated after a cease-fire.

N: Well, to be negotiated—does it mean—do we agree to that goal?

K: Well, I think it is unattainable, Mr. President, and in my conversations I have always fudged it and said that is an issue that should be addressed within the context of the Security Council Resolution 242 and the major point to make to these people is to separate the cease-fire from the post-cease-fire and the argument that I found very effective is—they want America to engage itself in the diplomacy afterwards—that you promised to do. But that means also now that the war has to be brought to an end under conditions which enable us to be in touch with all of the parties. And secondly, that if we now try to settle it as the result of the war, it will be an endless negotiation with the war going on.

N: That's right. Well, if we aren't there to work on the settlement, it leaves them with no other option—just beat the hell out of the Israelis.

K: To have an endless war to push them back.

N: We are the only ones who can influence the Israelis.

K: And that is a point to make. Another point to make is that the military situation has already changed as a result of the war.

N: Oh, it's changed? How do you mean?

K: Well, they [the Arab leaders] will say how do we know that after a cease-fire there won't be a stalemate? And one point to make to them is that the situation has changed strategically—that no country now can claim supremacy in the area anymore and therefore they have to rely on—

N: In other words, basically, that Israel can no longer claim supremacy.

K: Right. I wouldn't phrase it that way because—

N: I understand. All right, I've got the word.

K: I talked to the Foreign Minister of Saudi Arabia yesterday extending your invitation to the King and he was very pleased. In fact, you can hold him back for a few minutes when the others leave.

N: Yeah.

K: And do two things—thank him for the very moderate and constructive role he has played all week and, secondly, say you hope to see the King as soon as a cease-fire is achieved, as can be mutually arranged. I would tie it to the cease-fire, Mr. President, because otherwise they'll have another reason for delay.

N: Yeah.

K: And we don't want him—it's not in his interest to be in the forefront of the diplomacy because he will be stuck with all the problems.

N: After the cease-fire—

K: After the cease-fire—they may want to get him over here before.

N: We don't want that.

K: No. That would not be advantageous.

N: We don't want anybody.

K: I think by tomorrow this thing is going to break one way or the other. It may break unfavorably but then Kosygin goes back to Moscow—

. . .

DEPUTY SECRETARY OF DEFENSE WILLIAM
CLEMENTS–KISSINGER
Wednesday, October 17, 1973
9:35 A.M.

K: Bill, we feel very strongly, I'm at the White House now, that we should get that supplemental [spending bill, to pay for the airlift and expenses of the Middle East war] up today and to stop diddling around with exact figures. Let's just get a figure.

C: We're ready, Henry. I looked at the draft last night.

K: Good. What is it? $3.5 billion.

C: No, Henry, it's $2.9 billion. The reason it's $2.9 billion is because we found on investigation that the 1.7 that you heard me talk about in the meeting yesterday which is the credit to date, that cannot be cross-referenced to this supplemental. There's no way. So that 2.9 that we're coming up with is in fact a net increase greater than the other number.

K: Good. But you're putting in something for others.

C: Absolutely. There is $500 million in there plus Cambodia.

K: Good.

C: That's the whole thing now. I can get a draft of this, I mean I can get you a copy of this draft over there immediately but I think that Bill Timmons [Assistant to the President for Congressional Relations] has already got it.

K: We all feel that it is essential to get it in today in case the diplomacy breaks.

C: Fine.

K: Can you do that?

C: Yes we can, Henry. I was going to bring this up for review at the WSAG this afternoon and I feel like you ought to look at this thing and be fully aware of what we do before we drop it in that hopper. Would you like for some of us to come over there and brief you about fifteen minutes on it or something?

K: The trouble is I've got these Arabs coming.

C: That's right. We're ready, Henry. The only thing is I—

K: When would you drop it in after the WSAG? Tomorrow morning?

C: Yes, tomorrow morning.

K: That shouldn't be too much of a delay, should it?

C: I wouldn't think so but that was what our plan was within the morning so that it could be discussed at the WSAG.

K: That would be fine.

C: Okay, Henry. Good luck.

AMBASSADOR DOBRYNIN–KISSINGER
Wednesday, October 17, 1973
9:42 A.M.

. . .

D: . . . I have instructions to tell you on a very strictly confidential basis for you and for President Nixon, I am to mention to him and you that we are now having consultations with Arab leaders.

K: Yes, and Kosygin is in Cairo.

D: Yeah, this is exactly what they asked me to tell you. But you already know.

K: No, no we know a Soviet VIP is in Cairo. We've told the Israelis to stay away from Cairo and the Cairo airport.

D: This is Kosygin.

K: We didn't have it confirmed.

D: But they specifically asked to tell you and to the President—

K: I hope you have noticed that we have tried to keep things very quiet here.

D: No, I know. I noticed that it is on low-key under the circumstances. But this is really for your information.

K: You know we cannot help if there is speculation because—

D: No, no, I understand.

K: Frankly, we know a Soviet VIP plane is there. And therefore a lot of people know something.

D: No, I understand.

K: But you can be sure that we will not confirm it in any official way or leak it.

D: Yeah, I understand. This is just they asked me specifically to tell—he is there in connection with this consultation and including the proposal [a cease-fire coupled with negotiation to implement Security Council Resolution 242]—

K: Anatol, you should understand, because I don't want to mislead you, the cease-fire formula—the one on Saturday, we had discussed with the Israelis—this formula, we have not yet discussed with the Israelis.

D: About the 242?

K: Yes.

D: 242?

K: Yes. But we think they will accept it, but we didn't want, frankly, our press to be agitated against us.

D: Yeah, no, no.

K: So there may be twenty-four hours after if you come back with something.

D: Yes, I understand.

K: I just don't want you people to be misled.

D: Yes.

K: You can be sure that what we said to you we will stand by.

D: Hm, huh. And the last one, Henry, here is some oral considerations by Mr. Brezhnev to the President. It is not immediate in the sense of proposals, but, so to speak, of our relations in really good terms, I should say in a quiet way, it is on four pages—probably—it's oral, however, maybe I will send it to you—nothing really.

K: Can you send it over within the next hour?

D: I could send it right away.

K: Send it over, just for our records.

D: Just for your own. And if you have some comments or other, please let me know.

K: Okay.

D: I could come to you anytime—or by telephone.

K: You know our policy, as I have told you, is to try to really, to the utmost, to not only keep the détente going, but to strengthen it.

D: Yeah, this is really what—this too—this oral consideration—by Brezhnev. I think it is rather helpful, just for the whole background. There is nothing immediate or specifically new, but in general how it is presented, I think you will find it interesting.

K: Good.

. . .

THE PRESIDENT–KISSINGER
Wednesday, October 17, 1973
1:40 P.M.

. . .

K: Mr. President, I think it was a most successful morning. What's more important, they [the Arab Foreign Ministers] were happy—very successful morning.

N: Now, on to the Russians. When do you expect to hear from Kosygin?

K: We've got a long message from Brezhnev. Now, in itself, it doesn't say anything; he skirts the issue— Matters have not reached the point of no return and in détente— We will hear from them by tomorrow night.

N: Meantime, you might pick up Senator Mansfield's brilliant suggestion.

K: Mr. President, when have they not failed us?

N: Really something.

K: When have they ever stood behind the President?

N: No, but come up with a cockeyed scheme of going to the United Nations, having a six-power conference—

K: Never support what we are doing.

N: This meeting with the Arabs just about killed the damn press people. They expected all hell to blow up.

K: Of course.

N: There was a huge number out there today.

K: Well, we trotted out the poor Foreign Ministers.

N: At a time when we are supplying Israel.

K: At a time when American planes are landing in Tel Aviv every half an hour. People take everything for granted, no minor feat.

N: Anything doing with battle?

K: Seems to be a tank battle going on—

N: I think it's a stalemate, I really do.

K: I do too.

N: Both sides sort of bled.

K: I suppose the Israelis can barely win, but not at any price that's worthwhile.

N: Okay, have a good rest.

The reference in the conversation to "trotting out the poor [Arab] Foreign Ministers" was to a comment to the press made by Saudi Foreign Minister Omar Saqqaf on leaving the Oval Office: "The man who could solve the Vietnam War, the man who could have settled the peace all over the world, can easily play a good role in settling and having peace in our area of the Middle East."

AMBASSADOR DINITZ–KISSINGER
Wednesday, October 17, 1973
5:20 P.M.

K: Yes, Mr. Ambassador.

D: I don't trouble you with news of the front. I keep the general [Brent Scowcroft] informed. I have a message from Dayan, who just returned from the front and called about twenty minutes ago. He just returned from the front and wants to add to the congratulatory note that he sent you on the Nobel Peace Prize. He is sure he will not have any reasons to be ashamed of us at the Canal. He saw what he saw and liked it very much. Our position is such that his feeling is, we don't need to beg from anyone. He means you and us. Any initiative but rather wait for them to wait for one of us.

K: You know what is developing—

D: I have pointed it out to the Prime Minister.

K: The Foreign Ministers were heading in the same direction. It's not going to be easy to do this, to reconfirm a Security Council resolution that already exists.

D: I did not get from the Secretary General the sort of language. They—about the cease-fire and 242.

K: This should lay the basis for 242. They didn't give us a formulation. It would depend on formulation before we could make a judgment.

D: I understand. That is what I informed the Prime Minister. The point is that 242 has so many interpretations.

K: We are not going to accept any interpretations.

D: I expect by tomorrow morning I will have the response from Israel and I will let you know. I thought the Minister of Defense's message was important. That you would sense the—

K: I am delighted. What is the supply situation?

D: Very fine. Golda talked to me on the telephone. She said people are crying in Israel. She went to the airport and saw American guys coming with the planes and said it was one of the most exciting sights of her life. I want to add my own personal regards on the Nobel Prize. We here at the Embassy were all very pleased yesterday with the news.

K: Thank you. The President in this one feels that, just for your guidance, this [cease-fire linked to Resolution 242] is one that will be very hard to refuse. Of course, we have no language.

D: Right. I would suggest that after the answer, you would probably want to see something more specific.

K: We haven't a proposal.

D: When do you expect to get it?

K: My instincts are after Kosygin comes back from Cairo, if he is in Cairo.

D: We will not accept a specific reference to the '67 borders.

K: You can expect we will not accept a specific reference to the '67 borders and that we have told the foreign ministers that. We have also told the Arab Ambassadors.

D: I will pass the information along.

October 18, 1973

On Thursday morning, October 18, Israel announced that it was re-inforcing its bridgehead across the Suez Canal, which now extended about eight miles wide to the north and about four miles wide to the south. In getting Ron Ziegler ready for the morning press briefing, I told him that I expected a cease-fire by Sunday or Monday (October 21 or 22).

RON ZIEGLER, PRESIDENTIAL PRESS SECRETARY–KISSINGER
Thursday, October 18, 1973
10:07 A.M.

Z: What is your reading this morning on the general direction we should take on the Middle East.

K: Stay cool. Don't jazz it up. Just hold it where it is.

Z: Should we break off at your remarks last night.

K: I wouldn't do much beyond that. I said it now. I said it deliber-ately in a place where it couldn't get a hell of a lot of news. You know, I didn't distribute them ahead of time. I haven't seen them in the newspapers.

Z: It's on the wires.

K: But it isn't in the newspapers.

Z: It'll be in the afternoon papers. But it's not a boom headline story. But the breaking news from State yesterday and your re-marks indicate that there is diplomatic activity between the U.S.—

K: I scolded McCloskey. We should not—he shouldn't have done that. There is the slightly self-serving quality in all this briefing. I mean by McCloskey. It is not our custom to discuss diplomatic activity while it's going on.

Z: What do you feel is our best position to take on the oil thing [OPEC announcement of cut in oil production]? I'll be asked about the 5 percent reduction in production.

K: Say we can handle it. I know that is a token thing but if you say it's a token thing, that will force them to escalate it. Let's say you're aware of it. Isn't it possible for us in effect to say in this delicate phase we don't think any useful purpose is served by—

Z: I think that's the best answer and I think that would be useful. We had a very constructive meeting yesterday, we're in touch with all parties.

K: On the constructive side I'd refer to what the Arab Foreign Ministers said.

Z: That's what I mean. And we continue to be in touch with all parties of course in touch with the Soviets and in this delicate phase it would just not serve the interest of achieving a peaceful peace in the Middle East by commenting on the oil thing. Right?

K: That's right. I think that's the best thing to do and it will make us look better when it's all over. I must tell you that if we get through this without breaking it with the Arabs or Soviets it won't be a bad achievement.

. . .

SENATOR FULBRIGHT–KISSINGER

Thursday, October 18, 1973
1:15 P.M.

K: How are things in Arkansas?

F: Fine here. I have been traveling since I have been here. I am in Little Rock now.

K: Is it exhausting?

F: Pretty much.

K: What I would think. I wanted to bring you up-to-date where things stand. As you may know Kosygin is in Cairo. He is basically putting forward the proposition that you and I discussed the other evening. Cease-fire in place and linked to the implementation of the Security Council Resolution 242.

F: Good.

K: The Russians have told us they were supporting it. He has tough going because the Egyptians want a fixed date to withdrawal of '67 borders. The thing we all have to remember is with all of this détente talk, without the détente Kosygin would not be in Cairo. The Soviet press would not be accepting our airlift and all hell would be breaking loose. We have talked to the four Arab oilmen, including the Algerian, and made the same proposition. We made a commitment if there is a cease-fire we would put the whole prestige of the United States behind getting behind a solution to the causes of the war. Even though it seems quiet we hope within the next forty-eight to seventy-two hours something will break and we hope in the right direction.

. . .

AMBASSADOR DINITZ–KISSINGER

Thursday, October 18, 1973
8:28 P.M.

K: I called Dobrynin after you left, in a low-key way, and told him I had expected Kosygin to return soon and I just didn't want them to get impatient if they come up with any ideas—that it would take us a reasonable thirty-six to forty-eight hours to consider. I wanted his leader to know it so that they didn't think we were stalling. I asked his assessment of the military situation. He said his reports indicated a stalemate. I said ours did too. Three minutes ago he said in two hours they will come in with a message containing a proposal.

D: Even before Kosygin arrives?

K: He didn't say what the proposal was—what urgency it has. I can call you. I just wanted you to be aware.

D: I suppose the reports from the field are beginning to reach them.

K: He gave no indication. The President doesn't—I can call them and say the President is asleep.

D: I don't know about your President, but my Prime Minister is definitely asleep now.

K: I just thought if the diplomacy starts acting up, you'd better be

informed. Now you know everything I know. I haven't been able
to tell the President and you know more than he does.

D: I will be here in the office.

K: It will take about two hours.

D: I'm in no hurry.

K: I know. I'm not hurrying.

Ambassador Dobrynin–Kissinger
Thursday, October 18, 1973
8:45 P.M.

D: Mr. Brezhnev asked you to convince the President of the following: This is not exactly the text of the message but I'm reading—
"We continue to carry on very expansive consultations with
the Arab leaders. For its consideration, we need a little bit
more time. At the same time we—the Soviet Union, the Soviet
leaders—want to think of what kind of formulation should be included in the text of the draft resolution of the Security Council.
In our opinion this resolution should include the following main
provisions:

"1. A call to the sides to immediately cease fire and all military
action on the positions where the troops actually are.

"2. A demand to start immediately after the cease-fire-phased
withdrawal of the Israeli troops from the occupied Arab territories to the line in accordance with Resolution 242 of the Security
Council, with completion of this withdrawal in the shortest period of time.

"3. A decision to start immediately and concurrently with the
cease-fire appropriate consultations aimed at establishing a just
and honorable peace in the Middle East."

This is the main point. I will repeat it. [Repeats the above three
provisions].

K: Appropriate consultations with whom?

D: Our commentary involves the following conclusions. We feel that
the best thing would be to have a limited number of participants in

these consultations. We, the Soviet Union, are prepared, if it suits you and the immediately involved participants and Israelis, for this kind of consultation on the part of the Soviet Union and the U.S.

K: Why are you so hard on your allies?

D: On what allies? We have many allies. I would like a clarification.

K: The one ally you have as a permanent member of the Security Council.

D: For the sake of conversation, why not drop them?

K: Actually we are no more eager to have our allies there than you are. We are not much more eager to have our own allies there.

D: Let's have these conclusions between the U.S. and the Soviet Union. The question arises about a guarantee if the resolution is to be adopted. I agreed together with you, if it is acceptable to both of our clients, that the U.S. and the Soviet Union in a recent forum guarantee the fulfillment of this resolution. We also are prepared to guarantee the territorial integrity, security, and inviolability of the borders and the frontiers of all, including Israel, taking into consideration at the same time its right to sovereignty and independent existence. With these kind of guarantees from the U.S. and the Soviet Union, we feel that hardly anybody will have a doubt about the viability of the guarantee. So Mr. Brezhnev would like to share his thoughts along those lines with the President and he would like to receive the reaction of the White House. On my own, there are two basic things: the Middle East and our relationship to cement with you.

K: I understand. You will see in the message that the President will send to you at about 10:00 or 10:30—this he has and wants to work on it personally—which is not an answer to this—that he makes exactly the same point without going into details. Should I still send the message of the President's to you?

D: Yes, I will mention that it was received before this.

K: Because we won't have an answer in two hours. Thinking out loud without having talked to the President, [I would say] the most difficult point here is point number two, about immediately after [a] cease-fire the Israelis should withdraw to a line under Resolution 242 which really isn't established yet. First, let me say I realize you're making a very constructive effort—

D: Yes, I'm being very constructive.

K: Why don't we consider it later rather than debate it out now, and if we have a counterproposal we will get back to you.

. . .

THE PRESIDENT–KISSINGER
Thursday, October 18, 1973
9:35 P.M.

K: Hello, Mr. President. I just wanted to tell you we have had a preliminary message from the Russians. They are moving in our direction, but are not quite there yet.

N: I see.

K: It is from Brezhnev. It is their preliminary observations. Kosygin hasn't left Cairo yet. They are moving definitely towards the position you outlined yesterday. We have to stay very cool and not let on to anyone.

N: Yes, we don't want—

K: I have the impression the Israelis may be doing very well in the tank battle. They don't tell us.

N: That will move the Russians.

K: I think—well, we shouldn't count our chickens, but I think you have pulled it off.

N: That is good news.

K: It will take us another forty-eight to seventy-two hours. I'm sending—on your behalf—Brezhnev a response to his message yesterday which says nothing except you are holding things together here and want to—and that a constructive outcome is highly desirable.

N: Just assure him we are prepared to follow through. We don't want them to think we'll get in cement—Thank you.

In order to gain time—which would increase the pressure on both Moscow and Cairo—I sent a message, as discussed with Nixon, in the President's name to Brezhnev that avoided any specifics about Israeli withdrawals.

SOVIET DEPUTY CHIEF OF MISSION YURI VORONTSOV–KISSINGER

Thursday, October 18, 1973
10:20 P.M.

V: This is Vorontsov.

K: Yuri, the most depressing thought is to know you are in town.

V: That is called psychological warfare.

K: Now, I know things are going to get tough. The President had made some changes in the message to the General Secretary. He thought, in the light of the message we just received from you tonight, he should just send the general thoughts and not get involved in a debate at this point.

V: Of course.

K: They are just general thoughts about the Middle East and our relationship with the Soviet Union. What you are getting is—which you will see is very constructive and positive and pledges the U.S. to make a major effort but does not stress the one major point about withdrawals. We will be exchanging views on that at a later time. The President thought it might be too confusing right now.

V: I got it and will explain it by all means.

K: We have a messenger on the way over right now. It is a very warm message which we think you will feel and we believe this has to be ended by the two countries.

V: That is our approach. Thank you. I will report it to the Ambassador.

K: Just wanted to tell the General Secretary that it is slightly different than if we were handling complete negotiations. If you have any questions after you receive it, why don't you call me.

V: All right.

GENERAL SCOWCROFT–KISSINGER

Thursday, October 18, 1973
10:45 P.M.

. . .

K: The Soviets have sent us a three-point plan, which I will get over to you, of which points one and three are highly acceptable. Point two is not acceptable, however. It calls for a withdrawal to the line in Resolution 242 which they [the Israelis] will not accept. As to the frontiers, I called Dinitz and left out point three, so I will have something to use as an incentive tomorrow. They are as obnoxious as the Vietnamese.

S: I think you have it started just right. By the time we get something down we can live with, they will be relatively pleased.

K: [The Israelis] also told me they are going across with more tanks. I am afraid it will turn into a turkey shoot. If they keep going across, somebody is going to get killed—that's for sure.

S: The real danger is, the Egyptian army is going to panic.

K: Once they get across the division strength, that means the SAM belt is gone. When they see the army from top and bottom, they are going to disintegrate. They are not that good. They won't be able to get supplies. They'll die of starvation. What I can't understand is how they broke through the Canal.

S: That is a mystery to me. They had this new defense position. They broke through two divisions, one infantry and one armor.

K: Is that the detailed report?

S: Yes. They [the Israelis] attacked through a strong point because if they went through a weak point they would have two strong divisions surrounding them.

K: They broke through a strong point and went across the Canal. They are a good army, or the Egyptians are very bad.

S: The Israelis are very smart and audacious and willing to take chances and back them very strongly—

K: ... The Russians suggested negotiations be conducted between them and us and not have any other U.N. members, together with the Arabs and Israelis. You can imagine what Chou En-lai is going to say to this. Of course, the Europeans will go right up the wall.

S: Of course, the trick of trying to get negotiations with permanent members of the Security Council—

K: I am going to get a message out to Ismail. Do you think that is all right? I thought I would say this will remain my position regardless of the military outcome but it might make them suspicious.

S: I like it and you should send off a message, but telling them that might tip them and antagonize them.

K: I am afraid they will all get hung. I think this is the end of Sadat.

S: I think you are right. They might just run them out.

K: They have to be careful. The fact of the matter is, when all is said and done it is a Soviet defeat. The same reasons why we could not accept an Israeli defeat will operate against them, and even if they say the supplies did it, that should make them [the Arab states] realize they better get on our side.

S: In that sense it couldn't have been better.

. . .

October 19, 1973

The Israeli beachhead on the western side of the Suez Canal was growing and therewith the pressure for a cease-fire. The Kremlin was experienced enough to realize that we were stalling on Brezhnev's offer of the day before because we found the demand for immediate Israeli withdrawal even to unspecified lines unacceptable. To cut through this deadlock, Brezhnev invited me to Moscow.

AMBASSADOR DOBRYNIN–KISSINGER

Friday, October 19, 1973
11:04 A.M.

K: Hello, Anatol.

D: Hello. I received a short message from Brezhnev to the President. The text I will read you. Okay?

K: Yes.

D: "Dear Mr. President:

"The events in the Middle East become more and more dangerous. Our two powers, as we both have agreed, must do the utmost in order to keep the events from going beyond the limits, when they could take [an] even more dangerous turn."

K: Right.

D: "If they develop along this way, there is a danger that harm could be done even to the immediate relations between the Soviet Union and the United States. We believe that neither you nor we want to see it. If it is so, then prompt and effective political decisions are needed. We have conviction that with due willingness our two powers can facilitate the finding of such decisions."

K: Right.

D: "Since time is essential and now not only every day but every hour counts—"

K: Right.

D: "—my colleagues and I suggest that the U.S. Secretary of State and your closest associate, Dr. Kissinger, comes in an urgent manner to Moscow to conduct appropriate negotiations with him as with your authorized personal representative. It would be good if he could come tomorrow, October 20. I will appreciate your speedy reply.

"Sincerely, L. Brezhnev, October 19, 1973"

K: You are friendly, aren't you?

D: Hum?

K: That's a friendly suggestion.

D: Of course it is.

K: Well, I will have to get to the President and call you back.

The invitation solved most of our strategic problems. It would keep the issue out of the United Nations until we had shaped an acceptable outcome. It would discourage Soviet bluster while I was in transit and negotiating. It would gain at least another seventy-two hours for military pressures to build. Nixon and I talked in this vein together with Haig and Scowcroft. We concluded that a trip to Moscow would advance our strategy.

AMBASSADOR DOBRYNIN–KISSINGER

Friday, October 19, 1973
11:38 A.M.

K: Anatol, I have had a preliminary talk with the President and we agree in principle to a high level contact.

D: Yes.

K: And you give me your quick reaction, why should Gromyko not come over here?

D: Because I think my reaction is because Kosygin is back from there so they would like to discuss, I guess, the three of them. Brezhnev, Kosygin and Gromyko.

K: I see.

D: This is really the idea—not to send a telegram telling what was said by Sadat or what was said back and forth. They would like you for one day to come there and then I am sure Kosygin will [brief] everybody. This is my real impression why they are asking this one because he is fresh so to speak in what he was thinking and they could discuss with you.

K: Will you come back there with me?

D: Yes, if you don't mind I would like to go both ways.

K: With me?

D: Yes.

K: Well, as long as you sit in the front compartment.

D: (Laughter) All right. I would rather be in the tail but nevertheless.

K: Now what are we going to do about navigators and so forth?

D: There is no problem. We will give you a navigator and we will take care about this.

K: Well all right. I will call you back—oh, what is it now, a quarter to 12:00?

D: Yeah.

K: No later than two.

D: No later than two. Okay.

K: We are very sympathetic to the proposal.

D: I think this is really important, Henry.

K: Anatol, when the Soviet Government makes such a proposal on the basis of urgency it is not a matter we take lightly.

D: Yes. And leave tomorrow because they really feel it is urgent.

K: Well they want me to arrive—well I can't leave now until about midnight tonight.

D: No, I understand. So you will arrive tomorrow but—

K: I will arrive tomorrow but—I will arrive tomorrow night and we could talk Sunday.

D: Sunday, yes.

K: You know I would like to get a few hours sleep before your three men starting working me over.

D: (Laughter) Oh you are a beautiful fellow. Yuri saw it in Moscow.

K: One night I think I am entitled to.

D: No, because—

K: My present thinking is that I leave around midnight tonight.

D: As it was last time.

K: As it was when we went on the secret trip.

D: I think it is right. So you will arrive approximately around in the evening.

K: Around 8:00 or 9:00.

    . . .

Ambassador Dobrynin–Kissinger

Friday, October 19, 1973
1:35 P.M.

    . . .

K: Anatoly, about that letter. The President agrees that I should go to Moscow. You understand this will present us with enormous domestic difficulties.

D: Well—

K: Oh, never mind. I think it's important that we say publicly, it was done at the invitation of the Soviet government.

D: I see no difficulty in that.

K: In our interests to announce it about 1:00 this morning our time.

D: 1:00 A.M.?

K: Yes, I think we should leave about 12:30.

D: This is acceptable.

K: Then we should say it is [at] the invitation of the Soviet government. I am going on urgent consultations. Of course, we will be delighted to have you come with us and—we are assuming that no unilateral actions will be taken while I am in transit.

D: What do you mean?

K: No military threats. And I am assuming both of us will keep the situation calm— I don't believe while I am there I will be able to negotiate a final settlement. I will be able to negotiate a cease-fire.

D: A cease-fire?

K: But we can't expect to settle it in one day.

D: Okay.

    . . .

The visit to Moscow could not have taken place at a more complicated time from the point of view of our domestic situation. Nixon was negotiating the agreement on the release of his tapes with Senator Stennis, the refusal of which led to the resignation of Attorney General Elliot Richardson and Deputy Attorney General and Acting FBI Director William Ruckelshaus and the firing of Special Prosecutor Archibald Cox on October 20. Two days later, the House of Representatives started impeachment proceedings against Nixon.

GENERAL HAIG–KISSINGER
Friday, October 19, 1973
3:20 P.M.

H: On this thing we are working on. The President wants to go out tonight and announce your trip.

K: Impossible.

H: Why?

K: First of all, we have now told the Soviets we would do it at 2:00 in the morning and secondly, I will be at a Chinese dinner that the Chinese are giving me. When does he want to do it?

H: Whenever we put this other mess [the Stennis compromise] together, which could be anywhere from 6:00 to 8:00. He would assemble the press in the Press Room and with cameras.

K: And say what?

H: Say in consultation with Chairman Brezhnev and that he has been in communication with him.

K: Say at the invitation.

H: He wants you to prepare the statement that he should say. Very brief.

K: Why should he do it?

H: There are a couple of reasons. One is he feels it for the reason of what he is going to announce after that.

K: He is going to make them both at the same time?

H: Yes.

K: A disaster.

H: Why?

K: My honest opinion is that it is a cheap stunt. It looks as if he is using foreign policy to cover a domestic thing.

H: The domestic thing is not controversial [the Stennis compromise]. A very good one. A very good settlement. It would also look very weird for him to make a major announcement on Watergate and ignore the fact you are going to Moscow when everyone wants to know what is going on in the Middle East. I don't see it as a contrived phony. I think you have two very important things happening.

K: He is not firing Cox?

H: As of now, no. Just giving him a desist order, which will probably result in his resignation.

K: I would not link foreign policy with Watergate. You will regret it for the rest of your life. I don't think he has to do either of them himself.

H: He has Ervin [Sam Ervin (D.-N.C.), Chairman of the Senate Watergate Committee], Baker [Howard Baker (R.-Tenn.), member of Senate Watergate Committee], and Stennis [John Stennis (D.-Miss.), Chairman of the Senate Armed Services Committee]. We are doing a hell of a thing here. He has to do it.

K: But if he gets that mixed up with foreign policy, Al, then he has to do this with the Jewish community. It will forever after be said he did this to cover Watergate. I really would plead with you. If he wants to make it as an announcement separate from the other.

H: He wants to do that. That is his idea.

K: No, no, no. He is going to make both announcements together.

H: You meant at the same time.

K: Right. I would be opposed if he even wanted to make an announcement. Now, the Soviets have asked us—by his stepping out there it becomes high-profile.

H: You are the best judge of that.

K: That does not bother me nearly so much. I think that is poor tactics. Also, we would have to get back to the Soviets. This will be a situation where the President has put his prestige on the line. Right now the Soviets have asked us to come. We should do it as a reasonable, low-key thing—simultaneous announcement. We call some newsmen in the middle of the night. It is still a big thing, but not the President's going before TV announcing it.

H: Okay.

K: I tell you, it will do him more good that way. It will be a second story that will override the first. I really mean it.

H: I know you do.

K: If he is insisting, we will do it, but I think he will regret it.

H: Okay. I will see what I can do.

GENERAL HAIG–KISSINGER
Friday, October 19, 1973
3:35 P.M.

H: I have an answer to your problem. He says okay, but he wants an announcement of your trip to come from the White House.

K: Yes. Ziegler should make it. One other question: must you do it tonight?

H: Absolutely, no way out of it. We have a midnight deadline to file.

K: All right. You will explain that?

H: How do you mean explain it?

K: It is my problem, quite honestly. It is no joy to be in Moscow under these conditions, as it is. Anything the President says makes it tougher.

H: This will strengthen it dramatically.

K: You think so?

H: No question. All the press knows we have until midnight to file.

K: Actually that is a good cover for me to get out of town. I had already explained that Ziegler should call a few selected press people about 2:00 in the morning. Tomorrow morning he could give a briefing at the White House. It would be all White House. Not

State Department. Moreover, when I come back, whatever comes out of it, then he should step forward.

H: I understand you and you are right.

K: Thank you.

Ambassador Dobrynin–Kissinger

Friday, October 19, 1973
4:30 P.M.

D: —Could I tell them it will be a commercial flight?

K: Tell them I am coming on a B-52.

D: Laughter.

K: As it turns out I have to stop in Copenhagen.

D: And then they will go along route of commercial.

K: Let's say yes.

D: I think it would be safer. I will tell them you will stop in Copenhagen and you will use [the] route used by your Pan American.

K: Yes. You have to tell us what altitude.

D: All right.

K: Is the announcement all right?

D: I will be in touch with you.

Ambassador Dobrynin–Kissinger

Friday, October 19, 1973
4:30 P.M. [AS RECORDED]

D: —A short telegram from Brezhnev. He thanks the President and you for your positive answer on his proposal. He says no objection for your public statement concerning your visit to Moscow and I was told you may come without any of our men on your aircraft.

. . .

K: Try to understand. We are discussing in the framework [cease-fire] you and I have been discussing—not a final settlement.

D: No need for me to tell them that.

K: I just don't want them to be disappointed.

D: They have invited you, and you tell them the position of the President.

K: Exactly.

D: Okay, good.

K: Okay.

Signs were mounting that with victory imminent, Israel was developing second thoughts about linking a cease-fire to the implementation of Resolution 242, even though it had been on the books—with repeated Israeli endorsement—since 1967.

AMBASSADOR DINITZ–KISSINGER
Friday, October 19, 1973
7:09 P.M.

K: Mr. Ambassador, I am assuming that I can just announce myself to Israel if I think it is a useful way to get your views.

D: Sure. At any time. Would you let me know so I can go with you.

K: If I want to go from where I am going now, I will do that and let Scowcroft know and you can get over there.

D: I have not told the Prime Minister, but I am sure it is all right.

K: I have no desire to do it. It is just a possible delaying move.

D: I will call her right now and give you an answer within ten minutes.

K: I have the President's approval, which I didn't have earlier, to begin with your proposal instead of his. I will begin to sell our proposal— That presumes that if they accept your proposal, you will accept it immediately.

D: You mean by Sunday night?

K: I don't give you a time because I don't think they will, but I don't know how desperate the problem will be.

D: Very. The last report, we have taken a town thirty-five miles from Cairo, which is halfway between the Canal and Cairo. It is seventy miles between the Canal and Cairo and this is halfway.

K: It took you a little longer. I just like to give you a tough time.

D: We have gone together with very tough times, so we are allowed a little relaxation.

K: You understand my strategy as we have discussed it— The discussions will not start before Sunday morning Moscow time and cannot conclude before Sunday afternoon Moscow time and, depending on the outcome, cannot be implemented before we have discussed it with you. This I tell you for your own planning. May I make one request? The importance of maintaining the President's goodwill for diplomatic performances that must follow. Because the outcome you have achieved is the destruction of the Egyptian army—you lived six years with 242 and I didn't—

D: We won't go into this again.

K: I am not asking you to change the position of your government, which you cannot do. If the matters reach that point, which they will reach and which I cannot avoid, please keep in mind that after [a] cease-fire it is important for your sake that the President look good and is not accused of having sold anybody out. You will need him very much in the diplomacy that follows.

D: Sure, I understand. You mean while—

K: Supposing the worst happens, from your point of view? That resolution that I gave you will not happen. Nevertheless, praise him for his statesmanlike achievements.

D: You don't even imagine that any of the linkage—

K: No phrase of Section 2 [of the Soviet proposal of the previous day demanding immediate Israeli withdrawals] will be incorporated.

D: What I understand you to say is that you want some linkage with 242—negotiation in order to implement 242.

K: Exactly. I am not saying you can count on it being refused in all its parts. It is the sort of link I give you—should it turn out to be the best possible after long consultation, you should—in your heart to thank the President. You will need it.

D: I will call the Prime Minister on your proposal. Your trip to Moscow is secret?

K: Until it is announced at 2:00 this morning here.

D: I will try to give General Scowcroft the full situation in the field.

At 7:15 P.M., I had a brief session with my colleagues of two weeks of WSAG meetings: Secretary of Defense James Schlesinger, Joint Chiefs of Staff Chairman Thomas Moorer, CIA Director William Colby, and my deputy, Brent Scowcroft. We had conferred daily, sometimes tensely. We had not always agreed, but we had managed a difficult crisis to a favorable outcome. We had achieved our fundamental objectives: We had created the conditions for a diplomatic breakthrough. We had vindicated the security of our friends. We had prevented a victory of Soviet arms. We had maintained a relationship with key Arab countries and laid the basis for a dominant role in postwar diplomacy. And we had done all this in the midst of the gravest Constitutional domestic crisis of a century.

October 20–22, 1973

My associates and I left for the Soviet Union at 2:00 A.M. on Saturday, October 20, almost exactly two weeks after the outbreak of the war. I gave a lift also to Soviet Ambassador Anatoly Dobrynin, for whom this was the quickest means to get to Moscow. My departure was secret, but shortly after takeoff, the White House announced that President Nixon had sent me to Moscow for "direct discussions with the Soviet leadership on means to end the hostilities in the Middle East."

In order to gain time, I had told Dobrynin that I never negotiated immediately after a long flight across many time zones and would not be prepared to begin talks until Sunday morning Moscow time, more than thirty-six hours away. In the interval, as he and I both knew, the military situation could only change in Israel's favor. I had consistently told Israeli Ambassador Simcha Dinitz that Israel would be well advised to conduct operations in the knowledge that we would not be able to stall on a cease-fire proposal for more than forty-eight hours. (My trip to Moscow, in the end, doubled that interval.)

As things turned out, the military situation dictated the pace of negotiations. Despite a request to Dinitz to keep us minutely informed while I was negotiating in Moscow, we never heard from the Israeli government on any subject.

The Soviets went along with my request not to ask me to negotiate after a transatlantic flight—in a halfhearted way. We arrived in Moscow at 7:30 P.M. on October 20. After being served a heavy dinner at a state guest house, I was suddenly invited to another "private" meal with Brezhnev in the Kremlin at 11:00 P.M. The atmosphere was not without its bizarre aspects. The convivial second meal was taking place at the very moment when both sides were introducing thousands of tons of war matériel daily to opposite sides in a desperate war, each seeking to reduce if not eliminate the influence of the other. Brezhnev's contribution to the pleasant mood was the claim that the Soviets were doing nothing unusual in their air- and sealifts to the Middle East; they were simply fulfilling long-standing, four-year-old agreements "according to which we must send so many guns." The idea that Moscow, in fueling the Middle East war, was motivated simply by its well-known adherence to legal obligations was a bit much to take, even in the interest of maintaining a noncontentious atmosphere for an evening of stalling. "To us," I replied sarcastically, "it looks like you are fulfilling the four-year agreement in two weeks. It is an impressive performance."

Though Brezhnev did not press for the opening of a negotiation then and there, he informed me that Nixon had sent him a message granting me full powers—thus depriving me of the opportunity to plead the need for Washington approval as a negotiating maneuver. In any event, I learned within hours that Washington was in no position to monitor the details of any negotiation. It was the evening of the so-called Saturday Night Massacre: the firing of the Special Prosecutor, Archibald Cox, and the resignations of Attorney General Elliot Richardson and Deputy Attorney General and Acting FBI Director William Ruckelshaus. A firestorm was sweeping through Washington, which was within days to lead to the demand for Nixon's impeachment.

We learned also from our own sources that Moscow had alerted seven of its eleven airborne divisions. Though we heard nothing from Israel, a message from Egyptian security adviser Ismail conveyed that the military situation was favorable to our objectives. He informed us that Egypt no longer insisted on the withdrawal of Israeli troops after a cease-fire but would accept a linkage to a peace conference.

When the two teams met in the Kremlin at noon on October 21, I submitted a proposal that Sisco and I had elaborated during the night. Its first point called for a cease-fire in place. Our second point eliminated the Soviet demand for an immediate Israeli withdrawal to new lines; indeed, it made no reference to withdrawal at all, calling on the parties simply to begin implementation of Security Council Resolution 242 "in all of its parts"—a mandate sufficiently vague to have occupied diplomats for years without arriving at agreement. Our third point required immediate negotiations "between the parties concerned" under "appropriate auspices"; in other words, the cease-fire would lead to the direct negotiations between Israel and the Arab states that had consistently been refused and that a succession of Israeli cabinets had claimed would unlock the door to their concessions. We said nothing about guarantees.

To our amazement, Brezhnev and Gromyko accepted our text, with only the most minor editorial changes.* They then took a run at turning the "appropriate auspices" for the direct negotiations

---

* The text agreed between us became United Nations Security Council Resolution 338.

into a U.S.-Soviet guarantee of the outcome—a euphemism for an imposed peace. I rejected the proposition. I defined "auspices" as meaning the presence of Soviet and American diplomats at the opening of the negotiations and thereafter only when key issues were dealt with. That too was accepted by Brezhnev and Gromyko with a minimum of haggling.

After only four hours of negotiation, the text of the cease-fire resolution was agreed, together with a U.S.-Soviet understanding on the meaning of "auspices." This was extraordinary speed for any negotiation but particularly for one with Soviet leaders, considering the need for translating everything, checking the texts, and frequent interruptions as each side huddled together for consultation.

The agreement indeed improved what we had been proposing for two weeks. The original American proposal had been a cease-fire linked to a general reference to Security Council Resolution 242. Four months earlier in a summit communiqué, Brezhnev had refused *any* such reference. Then and during the war, the Soviets had insisted that we jointly spell out the meaning of Resolution 242 and impose terms that, in the Soviet formulations, were indistinguishable from the radical Arab program. The agreed text left the elaboration of Resolution 242 to direct negotiations between the parties. And the parties would, for the first time, engage in direct negotiations.

The United States had achieved its strategic objectives: (1) it had fulfilled its obligations to Israel; (2) it had reduced the Soviet role in the Middle East and was in a position to do so at an accelerated pace once the peace process evolved; and (3) it had maintained friendly relations with the Arab world—indeed, based on the messages with Ismail, there was every prospect of a fundamental shift in Egypt's heretofore sole reliance on the Soviet alliance.*

But the Middle East rarely sees hopes smoothly fulfilled.

---

* For the details of the implementation of the agreement, see *Years of Upheaval,* pp. 554–55.

October 23–27, 1973: The U.S. Alert and
the End of the Crisis

We stopped in Israel on October 22 to establish the cease-fire and re-turned from there via London, where I briefed British Foreign Secretary Alec Douglas-Home at the airport.

After arriving in Washington at 4:00 A.M. on October 23 and a few hours' sleep, I learned that the war in the Middle East had again broken out. At first we thought that the combat was the normal jostling after a cease-fire. We shortly learned otherwise.

Around 9:30 A.M., U.N. Secretary General Kurt Waldheim called to report that Egypt had formally complained of Israeli cease-fire violations and demanded a Security Council meeting. Waldheim suggested introducing an international force from Scandinavia and other countries to police the cease-fire. I told him I would consult my colleagues and the Soviets.

A few minutes later, I discussed methods of policing the cease-fire with David Popper, the Assistant Secretary of State in charge of United Nations affairs. He thought that the handiest means available was the U.N. observers group that had previously been stationed along the Suez Canal.

I then spoke to Soviet Deputy Chief of Mission Yuri Vorontsov, Dobrynin not having as yet returned from Moscow. To get matters started on a positive note, I asked him to thank Brezhnev for Soviet hospitality. At the same time, I stressed that the agreed joint "auspices" for negotiations—to which the Soviets had paid so much attention—presupposed the rapid fulfillment of Brezhnev's promise to bring about the release of Israeli prisoners of war. I then turned to the main purpose of my call, which was to inform Vorontsov of the reported cease-fire violations, with each party accusing the other. The best remedy, I said, would be to have the Security Council instruct Waldheim to call on the parties to observe the cease-fire immediately. We would go along if the Security Council wished to send

U.N. observers or a U.N. force. Vorontsov was clearly without instructions. He confined himself to cryptic grunts of "yep" and "right" to indicate that he had understood. When I offered Vorontsov the White House switchboard to speed up communications with Moscow, he declined, assuring me he would be able to get through "in no time." In other words, as I had assumed, Dobrynin had pleaded poor communications on the first day of the war and asked for our facilities as a device to demonstrate the absence of Soviet-Arab collusion.

Within five minutes, Vorontsov was back on the phone. Obviously, my message had crossed with one from Moscow, which by now was clearly alarmed. There was a note for me from Brezhnev—a highly unusual procedure, since in the past the General Secretary had invariably addressed his communications to Nixon. It took an hour for Brezhnev's message to be translated and sent over from the Soviet Embassy. In it, he told me that Israeli forces were moving southward along the west bank of the Suez Canal. This news came from Moscow's "own reliable information"—in other words, not from Egyptian sources but presumably from the supersonic MiG-25 Foxbats that were flying reconnaissance missions from Egyptian airfields. Brezhnev called Israeli actions "unacceptable" and a "flagrant deceit," from which one had to conclude that the Egyptians were in deep trouble. He suggested a Security Council meeting at noon—less than two hours away—reconfirming the cease-fire, and ordering all forces to be withdrawn to the line they occupied when the October 22 cease-fire resolution had passed, or twelve hours *before* the cease-fire was required to go into effect. (A clever Soviet ploy, this would have put the Israelis well behind the lines from which they obviously jumped off when the current fighting started.) Brezhnev enclosed a Soviet draft of a Security Council resolution embodying his ideas.

We were now in a serious predicament. The urgency of Brezhnev's appeal suggested that the plight of the Egyptian Third Army was far more serious than our own intelligence had yet discovered or the Israelis had told us. If the United States held still while the Egyptian army was being destroyed after a cease-fire negotiated in Moscow by the Secretary of State followed by a stop in Israel, the basis for trustful negotiations with moderate Arab states and even the Soviet Union would disappear.

At 11:04 A.M., I urgently contacted Simcha Dinitz. He did not know the location of the new battle lines. He could tell me, however, on behalf of the Prime Minister "personally, confidentially and sincerely that none of the actions taken on the Egyptian front were initiated by us." With all my affection for Golda, I thought she was imposing on my credulity with her definition of "initiate." It was not plausible that the Egyptian Third Army should launch attacks after a cease-fire that had saved it from being overwhelmed and that it should then immediately ask everyone within reach for yet another cease-fire, shooting all the time at passive Israelis who were only defending themselves while advancing.

But this was not the time for abstract debate. We needed time to assess our options.

Deputy Chief of Mission Vorontsov–Kissinger

Tuesday, October 23, 1973
11:25 A.M.

K: I just talked to the President. Two things, (1) we would really like a delay if at all possible.

V: Oh, oh, that doesn't mean that the Israelis will take some more 50 miles of territory during the delay.

K: No, no; I don't believe—I don't know how fast they are moving—

V: I don't know either but—

K: At least an hour.

V: Well, the Security Council never meets on the dot but still maybe just to have it started at 12:00 but then the time for agreement on the Resolution and everything like that and you will have your time. But to postpone the meeting is not very good in the eyes of the Arab countries.

K: Can you see whether Malik and Scali can't get some delay?

V: Malik said he has already engaged himself on the 12 o'clock with the Arabs and with the First Chairman or President of the Security Council.

K: You can then get a delay in the vote or something?

V: But later on they can do it. Yes, I know it for sure.

K: Okay. Well, do that then. Secondly, we definitely cannot accept your phrase "withdrawn to the position where they were at the moment of the adoption of the decision on the ceasefire."

V: How are you suggesting to change it?

K: Well, we have not yet decided. I have just talked to the President. What we could consider is "where they were at the moment the ceasefire went into effect."

V: Went into effect. Well, okay, I just warn Moscow about this, that you'll have these changes and warn Malik. But, again, let Scali and Malik talk on this.

K: Sure.

V: Okay?

K: Good. But this is not yet definite.

V: I would rather not see definite. I would rather see it as it is in the text.

K: No, that is out of the question.

V: Out of the question.

K: That we will not accept.

V: Okay, let's work on that.

I went through the Soviet draft U.N. resolution with Dinitz. I told him—as I had told Vorontsov—we would not go along with the Soviet formulation that the parties return to the lines existing when the cease-fire resolution was adopted by the Security Council. But I did not see how we could refuse an appeal to return to the lines existing when the cease-fire went into effect (twelve hours later). I said we favored the introduction of U.N. observers. Dinitz promised to seek instructions.

In the meantime, I sought to negotiate an acceptable resolution with the Soviets.

DEPUTY CHIEF OF MISSION VORONTSOV–KISSINGER
Tuesday, October 23, 1973
11:32 A.M.

V: Yes, Henry.

K: Yuri, I will let you know within half an hour, 45 minutes, but it must be where at the line established when the ceasefire went into effect.

V: It's firm now.

K: It's not yet firm but only one [formulation] we're now considering.

V: Went into effect. Right, I've got it.

K: On the other one, now, there's only one other point we have, which I know is no problem—where you say you think for that purpose, first of all, the personnel of the United Nations which is at present in Cairo.

V: Right.

K: What we would like to say is "using for that purpose U.N. personnel now in the Middle East but first of all—"

V: Now in the Middle East.

K: And first of all—

V: By this line, you mean—

K: The ones that are in Jerusalem, for example.

V: Un-huh. Not Syrian situation you have in mind?

K: No.

V: Since we are talking about Egypt and—

K: No, no. What we have in mind is the Egyptian situation.

V: Yeah.

K: It applies specifically only to Egypt.

V: Yeah, I see. So you mean from that line, from the Israeli side, yes, to engage—

K: Just to have more personnel available.

V: Yeah, all the personnel available there. First of all which is in Cairo. Well, I don't think there will be any problem here. But, Henry, there is a problem about postponement. Scali suggested to Malik 3 o'clock. It's terrible of course.

K: No, no; I have just instructed that they should start the meeting and delay the vote.

V: Yeah. Okay.

K: Okay?

V: Yeah, it's okay so far as I'm concerned. I don't have time to consult with the government in Moscow, you understand.

K: But tell Malik what I suggested.

V: I'll tell Malik. I'm just contacting him now.

At noon, Dinitz called with a rather complicated message. Its essence was that Israeli forces would not withdraw from the positions they now held. The Israeli government agreed, he said, with the argument that no one could tell where the original cease-fire line had been, so it could not accept a call to withdraw to it. Israel did not wish to undermine the authority of the United Nations by agreeing to an inherently unenforceable new resolution. Such delicacy showed a solicitude for the United Nations for which little in previous Israeli practice had prepared us. Nor did it solve our problem. We instructed Ambassador Scali in New York to stall until we had decided how to proceed.

At 12:36 P.M., an urgent message arrived from Brezhnev, this time to "Esteemed Mr. President." It spoke heatedly of Israeli "treachery"; it offered absolute assurance that the Arab leaders would observe the cease-fire. The message's passion was achieved at the cost of precision, for it omitted the issue likely to give us the greatest difficulty—whether Israel should withdraw and to what line. It concentrated simply on stopping the fighting. In the name of a nonexistent U.S.-Soviet guarantee of the cease-fire—perhaps misleadingly put about by the Soviets to induce Cairo to accept the original cease-fire—it asked us to take "the most decisive measures" jointly "without delay" to impose the cease-fire. My assessment was that if a new cease-fire was all that was wanted, our task would be relatively easy; if an Israeli withdrawal was envisaged, we were in for a tempestuous time.

To preempt a more concrete Soviet proposal, we interpreted Brezhnev's message in the first sense in our reply, which went out under Nixon's name within the hour and which treated the available facts as more clear-cut than we really felt they were:

> I want to assure you that we assume full responsibility to bring about a complete end of hostilities on the part of Israel. Our own information would indicate that the responsibility for the violation of the cease-fire belongs to the Egyptian side, but this is not the time to debate that particular issue. We have insisted with Israel that they take immediate steps to cease hostilities, and I urge that you take similar measures with respect to the Egyptian side.

We decided to proceed on the basis of a joint U.S./Soviet resolution reaffirming the cease-fire. Otherwise, the Soviet Union would be in a position to introduce a resolution of its own, facing us with the dilemma of vetoing the restoration of a cease-fire we had negotiated.

DEPUTY CHIEF OF MISSION VORONTSOV–KISSINGER
Tuesday, October 23, 1973
1:35 P.M.

K: I should have known with you in town we are in deep trouble. Let me tell you what we have [in the U.N. resolution]: Confirm decision about immediate cessation of all military action—and urge that the forces of the two sides be returned to the positions they occupied at the time the cease-fire became effective.

V: Yep.

K: And say the same thing—We are willing to accept this and make it a joint resolution if you will.

V: Good, yes.

K: In the second paragraph—Using for this purpose—personnel in Middle East—and personnel on Cairo. Now, between you and me, I would not hold up deliberations on that.

V: Not understand.

K: It should be included in—I think it is a reasonable proposal, don't you?

V: I do too. I will talk to Malik and I will confirm.

K: It is better to argue about where the line is—the principle of withdrawal. We would slow that debate.

V: Let them argue but just not fight—

K: Secondly, we attach great importance to the understanding between the Secretary General and me about the exchange of [prisoners]—

V: I repeat this to Moscow.

K: Emphasize it again. Let me know.

V: I need five minutes.

K: We will make it a joint resolution.

V: A joint resolution. Malik has insisted to make it separate.

K: Tell Malik not to. If you can accept my language—

V: Exactly, exactly. We can accept. I then need five minutes.

AMBASSADOR SCALI–KISSINGER

Tuesday, October 23, 1973
1:36 P.M.

S: Malik is acting like a goddamn idiot.

K: You tell Malik to calm down. We are in the process of working it out.

S: Tell him right now?

K: Yes. Tell him right now. Vorontsov is now in the process of getting instructions from Moscow.

S: He claims that he has talked to Vorontsov and has gotten—

K: I have just talked to Vorontsov and given him our proposal.
You tell Malik to hold his water or I will send him to Siberia. I
know Brezhnev better than he does. Ask him if he has ever been
kissed on the mouth by Brezhnev, as I have. Tell him to go to
Vorontsov. We have made a new proposal and we think we will—

S: Okay, I'll tell him.

DEPUTY CHIEF OF MISSION VORONTSOV–KISSINGER
Tuesday, October 23, 1973
1:40 P.M.

V: We accept the changes you wanted in the first case and second.
So we are accepting it together.

K: Give me ten minutes to let those maniacs in New York know.

V: I have contacted Malik and he has told Scali, so Scali knows.

K: Good.

We thought we had given Israel the maximum flexibility to bargain. But it wanted what we would not grant: a free hand to destroy
the Egyptian Third Army.

That Tuesday afternoon, October 23, we received a blistering
communication from Golda Meir, which Dinitz read to us. She
chose to construe the proposed new Security Council resolution as
an Egyptian-Soviet imposition growing out of an Egyptian violation
of the cease-fire: "It is impossible for Israel to accept that time and
again it must face Russian and Egyptian ultimatums which will sub-
sequently be assented to by the United States." It was, of course,
hardly an ultimatum to ask Israel and Egypt to cease firing while a
cease-fire was in effect and to negotiate a return to a line we had carefully not specified and while the U.S. airlift was still going full blast.

But all the frustrations of the three difficult weeks found expression in Israel's reaction. Golda informed us that Israel would not comply with the proposed resolution or even talk about it. Israel seemed determined to end the war with a humiliation for Egypt. We had no interest in seeing Sadat destroyed as the consequence of an Israeli challenge to a cease-fire we had negotiated and co-sponsored. And if Israel had been less shaken by the events of the previous weeks, it too would have understood that what it sought would end any hope for diplomacy and doom it to perpetual struggle. For if Sadat fell, the odds were that he would be replaced by a radical pro-Soviet leader; Soviet arms would, in a measurable time, reconstitute the equivalent of the Third Army; and sooner or later, there would be another Egyptian-Israeli war reviving the same dilemmas we had just barely surmounted. The peace process dominated by America would end before it was started; when restored in an uncertain future, it would be under much less favorable auspices.

At 3:02 P.M., I discussed the situation briefly with Schlesinger. A major problem was whether to end the airlift to Israel. The cease-fire had generated pressure in the Pentagon to end the airlift, largely for budgetary reasons. Schlesinger went along with my view that it should be kept going at least until the immediate crisis was resolved.

SECRETARY SCHLESINGER–KISSINGER

> *Tuesday, October 23, 1973*
> *3:02 P.M.*

S: How are you?

K: A little tired but I think we made it.

S: We now have the problem of post-cease-fire.

K: We are settling that. We are introducing a joint resolution at 4:00 with the Soviet Union.

S: My query is what about the airlift?

K: We have to keep it going till we get a handle on the others.

S: So, when they cut it off, we cut it off.

K: We have made a proposal and I think we should play it hard. We cut it unilaterally, and it will be bad.

S: No question. The Egyptians were pretty shaky.

K: I don't think so.

S: Make it harder in [the] same way.

K: Do you think we made a mistake joining a resolution calling for a new cease-fire?

S: I don't know enough at this stage.

K: Well, supposed the Soviets introduced a resolution alone; do we then veto it?

S: Yes—I mean no, we can't.

K: If we do it, we will be in trouble with the Arabs.

S: The name of the game is to keep the airlift going.

K: We will have a WSAG at 5:00. I may move it to tomorrow.

. . .

GENERAL SCOWCROFT–KISSINGER

Tuesday, October 23, 1973
4:20 P.M.

. . .

S: I understand you talked to Schlesinger. Everyone wants to cut back on supplies.

K: I will talk to them.

S: They [the Pentagon] need quieting down.

K: Why?

S: They have no idea of what is going on and now we have a cease-fire we should stop supplies.

K: At least tell them to stand by till I call. Why should we cut back on the Israelis when the Russians don't cut back on the Arabs?

. . .

Secretary Schlesinger–Kissinger

Tuesday, October 23, 1973
5:09 P.M.

K: I just saw a news ticker that Pentagon sources said because of Soviet slowdown on supplies we were slowing down. Will you keep your people quiet! We need the Israelis on a—they need an open supply line during [this crisis]. You will keep it going full blast. We will meet at WSAG tomorrow at 10:00.

S: Maybe Bill [Clements] will be there. Unless you want me there?

K: No, I told you everything today. Anyway, we are having lunch tomorrow.

S: We are? How is the cease-fire going? Are we going to crack down immediately? Or will we tolerate—down?

K: It is—is tremendous victories for us. The big pressures will have to come when we get into peace negotiations.

The President–Kissinger

Tuesday, October 23, 1973
6:50 P.M.

   . . .

K: . . . A lot of newsmen have sent notes and called in on the Middle East and realize what a role you have played. I think that is an asset.

N: In terms of—compare this with the Cuban confrontation. The Russians would never have called Kennedy. With a twelve-to-one advantage. But in the Middle East they might have— We have no ships. Moving the aircraft they had no choice—

K: That is my key point.

N: They realize it took some nerve to do this.

K: No question. It was a tremendous victory.

N: The thing you negotiated was fantastic. To change the wording to urging was good. Very good. Well, anyway you need a good night's sleep. Tomorrow you knock them dead.

   . . .

ADMIRAL THOMAS MOORER–KISSINGER

Tuesday, October 23, 1973
8:28 P.M.

K: I placed a call earlier. I think it is now overtaken by events. I just wanted to make sure the airlift continues full [blast]. It is not to be cut either in the sortie rate or tonnage.

M: We are running about five and sixteen now. We will just continue.

K: We will not cut it. If you get any orders to the contrary, let me get a chance to get that man into the President's office. Load the planes as full as they should be. I want to make sure that the tonnage and sortie rate is what we promised them.

M: Yes.

By the evening, Dobrynin had returned from Moscow, and we reviewed the state of play with respect to the new cease-fire resolution in a noncrisis atmosphere:

AMBASSADOR DOBRYNIN–KISSINGER

Tuesday, October 23, 1973
7:10 P.M.

. . .

D: When I left Moscow, all the members of the Politburo [were satisfied]— Now it looks really rather negative after your trip to Israel—all these developments.

K: We had another joint resolution this afternoon— You agree with the Egyptians on something.

D: The only point which I was surprised you refused to accept was Paragraph 2 about the cease-fire line.

K: What Paragraph 2?

D: Of the resolution calling for them to return to the position previously agreed upon.

K: First of all, that isn't true. The extraordinary difficulty is deciding where the line started. We didn't want to get into a hassle about where the line had been. Finally we joined you. I had to talk to the President.

D: It looks fine again. Were you surprised?

K: I had absolutely no knowledge of this.

D: I think nothing really.

K: Vorontsov called me at 10:00 this morning. By 1:00 we had agreed to it. That is not an undue delay.

D: What is the situation in the field?—

K: The Israelis swear that the Egyptians attacked them first. We have no separate information.

D: What is the situation? The fighting continues or stops?

K: I think it stops. We have urged the Israelis in the strongest terms to stop it.

D: Did they begin to—the position as they issued on Sunday?

K: They say they would agree to it. But who knows what that position was? They will never agree.

D: Don't you know through your reconnaissance?

K: We haven't done any air reconnaissance. Let's say we do not know what the actual situation is, frankly.

D: You don't know yet.

K: We have sent two urgent messages today to stop, and I have had the Israeli Ambassador in here to stop.

D: Brezhnev, when I left—

K: It isn't right for Vorontsov to say he had to complain to the Politburo. You can't give us a resolution and expect an answer in ten minutes. It is amazing. We—

D: It was agreed upon by you and Brezhnev that there would be a cease-fire in twelve hours.

K: Your resolution said they should return to the position at the time the cease-fire was agreed upon— We were reluctant to agree to something that nobody could enforce. The Egyptians say one thing, the Israelis another; you don't know and we don't know.

D: He [Soviet Ambassador to the U.N. Malik] had to call again to

Moscow. He agreed on the second line. Then in a few moments Sisco called.

K: He had no right to do that. I straightened that out. It wasn't easy to get a winning side to accept a cease-fire. From that point on, Israel was winning and we nevertheless agreed to it.

D: We didn't make any definition in Moscow as to who was winning.

K: We made a great effort to make the agreement.

D: I am more worried about our understanding than the Arabs—

K: We have spent all day today to get the Israelis to stop and I think they have now stopped.

D: I would like to see you tomorrow. If you don't mind.

K: I think we have the—in principle of the Israelis in our joint auspices.

D: They agreed to this one.

K: Not yet 100 percent. If we can get the prisoner thing settled they will agree to it. I had a long talk with the Prime Minister. I have already sent a message to Brezhnev to that effect.

D: Do you think we should talk tomorrow? You are having a press conference tomorrow?

K: No, on Thursday. I also wanted to talk to you. There will be a few ups and downs within the next few weeks. We have settled this in a very diplomatic way—

D: This is exactly the point. All right, Henry. The most important thing is the agreement between you and Brezhnev and the whole situation in the Middle East. If we hold that firm it doesn't matter what happens, we will survive. If we drag this anchor through the winds—

K: You have known me long enough. I will not trick Brezhnev. That is the stupidest thing I could do. Even if we win this one, we could never have a trusting relationship again. We cannot control everything the Israelis do. They swear that [the] Egyptians started it.

D: The question is to stop and continue discussions politically with
the Secretary General [Brezhnev].

. . .

While Dobrynin was in transit from Moscow, the situation had,
in fact, worsened. At 3:15 P.M., an urgent message from Sadat direct
to Nixon was delivered through intelligence channels—the first time
Sadat's name was cited explicitly as the originator, demonstrating the
gravity of the situation. Sadat made the extraordinary proposal that
the United States, with which Egypt had not had diplomatic relations for six years, should "intervene effectively even if that necessi-
tates the use of forces, in order to guarantee the full implementation
of the cease-fire resolution in accordance with the joint U.S.-
U.S.S.R. agreement." The letter went on to allege (based probably
on Soviet misrepresentation) that the United States had offered a
"guarantee" of the cease-fire.

The Egyptian proposal that we use American forces against our
ally Israel was, of course, no more tenable than the Israeli desire that
we run diplomatic interference while it strangled an Egyptian army
trapped *after* a cease-fire we had negotiated. So we decided to stick to
our course of working to stop the fighting and then to encourage a
negotiation over the location of the cease-fire lines. At 5:15 P.M., I
replied to the Brezhnev message of early in the day that had been addressed to me:

> As I said to Mr. Vorontsov, and as he confirmed, our willingness to
> accept the principle of your Security Council proposal was made
> possible when your government assured me that it will show mod-
> eration when differences ensue between the parties, as to the [cease-
> fire] positions in dispute.

Still believing that we were talking about a few miles in the
desert, I urged Dinitz to move back a few hundred yards to maintain
the principle.

Ambassador Dinitz–Kissinger

Tuesday, October 23, 1973
7:20 P.M.

. . .

K: We have had a message from Sadat pleading with us to produce a cease-fire. Dobrynin is back and they are [beside] themselves.

D: Of course, I will pass this message on to the Prime Minister.

K: We have been assured by Israel it is purely a defensive decision— Put that Jewish mind to work so that when the pressure starts you can start withdrawing a few hundred yards—

D: I will ask the Prime Minister if she can find some sandpile.

K: Not right now. The time to make moves is just a little bit before you are forced to and make them figure out what you just did. Then they have to generate new pressures. If you withdraw a few hundred yards— Tomorrow stop the fighting. Somebody will say, announce that as of Thursday you are returning to the original position. You see what I mean?

. . .

Ambassador Dinitz–Kissinger

Tuesday, October 23, 1973
8:30 P.M.

D: I just talked to the Prime Minister and have the authority to pass on to Moscow that you can pass to Sadat our solemn pledge. If the Egyptians stop shooting, we will not shoot either. Moreover, she gives you her personal pledge that if Egypt gives instructions to cease fire and actually executes it, we will not shoot, regardless of all the advantages we can get.

K: The second point is the same as the first.

D: No, she is giving you her personal pledge.

K: We can tell that to the Egyptians—

D: The Egyptians and Russians—

K: That we have been given assurances.

D: If they give orders to stop firing and execute it, we will not shoot. She tells you that we will stop in spite of the fact that it will cause disadvantages in the field. She said to tell you, that place you both talked about was under consideration last night? They decided to—it ought to give the cease-fire a chance. It was absolutely the decision of the Egyptians to break the cease-fire.

K: I will tell you what I would do if I was Israeli National Security Adviser—

D: She asked me to tell you she does not believe the question of the business of two hundred or three hundred will work. The Egyptians and Russians know where they were. She suggested this tactic. We are honestly and sincerely willing to accept the cease-fire and right now. The Egyptians resumed the war, and as a result of this, new territory was claimed. She asked me to tell you she honestly does not believe that two hundred to three hundred yards would work.

K: Well, she is in charge of Israel.

D: I suggest let us start with this and we will be in touch again.

K: We are in a tough position on this one. We are not saying who started it. As you are in Suez city, some people will be starving in the next day or two.

D: We have not entered the city proper. We have gone around it.

K: You have cut the road. Some people on the east bank will not have any water.

D: They had no business being there anyway.

. . .

Ambassador Dobrynin–Kissinger
Tuesday, October 23, 1973
8:35 P.M.

K: You really didn't want to sleep tonight.

D: I didn't know it myself but I was flying from Frankfurt on a plane that was going from Israel to New York. It was quite a coincidence.

K: After our call I called the Israelis and said the fighting must stop, and I have their pledge that if the Egyptians stop firing they will in any event stop any advance now, and if the Egyptians obey the cease-fire they will obey the cease-fire. I now have the impression they will stop. Let's get it stopped. They are now in defensive position. They are not advancing. If you could get the Egyptians to give another order to stop firing—

D: The next step should be coming back to the resolution line.

K: That is the next question. All Sadat has asked us to do is stop the fighting.

D: To stop and go back where they were.

K: The first step is to get the fighting stopped.

D: There is nothing else I want.

K: Right now they will still advance, as I understand it.

D: I will get to Moscow about this.

K: Then we will see about the next step.

D: All right, Henry. Good night.

SENATOR FULBRIGHT–KISSINGER

Tuesday, October 23, 1973
8:35 P.M. [AS RECORDED]

. . .

F: Well, you had a rough time. I'm delighted you're making progress.

K: Well.

F: Have they started again?

K: We passed another resolution—joining the Soviet Union—asking for a cease-fire immediately and return to the lines which existed when they started and finally the introduction of U.N. observers. Frankly, I think we can make the lines stick but we are not sure where they were—it will be difficult.

F: From what I read about your agreement with the Russians I was very encouraged.

K: Actually, you played a role—

F: Oh, I would hope I did.

K: I'm not saying decisively but Dobrynin referred to it a couple of times. It came out better—we got it down to negotiations between the Arabs and Israelis—and they say under appropriate auspices. For your information what Brezhnev and I decided was that the U.S. and the Soviets should provide the auspices under the general supervision of the Security Council.

F: That's real progress and it gets détente back on the road.

. . .

Israel's seemingly defensive proposal ordering its troops to stop firing amounted to an insistence on starving out the Egyptian Third Army. As soon as it became clear that the Israelis had cut the last supply route, a crisis was becoming inevitable. Even if the Israelis had stopped fighting, the Third Army was bound to try to break out. Israel's decision guaranteed a major crisis in which, if pressed to an extreme, we would stand by what had been negotiated in Moscow.

The U.S. strategy was to concentrate on a cease-fire as a precondition to dealing with the status of the Third Egyptian Army. Because its circumstances were perilous, tensions rose as the day progressed.

AMBASSADOR DOBRYNIN–KISSINGER
Wednesday, October 24, 1973
9:45 A.M.

K: Anatol, the madmen in the Middle East seem to be at it again. We got a message this time on the East Bank. The West Bank is quiet now. We just had a message the Israelis claim they're being attacked. The Egyptians don't say who's doing the attacking. I want you to know what we have done. We've sent first a message to the Israelis telling them it had to stop and we had their assurance that they're staying in defensive positions. We sent a message to the Egyptians of which I'll send you a copy, telling them that we will totally oppose any further military offensive military actions by the Israelis and recommending that they, too, stop offensive actions. And that is our impressions which we have no independent proof, that this time the Egyptians may have started it but we are not sure. We have no real basis for judgment. I just want you to know what we are doing. And I'm sending you the message we sent to the Egyptians but we have made a very violent representation to the Israelis.

D: All right.

K: But one thing that Moscow is to understand we are not playing any games here. We made an agreement and it's now going to be enforced.

D: This is the point.

K: Well, you have our assurance.

D: I will send a telegram to Moscow.

K: I'll send you the message to send out immediately.

AMBASSADOR DOBRYNIN–KISSINGER

Wednesday, October 24, 1973
10:10 A.M.

D: Henry, I just received a telegram from Moscow.

K: Well, I wanted to bring you up to date. We have just been informed by the Israelis that they will permit American military attaches from Tel Aviv to go to the battle area to help observe that they are not taking offensive actions, and we have informed the Egyptians to that effect.

D: From Tel Aviv?

K: Yes. That we are sending U.S. military observers to make sure, to reassure that they are taking only, they're only firing back. They're not advancing. [Unclear] that they will allow American military observers to come there to guarantee, you know, to make sure that this order is carried out.

D: [Unclear] a United Nations [unclear]

K: No, no, a United States military attaché.

D: You said first observers from United Nations.

K: No, I meant United States military attachés, in addition to U.N. observers.

D: In addition. How many are you sending there?

K: Well, as many, I don't know. I'm now talking to our people to find out how many we have in the military attaché's office. We don't have very many there.

D: Who requested this? Did you or they?

K: I was the initiator. I demanded to have proof that they're not taking offensive action and we were asking—

D: On a temporary basis you're sending them.

K: Just on a temporary basis. Yes, we'll withdraw them in a day.

D: All right.

K: But we were asked by the Egyptians to use American ground personnel to bring about an end to the action.

D: They did ask you?

K: Yeah.

K: And I'm sending you a copy of our message to President Sadat in which we inform him of that.

. . .

AMBASSADOR DOBRYNIN–KISSINGER
Wednesday, October 24, 1973
10:15 A.M.

K: Two things. We've just been informed by the Israelis firing has been stopped on the East bank. On the West bank there wasn't much going on anyway. We are sending ten of our people from Tel Aviv to observe it for about forty-eight hours until the U.N. observers are there.

D: Forty-eight hours.

K: Yes. We are willing to keep them longer if anyone asks you.

D: I understand.

K: Secondly, we've just been informed, which I can hardly believe that Brezhnev is leaving for Cuba at the end of this week.

D: To Cuba?

K: Yes.

D: This I heard for the first time. This I am hearing for the first time. I know that he had an invitation to go by the end of this year.

K: Our understanding was that he would leave in December.

D: This I know. And I'm sure when I was in Moscow if it was he were going, I would have been told so I am presuming, of course I didn't discuss this directly with him so I am make a small reservation in terms of unbelievable to me but 99.9 percent it is completely untrue.

K: OK.

D: I'm rather prepared to say 100 percent untrue because otherwise when I was in Moscow I was there a good 20 hours maybe—

K: You can't keep him from going to Cuba but you can imagine—

D: I am not going to mention it to him because I am sure, even when I was in Moscow he mentioned to me because he usually tells what his major plan is, where he goes. He is going to India.

K: That I knew.

D: I am sure he will mention to me about it but I am sorry you have some problem, however, it was in December he plans to go there. What is your information based on.

K: A clearance for Brezhnev's plane.

D: They are just making sure to know before and how and so on. It was only on this one. No, I knew about these planes. He doesn't know that that plane is going there.

K: I don't think you should—that this would be the time. I wanted to inform you also that the Chinese trip. We have proposed going there on the 26th of November and they have now strongly urged us to come on the 10th of November and I am accepting that.

D: On the 10th. Why is it urgent?

K: I don't know.

D: Maybe some special occasion.

K: I have assured there is nothing. I repeat to you we are planning nothing. Now you know if they want to—if something unbelievable is offered to us while we are there. At this moment or any time that I can foresee there will be nothing but general consultations.

. . .

AMBASSADOR DOBRYNIN–KISSINGER
Wednesday, October 24, 1973
10:19 A.M.

D: Henry, we have the following message from Brezhnev to President Nixon.

"Mr. President:

"We have precise information that the Israeli troops are attacking now with tanks and military ships on Egyptian forces on the western part of the Suez Canal. They are trying to capture this port by violating the U.N. Security Council decision on the Middle East ceasefire. At the same time Israel's military forces are attacking on the Eastern part of the Suez Canal and again Egyptian troops to the south of the Canal. These violent actions of the Israelis were taken only a few hours after the Security Council once again confirmed their decision on a mutual ceasefire and after your very firm statement made to us that the United States would take the full responsibility to assure the full ceasefire from the part of Israel.

"Mr. President, we are sure that you have responsibility to make clear to Israel that the troops should immediately stop their actions of provocation. We would like to hope that you and we would be loyal to our words which were given to each other and to the agreement we have reached with you. We would very much appreciate your message about the steps which are taken by you in order to insure that Israel will obey the second Security Council decision. Respectfully, . . ."

K: Thank you, Anatol. Now we will send you a message within a couple of hours on the substance but you can already tell him the following: We have told the Israelis that a continuation of these operations will mean a total reevaluation of our relations including supplies. Secondly, we have demanded that they stop the action. Thirdly, we have demanded that our own observers see, that they are not on offensive operations until the U.N. is [on the ground]. Fourthly, the President has personally called, in the last five minutes, the Israeli ambassador and has made the same point to him.

D: OK.

K: Now could you transmit this to Brezhnev and tell him that the spirit which [unclear] us over the weekend continues and we are not in a game of extracting five mile advantages which mean nothing to you or us.

D: Yes, this is exactly true. OK, Henry.

K: Thank you.

Simultaneously, there was a message from Hafiz Ismail claiming that Israel had broken the new cease-fire. Sadat followed with a message to Nixon demanding his intercession. In the middle of the afternoon, Sadat, in a message to Nixon, put forward a proposal bound to lead to decisions of grave consequence: the immediate dispatch of American observers or troops for the implementation of the Security Council cease-fire resolution on the *Egyptian* side. What was new was what I had feared throughout the crisis. Sadat told us that he was "formally" issuing the same request to the Soviets. Shortly after

Sadat's private message, I learned through a news bulletin that Cairo had announced publicly that it was calling for a Security Council meeting to ask that American and Soviet "forces" be sent to the Middle East. The makings of a major crisis were emerging.

We were not prepared to send American troops to Egypt, nor would we accept the dispatch of Soviet forces. We had not worked for years to reduce the Soviet military presence in Egypt only to cooperate in reintroducing it as the result of a U.N. resolution. Nor would we participate in a joint force with the Soviets, which would legitimize their role in the area and strengthen radical elements. Anti-Soviet moderates like Saudi Arabia, the Emirates (Trucial States), Jordan, and Kuwait might well panic at this demonstration of U.S.-Soviet condominium. The Soviet force might prove impossible to remove; there would be endless pretexts for it to intervene at any point against Israel, or against moderate Arab governments, for that matter.

We were determined to resist, by force if necessary, the introduction of Soviet troops into the Middle East, regardless of the pretext under which they arrived. I therefore told Dobrynin when he called on me at the State Department at 4:00 P.M. that we would veto any Security Council resolution calling for the dispatch of troops of any permanent member. The following telephone conversations show the process of consultation with allies and directives to associates that followed.

AMBASSADOR DINITZ–KISSINGER
Wednesday, October 24, 1973
3:40 P.M.

K: We have just been told by the Soviets; I'm not saying this is true; but I want to bring you up-to-date—that your forces are still continuing to attack.

D: I have just talked to Israel about five minutes ago and they told me all is quiet and we canceled the blackout in Israel today.

K: I want to inform you of our strategy at the U.N. If the meeting is called, we will take the following position: 1) We will support the strongest call for an observance of the cease-fire; 2) we will totally oppose introduction of American and Soviet forces (unless you are for it).

D: No. No. No.

K: 3) We will strongly favor strengthening of U.N. observers by bringing people in like the Scandinavians and elsewhere. 4) On the question of return to the original line, we strongly support the principle but have no thoughts on how to apply it. Scali will be instructed to delay and confuse it. Okay?

D: Fine. Do you have any idea if anyone is going to propose a resolution?

K: No. I have no word. I have seen that the Egyptians and Syrians are calling a meeting. I am seeing Dobrynin at 4:00 on another matter and I will tell them not to propose it because we will oppose it. Give us as much assurance as you can that you are not taking any military action.

D: I called five minutes ago. I will tell the Prime Minister about the strategy and repeat the concern that the Russians expressed to you.

Secretary Schlesinger–Kissinger
Wednesday, October 24, 1973
4:25 P.M.

K: Are we permitted to go to the front in Israel yet?

S: We are permitted, but I'm not sure it's a good idea anyway.

K: Well, is there any way we can find out if it's quiet for ourselves? The Israelis tell us it is, the Soviets are telling us it isn't, and—

S: We can send them [observers for the U.N.] down there; they're ready to go. We told them we would be moving them.

K: I don't want to send them in as a formal observer group. Don't want to send Soviets too— Why don't we send it as an informal group?

S: The problem is, if [we] send U.S. military down there, they're going to use it.

K: Can't we send somebody simply for our own information with no official status? Send two or three people and bring them right back to Tel Aviv, just so I can tell the Soviets what I think we've found?— I have no independent—

. . .

DAVID POPPER, ASSISTANT SECRETARY OF STATE FOR
INTERNATIONAL ORGANIZATION AFFAIRS–KISSINGER
Wednesday, October 24, 1973
4:50 P.M.

K: . . . only questions of possible observers.

P: Say American idea—I would think limiting number would not expose us. If you have limited number, say ten members from each side—of U.N. forces, about two hundred altogether— Can't think there would be any particular harm.

K: You can instruct Scali, if it comes up, to go along with that. One thing I want to make absolutely clear: the dispatch of military attachés is not to be construed as a military thing. They are going for twenty-four hours to report to us what is going on. We have the right to inform ourselves what's going on. The Soviets have the same right. We have no right to tell the Soviet military attaché what he can do. If he wants to go to the front, that's his business. I have informed [the] Soviets we are sending [a] military attaché to [the] front to report to us his judgment of who's doing the fighting. I don't want this to be confused with—

P: No, no. This is quite separate from the observers—

K: I know it's quite different, but I don't want it to be confused.

P: Any reasons why the dispatch of military attachés should arise this evening?

K: No, except the Egyptians and the Soviets know about it. My instructions are that this is to be treated as a separate thing from the U.N. observers group.

P: I understand fully.

K: Secondly, if the U.N. observers want to—we'll leave that open. Say we will consider it. Thirdly, Dobrynin felt there is no reason for [a] resolution at all. Don't think we should browbeat Malik—

P: Does that mean consensus statement by the President [of the Security Council] rather than—

K: Consensus statement by the President would be best, and that's what Scali should push. He should also, in [a] low-key way, present to Malik—

P: It's going to be difficult with Malik.

K: I know. Malik's not the easiest man to— But neither is Scali.

P: First priority after hearing parties—stop fighting—

K: Do not have impression Soviets will introduce any addition of U.S.-Soviet forces and—

P: [Deputy Press Secretary Gerald] Warren's statement—the White House recalled the statement and said Scali would articulate it later this evening. His statement should include something about how we felt. I'm just writing something now, a paragraph to—

K: Okay, but keep it low key.

Since it was already past midnight in Moscow, the general feeling was that the evening would end either inconclusively or with another cease-fire resolution.

At 7:05 P.M., we learned better. The Soviet Union informed us that it would support a request for the dispatch of U.S. and Soviet troops to enforce the cease-fire. A confrontation was inevitable if the Soviet Union persisted.

AMBASSADOR DOBRYNIN–KISSINGER

Wednesday, October 24, 1973
7:05 P.M.

D: —which our representative in New York has now received—but as we discussed with you today I don't want to mislead you on this one. If the draft resolution will be introduced with address to Soviet Union and United States to take urgent necessary measures—

K: Anatoly, I am having a call from the President. Will you call me back? Just give me a general idea of what it is.

D: He has instructions to go and vote even for sending troops to that area and for your troops.

K: We won't agree to that.

D: I am just telling you what we received.

AMBASSADOR DOBRYNIN–KISSINGER

Wednesday, October 24, 1973
7:15 P.M.

K: Anatoly, I was talking to the President. As I understand it, Malik has instructions to vote for the resolution if we go along with it, even to send troops. We won't go along with it.

D: If a draft resolution will be introduced which will contain the appeal towards the Soviet Union and the United States—

K: If the Egyptians introduce it.

D: —to take urgent necessary measures, including our sending over military contingents to insure the fulfillment of the resolution of the Security Council about cease-fire, then he is instructed to vote for such a resolution.

K: We will vote against it.

D: I would like you to know—when I talked to you I was wrong.

K: I think we should both discourage such a resolution.

D: He has already received instructions. I think it only fair for me to tell you, because of our discussions this afternoon.

K: Well, we will vote against it [that is, execute the American veto].

AMBASSADOR SCALI–KISSINGER

Wednesday, October 24, 1973
7:25 P.M.

. . .

K: I wanted to tell you something. I've just been told by Dobrynin that the Soviet instructions are that if somebody introduces a resolution calling on the United States and the Soviet Union to take urgent measures to enforce the cease-fire, including sending of military contingents, Malik is to vote for it. Your instructions are to vote against it.

S: I understand.

K: Veto it, and make a very strong speech on that. And we could try to get some others to veto it too, the British—

S: —The Secretary General will speak; Israel will speak; Guinea will speak and ask for an hour's delay and ask for the Nonaligned countries to come up with a resolution which would a) condemn Israel, and b) call for peace forces from smaller countries to back up the observers. Some of the smaller countries already have told the U.N. they have such peace forces allocated.

K: We can't condemn Israel, can we?

S: Of course not.

K: We will veto the condemnation of Israel and vote for the peace forces.

S: We will vote for the peace forces? I would think we would have to. However, as I understand it, Henry, from what McIntyre told me, we will have time during the one-hour delay.

K: We are not for peace forces. We favor strong augmentation of UNTSO [United Nations Truce Supervision Organization, the U.N. observers along the Suez Canal before the war], not in favor of military forces.

S: I understand that, but what if we are confronted with a resolution?

K: Veto it.

S: a) condemn Israel, b) peace forces—told the Soviets to go ahead and veto it. I wanted to tell you that Huang Hua [China's U.N. Ambassador] told me to pass on to you that the next time they get a resolution like we confronted them with, with no opportunity to consider it, they will veto it.

K: That's all right.

S: He [was] very anxious to know how we stood on sending Soviet forces.

K: Tell him we are violently opposed.

S: —most we would consider, sending limited number of additional observers.

　. . .

AMBASSADOR DOBRYNIN–KISSINGER
Wednesday, October 24, 1973
7:25 P.M.

K: I have been talking to the President and we really want to urge you not to push matters to an extreme because we will veto any resolution that calls for sending over any military forces. What we need is more observers.

D: Because, as I mentioned to you when I was in Moscow, it was completely out of the question to send any troops. Now they [Soviet leaders] have become so angry they want troops.

K: Why through us? What was achieved?

D: You allowed the Israelis to do what they wanted.

K: When this first operation started, I pleaded with you to get people to return from the lines and it took a week [to get the Soviet response].

D: It was already agreed upon by you and Brezhnev—

K: Be that as it may, if you want confrontation, we will have to have one. It would be a pity.

D: You know we don't want to have a confrontation.

K: It is inevitable that there will be mutual charges in the first

twenty-four hours of a cease-fire. We introduced two joint resolutions—

D: I will send this but I am sure this was what he [Malik] received—
I will send it right away but I am sure they [the Politburo] discussed it and put the instruction this way. I just didn't want you
to think—

K: But you have sufficient influence on the noncommitted to prevent this resolution from being put forward.

D: It is a guessing game. Maybe they already mentioned it to
Moscow.

K: We are going to veto and it would be a pity to be in a confrontation.

D: I will mention this and get in touch.

LORD CROMER–KISSINGER

Wednesday, October 24, 1973
7:28 P.M.

K: I have been informed the Soviets have instructions to vote for
a resolution, introduced by someone else, for the introduction
of peacekeeping forces into the Middle East, including Soviet
and American ones. I wanted you to know we are totally opposed. We will veto it. There are enough military forces running
around there now.

C: You are so right.

K: We would hope very much if you would join us in a veto—

C: Do you know who is introducing the resolution?

K: It is our impression it is the noncommitted. They are putting it
on. We believe the Chinese will veto it also.

C: We will get to that right away.

General Scowcroft–Kissinger

Wednesday, October 24, 1973
7:30 P.M.

K: . . . We want the Chinese to know we are going to veto it and are against the introduction of any military forces, not only American. Even if they are not American and Soviet they will be under Soviet influence. Tell them you are calling [the Chinese mission] because you have a direct line and I don't. We are in favor of augmentation of observers. Will you make sure of that?

S: Yes, I will call them right now.

Ambassador Dinitz–Kissinger

Wednesday, October 24, 1973
7:35 P.M.

K: Mr. Ambassador, I called to let you know we have just been informed that the Soviets will endorse a resolution which calls for introduction of peacekeeping military forces, committing American and Soviet Union— 1) We will veto any condemning of Israel, 2) we will veto any military peacekeeping forces, and 3) we will certainly veto any introduction of American forces. What I must have of you is your complete circumspection of this military operation. I wanted to inform you what we are doing and I assume you are doing.

D: I appreciate it.

K: Will you inform Israel?

D: I talked to the Prime Minister about a half hour ago and she asked me if she could go to sleep.

K: Just keep her informed.

GENERAL HAIG–KISSINGER

Wednesday, October 24, 1973
7:50 P.M.

K: I wanted to bring you up-to-date on what is happening. The Soviets are taking a nasty turn. They realize they were taken. They now are telling us they are approving a resolution introduced by the noncommitted members which 1) condemns Israel for violation of the cease-fire and 2) asked for introduction of military peacekeeping contingents, including Soviet and U.S. troops— I told Dobrynin this is mischievous and outrageous. We will condemn both sides— We are totally opposed to the introduction of any military forces.

H: Is it going that far?

K: We may have to take them on.

H: We knew this wouldn't be easy.

K: I think we have to be tough as nails now.

H: Sure we do. Absolutely.

K: Of course, if the Israelis had just stopped yesterday, we would be that much better off.

H: I have the President calling me.

AMBASSADOR DOBRYNIN–KISSINGER

Wednesday, October 24, 1973
8:02 P.M.

K: I am calling you again at the request of the President.

D: What is it now?

K: It is to urge you to avoid the confrontation between us and the U.N.—

D: I spoke with Malik at 6:30. The hall was full of people and there were discussions but he didn't know what the Council had prepared. They were discussing the Third World.

K: Our information is, there is no fighting going on now.

D: What is the actual situation now? Is it easy for you to check it. Is anybody introducing the resolution?

K: Let me check with Scali.

D: Let me know what the exact situation is and I will send a telegram.

K: Good.

Ambassador Dobrynin–Kissinger

Wednesday, October 24, 1973
8:25 P.M.

D: He [Malik] said that he asked U.S. and Soviet Union to send their forces. He is already making a speech. It is on UPI 304. Just because—

K: I would still urge you to show great restraint. It is not yet a resolution.

D: I am only saying what he said in the Security Council.

K: It would be that from the closest cooperation we turn to a very dangerous course.

D: I am only telling you.

K: Okay.

Ambassador Scali–Kissinger

Wednesday, October 24, 1973
8:52 P.M.

S: He [Malik] stopped short of attacking us directly—he just lambasted Israel and then he said, as far as the Sadat request goes, it would be entirely justified and in accordance with the charter. But he didn't say flatly he would buy it. He did call for everybody to break diplomatic relations and support sanctions against Israel. He noted that you had been to Tel Aviv and had great responsibility. He believes that the U.S. is in a position to force Israel to do what it wants it to do. Said Israel is ignoring the U.N. resolutions.

K: What are you going to do?

S: Let me finish one other point. He deplored the makeup of the observer corps and implied that it should be sent there but didn't say so directly. I have a speech which I can make.

K: I would not reject something that hasn't been proposed.

S: El-Zayyat formally asked us in the Council.

K: You had better give that speech.

S: Sadat says he wants the "great powers to interfere and move their forces in there."

An hour later, the looming confrontation in the Security Council escalated into a direct U.S.-Soviet confrontation when Dobrynin dictated a letter from Brezhnev to President Nixon.

The operative parts of Brezhnev's letter read:

> . . . Let us together, the USSR and the United States, urgently dispatch to Egypt the Soviet and American military contingents, to insure the implementation of the decision of the Security Council of October 22 and 23 concerning the cessation of fire and of all military activities and also of our understanding with you on the guarantee of the implementation of the decisions of the Security Council.
>
> It is necessary to adhere without delay. I will say it straight that if you find it impossible to act jointly with us in this matter, we should be faced with the necessity urgently to consider the question of taking appropriate steps unilaterally. We cannot allow arbitrariness on the part of Israel. . . .

It was one of the most serious challenges to an American President by a Soviet leader, from its peremptory salutation, "Mr. President," to its equally peremptory conclusion demanding an "immediate and clear reply." In between, it proposed that American and Soviet military forces impose not just a cease-fire but a final settlement on terms that were not specified but that had been repeatedly spelled out by Moscow during the year and had just as often been rejected by us. And it threatened to send troops unilaterally if we refused. The fact that it was dispatched from Moscow at 4:00 A.M. Moscow time showed how frayed nerves were at the Moscow end.

GENERAL HAIG–KISSINGER

Wednesday, October 24, 1973
9:50 P.M.

K: I just had a letter from Brezhnev asking us to send forces in together or he would send them in alone.

H: I was afraid of that.

K: I think we have to go to the mat on this one.

H: This is a reaction to your tough response?

K: No, we just said we would veto any U.N. resolution. What they said is, they would join if someone else proposed it.

H: Where are the Israelis at this point?

K: They've got the Third Army surrounded.

H: I think they're playing chicken. They're not going to put in forces at the end of the war. I don't believe that.

K: I don't know— What's going to keep them from flying paratroopers in?

H: Just think of what it will do for them. Of course, their argument is that Israel is not complying.

K: I think the Israelis should offer to back up. That is dangerous, for they might insist they back up beyond the point where they were.

H: We don't expect the Israelis to take that sort of thing. Do the Israelis know? I mean, have you brought them along?

K: I've kept them informed. Should I wake up the President?

H: No.

AMBASSADOR DINITZ–KISSINGER

Wednesday, October 24, 1973
10:00 P.M.

K: —joint resolution by the Soviet Union and the United States that we would put forces in jointly or they would go in unilaterally to stop the fighting. We obviously will not agree to join—

D: What do they have in mind?

K: They claim all they want is to get the fighting stopped.

D: I have two items to bring to your attention. I just got information that in the city of Suez a unit of our paratroopers has been under constant fire for several hours. It has been trapped and attacked by heavy guns and fire for several hours by their commando unit. We have to rescue these units or they will be slaughtered. What we intend to do is have air assistance given to them so they can break out of the trap.

K: All right. If the Soviets have decided to go in, I just think we turned the wheel yesterday one screw too much.

D: We won't go into it again.

K: Let's look at the tactics of this. We have to offer them something, which puts them totally in the wrong— I want to know if you can agree to return to the position you occupied before it all started.

D: How can this be done! I can inform the Prime Minister if you want me to, but I will tell you in advance—

K: I don't have time for this—

D: The Soviets will put forces to fight us?

K: That is not impossible. In fact, I think that is what they will do. I will read the letter to you as soon as I have it transcribed. The Soviets say if we don't put forces in jointly, they will go in unilaterally.

D: Contingents to peace or contingents to fight?

K: They are talking about peace—

D: I am just a representative of a very small country.

K: Look, I have no time for this! You have to check— They said either we will do it jointly with them or they will put in forces unilaterally. If there is nothing you can do, I will accept that too. What should we reply, as far as you are concerned?

D: I will put that to the Prime Minister.

Ambassador Dobrynin–Kissinger

Wednesday, October 24, 1973
10:15 P.M.

K: We are assembling our people to consider your letter. I just wanted you to know if any unilateral action is taken before we have had a chance to reply that will be very serious.

D: Yes, all right.

K: This is a matter of great concern. Don't you pressure us. I want to repeat again, don't pressure us!

D: All right.

General Haig–Kissinger

Wednesday, October 24, 1973
10:20 P.M.

H: —the WSAG.

K: The principals, the WSAG now practically is the principals.

H: Have you talked to the President?

K: No, I haven't. He would just start charging around—until we have it analyzed.

H: It seems to me if the Soviets have acted in good faith, in your judgment, and if this would quiet it down, it is not going—and if it would be necessary to put a joint force in there, I am not so sure it is totally tragic in the— I think they caused it to have a Soviet force in alone.

K: Right now it would be an absolute storm in the U.S., a storm in Europe and eventually operate against the Israelis. In other words, they would have to attack us to get at them. I would rather put our force in after they put theirs in.

H: There could be commitments, discussions, and willingness. What we don't want is to have them go in. I am afraid there would be some fighting and then we have a problem.

K: What do you mean?

H: Between the Soviets and Israelis. Isn't there some way of deciding the modality? If we go back, tough, we have to be prepared to be really tough—

K: You cannot be sure how much of this is due to our domestic crisis.

H: I think we owe a lot to that.

K: I don't think they would have taken on a functioning President.

H: They wouldn't. The only way we could do this is if it is necessary to put something in there—convince the leadership in the morning to work out [the] modality in the meantime. If the peacekeeping forces that I cannot think— It even brings us together, even more than the resolution.

K: It would wreak havoc with the Chinese and the Europeans. The bastards may have originally had this in mind as a way of getting in there— We sent him [the U.S. military attaché] to the front today—

H: The Israelis were very, very believable, from what I heard from them today.

K: That is what I believe.

H: But if they have lied to us—

K: Yesterday they trapped the Third Army. That army is probably starving to death right now.

H: They are all on the east bank and have no supplies, I presume.

K: There was one road also, which Israel cut.

H: That is not that big an area—that they cannot handle that. To let that unit survive and get the hell out of there if it has to. In any event the key point is questionable. You can work a peacekeeping force—

K: Jackson has already called this afternoon protesting violently.

H: Any conception of that?

K: Yes.

H: How did he know that?

K: It leaked out of one of my meetings.

H: On top of our other problem it could be the end—or the beginning.

K: Don't forget that is what the Soviets are playing on. They find a cripple facing impeachment and why shouldn't they go in there.

H: If they do and start fighting, that is the serious thing. They go in there and that— They genuinely believe [the] Israelis are— I am sure the Soviets are on the ground all over the place.

K: Sure, they have their intelligence.

H: It is really a question of [the] Israelis leveling with us and if they say—

K: The Israelis yesterday grabbed a hunk of territory and cut the last supply line for— Today the Third Army has been trying to cut its way out and has failed. That is the problem.

H: Okay.

K: I don't believe that the Israelis started it.

H: I don't after Dinitz—

K: That was the issue. If the Russians had wanted to play fair, they could have had the Israelis return to the original line rather—

H: It seems the Israelis must have—

K: I told Dinitz to come up with some offer we can make. It will be hard as he will have to justify it. I don't think we should bother the President.

H: Are you meeting at the White House or—?

K: The State Department.

H: He has to be a part of everything you are doing.

K: Should I get him up?

H: I wish you would hold it at the White House.

K: All right.

Nixon recounted in his memoirs:

> When Haig informed me about this message, I said that he and Kissinger should have a meeting at the White House to formulate plans for a firm reaction to what amounted to a scarcely veiled threat of unilateral Soviet intervention. Words were not making our point—we needed action, even the shock of a military alert.

The proposed meeting started in the White House Situation Room, in the basement of the West Wing, with me in the chair, at 10:40 P.M. It went on with various interruptions until 2:00 A.M. early Thursday, October 25. Present were Secretary Schlesinger, Director of Central Intelligence William Colby; Chairman of the Joint Chiefs Admiral Moorer; presidential chief of staff Alexander Haig; Deputy Assistant to the President for National Security Affairs General Brent Scowcroft; Commander Jonathan T. Howe, my military assistant at the NSC; and me.

Brezhnev's proposal of a joint U.S.-Soviet force was unthinkable. If we agreed to a joint role with the Soviet Union, its troops would reenter Egypt with our blessing. Either we would be the tail to the Soviet kite in a joint power play against Israel, or we would end up clashing with Soviet forces in a country that was bound to share Soviet objectives regarding the cease-fire or could not afford to be perceived as opposing them.

But the impact would go far beyond Egypt. If Soviet forces appeared dramatically in Cairo with those of the United States—and even more if they appeared alone—our traditional friends among Arab moderates would be profoundly unnerved by the evident fact of U.S.-Soviet condominium. The strategy we had laboriously pursued in four years of diplomacy and two weeks of crisis would disintegrate: Egypt would be drawn back into the Soviet orbit, the Soviet Union and its radical allies would emerge as the dominant factor in the Middle East, China and Europe would be dismayed by the appearance of U.S.-Soviet military collaboration in so vital a region. If the joint effort collapsed and turned into a U.S.-Soviet crisis—as was probable—we would be alone.

There was no question in my mind that we would have to reject the Soviet proposal. And we would have to do so in a manner that shocked the Soviets into abandoning the unilateral move they were threatening—and, from all our information, planning. For we had tangible reasons to take the threat seriously. The CIA reported that the Soviet airlift to the Middle East had stopped early on the 24th, even though ours was continuing; the ominous implication was that the aircraft were being assembled to carry some of the airborne divisions whose increased alert status had also been noted. East German forces were also at increased readiness. The number of Soviet ships in the Mediterranean had grown to eighty-five—an all-time high. (It later reached more than one hundred.) We discovered the next day that a Soviet flotilla of twelve ships, including two amphibious vessels, was heading for Alexandria.

I began the meeting with a detailed briefing. There had been no particular cause for alarm for most of the day. In fact, matters had seemed to be calming down when suddenly, at about 7:00 P.M. our time (or 2:00 A.M. Moscow time), the Soviets decided at first to support and then to insist on the introduction of a joint U.S.-Soviet military force into the Middle East. I said that, in my view, joining the Soviets would be "a mug's game" for us, with devastating consequences to our relations in the Middle East, China, and Europe—all fearful, for various reasons, of a U.S.-Soviet condominium. There were three possibilities: (1) The Soviets had intended this move all along and had invited me to Moscow to gain time for it; (2) they decided on it as the consequences of the Arab defeat began to sink in; or (3) they felt tricked by Israel and by us as the Israelis moved to strangle the Third Army after the cease-fire. I thought that the likely motivation was a combination of 2 and 3.

This was preliminary to one of the more thoughtful discussions that I attended in my government service. The participants weighed Soviet actions, motivations, and intentions. During the night, the consensus emerged that the Kremlin was on the verge of a major decision. We expected the airlift to start at dawn in Eastern Europe, about two hours away. At 11:00 P.M., I interrupted the meeting to see Dinitz in the deserted lobby of the West Wing of the White House. I repeated to him that we would reject the Soviet proposal out of hand; only the tactics remained to be decided. We still were eager to hear Israeli views on this.

When I returned to the Situation Room, agreement was quickly reached to test whether we could slow down the Soviets' timetable by drawing them into talks. This suggested an American reply conciliatory in tone but strong in substance. There was consensus too that this would have no impact unless we backed it up with some noticeable action that conveyed our determination to resist unilateral moves. Ideally our response should be noted in Moscow *before* our written reply reached there. We therefore interrupted the drafting of a reply to Brezhnev for a discussion of various readiness measures.

American forces are normally in various states of alert called DefCons (for Defense Condition), in descending order from DefCon I to DefCon V. DefCon I is war. DefCon II is a condition in which attack is imminent. DefCon III increases readiness without the determination that war is likely; it is in practice the highest stage of readiness for essentially peacetime conditions. Most of our forces were normally at DefCon IV or V except for those in the Pacific, where as a legacy of the Vietnam War, they were in 1973 permanently in DefCon III. The Strategic Air Command was usually at DefCon IV.

We all agreed that any increase in readiness would have to go at least to DefCon III before the Soviets would notice it. Even then, they might not recognize the significance of the change rapidly enough to affect their diplomacy. We agreed to discuss additional alert measures not foreseen in DefCon III. In the meantime, Admiral Moorer—at 11:41 P.M.—issued orders to all military commands to increase readiness to DefCon III.

At 11:25 P.M. Dinitz brought an Israeli proposal on how to deal with the Soviet overture. It was in effect to offer a variant of the Israeli disengagement proposal of 1971: Israeli forces would withdraw to the east bank of the Suez Canal, Egyptian forces would withdraw to the west bank in a territorial swap; a demilitarized strip of ten kilometers would then be created on each side of the Canal. It was an impossible scheme. Sadat would consider it an insult to be asked to vacate Egyptian territory. Nor could he end the war by withdrawing ten kilometers from where he had started it. And it was too complicated to negotiate in time to head off a Soviet intervention if indeed one was imminent. It might even accelerate the move if Sadat was sufficiently infuriated by it to *insist* on great-power participation. I told Dinitz that I would discuss the proposal with my colleagues but that I knew it would not work. In the event, we were too preoccupied with forestalling the Soviet move to take up the Israeli scheme.

Our next decision was to seek to close off Moscow's diplomatic options by inducing Cairo to withdraw its invitation to the Soviets to send in troops. At 11:55 P.M., the meeting approved a message to Sadat in Nixon's name reiterating our previous rejection of a joint U.S.-Soviet force. In its operative paragraph, the message warned that should Soviet forces appear, we would have to resist them on Egyptian soil. At the very least, in these circumstances my planned trip to Cairo to start the peace process would have to be canceled:

> I ask you to consider the consequences for your country if the two great nuclear countries were thus to confront each other on your soil. I ask you further to consider the impossibility for us undertaking the diplomatic initiative which was to start with Dr. Kissinger's visit to Cairo on November 7 if the forces of one of the great nuclear powers were to be involved militarily on Egyptian soil.

Immediately after we instituted DefCon III, I asked Scowcroft to leave the meeting to call Dobrynin with the following instructions:

> [T]ell him to desist from all actions until we have a reply. Tell him you are not empowered to give any reply. I am in a meeting and can't be pulled out. There should be no unilateral actions and if they are taken it would have the most serious consequences. If he says anything, you can say you have instructions not to comment. They may as well know that we mean business.

But two could play chicken. Dobrynin made no comment except that he would transmit our message to Moscow. No reassurance; no claim of having been misunderstood; no suggestion that at midnight we all go to bed and resume our discussions in the morning because there was no intended threat. Only the laconic comment that he would stand by for our reply.

If Dobrynin's pose was designed to heighten our sense of menace, it succeeded admirably. Our conviction that we were facing an imminent Soviet move was hardly diminished when we learned during the evening that eight Soviet An-22 transport planes—each capable of carrying two hundred or more troops—were slated to fly from Budapest to Egypt in the next few hours. And we discovered too that elements of the East German armed forces had been put on alert effective at 5:00 A.M. Washington time, or five hours away. We estimated that the Soviets could lift five thousand troops a day into Egypt. We decided that going to DefCon III would not be noted quickly enough by Soviet decision-makers. Something more was necessary. At 12:20 A.M., we alerted the 82nd Airborne Division for possible movement. At 12:25 A.M., we ordered the aircraft carrier *Franklin Delano Roosevelt*—now off Italy—to move rapidly to the eastern Mediterranean to join the carrier *Independence* south of Crete. The carrier *John F. Kennedy* and its accompanying task force were ordered to move at full speed from the Atlantic to the Mediterranean.

At 12:30 A.M., we returned to drafting the formal reply to Brezhnev. We decided to deliver it around 5:30 in the morning Washington time. Insofar as the Soviet decision to intervene depended on our message, it gave us additional time to complete our preparations. And by then the Soviets would notice our troop movements. At 1:03 A.M., I informed Ambassador Cromer of our various alert measures and of the letter from Brezhnev. I told him that we would formally brief the North Atlantic Council, the permanent body of ambassadors assigned to NATO headquarters in Brussels, an hour after delivering our reply to the Soviets, or about noon Brussels time. We hoped that Britain would support us in the North Atlantic Council as well as in other capitals.

At 1:35 A.M., Dinitz reappeared. He urged on behalf of the Prime Minister that we not ask Israel to pull back to the line it occupied at the time the original cease-fire went into effect (on October 22). I assured him that we had no intention of coercing Israel in response to a Soviet threat.

At 1:45 A.M., Scowcroft, at my request, called Dobrynin again with the same message as before, adding only that we had still several more hours of deliberation ahead of us. Dobrynin could infer from my refusal to talk to him that we were in no mood for negotiations. Once again he replied that he would report, offered no reassurance, and said that he would stand by. Concurrently, we notified the commander of our forces in Europe that he was to delay the scheduled return to the United States of troops participating in an annual NATO exercise designed to test our ability to reinforce Europe rapidly.

At 5:40 A.M., the reply to Brezhnev was delivered to Dobrynin in Nixon's name. It rejected all Soviet demands. We sent it by messenger, avoiding any softening via an explanation. The letter offered American approval of—and willingness to participate in—an expanded U.N. truce supervisory force composed of noncombat personnel on a temporary basis whose sole task would be to provide "adequate information concerning compliance by both sides with the terms of the cease-fire." Our reply added:

> You must know, however, that we could in no event accept unilateral action. This would be in violation of our understandings, of the agreed Principles we signed in Moscow in 1972 and of Article II of the Agreement on Prevention of Nuclear War. As I stated above, such action would produce incalculable consequences which would be in the interest of neither of our countries and which would end all we have striven so hard to achieve.

At 8:00 A.M. on October 25, we received the first indication that we had faced down the Soviets. It became apparent that Sadat was betting on the United States, not the Soviet Union. For two messages from Egypt were waiting for me at my White House office (in my capacity as National Security Adviser).

Showing a degree of care appropriate to the seriousness of the situation, the Egyptians had numbered them sequentially to help us follow the evolution of their thinking. Message number one was Ismail's answer to my account (midday on October 24) of the efforts we had made to secure Israeli compliance with the cease-fire. Despite the plight of the Third Army—to which he proudly did not refer—Ismail expressed his appreciation for our offer of help. He did not consider the sending of American military attachés adequate; he maintained that a combined U.S.-Soviet force was the best guarantee. However, "since the U.S. refuses to take such a measure, Egypt is asking the Security Council to provide an *international* force" (emphasis added). This meant that Egypt was withdrawing the request that had produced the crisis. And it was substituting a proposal for an "international force," which by United Nations practice *excluded* forces from the five permanent members of the Security Council and therefore the U.S.-Soviet force urged by Brezhnev.

This was made explicit in message number two from Sadat to Nixon. It agreed with not only the substance but also the reasoning of the message sent in Nixon's name the previous night:

> I understand the considerations you have put forward with respect to the use of a joint US-USSR force, and we have already asked the Security Council for the speedy dispatch of an international force to the area to review the implementation of the Security Council Resolutions. This we hope will pave the way toward further measures as envisaged in the October 22 Resolution of the Security Council aimed at establishing a just peace in the area.

We were on the verge of winning the diplomatic game. Without Egyptian support, it was very unlikely that there could be a U.N. resolution calling for a U.S.-Soviet force. If the Soviets sent troops, it would be unilaterally, without the sanction of either the host country or the United Nations. This would be much easier for us to resist, and we were determined to do so. It showed—though we could only guess this at the moment—that Sadat was staking his future on American diplomatic support rather than Soviet military pressure.

The second hopeful sign was an early morning report from John Scali at the United Nations. After his strong opposition to a joint U.S.-Soviet force the previous evening, enthusiasm for the idea had cooled noticeably. The Security Council was rarely prepared to vote against the determined opposition of one of the superpowers if it was given any alternative. And it can be ingenious in finding alternatives. The Nonaligned, faced with a United States veto, had early on October 25 tabled a draft resolution asking the Secretary General to increase the number of U.N. observers and "to set up immediately a United Nations Emergency Force under [Security Council] authority." Though vaguely phrased, the draft resolution would open the way to excluding the superpowers from the Emergency Force. The Council was to meet at 10:30 A.M. to consider the draft.

Later in the morning, we received the British reaction to Brezhnev's letter—which was the same as ours. Cromer informed us that "they [London] certainly take Brezhnev's message just the same as you do." The British Ambassador to Moscow had been asked to make urgent representations to Brezhnev to warn against unilateral military action.

It was thus in a hopeful, if still tense, mood that Haig and I briefed Nixon shortly after 8:00 A.M. that Thursday, October 25. During the night Haig had repeatedly left the N.S.C. meeting presumably to have liaison with Nixon. I now reviewed the diplomatic and military moves of the night before. As always in crises, Nixon was clearheaded and crisp. We agreed that it would be unprecedented—and hence a major challenge—if the Soviet Union put organized combat units into an area far from its periphery and against the will of the local government. Despite the War Powers Act passed a few days earlier, Nixon was determined to match any Soviet troop

buildup in the area and leave it to Congress to terminate his move—
as the new law made possible.

After the meeting with Nixon, a presidential reply to Sadat was
dispatched. It welcomed Sadat's "statesmanlike approach to the issue
of peacekeeping" and indicated American support for an international force excluding the permanent members of the Security
Council.

From 8:40 to 10:00 A.M., Nixon and I briefed congressional leaders about the night's events. They were at once supportive, rudder-
less, and ambivalent. They approved the alert; they were enthusiastic
about our refusal to accept a joint U.S.-Soviet force. But their support reflected more the Vietnam-era isolationism than a strategic assessment. They opposed a joint U.S.-Soviet force because they
wanted no American troops sent abroad; the *American* component of
the proposed force bothered them a great deal more than the Soviet
one. By the same token, they would object to the dispatch of American forces even if, in our view, they were needed to resist a unilateral
Soviet move. The spirit of cooperation thus cooled noticeably when
Nixon outlined our determination to match a unilateral Soviet troop
presence with an American one either in Israel or in friendly Arab
countries. Several of the congressional leaders expressed the gravest
reservations. And while they did not go so far as to indicate outright
opposition, they made it clear enough that support for the alert
should not be interpreted as endorsing the movement of troops.

At noon, I held a press conference in which I reiterated our
heretofore private position publicly:

> The United States does not favor and will not approve the
> sending of a joint Soviet–United States force into the Middle East.
> The United States believes that what is needed in the Middle East,
> above all, is a determination of the facts, a determination where the
> lines are, and a determination of who is doing the shooting, so that
> the Security Council can take appropriate action. It is inconceivable

that the forces of the great powers should be introduced in the numbers that would be necessary to overpower both of the participants. It is inconceivable that we should transplant the great-power rivalry into the Middle East or, alternatively, that we should impose a military condominium by the United States and the Soviet Union. The United States is even more opposed to the unilateral introduction by any great power, especially by any nuclear power, of military forces into the Middle East in whatever guise those forces should be introduced.

The alert was immediately engulfed in the cynicism spawned by Watergate. Two kinds of questions were put forward: whether Soviet actions had been caused by our domestic disputes; and its opposite, whether we had generated the crisis for domestic rather than foreign policy reasons—whether, in the unsubtle question of one journalist, our actions had indeed been "rational." The query about Soviet motives gave me an opportunity to stress my Watergate nightmare: "One cannot have a crisis of authority in a society for a period of months without paying a price somewhere along the line."

The queries as to America's motives showed how narrow was our margin for policy. If we courted confrontation, following the advice of the anti-détente zealots, we would almost surely be undermined by the Watergate-obsessed who would treat every challenge to the Soviet Union as a maneuver by which their hated quarry, Nixon, was trying to escape them. To broaden our maneuvering room, I replied rather heatedly:

> We are attempting to conduct the foreign policy of the United States with regard for what we owe not just to the electorate but to future generations. And it is a symptom of what is happening to our country that it could even be suggested that the United States would alert its forces for domestic reasons.

And in reply to another question:

We are attempting to preserve the peace in very difficult circumstances. It is up to you ladies and gentlemen to determine
whether this is the moment to try to create a crisis of confidence in
the field of foreign policy as well. . . .

There has to be a minimum of confidence that the senior officials of the American government are not playing with the lives of
the American people.

By the time the press conference was over, a call from Waldheim
informed us that the crisis was over. The Egyptian resolution about
introducing U.S. and Soviet forces had been dropped. On the table
was a Nonaligned resolution for an observer force excluding the permanent members of the Security Council. Diplomacy would now
focus on the composition of the force and its size.

SECRETARY GENERAL WALDHEIM–KISSINGER

Thursday, October 25, 1973
1:18 P.M.

W: I am very grateful for [your] returning the call. I have, of course,
spoken to Joe Sisco and informed him, but I wanted to keep you
informed of the situation here. The situation is that, as you
know, the Russians got instructions to accept the new American
amendment. Only the French position is reluctant. The French
Ambassador was just here and he said they would ask for a separate vote on the amendment—excludes the permanent members. They will vote for the resolution, but ask for [a] separate
vote on the amendment in order to show they are not in agreement with this.

K: You are in no doubt, Mr. Secretary General, that we will veto any
resolution which doesn't have it in it?

W: Yes, I was informed of this by Joe Sisco.

K: We will not compromise on this.

W: Yes, that is understood. No problem. Any more, Nonaligned—change and the Russians, only the French want a separate vote.

K: Well, that's their privilege.

W: But, after that, the French will vote for the resolution as it stands.

K: Excellent. There is one thing that concerns me, Mr. Secretary General. We are fundamentally opposed to the introduction of any East European contingents, any Communist countries. There must be enough neutrals in the world to do it. If there were Eastern European countries, it would produce a crisis of confidence here, if any contingents from Communist countries were included.

W: Well, there is a strong trend to have in addition to the Nordic countries one African, one Asian like Malaysia, African like Nigeria.

K: Well, we have no objection to that as long as it isn't an East European country.

W: There is an idea of including Poland.

K: We think it's a great concession to permit Sweden.

W: How is it with the Russians?

K: —can't accept any Eastern Europeans.

W: Could lead to situation where we would have a problem with Canada.

K: Canada?

W: Yes, because of NATO.

K: That's all right with us.

W: Neutral countries.

K: We will trade Canada. Also won't accept Yugoslavia.

W: There was no question of taking them— But I take note of your information and I hope we can proceed on that line.

K: Mr. Secretary General, when this is all over, and I hope it will be soon, you and I must have a drink together and reminisce.

. . .

At 2:40 P.M., Dobrynin made it official that the confrontation was over by a letter to Nixon from Brezhnev.

AMBASSADOR DOBRYNIN–KISSINGER

Thursday, October 25, 1973
2:40 P.M.

K: Anatoly?

D: Hello, Henry. I would like to read to you a letter from Brezhnev to the President and then I will send you. Have it now in writing, I mean handwriting.

K: Is it going to calm me down or make me go into orbit again?

D: No, not orbit— Prefer to stay in orbit quietly. "I have received your letter in which you alleged once again the Israelis have cease[d] firing—contradictory to the facts we have received in Moscow—Israel was bombing the city of Ismail, and fighting was continuing in the straits of [unclear], which has until this moment not been a scene of military action— President of Egypt, Mr. Sadat, in which addressed— We have already dispatched, on October 25, Soviet—which counted seventy persons at the Egyptian-Israeli front, of observers of—Security Council decision. Since you are ready now, as we understand it, to send to Egypt a group of American observers, we agree to it jointly in this question. Soviet group of observers instructed to get into contact immediately in a businesslike operation with the U.S. group of observers, with the American group as soon as they arrive in Egypt, and without delay and discharging their tasks—in the situation without delay. We are ready to cooperate with the American side in taking other measures which will be dictated by the situation, to insure immediate—implementation of the Security Council resolution of the 22nd and 23rd of October— Following dispatch of observers, we, in an urgent memo, will continue also other political measures and corresponding to decision of the Security Council and—to the understanding in

Moscow with Kissinger, who conducted negotiations on your behalf, on part of U.S. really effective steps will be taken to guarantee implementation by Israel of decisions of the Security Council about what you, Mr. President, write in your letter. Respectfully, Brezhnev." That's all.

K: Okay, Anatoly. Did you hear my press conference?

D: Of course, I hear, Henry. I couldn't miss you. I see on television.

K: I tried to be gentle with you, so—

D: Yes, so I noticed, from yesterday 4:00 in the morning.

K: Oh, no. At 4:00 in the morning I didn't try to be gentle. I thought you were threatening us. Don't— I take threats very badly. We will talk about it sometime.

D: No, isn't anything to discuss now—

K: Will you get it over to me at the White House, to Scowcroft?

D: To Scowcroft. Okay. We will type it up and send to him. Good. In the usual way.

K: Good.

AMBASSADOR DINITZ–KISSINGER

Thursday, October 25, 1973
5:35 P.M.

K: We have now had a reply from the Soviet Union. All they are doing is offering seventy men as individual observers. So we have managed to face them down again.

D: You are going to offer—

K: We are going to tell them we don't think it requires seventy.

D: Yes, I see. These observers will be strictly— We will have an observer force as well as a—force. The Russians will be coming in the framework of the observer force, and you are going to tell them they don't need to offer that many. Do you have any idea what was in the five planes that landed in Cairo today?

K: No.

D: Maybe the seventy observers have landed today.

K: Yes, that is my impression.

D: All right. I will pass it on. Our policy will be, the less of them that come the better.

K: That is exactly our policy too.

At 2:45 P.M., I thanked Schlesinger for his contribution to the successful outcome.

SECRETARY SCHLESINGER–KISSINGER

Thursday, October 25, 1973
2:45 P.M.

K: I think it is working.

S: You think you have won.

K: Yep. They have agreed to the Security Council resolution.

S: Have we heard back from them directly?

K: Yes, and it is conciliatory. Keep that quiet for the time being.

S: Good.

K: Otherwise it looks as if we ginned this thing up.

S: Okay. I am exploring with Tom [Admiral Moorer] and Bill [Clements] here. We have a worldwide DefCon and I think there are some places that we can relax now after this vote.

K: I think we should hold it until midnight.

S: We have the Alaskan Command which is sort of irrelevant to this thing and a few other places. I'm not talking about SAC [Strategic Air Command] or EUCOM [United States European Command].

K: Do not relax after the vote. It looks as if it is a pressure play.

S: Do it at midnight.

K: Start standing down at midnight and tomorrow let's talk at 8:00 in the morning. Do Alaska at midnight and we will talk in the morning and stand down the rest then.

S: Very good.

K: You all were great last night and this morning.

. . .

There was a little time for some self-congratulation and briefing of senators and journalists.

THE PRESIDENT–KISSINGER

Thursday, October 25, 1973
1:15 P.M.

K: Mr. President. Well, I got through this hour.

N: I didn't get to hear it, Henry. I'm sorry.

K: [Clark] Mollenhoff said was this [alert] a rational decision by the President? [I] said it was [a] combination of the advice of all of his advisers—that the President decided to do this. When it is all over, we will put the facts before you, and then the American people will judge for themselves. It's a sad commentary that in a national crisis such a question could even be asked. The Soviets are blinking, Mr. President—agreed to our draft of the Security Council resolution—

N: British are screwing it up.

[. . .]

K: When it's over—

N: If it's ever over—cease-fire isn't going to be one damned—send plane loaded.

K: Already screaming about—

N: Be sure they know we hold them responsible. If they embarrass us, by God—

GENERAL HAIG–KISSINGER

Thursday, October 25, 1973
2:35 P.M.

H: You did a hell of a job.

K: Was it all right?

H: Superb.

K: We have won. They have accepted the Security Council resolution without permanent members and we have just had a message from Brezhnev saying they are sending seventy observers to Cairo and they will be glad if we send seventy observers too.

H: Well, well, well. And the staredown, Henry.

K: And one move less and we would have had it.

H: I think you are exactly right.

. . .

THE PRESIDENT–KISSINGER

Thursday, October 25, 1973
3:05 P.M.

K: Mr. President, you have won again.

N: You think so?

K: The Soviets have joined our resolution at the U.N. barring permanent members after screaming like banshees and we have had a reply from Brezhnev.

N: What does it say?

K: It accepts your proposal and says he is sending seventy observers and we should send seventy observers also and that is it.

N: That is easy. We will send 170 if they want.

K: That is it. It is done.

N: You think it is?

K: Yes. We should stay on alert until midnight and start standing down in Alaska at midnight and so on.

N: How should we handle the press tomorrow?

K: I will be glad to step out in the Press Room tomorrow and explain it.

N: Not until tomorrow? Will the evening news carry the U.N. resolution?

K: They will carry it. I will explain it at the press conference. The @#$%xs are saying we did all of this for political purposes.

N: I know. Like Kalb [Marvin Kalb, CBS correspondent] and who else?

K: Kalb, McCarthy. Reston [James "Scotty" Reston, *New York Times* correspondent] called here with a similar question.

N: In other words we set this up.

K: At 4:00 in the morning.

N: And that we created a crisis. I hope you told him strongly.

K: I treated Kalb contemptible at the press conference.

N: What about Scotty [Reston]?

K: I gave him a few facts. I said what would you do if seven of eight airborne divisions were put on alert. I did not tell him about the Brezhnev letter.

N: Why does he think the President is up until 3:00 this morning?

K: I said, you think we staged all of this? He said no, but we had to give all of the information.

N: I thought you had.

K: I had, but I did not tell them about the Brezhnev letter and the air alert. We don't want to force him to hit you back. What you did was just another one of these moves.

N: Just as well I will not be doing the press conference. I am not in the mood to do it tonight.

K: Absolutely not. I think I would do it tomorrow or Monday.

N: I don't think I can wait until Monday.

K: Do it tomorrow night. I would treat the bastards with contempt, Mr. President. They asked me about Watergate. I said you cannot play with the central authority of the country without paying a price.

N: You are rather confident that this is going to do it.

K: Mr. President, you were prepared to put forces in . . . and that was way before you knew what was going to happen. I told Kalb that the President is attempting to conduct foreign policy of the U.S. regardless—that it would be suggested that the U.S. would alert its forces for domestic reasons—

N: Good. Al told me you slaughtered the bastards. Keep it up.

K: That is what I am here for.

N: Keep it up. We will survive.

K: No question.

THE PRESIDENT–KISSINGER

Thursday, October 25, 1973
3:13 P.M.

K: Mr. President.

N: Henry, will this be announced in time, that is, the U.N. resolution—has it been announced yet?

K: It has not been voted on yet.

N: Do you think it will be voted on?

K: Yes, in time for the evening news.

N: Yes.

K: No question.

N: I was thinking of going up to Camp David.

K: I think you can safely go now. The Soviets have agreed and it has
been announced.

N: You don't think you could go up too?

K: I, uh, uh—

N: No, I understand. You think there is no problem, then.

K: No problem. It would be normal for you to go up there. It is now
known by the press.

N: Don't you think you should call a few of those damnable leaders
[congressional leaders] and tell them?

K: I will do that now, Mr. President.

N: Good boy.

THE PRESIDENT–KISSINGER

Thursday, October 25, 1973
3:30 P.M.

K: Mr. President.

N: I think it would be well for semantics, no semantics, I mean, if
you could come over here, make an appearance, dash over to say
hello. You know, to sort of, what are you doing now?

K: I was having a staff meeting.

N: Well, what time will you be through?

K: About fifteen minutes. I can come over. I've got the Chinese coming in but I can shift them half an hour. I'll come over in about twenty minutes.

N: Well, I don't want to, you name the time. You could have them over here.

K: No, I'll be over in about twenty minutes.

N: Okay.

SENATOR MANSFIELD–KISSINGER

Thursday, October 25, 1973
4:45 P.M.

M: I hate to bother you so soon again—Senator [Robert] Griffin (R.-Mich.) came in to the office about an hour ago. He said he had been solicited by television to come over and make a statement. He decided he was not the proper one to do it and he came to me— Most unusual, coming from Griffin. Never done that before. He said I would be a better person to go explain I was supporting what's going on there, etc. I didn't want to do anything until I checked with you.

K: If you would do that it would be a very good thing to do. Let me bring you up-to-date. The Security Council voted forty to nothing, I mean fourteen to nothing, so the resolution has passed.

M: Did somebody abstain?

K: The Chinese.

M: Uh huh.

K: Also, and this is strictly for you and you cannot refer to this now. We had a note from the Soviets saying they accepted the proposal to send observers and they are sending seventy.

M: Seventy.

K: Yes, so the crisis is practically over. I mean, last evening they were talking about military intervention, and—

M: Yah. Well, if you think it would be useful, I will.

K: I would not yet say the crisis is over, wait a day to see how they interpret the resolution. You can say you are hopeful, you support it, if you felt you could say that—

. . .

THE PRESIDENT–KISSINGER
Thursday, October 25, 1973
7:15 P.M.

K: Hello, Mr. President.

N: I thought you should know that Mrs. Nixon and Tricia [Nixon's daughter] thought you did a hell of a job. They are pretty good critics.

K: Well, Mr. President, you rate the remarks.

N: I talked to Al and I want you to do this on a crash basis to follow up. This is the group I want you to fly down tomorrow from New York. [Names off the heads of CBS, NBC, ABC, the *New York Times* and the *Washington Post.*]

K: Right, Mr. President.

N: I think you can have an enormous influence on them. Their major concern is Israel. Who saved Israel? Would anybody else have saved it? You have to tell them that. And with the fact that if Albert [Speaker Carl Albert (D.-Okla.)—next in line for the presidency, since Agnew had resigned and Ford had not yet been named] had been faced with it— It has to be done on a crash basis.

K: One thing for sure, if we can't do it tomorrow, we can do it Monday. I will call them. We have completely dominated the news. They gave about fifteen minutes.

N: I understand there was over six minutes with regard to the fact that we faked this whole thing on CBS. That we made it all up. Do you remember the—Kalb and [Dan] Rather were both shocking.

K: I killed them with the answers.

N: Anyway, they used six minutes on that bad point, which plants in the public's mind that we made it all up. Ziegler has to make sure that that line doesn't get through. You know we were close to a nuclear confrontation this morning.

K: Mr. President, I have seen the CBS news and I think it was very good for us. They presented all the tough answers to these charges.

N: Do they point out the fact that the President—

K: No, as a leadership role.

N: They spent half an hour— Not individually. Get the whole bunch in a room and say you are American first, and members of the American Jewish community, and interested in Israel. Who is going to save Israel and who will save it in the future?

K: I will do my best to get it done tomorrow.

N: You did a hell of a job.

On Friday, October 26, Dobrynin and I sparred about the size of the U.S.–Soviet observer contingent. Finally, there was an agreement on contingents for U.S. and Soviet observers numbering thirty-six for each side. It was a needless effort, for Egypt promptly changed its mind about the desirability of any observers. Egypt's new Acting Foreign Minister, Ismail Fahmy, said in Cairo that Egypt neither wanted nor needed the observers. The Soviet ploy for a special U.S.-Soviet contingent never got off the ground, and the issue was buried in the diplomacy that followed.

During the course of the afternoon, Security Council Resolution 340 was passed. It reiterated the call for a return to the lines of the original cease-fire of October 22; we had succeeded in substituting the more neutral word "return" for the original word "withdraw." It established an international force comprised of U.N. members, excluding the great powers.

We had achieved three of our four principal objectives in the midst of the worst Constitutional crisis of the century: (1) we had helped assure the security of Israel, our ally; (2) we had faced down a threat of Soviet military intervention—though we remained sensitive not to offend Soviet *amour-propre;* and (3) we had maintained the option of improved relations with the Arab world.

But the fourth problem that had given rise to the crisis remained. The Egyptian Third Army was still trapped; it was not under assault but was slowly being starved into submission. The medical convoy we had been attempting to arrange for twenty-four hours had been stalled by the Israelis under one pretext or another at the outskirts of the city of Suez. Israel claimed that it was transferring medical supplies directly. We had no means of checking. At any rate, this too was designed to humiliate the Egyptians by emphasizing their dependence on the Israeli armed forces. It was not a circumstance that Sadat could accept indefinitely.

And he did not. Shortly after 9:30 A.M., Friday, October 25, Sadat sent an urgent message to Nixon charging that the Israelis were exploiting the situation "to establish themselves astride the lines of communication of the Third Egyptian Army in an attempt to isolate and oblige it to surrender" and that the Israelis continued to prevent U.N. personnel from reaching the area. Sadat threatened unilateral action to reopen the supply lines. He was also informing the Soviets, he told us. He went on to suggest that prolongation of the impasse would jeopardize the atmosphere for "constructive" talks with me. "I would like to inform you," he wrote, "that in preparation for this visit, we are working out comprehensive proposals which we hope will provide a turning point toward a final peace settlement."

We had supported Israel throughout the war for many historical, moral, and strategic reasons. And we had just run the risk of war with the Soviet Union, amidst the domestic crisis of Watergate. Nor would the destruction of an Egyptian army after the cease-fire have been in Israel's long-term interest. Maddened by the fact that they had been surprised, beside themselves with grief over the high casualties, deeply distrustful of Sadat, who had engineered their discomfiture, Israel's leaders wanted to end the war with his destruction. Their emotion was understandable. But one of our interests was to give Arab leaders an incentive for moderation. Our exchanges with Cairo had convinced us that Anwar Sadat represented the best chance for moderate peace in the Middle East.

Now that we had prevented Soviet intervention, it was essential to begin the peace process. This required some immediate relief for the Third Army—a difficult tactical problem. There was unanimity in our government as to goals, disagreement as to methods. The Defense Department proposed resupplying the Third Army as an American undertaking using C-130 airplanes. There was also much pressure to cut off our airlift to Israel. I was uneasy about both ideas. We could not in the space of two weeks operate an airlift to the two opposing sides in a Middle East war. At the same time, an abrupt halt of the airlift to Israel would risk being interpreted as dissociation from our ally and thus would tempt Arab intransigence and perhaps renewed Soviet intervention.

So we spent Friday, October 26, attempting instead to persuade Israel to volunteer some relief for the Third Army and thus avoid forcing us into open opposition. It turned out to be an impossible assignment. A prickly, proud, and somewhat overwrought ally had to be convinced not to persist in a course promising great domestic benefits in the run-up to its election,* and we had to accomplish the goal while maintaining a public posture of close association. We had to preserve Egypt's confidence in us through the agonizing hours required to convince Israel. It was a close race between our persuasiveness and the endurance of the Third Army and with it the prospect of a moderate government in Egypt. And, having just coaxed and pressured the Russian bear back into his cage, we had to be watchful lest he have second thoughts and charge out again.

It turned out to be another long day. We needed no special incentive. The increasingly frantic appeals from Sadat left little doubt

---

* The Israeli general election, originally scheduled for October 30, was rescheduled during the war to December 31.

that time was running short if the Third Army was going to survive. We did not want Egypt to rush back into the Soviet camp, nor did we think it desirable to tempt Moscow into a second round of confrontation. Starting in the morning of October 26, we began urging Israel to put forward some solutions to this conundrum. It proved impossible and finally drove us to issue the equivalent of a diplomatic ultimatum to Israel.

Within minutes of receiving Sadat's message, I contacted Dinitz. Meanwhile, the Third Army was trying to break out of Israeli encirclement north of Suez city. This indicated its desperation and would aggravate its plight by depleting its resources. It would also face us with another round of disputes over cease-fire violations. I urged that Israel take two steps: invite U.N. observers to proceed immediately to points between the two armies to monitor the cease-fire; and permit convoys of food, water, and medical supplies to the Third Army. The latter would remain surrounded, incapable of combat, useful as a bargaining counter but not subject to the humiliation of surrender. I also told Dinitz of my plan to visit Egypt. Dinitz promised an answer within a short time.

AMBASSADOR DINITZ–KISSINGER
> *Friday, October 26, 1973*
> *11:30 A.M.*

(missing first part)

K: No, no, I told you what I think the problem is. You don't have one man who can make foreign policy decisions.

D: That's correct.

K: If you and the Prime Minister could act like the President and I do—

D: You're right. That's what the Prime Minister has said on several occasions.

K: By the time you have the Cabinet, each of which is knifing each other—

D: That's correct. Everybody having discourse and adding their suggestions. Absolutely right. One of the ills of the parliamentary system. And I don't think the British are any better.

K: English are putting out, we have overreacted too. That's extremely dangerous.

D: Did you see the editorial in the *Post*? Very good. In support of the President, in support of your press conference, for the *Washington Post* that's something. I am happy to see some result. . . .

. . .

D: Something else, Brezhnev made a statement in Moscow—

K: I have seen that.

D: Urgent and necessary measure required to—cease fire, referred to personnel sent, linked with U.N. observers.

K: Yes, I saw it.

THE PRESIDENT–KISSINGER

Friday, October 26, 1973
11:58 A.M.

N: Hello, Henry.

K: Mr. President.

N: What, ah, how are things going? Still the same?

K: Still about the same. Some back and forth on whether the Soviets and Americans can be in the observer force. We have taken the position that, on the whole, we prefer the observers be the same type of people as the military force. But if the Secretary General requests Americans and Soviets, we will accept. The Soviets have sent in seventy people they call observers. We are saying they can send anyone they want but they have no status as far as we are concerned, except for what the Secretary General recognizes. You had another message from Sadat about the Third Army. A lot of technical stuff and needn't be brought to your attention. We should get the Egyptians to check this with the U.N. We will pass it on to the Israelis.

N: I want it passed to the Israelis—strongly. Let's keep our side of the bargain.

K: When we can determine that the Israelis are doing something wrong, we lean on them very hard.

N: I understand.

K: The Egyptians have made a proposal and they have sent this message about a comprehensive proposal on my visit. And we have sent a warm message to Sadat from you saying you have instructed me to take a constructive and positive attitude.

N: Good, good. How about the reviews? Still getting positive reviews?

K: Oh, yes. The *Post* was supportive of you on the editorial page. I haven't read the other. On the whole, the news play was very positive.

Not having received an Israeli reply to our request for some proposal to ease the situation of the Third Army, I contacted Dinitz that afternoon.

AMBASSADOR DINITZ–KISSINGER
Friday, October 26, 1973
1:17 P.M.

. . .

K: You offered to let food and water through—[a refusal] could cause very serious consequences with [the] Russians.

D: I want to ask you about something that has been on my mind, not my government's mind. Suppose we offer to return all the people free without equipment, wouldn't take prisoners, let them have food and water and let them return home safely if they wanted, open the road.

K: In my view, the best thing to offer is food and water, nonmilitary supplies.

D: Okay, I will pass that on. That also will not solve the problem, though. Will delay confrontation we are going to have with Egypt.

K: You will wind up, in my judgment, we will end up on the wrong side of the confrontation. It would be a whole hell of a lot better to establish the principle of limited supply now.

D: I'm not negating this.

K: In addition, and to offer that anybody who wants to leave will be permitted to leave, the Egyptians will consider that insulting.

D: We don't want to insult Egypt, but there must be a solution to the problem; we don't want to allow them to become fighting forces again.

K: I understand—eventual solution will be to open the road to non-military supplies.

D: Yes, I understand.

K: You will get under irresistible pressure if you keep it up.

D: Not keeping it up; we started with nonmilitary, humanitarian things, and I think the possibility—

K: My personal advice, you understand, it's not an official position yet, but it is my usual tactic of anticipating in order to gain time.

D: As I said last night.

K: You will not be permitted to capture that army. I am certain.

D: It's not first priority. We would rather have them go home.

K: I don't think that will be possible either. Unless you withdraw your forces.

D: Well. That comes back to your suggestion—that we suggested to you that night.

K: You won't [withdraw] in the north.

D: Don't want both sides of the Canal in the north.

K: I frankly think you will make a mistake if you push into a total confrontation.

D: We're not trying for a confrontation, just want to find the best way to solve it.

K: Well, I have given you my views; it would be helpful if we could get an answer in the early part of the afternoon. . . .

 . . .

The President–Kissinger
Friday, October 26, 1973
3:45 P.M.

N: Yah.

K: Mr. President.

N: Henry, I can't make out something your staff sent over here with regard to sending Soviet observers. I understand we did receive a message from Brezhnev.

K: Mr. President, the situation is the following: we don't want to get sucked into a separate U.N. observer force.

N: I understand; the point that I am making is this. The Secretary General would say—

K: The Secretary General should suggest—should be willing to contribute to an augmented—

N: My point is, suppose he doesn't want to, what do we say with regard to the Soviets sending—?

K: For your information, we are working out this afternoon a situation where the Secretary General will request twenty American and Soviet observers, so the question you raise will be hypothetical, Mr. President. As you say, there are two points to be made—

N: I understand and there should not be a separate U.S. force—

K: Also, should be no self-appointed forces of any one nation. We believe there will be small numbers of Soviet and U.S. personnel requested.

N: I have reason to believe that will be done.

Assistant Secretary Sisco–Kissinger

Friday, October 26, 1973
4:00 P.M.

K: (The Egyptians have asked) Waldheim to help them with the Third Army. I think we have to do something.

S: Larry [Eagleburger] just showed me the message prepared to go to the Egyptians. Let's send that off and see what happens [urging direct Israeli-Egyptian negotiations]. As I said earlier this morning, I think that we have got to be satisfied that they are really doing what they say they are doing and I don't know how we do that.

K: There are two problems. One is that and, second, is for the Israelis to do something on that @##$% line.

S: You mean by way of pulling back.

K: Yes.

S: I felt that the trade-off was that they would get those observers there and there would be some pullback. As I say, I don't feel like we are going to get the Israelis to do this in the next twenty-four hours but it is worth trying.

The President–Kissinger

Friday, October 26, 1973
4:05 P.M.

K: Mr. President.

N: It is necessary to be somewhat precise on this now. What can we say? That the United States will participate in providing observers if requested by the Secretary General? I don't want to be behind the news. I would like to be ahead of it.

K: If requested by the Secretary General.

N: Fine. The Soviet Union is sending unilaterally. Are we going to object?

K: They cannot do anything until the Secretary General asks for them.

N: Henry, I am getting at this. It is already in the news. To the effect that Soviet Union is sending observers and has asked us to—

K: We have responded to that— We have to avoid, Mr. President— They are pouring people in there and calling them observers and they have to be observed.

N: I am trying to see what we say tonight.

K: The U.S. is—we think a small number of U.S. observers—we are prepared if the Secretary General asks for them and we have every reason to believe this is what will happen.

N: This is being discussed now and we think it will be worked out this way? And that can be said?

K: Yes, Mr. President.

N: Thanks, Henry.

AMBASSADOR DINITZ–KISSINGER

Friday, October 26, 1973
4:15 P.M.

D: You wanted me.

K: The Egyptians have asked for a Security Council meeting tonight. They have now made another appeal to us from Sadat and from New York—el-Zayyat through Waldheim in which they say the Third Army will never surrender no matter what you do and that they will take drastic measures if you continue blockading them. They don't care what line you go back to. They won't quibble about that and they are willing to talk about prisoner release and other matters. It seems to me you are going to come to a crossing point tonight of either making concrete proposals or [not]. I tell you this as a friend, I have kept this from the President, who is preparing for a press conference. I don't want him to say something you will regret. I have no doubt what he will do when it [the information] gets there [to Camp David]. We also have a hot line message coming in from Moscow.

D: Can I tell you what the military situation is. I will not elaborate.

K: Our own information is that you did not start it.

D: Thank God.

K: But that does not make any difference. What produces the fighting is that they are desperate.

D: Absolutely correct. They are attempting to break out.

K: Why don't you let them break out and get out of there?

D: We would be willing to let them break out and go home but they are not trying to break out and run. They are shooting at our forces and—

K: Why can you not let them take the tanks with them? The Russians will replace them anyway.

D: We will not open up the pocket and release an army that came to destroy us. It has never happened in the history of war.

K: Also it has never happened that a small country is producing a world war in this manner. There is a limit beyond which you cannot push the President. I have been trying to tell you that for a week.

D: We are not trying to push the President.

K: You play your game and you will see what happens.

D: The Prime Minister [Golda Meir] is sitting now on suggestions on what to do.

K: I am suggesting to you to make a constructive suggestion.

D: I understand and I asked you if you have anything in mind.

K: I gave you what I have in mind.

D: About the food.

K: That while talks are going on you permit nonmilitary supplies to go in there and perhaps you can establish the principle that no military supplies can come in from the road and you pull back from it.

D: One of the suggestions from the Prime Minister as I left the phone to come to you is that she thought she would send to you

General [Riva] with a complete proposal of how to solve the situation.

K: That would take ten hours.

D: At least. She thought he could convey that would mean either swapping people, territories. Things that would solve the question. We cannot let them out without getting something in return.

K: That is right, but you have to buy time for this discussion. We will be glad to propose that there will be immediate discussions between you and the Egyptians to solve this problem. We are willing to be cooperative but I tell you what will happen is another maximum Soviet demand and you cannot put the President in confrontation day after day.

D: We don't want to.

K: It has rarely happened that after a cease-fire one country traps the army of another.

D: It is not exactly what we want to do. I will pass your urgent message to the Prime Minister.

K: I am telling you as personal advice. I guarantee if you want me to take it to the President you will get a much worse answer.

D: I am completely confident in accepting your advice. Believe me.

K: I have got to see the German Ambassador now and raise hell with him about your ships [supply ships for Israel held up in Bremerhaven].

D: Yes. Okay. I will talk to the Prime Minister and I will tell her it may be—

K: I think you have a bargaining situation and I think you can get something for it. There has to be a bargain.

D: How do we go about it?

K: By at least getting talks started on that narrow issue.

D: On the food?

K: By getting a certain standstill enough so they don't get so desperate you do not get constant fighting.

D: Our people say at least two to three days of food and water [for the Third Army]. We hear talk from the commander—they say in two to three days the U.N. will get us out of here. That is the situation there. We must strike some sort of a bargain out of it.

K: Make a proposal.

D: All right, so that is what I was trying to ask you. I will tell the Prime Minister that if she does not think—

K: But before 9:00 tonight make a proposal to confuse the issue. Or you will get a condemnation on you.

D: I will talk to her again.

Ambassador Dobrynin–Kissinger
Friday, October 26, 1973
Before 6:30 P.M.

K: Anatoly, we were told a couple of hours ago that a hot line message was coming.

D: It could be. I don't have any information. They don't usually take more than two or three minutes to pass by hot line.

K: There is a meeting at 9:00 of the Security Council.

D: You get the news from your Embassy?

K: I don't know who we got the information from. If it is important, whatever judgments we should eventually make on this, we would try to avoid another one [crisis].

D: I know the President makes a speech today and I just have routine telegrams. I don't have a single telegram that is on a top issue except one issue about U.N. socialist countries [refers to East European satellite states]. I cannot answer your question. They sometimes send me a flash.

K: Let me find out where we got the information from and I will call you back.

The President–Kissinger

Friday, October 26, 1973
6:30 P.M.

K: Mr. President.

N: Have we had any further developments with the U.N. or Secretary General requesting us to participate in—

K: Not yet.

N: In the one case it is a peacekeeping force and in the other case an observer force.

K: We will under no circumstances approve the peacekeeping force. That is what the Security Council ordered.

N: They agreed to that—

K: On the observer force we have not yet been asked but we can say that we have reason to believe we will be asked.

N: And the Soviets indicate they so desire. Is it sent in already?

K: They send seventy people but we should not praise them because of that.

N: No, no. Okay, I will try to dance around it.

Ambassador Dobrynin–Kissinger

Friday, October 26, 1973
6:45 P.M.

K: Anatoly, we understand it was alerted from your end, just on the hot line.

D: It could be that fighting is going on in the southern part of the Suez Canal. That is my guess.

K: For your information, we are urging Israel very much to make some sort of offer to the Egyptians on this.

D: Is the Security Council already in session?

K: No, at 9:00 tonight.

D: If we have anything, of course I will be in touch.

K: Good, I would appreciate it.

CIA DIRECTOR WILLIAM COLBY–KISSINGER

Friday, October 26, 1973
6:55 P.M.

K: We have been alerted for two hours on the hot line that a message is coming, which is [an] odd procedure. We are getting so paranoid I just wonder whether that is an indication of a fait accompli. Have you picked up anything?

C: Those down near Egypt apparently moved out. They have been reasonably quiet. There is only the Sadat thing. He is really getting very upset. You saw his message.

K: You mean his message to me?

C: Yes, I don't blame him. It is quite a jam. Let me run a check and call you right back.

WILLIAM COLBY–KISSINGER

Friday, October 26, 1973
7:02 P.M.

C: We don't find anything in particular. There was the Soviet airborne thing. [. . .]

   [. . .]

C: No—those guns are too far away to be any good at Alexandria. There is that remote possibility that they made some kind of threat.

K: Do you think we overreacted on Wednesday to that letter?

C: I don't think you had any choice. The Soviets may not have had the intention of going much further, but they sure sounded like it. Your letter was straightforward and good. You mean the alert?

K: Yes.

C: We may have gone a little further with the worldwide alert.

K: I am just wondering about the impact on them. Whether they—

C: The worldwide is the only thing. I think you were giving them an important message.

K: Okay, thanks.

   . . .

On the evening of October 26, the President held a press conference. He had been through three weeks of extraordinary strains: the negotiations over the Agnew resignation and its completion, the selection of a new Vice President, the beginning of the Middle East war, the Stennis compromise, the Saturday Night Massacre, the beginning of impeachment processes, the Brezhnev letter and alert. All this combined to produce a somewhat overwrought description, comparing the Soviet challenge of forty-eight hours earlier to the Cuban missile crisis and the President's action toward the Soviet Union as similar to the mining of North Vietnamese harbors.

History offers many examples of crises seemingly surmounted rekindled by claims of victory and second thoughts by the loser. There was also the unprecedented notice of an imminent hotline message that, contrary to the purpose of the hotline, which was speed, had not arrived two hours after we had been notified. I raised concerns with Haig, who took them up with Nixon, resulting in the following phone conversation:

GENERAL HAIG–AMBASSADOR DOBRYNIN
Friday, October 26, 1973
8:04 P.M.

. . .

H: Listen, I just came back from the President and I told him that his remarks tonight were I thought overdrawn and would be interpreted improperly.

D: Yeah.

H: And I wanted you to know that he did not in any way have the intention of drawing the situation as sharply as he did. What he was trying to do—and I don't think it came across—he thought he was doing it but as being a member of the audience, I didn't think he did it, was trying to emphasize his strong personal relationship with Mr. Brezhnev and it did not come across that way to me at all.

D: Yeah, it didn't come to me either.

H: No. And he's quite upset about it because he did not intend it to be that way.

D: You see, General, I would like to say only one private observation. It is my own but maybe it's good for you to understand and for the President.

H: Sure.

D: What is really in Moscow, they very much upset and if I may use a word—I am speaking on my own, you should be very clear on this.

H: I understand.

D: Because I didn't know that you would phone me.

H: Right.

D: But I think understanding between us on this is very important. But they are very angry because they consider that you created all these things by reasons we don't know—we don't want to discuss it—but artificial crisis, why? And when you compare it with the even Cuban crisis, it is really—excuse me—but it is going beyond any comparison. Because why? It's only one detail I would like to mention, we are [constantly] in touch with Henry on all the matters, big and small.

H: Yes.

D: Every hour on the hour. But what happened in the night? When I give this letter, it was as the President said: I determined he answered firm. It's quite all right. The usual procedure is through the confidential channel. But until we received letter, Henry didn't mention a single word that you are going to put this on an alert. It's the easiest way—just to call and say to Ambassador: Look here, the President feels very strongly so if you really going to persist sorry—well, you may use any language you like, tough or no tough or diplomatic—but we will be forced to do it. Then I will be in touch with Moscow; Brezhnev will answer and then it's natural.

H: Yeah.

D: But you were holding for five hours—Henry and Scowcroft calling me and they say a reply, wait a reply, then I will receive a reply. Reply was, well, firm, right as President said. But he didn't even mention about this alert. We find out on the radio, by the way.

H: Yeah.

D: But for me, it looks really it was not real. Because if you really were concerned, I am sure you will first be in touch with Brezhnev to find out what's going on, if it's real. But you were not really concerned so it was the easiest way to make up an alert without telling us. So I am a little bit, quite frankly, I'm telling you without anger, without specific emotions, but I'm really feel sorry about this episode because it damaged very much of what was done, by what reason we don't know really. It was so good trip of Henry to Moscow. Brezhnev spend with him so many hours that the President never spends with Gromyko, by the way. And it looked so it was quite all right. But then he created this [unclear] crisis that you are real and we are just weaker partners standing looking against braver United States. Really, we have our people too around Moscow. Of course, he looks differently.

H: Yeah. Well, Mr. Ambassador, what worries me, I don't think it's a reflection of the attitudes here at all.

D: Yeah.

H: For example, what was done on the alerts I am sure you know that's been done on countless occasions and for some reason none of the fanfare.

D: Yes, without fanfare. Why you make it without even telling us, why? If it was really war, I am sure you will try to prevent the war.

H: No, no—

D: And you will tell us if so. But if it was not the war, why to play the game publicly about it because you put us in a very difficult position domestically really. Well, we are just thinking what to do—to make a public statement denying all these things really because after all, one impression in the letter couldn't justify or just to be quiet but remember this thing. This is not the thing to be done. I have spent too many years and I'm telling you rather frankly—that is not necessary to do but it is better for us mutually to understand what is going on.

H: Well, obviously, I wouldn't call if I was at all comfortable with what was said tonight.

. . .

Dobrynin's description was a caricature of what had happened, but it showed that Washington was not the only capital on edge.

In any event, for our own reasons, we had decided not to permit the Third Army to be destroyed. I therefore returned to my urgent request to Dinitz for some Israeli initiative, which had been ignored for twelve hours.

AMBASSADOR DINITZ–KISSINGER
Friday, October 26, 1973
8:45 P.M.

K: Mr. Ambassador, this is a call not as Secretary but as a friend.

D: I understand.

K: We are going to get a hot line message within an hour. I just wanted to tell you it is my honest judgment if you don't move in some direction to get serious motion on the enclave, you will lose everything.

D: Maybe. I don't know what your suggestion is.

K: My suggestion this morning was to offer some time— You should know: once the President is involved, he will order that we should join the others because we have nothing to hold on to. It is water over the dam at this point.

D: The supply business? That is what you mean?

K: The supply business or something else Israeli ingenuity could produce. His suggestion is a negotiation.

D: I told you that is what we intended to offer them.

K: You told me it might be. I didn't know you wanted us to pass it on to them.

D: We don't want to reveal all of the cards. Maybe I didn't make myself very clear. I did not mean for you to withhold it from them.

K: That would be considered humiliating and it's just as well. I know what you are trying to do. Maybe you should play it your way for a while and they may buy it.

D: We have a mutual friend and he just called me on the direct line and he said something that I wasn't going to tell you. But since you called, he said tell my friend Henry, that if Golda Meir or any other government opens this route he will not survive twenty-four hours in Israel. I didn't—

K: The tragedy is that my judgment is that Israel will lose everything on this route but it is better for them to be forced than to make it as a decision.

D: In this Embassy we have three girls who lost either a brother or a cousin in this fighting. This is an example of what it has done to our country. In the closing of this route we have lost scores and scores of lives. If we open the route, we vitalize two or three divisions that will be a threat to our bridgeheads. We know what their intention is as of this evening. They are threatening us and the President of the U.S. We cannot let them execute these plans. We are not trying to—We cannot afford to have this army revitalize and they will be. They have the missiles and tanks ready for reloading. We saw them and we have tapes as of this afternoon.

K: I am trying to tell you it doesn't make a bit of difference. You will be forced if it reaches that point.

D: The Prime Minister asked if she should write a message to the President.

K: Write if it makes you feel good. It is almost totally impossible—

D: We are prepared to release them but should we—them. Should Israel take these enemies—

K: There is one—that you can hold the road after the cease-fire.

D: It is not a realistic argument here. The Soviet Union decided they cannot have the Egyptian army humiliated, so we are trying to—

K: Let's see what the hot line message says. We don't know what it says yet. We may not have a problem. I am honestly very pessimistic. At least there should have been a proposal that is being considered.

D: By the way, now we have allowed the Red Cross to go in for the wounded. This evening.

K: You know I am on your side. If that Third Army could disappear tonight, nobody would be happier than I. I have no interest in the Third Army, but this thing is going to get too big for us. It is my judgment, but in no official capacity whatever. What I advised you this morning I advise you as a tactic for what I was sure would happen. It hasn't happened yet. Let's not worry about it now.

D: We will wait and face the situation as it comes. I don't think we have any other choice.

K: I think you have practically— If you turn out to be right, I will celebrate with you.

D: In any event we will celebrate that you were wrong.

K: Never have I more wanted to be wrong.

D: This is the only thing that keeps me believing, is that we can work together with this.

K: You won't be pressured one second before it becomes inevitable.

D: I appreciate it.

Finally at 9:00 P.M., four hours after notification, the hotline message arrived.

GENERAL SCOWCROFT–KISSINGER

Friday, October 26, 1973
9:14 P.M.

S: They are just bringing the next three pages in. [Reads the note from Brezhnev.]

K: That is going to be a lollapalooza.

S: It's a dandy.

K: [. . .] They [the Israelis] are mad heroes. If they had let us communicate to them. It is just enough to be sick.

S: It has been another great day. I will call you as soon as the last two pages come through.

K: I don't know how we could have forced them to do it.

S: We can't really. It is so hard to see how they are not able to realize what they are doing. I don't know what more we can do without over-brutalizing the whole thing.

LORD CROMER–KISSINGER

Friday, October 26, 1973
9:35 P.M.

C: I thought the President was absolutely great. By allusion to the State Department remarks this afternoon, I think you might have a hornet's nest. I was at a lunch today—as you know, I have no complaint, but they were full of complaints over no consultations on anything. So when the President goes on the air and says he has received less than cooperation from the Europeans, this can cause a lot of unhappiness. I know what—

K: Well, we are willing to take this, Rollie. We have just about—the Europeans have to face the fact that the President is fed up.

C: They weren't called in to be told.

K: That's not true of you.

C: That is what I am saying. I am ringing you up as a friend, not as an Ambassador. I have no complaint whatsoever. I'm ringing just to say you might get a blast.

K: Let's be honest. We could have consulted to the devil and back with the Europeans and they would not have changed one iota.

C: That might be true. I am not getting into the right or wrong of the thing. From what I heard at lunch today, they are pretty unhappy.

K: We might reach a point where on both sides of the Atlantic there will be a need to reassess U.S. relations. . . .

. . .

AMBASSADOR DINITZ–KISSINGER

Friday, October 26, 1973
9:40 P.M.

K: We have received a message which gives us another day. They [the Soviets] claim Sadat requested us to send nonmilitary supplies. This they [the Soviets] did not do but they say within a day if this isn't done they will take appropriate measures. I will now have to take it up with the President. I tell you now, you can't expect a repeat of the performance of the other night.

D: I understand.

K: You read it and let's talk.

D: I will.

K: They are discussing a confidential understanding with us. I want you to know, the only confidential understanding we have is on joint auspices, which I discussed with the Prime Minister. There is no other confidential understanding.

D: For your negotiations?

K: Yes.

D: Would you like me to send somebody?

K: No, call Scowcroft.

D: Can I call him now?

K: Yes, he has it [the message].

Ambassador Dinitz–Kissinger

Friday, October 26, 1973
10:28 P.M.

D: I did not get the note yet.

K: Have you talked to Scowcroft?

D: Yes, right away. He told me he would send it within ten or fifteen minutes.

K: Okay. I will see about it.

General Scowcroft–Kissinger

Friday, October 26, 1973
10:30 P.M.

K: Brent, Dinitz has not gotten the note yet.

S: We have been giving it some final word changes and retyping.

K: Never mind about the word changes. They don't change the substance. Please get it to him so they can make a decision.

S: We have a car waiting.

K: Speed is more important than word changes. It is delaying us another hour now that they have another excuse not to talk about it.

S: Okay. It's going in right now.

As it turned out, the hot line message was a strange document. It spoke of threats to universal peace, but not about what the Soviet Union would do about them. It asked for an American response within a few hours, but threatened no consequences other than serious doubts about our intentions. It was plaintive about the alert, but the cautious phrasing indicated that some important lessons had been learned during the previous nights. Still, there would be a limit to the demonstrations of their impotence that the Soviet leaders would tolerate.

I had resisted the bureaucracy's pressures to undertake an *American* resupply of the Third Army. The thought of two airlifts to opposing sides was more than any diplomacy could sustain. I understood that Israel's intransigence reflected a combination of insecurity and despair—molded of a fear of isolation, a premonition of a catastrophe burnt deep into the soul of a people that had lived with disaster through the millennia of its history, and the worry that if it once yielded to pressure, it would invite an unending process of exactions. It also reflected the deadlock of a divided cabinet, none of whose members dared to appear "softer" than his colleagues. I had maneuvered all day to avoid a public American dissociation from Israel, to preserve Israel's psychological substance even while persuading it not to press its advantage to an extreme. But it was becoming clear that Israel was in no position to make a decision. It seemed to prefer being coerced to release its prey rather than relinquishing it voluntarily. My ultimate responsibility was as Secretary of State of the United States, not as psychiatrist to the government of Israel. With the utmost reluctance I decided that my duty was to force a showdown. The only act of friendship I could show to Israel was to keep it private, if Israel would let me.

Thus late Friday evening, I called Dinitz on behalf of Nixon. I do not remember checking in advance with the President; whether I did or not, there was no doubt from his conversations all day the President would back me. In all probability, he would have forced the issue earlier or accepted the option of American resupply of the Third Army had he not been preoccupied with his press conference and Watergate. I said to Dinitz:

AMBASSADOR DINITZ–KISSINGER

Friday, October 26, 1973
10:58 P.M.

. . .

K: Let me give you the President's reaction in separate parts. First, he wanted me to make it absolutely clear that we cannot permit the destruction of the Egyptian army under conditions achieved after a cease-fire was reached in part by negotiations in which we participated. Therefore it is an option that does not exist. We will support any motion in the U.N. that will [achieve this end]. Secondly, he would like from you, no later than 8:00 A.M. tomorrow, an answer to the question of nonmilitary supplies permitted to reach the army. If you cannot agree to that, we will have to support in the U.N. a resolution that will deal with the enforcement of 338 [the Security Council resolution passed that week to end the war] and 339 [the Security Council resolution passed earlier that week to enforce the cease-fire]. We have been driven to this reluctantly by your inability to reach a decision. Whatever the reasons, this is what the President wanted me to tell you is our position. [We require] an answer that permits some sort of negotiation and some sort of positive response on the nonmilitary supplies, or we will join the other members of the Security Council in making it an international matter. I have to say again, your course is suicidal. You will not be permitted to destroy this army. You are destroying the possibility for negotiations, which you want, because you are not making possible—

D: Your proposal to let the army go is very close to our proposal.

K: You can make any proposal you want to us and we will transmit it. We are not transmitting anything [of our own] to the Egyptians. We have not had an answer to the last message, but that only went out two or three hours ago. Maybe it will turn out they will accept your proposal and I will have a drink with you. As it stands now, it is our official position that if you do not make some proposal along these lines, we will have to go along with the majority of the Security Council. We can probably make a proposal and you can delay the implementation of it on practical grounds and get a little more time.

D: If we make an offer on the supplying of nonmilitary supplies?

K: That is right. Then we could at least point to something that we have managed to achieve in the— I must tell you that you are perfectly free to play it your way and see what happens. Maybe the Egyptians will be so desperate they will accept your proposal. It is not my judgment. It is inconceivable that the Soviets will permit the destruction of the Egyptian army and that the Egyptians will withdraw their army. It will bring down Sadat. It is not something he will agree to.

D: I am not authorized, or feel competent, to give advice. But why can't I answer that Israel offers to let this army go intact, with all side arms, but cannot have two hundred tanks go with these people so they can go back on us?

K: The agreement was cease-fire in place. Now they won't accept losing all that equipment and giving it to you.

D: They can blow it up.

K: You are asking them to destroy two hundred tanks and pull their army out. They will never do it and the Soviets won't take that. Why don't you bluff for a day and see if you can get it.

D: That is what we tried to do.

K: If that is going to be your formal answer, we will of course transmit it. It can be under no—

D: Mr. Secretary, if I asked my government to transfer to you the military plans we were able to obtain about the defenses of this army, will it make any difference? What is their operational plan?

K: Right now I don't think they have any plans.

D: They do, as of today. We have it on tape.

K: That is their way of breaking out.

D: If they want to break out and go home we could help them. They don't have to kill our people. Their plan is to cut us and fortify themselves with tanks and missiles. It is suicidal for us in either way.

K: It is.

D: Ten thousand tons of supplies that the Soviets have provided them. Twenty-four hours and we would have to rush to you like last Friday night.

K: I have given you the President's views of the cease-fire agreement.

D: It is not we who force your confrontation with the Soviet Union. By its actions they have forced it.

K: If the Soviet Union did this to you or Egypt after a cease-fire agreement, I would urge on the President the most drastic measures.

D: We did not do this without them fighting us after the cease-fire. You say it's immaterial. The note of Brezhnev is full of mistakes and you know it, Mr. Secretary.

K: I know only the basic situation is produced by bottling up of the Third Army, and I think you can make demands that no additional military equipment go into there.

D: Under what auspices?

K: U.N. personnel.

D: Including Soviet personnel?

K: That is one of the things that can be raised. That will be reasonable.

D: I will transmit it to the Prime Minister, of course, and get her reaction. Maybe she would want to send a note to the President. She has wanted to and I have been talking her out of it.

K: She can send a note to the President. It won't make the slightest difference. I will get the— It is the mildest possible reaction you will get in the bureaucracy. If everybody got—

D: I think what is at stake here is so important to us, I cannot come— What I have said to you.

K: If you will call me at 8:00 in the morning.

D: If the Prime Minister asks some more questions, can I still get you?

K: I am going home.

D: I will try not to call you.

K: But, of course, if it is important you can call me.

We did not inform any other government of the time limit on Israel. We sent a message to Ismail urging direct military talks between

Egypt and Israel regarding supplies for the Third Army. I briefed
Dobrynin that we had made a démarche for which we expected an
answer by late afternoon the next day. The reason was to avoid Soviet
ultimatums by riding piggyback on our deadlines.

AMBASSADOR DOBRYNIN–KISSINGER
Friday, October 26, 1973
11:15 P.M.

. . .

K: Have you seen the hot line message now that we got from
Moscow?

D: No, I have not gotten it. I probably will receive it in a few minutes.

K: It is about the Suez situation.

D: That was my impression.

K: One of our problems is, we get totally conflicting reports from
the two sides, and we have almost no means of telling it.

D: I think your people and ours could judge it better.

K: Yes, I wanted to tell you, we will send an answer in a couple of
hours. We will discuss the issues that are raised on a really urgent
basis with the Israelis and we hope to get an answer by tomorrow
afternoon our time, but it is a real tough problem.

D: Do you want me to tell Moscow, or will you use the red phone?

K: Red phone?

D: Hot line, so to speak.

K: We will say something to that effect but we're wondering if you
could transmit it. They will get an answer from us now, but I
cannot give you a conclusive answer until we talk to the Israelis.

D: Sometime tomorrow afternoon. Okay. Good night.

A presidential letter in the same sense was sent to Brezhnev at
2:30 A.M.

Barely had that message been dispatched when we heard from

Israel in the form of a message from Golda Meir to me. Even though I had transmitted our demand in the name of Nixon, Golda was too surefooted to tackle the President head-on. She made sure that her quarrels were always with subordinates. Placing the President on a pedestal gave him one more opportunity to change course by disavowing those who were undermining the harmony Golda postulated. And, if this failed, an ultimate concession to the President, with some skill and luck, could at least be turned into a claim for a future favor.

The letter itself was vintage Golda, passionate, self-centered, shrewd. It was written as much for its impact on the Israeli Cabinet as for the United States government. She chose to put the matter into the context of superpower imposition, implying that we were yielding to the Soviets—an argument that, if it surfaced, was certain to mobilize maximum domestic pressure against us: "I have no illusions but that everything will be imposed on us by the two big powers." This, about a request she had refused to answer for eighteen hours, that Israel make *some* proposal we could defend before the Security Council *against* Soviet pressures and after two weeks of a U.S. airlift to Israel. All she asked, the letter said, was that we tell Israel precisely what it was to do "in order that Egypt may announce a victory of her aggression." This, about the proposal to let food and water through to an army trapped forty-eight hours after a United States–negotiated cease-fire and that would remain trapped even after having received these minimal supplies. But if she had to make some concession, nothing could force the lioness to be graceful about it: "There is only one thing that nobody can prevent us from doing and that is to proclaim the truth of the situation; that Israel is being punished not for its deeds, but because of its size and because it is on its own." This was a warning that she would take her case to her supporters publicly.

Golda's profession of outrage again evaded the central point: she was still refusing to put forward a proposal. She was insisting that we impose it.

Side by side with these passionate exchanges, the U.N. deliberations regarding the projected U.N. forces were proceeding together
with our attempts to reduce the Soviet role in it to a minimum.

AMBASSADOR SCALI–KISSINGER

Friday, October 26, 1973
11:25 P.M.

S: Did you hear my defense of you?

K: What were you defending me against?

S: They quoted you out of context.

K: Who did?

S: None other than your friend Malik, who said you had admitted
the Israelis violated the cease-fire in your press conference. In
my right of reply I—.

K: What did he quote?

S: He said you said the cease-fire broke down and Israel made some
territorial gains. In any event I thanked him for the tantalizing
reference to the news conference because I had already sent the
complete text to all other missions of the Security Council and I
just said I wanted to thank the Ambassador for exciting interest
because I thought it was so fair-minded. They will all read it and
see you were more balanced than anything that has been said
here. We had this meeting with him afterwards.

K: How did it go?

S: He insisted on the Poles. I retorted by offering Romania. I said it
is Romania or none at all—no blocs, neither the Warsaw Pact
nor NATO.

K: What did he say?

S: That is discrimination. That is like going back to the Cold War.
On the observer side I said we would send fifty or twenty or were
willing to withdraw ours completely in return for none of yours.
It hit him like a sledgehammer.

K: He also is pretty dumb.

S: He said that he didn't understand this. We were trying to dictate to the Secretary General. He is furious because we won't accept Poland. We are trying to dictate to the Security Council and that Poland is a great country.

K: Poland, with a long and distinguished history of affection for the Jewish people. They haven't had a pogrom since the last Jew left.

S: He said he had very firm instructions on this.

K: Has anything changed in their attitude—since the alert?

S: He [Malik] has become more obnoxious.

K: More obnoxious since the alert? Are they beginning to hit us harder?

S: In the language they are using, yes. I gave a very reasoned answer and said we both had a responsibility at a time when there are charges and countercharges, none of which can be verified.

K: What is your view as to what we should do now?

S: We should stick firm on this offer we have made them.

K: I mean if the issue of withdrawal of the Israelis to the October 22 line comes up.

S: I think unless we get the Israelis to back up we are not going to have a friend in the house.

. . .

At 4:07 A.M. that Saturday, I received word from Hafiz Ismail that Egypt accepted direct talks between Egyptian and Israeli officers of the rank of major general "to discuss the military aspects of the implementation of Security Council Resolutions 338 and 339 of October 22 and 23, 1973." Talks should take place under U.N. supervision at the route marker denoting Kilometer 101 on the Cairo–Suez road. The only conditions would be a "complete" cease-fire, to go into effect two hours before the meeting proposed for 3:00 P.M. Cairo time that day (Saturday), and the passage of one convoy carrying nonmilitary supplies to the Third Army under U.N. and Red Cross supervision.

Through our mediation, Israel was about to enter the first direct talks between Israel and Arab representatives since the independence of Israel in 1948. Israel would retain control over the access route to the Third Army even while the United Nations almost unanimously was pressing for Israeli withdrawal to the October 22 line. All this in return for permitting one convoy of nonmilitary supplies to pass as we had been urging for twenty-four hours.

At 4:31 A.M., I informed Hafiz Ismail that his message, with our strong endorsement, had been passed to Israel "on a most urgent basis." By 6:20 A.M., Israel accepted the Egyptian proposal in total; I immediately informed Sadat. Three hours later—we wanted to reduce the time available for Soviet mischief—a letter was sent in Nixon's name to Brezhnev informing him of the imminent Egyptian-Israeli talks and of Israeli agreement to the convoy.

GENERAL SCOWCROFT–KISSINGER
Saturday, October 27, 1973
8:45 A.M.

S: [Reads proposed text of message to be sent to Secretary General Waldheim]

"I am pleased to be able to report to you that, as the result of an offer of our good offices to the Israelis and Egyptians, the two warring sides have agreed to meet together today under UNTSO [United Nations Truce Supervision Organization] auspices. The purpose of the meeting will be to discuss the military aspects regarding implementation of the United Nations Security Council Resolutions 338 and 339.

"At our urging, the government of Israel has agreed to permit a convoy of nonmilitary supplies to pass through its lines, under United Nations and Red Cross auspices, to reach the Egyptian Third Army today.

"I fervently hope we will continue to work closely and cooperatively to the achievement of a true cease-fire; a cease-fire that will make it possible for the warring parties, with our joint help, to arrive at a just settlement and a lasting peace in the Middle East.

"I will inform you immediately as further developments occur."

K: Add sentence from the first draft "hope we are well on the road, etc." and don't say "fervently."

S: Fine.

SENATOR FULBRIGHT–KISSINGER

Saturday, October 27, 1973
10:00 A.M.

K: Hello, Mr. Chairman.

F: How are you this morning?

K: It has been another sleepless night. That is why I started to call you.

F: We are not having another one?

K: No, this one has had a happy outcome. All day yesterday we received messages from the Russians and the Egyptians. The basic problem is the Israelis have an Egyptian army bottled up by cutting their road after the cease-fire that was to last. This is the basic problem from which stems most of the fighting. It is hard to tell who is trying to break out and who is whittling them down. All day frantic appeals have come in— The Soviet note was not nearly as brutal as before. It was much more civil than Wednesday. We decided that we could not permit a situation to continue in which there was a danger of constant confrontation with the Soviet Union as a result of action taken after a cease-fire negotiated with the Soviet Union. We, therefore, decided that Israel would have to permit nonmilitary supplies to reach the army. After receipt of the message by the hot line which more or less requested nonmilitary supplies we told the Israelis if by 8:00

this morning they won't agree to this, we would join the majority of the Security Council in expressing the sense of humanity that something like this would have to be permitted and told him [Dinitz] they would have to get in touch with the Egyptians and discuss the matter of implementation of the cease-fire. I told them we were in a position of being besieged by Sadat and Brezhnev with claims of bad faith. They are ready for talks on that last subject but went into orbit on the first one. They claimed they would go public and say they were being raped by the superpowers for the crime of being small. This consumed hours of time last evening. We held our position. At any rate, at 4:00 this morning the Egyptians accepted direct talks with the Israelis on the Suez Canal to discuss the military problems that exist, provided one convoy was permitted through today. This is the situation now. One nonmilitary convoy is going through and the Egyptians and Israelis are meeting within the hour.

F: If you can make them meet and start talking, it is a great accomplishment.

. . .

But in the Middle East every step forward requires testing the ground ahead for shifting sands. At 11:00 A.M. Washington time (or 5:00 P.M. in Cairo), we were informed by Israel that the Egyptians had not showed up at the appointed time or place. A flurry of exchanges followed. It transpired that the Egyptian military representatives en route to the meeting at Kilometer 101 had been stopped at the Kilometer 85 marker by Israeli sentries who claimed not to have received instructions to let them through. They seemed strangely lax in communicating with their headquarters on the unprecedented phenomenon of an Egyptian major general who appeared to insist on speaking directly to his Israeli counterpart! The mix-up was soon straightened out. I talked personally to Golda. Apparently, Israel had neglected to notify General Ensio Siilasvuo, head of the U.N. forces, to make the necessary arrangements as I had told Ismail he would.* I urged that a new time be set and all notifications be decided ahead of time. After considerable back-and-forth—produced by the need for messages between parties a few hundred miles apart to travel via Washington, or a total distance of twelve thousand miles—it was decided that the two generals would meet at midnight.

Ultimately, at 1:30 A.M. local time on Sunday, October 28, an hour and a half behind the new schedule, Israeli and Egyptian military representatives met for direct talks for the first time in twenty-five years, under the auspices of U.N. observers. But throughout that day the Israelis managed to delay the passage of the convoy. They had told me late on the 26th that the Third Army had food and water for forty-eight hours; they were determined to keep it on short rations; if the army collapsed while a convoy was on the way, no tears would be shed in Jerusalem. Finally, on Monday morning, October 29, I was able to report to Hafiz Ismail that the convoy had arrived at its destination. Egypt agreed to further meetings. While these remained inconclusive, the turn toward negotiations had begun. It soon became irreversible.

FOREIGN MINISTER ZAYYAT–KISSINGER

Saturday, October 27, 1973
12:04 P.M.

K: How nice of you to call.

Z: I want to thank you very much for your conversation. The problem is that it has not been implemented. I have seen a message from Israel—Cairo says they are resisting until they go into Suez.

K: No! I am told that as of this moment the Israelis are waiting [at] Kilometer 110 on the Canal and have been there since 3:00 and are prepared to permit the convoy to come through.

---

* I have since had an opportunity to check my impressions with General Siilasvuo. He confirms that it was a genuine mix-up, even though at the time I suspected an Israeli maneuver.

Z: Our information is good information. This morning they were there waiting. The Israelis say they have no instructions.

K: That is impossible. Mr. Foreign Minister, we will stand behind what we said to you. You send your convoy. The Israelis are waiting at Kilometer 110. Send your man there and we will work on it immediately. We are trying to help.

Z: I will get in touch with my people right away.

K: I will get in touch with the others to call Dayan.

Z: Thank you very much.

K: I will have someone from my office call and help you get the call through immediately.

Z: Thank you very much.

GENERAL SCOWCROFT–KISSINGER
Saturday, October 27, 1973
12:05 P.M.

. . .

K: I have just had a call from Zayyat saying the Israelis say they have no instructions to let a convoy through. Zayyat wants to call Cairo. Can you get someone to get in touch with his hotel and get a line cleared or put him through our nets?

S: We can put it through our switchboard.

K: We need it fast.

S: Yes, I will do it.

GENERAL HAIG–KISSINGER
Saturday, October 27, 1973
12:28 P.M.

K: The press conference reached Moscow, and Brezhnev asked Dobrynin if this could possibly be true. What happened Wednesday was compared to the bombing of Hanoi.

H: Oh, no! How is Dobrynin's morale?

K: He thinks there should be direct confrontation between the two gentlemen [Brezhnev and Nixon] but you know what happened overnight. It was put to the Israelis that we couldn't tolerate them squeezing Egypt this way—put to the Egyptians that they should meet with the Israelis and work out details. The Israelis blew their stack and said they would go public and that they were being brutalized for the claim of being small. At 4:00 [the] Israelis accepted this meeting, permitting one convoy to go through. I thought all was settled but now the Israelis are sitting at the meeting place and the Egyptian convoy is sitting somewhere within Israel [Israeli lines].

H: We cannot let the people starve.

K: You may help me to settle down those maniacs at Defense. He [Schlesinger] is now flapping all over the place—we cannot airlift supplies to Egypt.

H: One thing he did mention was putting troops in [the] Trucial States [Emirates] to get oil.

. . .

H: I told him he should not come to you. He said we could not let people die in the desert and that the Israelis are lying to us and that we must be tougher. The big thing is to get the two parties to work it out.

K: That way it has a chance. If we go in, it will start war again. I have asked him not to send a military mission to Israel. Schlesinger wants to check on whether the Israelis are lying—will you please help me with him?

H: I will do my best.

PRIME MINISTER GOLDA MEIR–KISSINGER
Saturday, October 27, 1973
12:40 P.M.

K: Hello, how are you?

M: I just want to say to you that there is one thing you just cannot accept, and that is that this was something deliberate.

K: What we did was to make all arrangements.

M: Our man went to the point of destination—waited and when the group from Cairo did not arrive he went to the U.N. headquarters—ten kilometers away and asked him if we were expecting something and he attempted to get in touch with Cairo. Our man was on the spot from 3:00 to 5:30. It is true that someone from here should have gotten in touch, but it was our assumption that from the Cairo side something went astray.

K: With all due respect, we passed the message to Egypt and to request all conditions be accepted and you would be in touch with Zayyat to work out details. If that did not happen, Egypt did not have any way of knowing. I just told them the set plan was accepted and you would work out details with the general. The fact is that your people did not make contact—they were waiting. You told us what to pass on to them—we did that. One person should have gotten in touch with the general—up to that point everything was worked out but from that point the Egyptians were waiting.

M: Mr. Secretary, they got the message we accept.

K: I have tried to explain to the Ambassador [this] is totally irrelevant. We are faced with a situation here beyond any control.

M: You have the message I sent.

K: Yes, that is what we passed on to Egypt. They had every reason to believe it was all right. They called me at 12:00 to say nothing has happened—about forty-five minutes ago. The U.N. man is at the checkpoint. [The] Egyptians had every reason to expect from our message that all would go well and now our own good word is involved. Zayyat was just telephoned that the Egyptian convoy was ready.

M: But, Mr. Secretary, we don't know about such—we don't see any convoy—what can be done now? An hour for early in the morning must be set and where is the convoy?

K: I will get in touch immediately with the Egyptians—five o'clock in the morning. I will be in touch with Dinitz and Zayyat. Let us make it 6:00 A.M., to make sure.

M: Six A.M. at the point on which was decided upon. I will also get in touch with the general right now.

K: Thank you, Madam Prime Minister.

AMBASSADOR DINITZ–KISSINGER

Saturday, October 27, 1973
12:55 P.M.

K: We have made an arrangement—saying all right for 6:00 A.M. We have just talked to the Egyptians. They tell me, and I tend to believe them, they were not permitted to pass through Kilometer 85—your people on the ground did not have instructions. We told the Egyptians to meet at ten o'clock tonight Israeli time at the agreed place and they have accepted it. Also a further meeting and convoy. To put off seven more hours we see no reason.

D: Frankly, technically we must see if it can be worked out. What I am going through is not less than what you are going through.

K: I said we were doing it in his interest at the agreed place at 10:00 P.M. for the convoy. Whether it can deliver is another question.

D: I will talk to the Prime Minister right away.

K: You must come back with a positive answer. Please let me know right away as soon as you check.

FOREIGN MINISTER ZAYYAT–KISSINGER

Saturday, October 27, 1973
12:55 P.M. [AS RECORDED]

K: I have just talked to the Prime Minister of Israel.

Z: Yes.

K: And here is what will happen if it is agreeable to you. If your representatives appear at the agreed place at 6:00 A.M. tomorrow morning Cairo time and if your convoy appears at 6:00 A.M. at whatever place it is ordered to go through, the convoy will be passed through and the Israeli representative will be there. I give you the assurances that the American government stands behind this arrangement and if anything else goes wrong we will take a very definite stand. They claim your people did not show up.

Z: Our people did not show up? They were prevented from doing so. I talked to Mr. [unclear] and told him about this. He said the reason our people were not at Kilometer 101 was because at K 85 the Israeli forces said they had no information about this arrangement and prevented them.

K: Would you like to do it at night?

Z: Certainly. We think they want to wait until morning—

K: Let's give it a reasonable time. What time is it in Cairo?

Z: It is six hours different. In Cairo it is ten minutes to 7:00. If they can make it at 9:00.

K: Two hours is too short. I am afraid of communications breakdown.

Z: Yes, 10:00 this evening Cairo time.

K: I understand. We have given you our word and we will stand behind it. When the U.S. makes a promise, we keep it.

Z: I appreciate it.

K: Ten tonight, then.

. . .

SECRETARY SCHLESINGER–KISSINGER

Saturday, October 27, 1973
1:00 P.M.

S: How are we doing on the Third Army question?

K: —We have a posture now for getting this thing on the way. We can't land troops in the Trucial States and resupply the Third Army.

S: Of course not.

K: We should get these two things going. The convoy will go through tonight and the meeting will take place.

S: Splendid.

K: The reason we don't want major generals running loose over there is not to get the pot stirred up. Can we settle it now?

S: Sure. The important thing is the Third Army.

K: No, getting the cease-fire straightened away is the most important. If the Israelis and Egyptians get something worked out on the Third Army that is— We have no interest in the Third Army—

S: We have some interest in the Third Army. It is our help arranging the cease-fire, and they were captured after that, which compromises somewhat our position in being the peacemaker in the area.

K: You can be sure I have talked at great lengths with them. We have spent the whole night. I have been on the phone all morning with Zayyat and Ismail and the Egyptians are extremely pleased with what we are doing.

S: Good piece of work.

K: Do you think a convoy can travel on that road at night?

S: We will have to check. My own belief is, yes, they can handle it.

K: Give me your judgment.

S: Did you indicate to the Israelis you would cut off their airlift if they did not acquiesce?

K: I said that we would be very tough, but did not indicate what we would do.

S: In any event, I think if they run convoys in, that problem is settled.

K: We did not talk about the airlift. I said we would vote at the Security Council against them.

S: If they prevent these guys from getting water and food, it is criminal.

K: Ten tonight is three hours away.

S: Good. In any event, if they fail to do it we should think about cutting off the airlift. It is a way of making clear our point of view.

K: I think it is one of the things we should consider at that point.

. . .

S<small>ECRETARY</small> S<small>CHLESINGER</small>–K<small>ISSINGER</small>

Saturday, October 27, 1973
1:10 P.M.

S: Henry, we have just had a cable from Tel Aviv from our DAO [Defense Attaché Office] that you should be aware of immediately. The Third Army has built two bridges across the Canal and the Israelis plan to attack them. Is the convoy coming from Cairo or Tel Aviv?

K: Cairo.

S: R[unclear] indicated that the IDF [Israeli Defense Forces] will attack both from the ground and the air.

K: I will tell you, I made it clear to them in the strongest possible terms that we are backing this stand [U.N. resolution]. I will get on the horn with Dinitz again.

S: Well, good. Just put that into your hopper.

K: Good.

Great events usually culminate not in great drama but as a series of technical decisions.

A<small>MBASSADOR</small> D<small>INITZ</small>–K<small>ISSINGER</small>

Saturday, October 27, 1973
1:15 P.M.

K: I just heard from Egypt. They want a midnight meeting [local time].

D: At midnight. It is better for us. We discussed 11:00. I will suggest midnight.

K: They also want to move the convoy at midnight.

D: Yes, the convoy and meeting.

K: The Egyptians also told us that there are some U.N. truce observers you are keeping out of Suez city. Could you let them in too?

D: I will check on that. Of course, I have no authority to say that.

K: If you could, for once, be positive quickly. I have requests to stop the airlift, to have U.S. forces do the supplying. Our government is going crazy.

D: If you only saw what I am going through here on this end.

K: Get me a very quick answer, will you?

. . .

SECRETARY SCHLESINGER–KISSINGER

Saturday, October 27, 1973
1:35 P.M.

S: Hello, Henry. That is a hard surface road. We took pictures on the 13th.

K: And it could be traveled at night?

S: Even if it has been hit, it has hard shoulders.

K: Good. The Egyptians asked to make it midnight. They moved it back two hours, which is 6:00 our time. I have told Israel that, on pain of the most drastic sanctions, it better happen.

S: Good. Bye.

AMBASSADOR DINITZ–KISSINGER

Saturday, October 27, 1973
1:55 P.M.

. . .

D: The first point is that U.N. force [is] in Suez city. They arrived with Egyptian liaison officers, which was not according to the agreement. So after certain discussions they decided to proceed without them. We passed them and they came to the gates of the city. It was dark. They asked for permission to stay overnight at the gates of the city and enter at daybreak.

K: They told us you are—

D: I am telling you the last information from Dayan. Everybody is happy and there is agreement.

K: Can I tell the Egyptians that if the force wishes to enter, you will allow it to enter?

D: From what I hear, they are sleeping outside the city until morning and entering then.

K: It may be that is a misconception.

D: Then I will phone my people and say that they want to go in. It is not because we prevented them but because it is dark.

K: The allegation is, you are planning—

D: I will get to the cease-fire business in a moment. There is no fighting now.

K: How about the convoy and meeting?

D: We are prepared, in spite of all difficulties, to hold the meeting at the same place. We have been in touch with the U.N. people and they have been in touch with the Egyptians. Arrangements are being worked out by the U.S., U.N., and Egyptians at exactly what time they will reach there. It would be—impossible for us to fix exactly 12:00. Maybe 12:15 or 11:45.

K: Fine.

D: We are working now with General Siilasvuo [Finnish commander of the U.N. forces] on all points and the Egyptians have already been in touch with the U.N. completing their arrangements. With regard to the convoy, it will also be allowed to proceed in spite of all difficulties. Our one problem is, if they come with Egyptian drivers we will ask them to change for the portion they go in Israel either to U.N. or Israeli drivers. Then they can change back to Egyptian drivers.

K: Can you explain the reasoning for this?

D: We have intelligence information that they will put intelligence officers instead of drivers. They have to go seventy kilometers inside our territory and you see all our placements and tanks.

K: I don't get into that—

D: No, I just wanted you to have this information.

K: Can't you tell them that now?

D: I am sure our people are telling them now, to the U.N.

K: I urge you, Mr. Ambassador, not to appear tricky and do not make this look like a delay or it will not be understandable.

D: I will phone them to make it in advance. About the cease-fire. Dayan said that he wants you to know that there is consistent shooting and attempts to build bridges twenty-four hours a day. My people have orders never to incite anything, only to return fire. Right now it is quiet on the front. Except an attempt to bring helicopters and back in with boats, they are to only shoot on these things and not on the front. Could you also ask the Egyptians to keep the cease-fire because we are under very strict instructions.

K: I will urge the Egyptians to do that.

D: That is all the information we have.

K: I will communicate immediately with the Egyptians.

D: Fine.

SECRETARY SCHLESINGER–KISSINGER

Saturday, October 27, 1973
2:10 P.M.

S: Hi.

K: Twelve midnight is all set.

S: Superb.

K: Everything is ordered. All the Israelis insisted on was that Egyptians not drive the trucks themselves but that U.N. drivers were all right. That is all right with Egypt.

S: That is wonderful.

K: Now, I don't know what can screw up.

S: Give credit for this to the President. He needs it.

K: We are giving it all to the President.

S: Yes, I mean get it to the press.

K: All right.

Ambassador Dinitz–Kissinger

Saturday, October 27, 1973
2:13 P.M.

K: I have passed the information to Zayyat. He thinks they will accept U.N. drivers.

D: Yes, fine.

K: He says the Security Council passed a resolution that this force must enter Suez city tonight.

D: I have talked to my people. If they want to enter tonight, we will make arrangements.

K: As long as you made the offer, you can't force them into the city. He also said they will give another—

D: I think everything is going to be well.

K: I frankly must tell you, as a friend: I have held this message from Sadat from the President. Now I will not send it to him.

D: —all the pressure that I can take from— When there was bungling on our side, that was the biggest shock.

K: Mr. Ambassador, we deserve a drink when all of this is quiet.

D: When I talked to the Prime Minister, she said why don't you take Dr. Kissinger to dinner tonight, after the convoy.

K: I can't do it tonight. We will do it when all of this comes out fine.

D: I feel this has come out all right.

K: Give her my warm regards.

Ambassador Dinitz–Kissinger

Saturday, October 27, 1973
3:05 P.M.

D: I don't want to disturb you long. This isn't that important. I spoke to the Prime Minister after I spoke to you and this is what she asked me to reaffirm. 1) The city of Suez—the Finnish commander himself, who arrived at the gateway of the city of Suez, decided on his own authority not to enter with his troops during the night because of danger. In the meantime, in addition to fifty people, he received two hundred more and they are camping outside of the gate. This was their own decision. We have no objections if he wants to enter the city, but we will not help him to do this because we do not want to be responsible for the people.

K: Good.

D: 2) We took note of the statement of Zayyat on the Egyptian consent that drivers will be U.N. drivers, not Egyptian. We will inform this to General Siilasvuo.

K: Good.

D: 3) We took note that Egypt will issue new orders for observation of the cease-fire. We appreciate your intervention. We passed this message on to our chief of staff.

K: Good.

D: The situation itself is quiet and we hope it will remain that way. This is passed on as sort of humorous. The Prime Minister sends you her greetings and felicitations. She wants to meet with Sadat at 3:30 this evening on Kilometer 111½. If you receive a positive answer from Sadat— She understands your impossible task of getting the real truth when you get him to answer.

K: I am glad she still has a sense of humor.

D: Yes, I was beginning to lose mine myself.

K: We have navigated another difficult problem.

D: I am sure it will be all right.

K: We are over the worst today.

D: I said to my wife this morning when I got home, "You know, this is the first night I am going to sleep quietly because I am beginning to see the ray of light." Then I woke up to this. I think we have it worked out now.

K: Yes.

Finally, at 1:30 A.M. local time on Sunday, October 28, an hour and a half behind the new schedule, Israeli and Egyptian military representatives met for direct talks for the first time in twenty-five years, under the auspices of U.N. observers.

On Monday morning, October 29, I was able to report to Hafiz Ismail that the convoy had arrived at its destination. Egypt agreed to further meetings with Israel for more permanent arrangements. While these remained inconclusive, the turn toward negotiations had begun. It soon became irreversible, culminating in a disengagement agreement between Egypt and Israel in January 1974, a political agreement in September 1975, and a peace treaty in 1978 that is in force at this writing.*

---

*For the conduct of these negotiations, see *Years of Upheaval* p. 799f. and p. 1032f. and *Years of Renewal* p. 347f.

The Last Month of Indochina

In the Middle East crisis, policy was designed to shape events in conformity with America's values and national interests. In the last month of U.S. involvement in Indochina, policy was confined to damage limitation. It more and more focused on rescuing as many as possible of the people whom America had tried to protect through five administrations of our two major parties. In the Middle East crisis U.S. policy had a theme, however controversial; the decisions of the last month of the Indochina crisis have a jagged quality. Issues received attention because of the daily need to manage human tragedies or to establish justifications for emergency measures. The Ford administration had become a passenger on a vehicle hurtling with ever accelerating speed down an ever steeper slope. But it felt that it owed it to the peoples of Indochina and to America's central position in the world to weather this process with the maximum of dignity and by easing so far as possible the fate of those who had relied on us.

The effort tore at our hearts; but the tragedy evolved as a series of bureaucratic or congressional wrangles over issues that appeared to be technical or legal. In fact they marked the collapse of an effort to which America had sacrificed twenty-five years of blood and treasure.

The Nixon administration had negotiated a peace agreement on Vietnam, signed in Paris on January 27, 1973, based on the conviction that it had achieved America's central objective: to give the peoples of Indochina an opportunity to determine their own fate. I have described elsewhere the details of the domestic debate and the evolution to the final catastrophe.* I will confine myself here to a summary of those issues that were relevant to the discussions of the last month.

The military provisions of the agreement were designed to prevent a recurrence of the conflict through a series of prohibitions: against the infiltration of North Vietnamese personnel into the countries of Indochina including South Vietnam; against the presence of North Vietnamese forces in Laos and Cambodia; against the entry of new military equipment (except to replace old equipment through international checkpoints); against the use of Laotian and Cambodian territory as military bases. The United States would withdraw its armed forces within two months. Prisoners would be returned.

The agreement's political provisions required national elections supervised by a council composed in equal parts of North and South Vietnamese participants, giving each side a veto.

North Vietnam violated all of these agreements. North Vietnamese forces remained in both Laos and Cambodia. Infiltrations of personnel into South Vietnam took place on a massive scale, culminating in the movement of eleven of North Vietnam's twelve divisions into South Vietnam in early 1975. Quantities of military equipment far exceeding the permitted replacement were introduced throughout.

The domestic disputes that had characterized the war continued into the postwar period, and the Watergate crisis prevented enforcement of the agreement. The controversy began with a debate over whether the United States had the right to defend an agreement for which over 55,000 Americans had died. And then, within six months, Congress in June 1973 prohibited any U.S. military action or military deployment in Indochina. It was the first time that the United States had deprived itself of the ability to enforce an agreement for which American forces had fought and died.

---

* Henry Kissinger, *Ending the Vietnam War* (New York: Simon & Schuster, 2003).

At the same time, congressional appropriations to Vietnam were reduced by 50 percent in each year from $2.5 billion in 1973 to $1.4 billion in 1974 and then to $700 million in 1975. The impact of these cuts on Saigon's forces was described by the authoritative journal of the North Vietnamese Communist Party, *Hoc Tap*, in January 1975 on the eve of the final North Vietnamese offensive:

> The intensity of firepower and the amount of mobile equipment of the puppet troops [Saigon] have markedly decreased. In the third quarter of 1974, the monthly number of artillery rounds fired by the puppet troops decreased approximately by three-fourths, compared with the monthly number in 1973. The number of daily tactical sorties of the puppet air force only equaled approximately one-fifth of those conducted in 1972. The present number of aircraft in the South, compared with the greatest number of aircraft on hand in the period of the limited war, has decreased by 70 percent, with the number of helicopters decreasing by 80 percent. . . . The bomb and ammunition reserves of the puppet troops have decreased and they are encountering great difficulties in fuel and in the maintenance, repair and use of various types of aircraft, tanks, combat vessels and heavy weapons.

Matters were brought to a head in early 1975 when President Gerald R. Ford, who had succeeded President Nixon in August 1974, asked Congress for a supplemental budget for Vietnam of $300 million to raise the total to $1 billion, 40 percent of the total aid appropriated for 1973, the first peacetime year. That sum had been promised by the chairman of the Senate Armed Services Committee, the venerable John Stennis (D.-Miss.) in 1974, in case of need. The request was fiercely resisted in a Congress which had been elected in the previous November under the impact of Watergate and contained a majority of members supporting the views of George McGovern—the 1972 Democratic presidential candidate—who had advocated a unilateral withdrawal from Indochina during the campaign. One idea that was gaining ground was to arrange a one-time terminal grant, which treated Vietnam as if it were a welfare case supported by foundations. Once the administration began to explore the concept, the amount for it became controversial, so that by March 1975, no new money had been voted, while eleven North Vietnamese divisions were invading the country. Additional aid to Cambodia was rejected altogether.

Confronted by the entire North Vietnamese army and with uncertain prospects for American aid, the South Vietnamese government decided to contract its defensive perimeter and to withdraw from the so-called Central Highlands. But no preparations had been made for a redeployment that gave up about 30 percent of the country. The retreat was all the more complicated because South Vietnamese military units always traveled with their dependents. A rout ensued; a quarter of the regular forces and half of the strategic reserves of South Vietnam were lost, together with the northern third of the country. The United States was left to watch events unfold as spectators—some tormented, others jubilant at the approaching end.

As this drama evolved, I was in the Middle East, conducting shuttle diplomacy for what later became the first political agreement between Israel and Egypt. Like my colleagues in Washington, I had observed the unfolding of the tragedy, unable to affect events. By the time I returned on March 23, Da Nang—the linchpin of the defense of the northern third of the country—was falling; catastrophe was certain for neglected Cambodia, probable for Vietnam.*

Washington was rent by three debates during the last month of the Vietnam tragedy:

- whether to extend additional aid to Vietnam and, if so, how much; this had been promised at the end of the previous year as a supplemental budget if the need arose. The figure then on the table was $300 million.

---

* For a full account, see Kissinger, *Ending the Vietnam War*, pp. 532–33.

- the rate of withdrawal of the six thousand remaining Americans, and of as many Vietnamese who had worked with us as possible;
- the prospects of mitigating the looming catastrophe by negotiation.

The controversy about aid raged on even as it became ever clearer that no new supplies were likely to reach Saigon before its final collapse. Congress was determined to prevent even a symbolic assistance, arguing that blocking it would thwart the administration's alleged efforts to recommit itself to the conflict—which was a figment of congressional imagination. The congressional majority was determined to impose a demonstrative end to America's involvement by refusing additional aid in order to teach the lesson of the futility of American commitment to distant regions. They did this by stalling deliberations on aid to Vietnam and refusing aid to Cambodia altogether.

President Ford and I had no illusions about the outcome of the tragedy. But we thought it important not to compound the evolving calamity by a deliberate and public abandonment of peoples who had linked their fate to American promises. We thought cutting off aid to an ally *in extremis* was shameful and could have a disastrous impact on nations relying on America for their security. And we faced two immediate operational problems. If the United States abandoned the aid request, the Saigon government would panic. In the ensuing chaos, the over six thousand Americans (mostly civilians) remaining in Vietnam might be made hostages by an enraged population and the abandoned South Vietnamese military. Above all, we were fully determined to save as many Vietnamese who had cooperated with America as we could. All this imposed a need for gaining time. President Ford therefore sent General Fred C. Weyand, the Army Chief of Staff, to Saigon to study Vietnam's requirements. The $300 million supplemental had become irrelevant. As long as we asked for aid from Congress, we might as well do so with a realistic, hence plausible, figure. I summed up this reasoning when briefing a State Department staff meeting about a request by the President for $722 million in aid on April 10:

> If the President last night had said what so many congressmen say he should have said—namely "We've done enough; we can no longer give military aid," I think Phil Habib [Assistant Secretary of State for East Asia] will agree there will be total uncontrollable, chaotic collapse in Saigon starting this morning. Once the President decided he was not going to do nothing, he might just as well ask for what is right on this because the opposition on the Hill is not hinged on a figure; it's hinged on the principle. . . .
>
> This thing is now going to go its course; its course is reasonably predictable. And what we are trying to do is to manage it with dignity and to preserve a basis for which we can conduct the foreign policy, in which people can have some confidence in us.

That request, on which Congress never acted, consumed the last month of South Vietnam's collapse.

The issue of the rate of withdrawal produced a dispute between the Defense Department and State Department, backed by the White House. The Department of Defense had been tormented by the conflict, obliged to conduct a war without controlling its strategy, its efforts thwarted on the battlefield, its forces vilified at home. It wanted to run no further risks and therefore constantly pressed for the most rapid evacuation from Vietnam. And since any evacuation would have to use Defense Department resources, the Pentagon had a special claim to attention. At the same time, the President (and I) feared that a sudden evacuation would produce panic, risking American lives and thwarting the attempt to save Vietnamese endangered by having cooperated with the United States. All these themes recurred throughout that fateful month of April 1975.

Finally, there was the pressure for negotiations to solve the catastrophe looming before us. Having negotiated with the North Vietnamese for five years, I had no illusions. Hanoi had been intractable when there was a military stalemate; it would not let us salvage a military defeat at the conference table. Nevertheless, in the desperate straits of Vietnam, we tried diplomacy as a means of gaining time for evacuation.

These three themes dominated the Washington political debates as Indochina was in its death throes during that fateful April of 1975.

And they were all essentially irrelevant and conducted for largely symbolic reasons. Those of us who favored going through the motions of giving aid knew it would never get there before the collapse. Those who opposed it knew that they were not hastening—as they professed—the end of a war; the end was imminent no matter what the fate of the aid bill. And those who were pressing negotiations— and those of us who fell in with it in desperation—knew in their hearts that the North Vietnamese, having been obdurate when America was strong, would extend no act of grace in the face of catastrophe.

So all the participants in what follows were adhering to a script established in a decade of bitter domestic strife: the administration pursued its definition of honor; the opposition its view that only extirpation of the Indochina adventure could preserve American values. And the advocates of negotiation insisted until the last month the illusion that there was some negotiating proposal that could extricate America from its dilemmas.

The Beginning of the End

During the first few days after my return from the Middle East on March 23, the administration was preoccupied with the stalled negotiations.

Vietnam reached my agenda at first because of the plight of Vietnamese refugees in Da Nang, the hub of the northern part of the country, which was on the verge of falling. The Assistant Secretary of State for East Asia, Philip Habib, had come up with a plan to rescue as many Vietnamese as possible by evacuating them on American

LSTs (flat-bottomed landing ships) in Da Nang harbor. This raised concerns at the Pentagon, reluctant to jeopardize American personnel and equipment. Lawyers in both the White House and the State Department objected that such an initiative would be contrary to the 1973 peace agreement, which prohibited the introduction of outside military forces (this while eleven of the twelve available North Vietnamese divisions were illegally in the country). The Pentagon's concerns surfaced first, in a conversation with the Secretary of Defense, who had apparently made some statement objecting to State Department requests to use naval ships to evacuate refugees.

SECRETARY SCHLESINGER–KISSINGER
Thursday, March 27, 1975
6:12 P.M.

S: Hi, Henry. Say, don't take this stuff personally, for Christ sake—you did as much as anyone could do in Southeast Asia. How the hell could you imagine what these constraints would be at the close?

K: Oh no, I—

S: When I referred to the effectiveness of the U.S. policy, if we are going to go into Da Nang we ought to be able to—

K: No, no, I didn't think you were aiming it at me.

S: Yeah, okay.

K: No, really, I think that you and I are now exactly on the same wicket.

S: The reason I came today, when I read Habib's paper [recommending evacuation of civilians by American military ships], I thought that there was an assumption that DOD [Department of Defense] was going to be some kind of deus ex machina and could pull a rabbit out of a hat.

K: Well, he wanted me to run it past the President and I wouldn't do it. And that's why we called the WSAG [Washington Special Action Group, a committee at the Deputy Secretary level to deal with crises, which was often attended by principals]. Jim, no, no, believe me, I didn't think you were aiming these remarks at me and I really think that you and I are perhaps among the few who understand the nature of what's happening to our country right now.

S: Just tragic, just tragic.

K: And we will pay dearly for this.

S: Well, we already have, as you know.

K: But in parts of the world outside of Indochina.

S: Well, I think you were very gentle and I think you were right to be gentle yesterday in your conference when you mentioned it [the collapse of Vietnam] was a factor but probably not the dominating factor [in the stalled Middle East negotiations].

K: Well, I didn't want to use it as an alibi—it sounded like sour grapes.

S: If the prestige of the United States were high, I think you could have pulled—

K: Look, if the prestige of the U.S. were high and if our assurances meant anything, it [the Egyptian-Israeli negotiations for a political agreement which stalled in March but were completed in September] would have worked.

S: Right, the damn thing is tragic.

K: Jim, if there is some way we can get out the fact that there hasn't been much fighting and that this collapse has really been caused by us—

S: The only reason, I haven't done so, to this point, is to say that there hasn't been that much fighting—kind of puts the tail on the incompetency of that retrograde operation [Thieu's retreat from the Central Highlands] Thieu [General Nguyen Van Thieu, President of South Vietnam] started.

K: Yeah, but the retrograde operation in itself was a panic.

S: Oh, quite right, quite right. We will—that is the line I've been taking and I shall continue to take it. As you know, I did that last week, I think sometime or other—some briefing.

K: I think it would be helpful.

S: If you look at that aircraft situation—when Thieu looked at his inability to get mobility forces into Damytuet, which has never been taken and it is the main juncture—once Damytuet fell they couldn't use their highway down through the Highlands. And naturally, he panicked. Now the handling of that withdrawal—

K: Oh, it's been a disaster. Disaster. But you can see how he came to the conclusion. His execution was a disaster.

S: Well, that's right, but in addition to that, when he didn't consult with anyone—well, some of those fellows over at State have this notion that don't just stand there, do something and I don't mind that as long as what we are doing is going to be effective.

K: Jim, we don't want—the exit from Vietnam *shooting* its fleeing refugees—that is the conclusive argument here.

S: Right, we'll take a good hard look tomorrow at that MSC boat—we may try that as a test case—

K: The what?

S: The commercial boat that we are talking about putting in there.

K: Are you against that?

S: I'm worried about it because, once again, you get the U.S. involved in a token operation and it can turn into a very questionable outcome.

K: That boat won't put in before we hear from Lieutenant General Ngo Quang Truong [Vietnamese commander of region].

S: Right, I will make sure we don't move it until we hear from Truong.

K: Make sure about that and then let's you and I consult.

SECRETARY SCHLESINGER–KISSINGER

Saturday, March 29, 1975
12:55 P.M.

S: The USN's [U.S. Navy] LSTs are at Subic Bay [Philippines]. Preparations are being made to put them to sea to pick up refugees.

K: What is your view?

S: I am very skeptical, but we now have a kind of widespread universal view in our bureaucracy; State is perhaps more pungent on this. They are saying you can save people and so forth. We've even had a request from the Vatican. We have the ships going in and if people can be lightered [ferried out to the LST, which would stay offshore], then I can see using the LSTs.

K: If we go in with LSTs, can we hold rioters?

S: No. We would have to require them to be lightered out. I think you will have a repetition of the Chu Lai incident [evacuation accompanied by panic].

K: I agree with you. I would not hesitate sending naval ships now. But I agree with you on lightering.

S: Okay. Very good.

K: Is there enough lightering capacity there?

S: We are taking a look at it and will see if there is enough capacity.

K: Okay. I agree with you. Thank you, Jim.

S: Okay. Bye.

I checked next with President Ford.

THE PRESIDENT, GERALD R. FORD–KISSINGER
Saturday, March 29, 1975
2:15 P.M.

K: I have two things. One is, you know we have had an urgent appeal from the Pope and many others about evacuating the refugees and others from Da Nang. We have countries who have sent LSTs. Australia has sent military airplanes. We would like to send LSTs from the Philippines. Schlesinger is aboard on this. We would not have them land on the beaches, but have the refugees lightered out. Our lawyers feel this requires notification to key congressional leaders.

F: What kind of notification?

K: Just tell them we are doing it.

F: I think we ought to do it, notify them and make a public statement.

K: Let's notify them first and then make the public statements. I think it is a humanitarian gesture.

F: Right.

K: The British are sending a frigate.

F: How quickly can they do it?

K: We let them leave the Philippines and they should be there tomorrow.

F: I think we should notify the members of the Congress, then announce it.

. . .

Within days, the tragedy of Da Nang shaded into the greater tragedy of Indochina. Constant rumors were fed by wishful thinking that at the last moment a negotiated solution might be available.

DAVID BINDER, *NEW YORK TIMES*–KISSINGER
Tuesday, April 1, 1975
3:00 P.M.

. . .

B: . . . I am calling about these flash stories coming out of Palm Springs [where President Ford was vacationing] saying we have started a diplomatic initiative, or effort, to settle the Vietnam problem.

K: Bullshit.

B: Have we got anything going at all? Russkies? Hanoi?

K: Look, David, you know North Vietnam and you know diplomacy. Under these conditions what can be done?

B: You under—I am working on this story today—and when we get a flash—

K: You cannot say I said bullshit, but I am not aware of anything.

But I don't see how they can be aware of anything. I don't know since they get their information from me.

B: Reuters did a flash on this and it is absolutely incorrect?

K: Yes.

B: We are not talking to anybody? Waiting for the blood to dry and the dust to settle?

K: What is there to say?

B: Habib got a lot of these same questions today and these bulletins from Reuters.

K: I appreciate your checking but there is nothing unusual going on.

. . .

GENERAL SCOWCROFT–KISSINGER
Tuesday, April 1, 1975
3:51 P.M.

. . .

S: The President is going to have a press conference on Thursday. We are going to have to get some Qs and As on Vietnam.

K: He has to pinpoint the responsibility.

S: On Indochina.

K: On Indochina. Just explain what happened. Can I see it [proposed answer] tonight?

S: Yes.

K: Good.

THE PRESIDENT–KISSINGER
Tuesday, April 1, 1975
7:15 P.M.

K: I'm really looking forward to coming out [to Palm Springs] on Thursday evening. I understand Fred Weyand [Army Chief of Staff sent by Ford to Vietnam to assess military needs] was delayed in Saigon because Thieu could not see him until today or tomorrow.

F: That's what Jim Schlesinger told me this morning. I talked with [unclear] and Fred would meet me in San Francisco on Friday before coming down here with us, so I would see him in San Francisco on Friday and then he could come down and the three of us could meet here.

K: That's very good. One thing, I know Jim has talked with you on the evacuation in Phnom Penh [capital of Cambodia]? My suggestion is that we tell the [Cambodian] government that you're planning to give a speech on the 9th or 10th. I would recommend the 10th.

F: It has to be the 10th because of the Speaker's [of the House of Representatives, Carl Albert] plans. It's definitely set for the evening of the 10th at 9:00.

K: That gives us a little more time to work on it. I would propose that we tell them that you're going to make any effort for aid in that speech, just to give them something to hold on to in the meantime rather—

F: I think it's wise.

K: If we start moving people out, there's going to be a total collapse before you could— With your permission I would like to send off a cable and do it on that basis. We'll tell them [Cambodian government] your plans for a speech. This will give them something to hold on for and in the meantime we'll pull out two hundred Americans.

F: Jim tells me sixty to seventy who had not really [garbled] over the present situation.

K: That's right and there are some people in other agencies.

F: I think we should present this.

K: I think we plan to pull out 150 people [from Phnom Penh] over the next few days. It may trigger the collapse but I don't see that we can do much about it. If we send them the message I discussed with you, I think that would sort of balance it.

F: It seemed to me that if we send it to them, they would have to hold out until the 10th because of what I was going to say and if

anything went wrong, it could be badly misunderstood and ex-
ploited. As long as we do—

K: What I would propose to put into the cable is this. We would inform them of your plan for a speech and you could ask for aid.
We leave the decision up to them and we'll inform their government of the decision and that we'll take out nonessential personnel and we'll tell them you're giving a speech so they don't
collapse the day we start pulling out Americans.

F: I think that's the right way to handle it.

K: We have to start developing evacuation plans for Saigon. It
hasn't reached that point yet, but there are more Americans
there. We should have the plan but not necessarily do it.

F: I think the development of plans should get started right away
but closely held.

. . .

At the same time, the White House was preparing the speech for
the President referred to in the previous conversation, recommending aid to Vietnam, based on the report about to be submitted by
General Weyand. I discussed these subjects with Donald Rumsfeld,
who had been made White House chief of staff by President Ford in
August 1974.

DONALD RUMSFELD, WHITE HOUSE
CHIEF OF STAFF–KISSINGER
  Wednesday, April 2, 1975
  4:57 P.M.

  . . .

R: When will you have your draft?

K: By tomorrow noon your time.

R: And you'll send it out?

K: Yes.

R: Are you going to get into international economics at all in this
speech?

K: I don't think so. We can put something in.

R: It seems to me—I just don't know if I think it's a good idea. The question is, can you separate international economics completely out.

K: That's a good point. We'll add a few pages to it.

R: I think, also, you and he were thinking this speech is a kind of— the fact you didn't touch on this in the State of the Union.

K: I'm looking at it more in terms that we have a critical situation. Foreign policy is basically in good shape. If we pull together we can still salvage it and do good things.

R: You're going to get into CIA [investigations of the Central Intelligence Agency headed by Senator Frank Church, D.-Idaho]?

K: Yes.

R: Good. NATO?

K: Yes. But that is a success story.

R: Yes. I'll ask him about Thursday night. He might want to see you if it's as early as 10:00.

K: We can leave it open. I think my plane is due in at 10:05 or something like that.

R: You'd be another thirty minutes at least.

K: Then let's skip it. It's three hours later, for me anyway, but I'll be glad to see him.

R: I'll mention the Weyand thing and then we'll look for a new draft of the speech.

. . .

BRUCE VAN VOORST, *NEWSWEEK* DIPLOMATIC
CORRESPONDENT–KISSINGER

Wednesday, April 2, 1975
7:45 P.M.

. . .

V: On Vietnam, the Secretary of Defense today said and the Vice President [Nelson A. Rockefeller] said about the same thing, that Saigon will fall.

K: The Vice President claims he did not say that.

V: In any case, for guidance, is your operational assessment the two governments will fall shortly?

K: I can't say until I talk to Weyand.

V: What will be the impact on the American political scene on the [unclear].

K: I know what it will be abroad, it will be very serious. You know my view, you heard me on the plane. You know I'm right.

V: There is a school of thought around town that there is a question of whether this [crisis] is sort of self-created.

K: When you predict things, you're accused of causing what you predicted.

V: The question really is how serious.

K: This is all on deep background.

V: I realize that. The Vietnam thing, is it not, more your personal involvement?

K: Come on. What is my personal involvement?

V: Getting the agreement.

K: Which was [unclear] after the U.S. was deprived the means of enforcing it. You tell me, would any treaties have been maintain[ed] when no party was willing to enforce it?

V: It has happened.

. . .

GENERAL SCOWCROFT–KISSINGER

Wednesday, April 2, 1975
7:55 P.M.

K: Did Schlesinger say today that Thieu is done for?

S: On that, I don't know.

K: That's what *Newsweek* is asking me.

S: I just got his briefing. Do you want me to look it over and call you back?

K: Yes.

S: It's several pages.

K: Did he say that? It's a goddamn disgrace.

S: The Vice President sort of did. It says, "How long do you think President Thieu will remain in power" and he said, "That's what Vietnam will have to decide themselves." That's all right. I don't see anything else about Thieu.

K: Schlesinger should have said what led to the collapse.

S: He maybe did. I have eight pages of single space here. I'm looking for the one thing.

K: Okay. Thank you.

THE PRESIDENT (FROM CALIFORNIA)–KISSINGER
Thursday, April 3, 1975
11:22 A.M.

K: Mr. President, I just wanted to check one thing with you. Gayler [Noel Gayler, Pacific Fleet commander] and Dean [John Gunther Dean, U.S. Ambassador to Cambodia] have come in with a recommendation to begin accelerating the pullout from Phnom Penh.

F: Right.

K: And I think we should do that.

F: That's beyond the twenty-nine or thirty plus the sixty or seventy [the previous tranches of withdrawal recommended]. In other words, do more than just the nonoperational people.

K: In effect, really, get it down to the minimum needed to run the airlift.

F: Well, if they recommend it I think we ought to undertake it. Don't you?

K: That's right. And I think, Mr. President, if you concur, we should call some congressional leaders and inform them of the fact that you have ordered this.

F: I agree, Henry. Tell them to go ahead.

K: Right. Okay. I will do that. Now, I have had a talk with Jack

Marsh [presidential aide brought into the White House by Ford]. He wanted you to make a very conciliatory statement about the Congress.

F: Right.

K: I personally disagree with that. I think you need a Churchillean posture now. I don't think you have to belabor this—them.

F: My inclination is to just point out the facts, Henry, and say that if the facts had been different the situation today would be different.

K: That's fine. You don't have to cast blame. I think—first of all, I think you should be very violent on North Vietnamese—

F: Violations.

K: Violations. They have totally abrogated an agreement solemnly signed by them and endorsed by eleven other nations and have turned it into a scrap of paper. That I would make very strong.

F: Right.

K: Secondly, I would say that—I would keep making that point. There were two aspects of it—our ability to enforce it [the peace agreement] and the amount of aid we gave. Both of them were reduced over the years.

F: Right.

K: And those are the facts. In addition, all of this contributed to the panic which we are now seeing. Then if you want to say, now we have to face the future, that would be—I'd have no problem with that.

F: If I am asked about an assessment of where we are, what the situation is—my feeling is that I should say I do not think I should publicly evaluate the military situation in Indochina.

K: Until you have talked to Weyand.

F: That's right, because I don't want to say anything that will encourage the Communists and undermine our allies of South Vietnam.

K: Absolutely right.

F: For me to make anything beyond what I think would be completely inappropriate at this time.

   . . .

K: . . . I am absolutely convinced, Mr. President, if you play it for
the two years period rather than two weeks—now everybody
wants to be taken off the hot seat.

F: Right.

K: But if you come out with a somewhat Churchillean stance—say
yes, there are major problems but we can master them along the
lines we handled yesterday. Then the American people would really rally.

F: Well, along that line I thought I would use three points: 1) I am
saddened by what I see and what I read.

K: I would frankly say we have to face the fact that we bear a certain
responsibility as a nation for—

F: Right. And then I would add, I am frustrated by the fact that
there wasn't sufficient aid given from a military point of view and
I am frustrated by the fact that our hands were tied in doing anything militarily.

K: Excellent.

F: Number three, I am totally determined that we are not going to
let this present setback interfere with our world leadership.

K: Because the peace of the world depends on our world leadership
and this is the American stake in it.

F: Right. . . .

   . . .

As Cambodia was unraveling, the deteriorating situation in Vietnam required us to begin arranging for the evacuation of Americans
from that country as well. That planning ran up against the formida-
ble personality of the U.S. Ambassador, Graham Martin. Martin
performed heroically and upheld to the bitter end the American
commitment to a free South Vietnam for which so many thousands,

including—as it happened—his adopted son, had given their lives. To induce Washington to go along with his recommendations, Martin was not above shading his analysis to accord with his preconceptions.

Faced with imminent disaster, Martin decided to go down with the ship and battled for his convictions until the last second of the last day. Believing that the United States Congress had erred grievously in abandoning South Vietnam, he resisted conventional media and congressional wisdom and made no concessions to the illusory "compromises" with which they salved their consciences. I knew very well that Martin's many hortatory messages were designed in part to create a record that might later be published—perhaps even to my disadvantage. For Martin tended to consider anything less than 100 percent support as betrayal. But whatever the record, it would show Martin struggling to maintain America's moral commitments. I agreed with his objectives, if not always with their feasibility. And I considered him an ally, albeit an occasionally aberrant one. In the meantime, my heart went out to Martin as I watched him mask his anguish with bravado.

Martin was reluctant to evacuate any Americans because he feared that such an act might accelerate Vietnam's disintegration. Though I was struggling to temper the Pentagon's sense of urgency for a more rapid evacuation, I considered Graham Martin's stonewalling dangerous.

AMBASSADOR PHILIP HABIB, ASSISTANT SECRETARY OF STATE FOR EAST ASIA–KISSINGER
   Thursday, April 3, 1975
   5:07 P.M.

K: Could you send that note to Martin about evacuation in a friendlier tone?

H: I thought it was polite. His tone wasn't that friendly. I thought I put it very businesslike to him. When a man doesn't carry out in-

structions from the Secretary of State and says he's been waiting
for three Marines he asked for, it is like he's not going to do this
until we do something for him.

K: I know what problems Graham Martin has.

H: He's got to learn to take orders.

K: I would just give him a specific order in a more polite way.
We want him to get the dependents out and he is to move on
this.

H: Did you see what I said?

K: Yes. It's a little too harsh.

H: I'll do anything you want. Except I'm beginning to run out of patience.

K: I understand why.

As Vietnam was disintegrating, Washington was searching
for scapegoats. Senator Henry "Scoop" Jackson (D.-Wash.), who
had already announced that he would vote against aid to Vietnam,
started a brushfire by charging that President Nixon had made "secret" commitments to Vietnam by personal letters to President
Thieu, promising that the United States would help enforce the
Paris Agreements.

That particular debate went back to the days the agreement was
signed and depended on the legal significance of presidential letters.
Presidential letters are not legal commitments but expressions of
intent of the incumbent President with respect to foreseeable con-
tingencies. They impose a moral, not a legal, obligation on his
successors (which inevitably declines with the distance from the
presidency). And, of course, no President is able to commit Congress
by a unilateral declaration.

In the case of Vietnam, Nixon's letters were written in the interval between the election in November 1972 and inauguration at the
moment that negotiations were coalescing into an agreement. Thieu
therefore had every reason to expect that Nixon would have four

years to carry out statements of his intentions totally compatible with his previous record and America's conduct toward previous agreements. Moreover, the President's associates repeatedly avowed the administration's determination to enforce the agreement publicly.* These pronouncements repeated the substance of what was in the presidential letters to President Thieu. The letters were similar to letters on comparable subjects written by Nixon's predecessors, for example, President John F. Kennedy's secret pledge to defend Pakistan against aggression.

In any event, the argument about the nature of America's obligation missed the central point. Neither the Ford nor the Nixon administration ever invoked a legal obligation to assist Vietnam. What they insisted on was something deeper—a moral obligation. America owed assistance to the peoples who had stood with us, to the casualties we had suffered, and to the common efforts in which we had been involved—in short, to ourselves.

When the United States concludes a peace agreement, the other party should be on notice that it will not be permitted it to violate its terms with impunity. Without a penalty for violations, a cease-fire turns into a subterfuge for surrender. Every previous and subsequent administration has held that view. The Jackson accusation led to an intense controversy essentially repeating what had become a standard dispute for two years.

GENERAL SCOWCROFT–KISSINGER

Tuesday, April 8, 1975
5:20 P.M.

K: We're being pressed very hard about these Jackson statements.

S: I'm drafting a statement right now to send over to you.

K: And we'll say the White House will comment on this.

---

* See Henry Kissinger, *Ending the Vietnam War* (New York: Simon & Schuster, 2003), p. 601ff.

S: I think that's better—from the White House. Weyand was at lunch on the Hill and is still there and I understand he talked about the letter [Nixon's letter to Thieu of December 1975] to the JCS [Joint Chiefs of Staff]. Wickham [General John Wickham, Army Chief of Staff] mentioned it to me.

K: What gives him the right to do that?

S: I have no idea. What was the discussion in California?

K: Ford kept me out. He [Weyand] showed [the letters] only to the President [Ford].

S: And then he talked to the Chiefs about them.

K: That's how it came out. That's obvious.

S: That's apparent now.

K: Does the President understand this?

S: No.

K: Well, you better send the statement over here.

S: I'll get it over in a couple of minutes.

JAMES "SCOTTY" RESTON, *NEW YORK TIMES*–KISSINGER
Thursday, April 8, 1975
6:40 P.M.

R: I am calling about your friend Jackson.

K: Oh, Jesus Christ.

R: Well, I am going to skin him alive.

K: Look, let me tell you there were a number of presidential letters, this is off the record, to convince Thieu to accept the agreement. There is nothing in these letters that I have been able to find different than Nixon said publicly. There were no secret agreements, even on the—

R: I have read the record about what Nixon said at that time and it is clear that the U.S. would perform a kind of watchdog function.

K: That is right and that is all he said privately.

R: Did Ford ever do anything about these presidential letters to Thieu?

K: No.

R: What he [Jackson] is doing is making charges of treachery.

K: It is one of these double things. He is saying that [we] are betraying the South Vietnamese and we are betraying the country while he is opposed to doing anything publicly. Nixon said nothing privately that he did not later repeat publicly. General statements about providing the watchdog role were later told to Congress and the Congress prohibited the watchdog role in July 1973. Ever since July 1973 it has been obvious that we were legally prohibited from doing anything. In July 1973 the President never invoked this legally.

R: What did Congress provide?

K: In July 1973 they prohibited military action in, over, and around Indochina.

R: Military action by us?

K: By us. At no time during that debate did we invoke any agreement and then when the War Powers Act came up, then there was some [disagreement]. Consequently, the understanding on Indochina is that we could make a plausible case to that effect.

R: [Quoting from Nixon that:] "We shall insist that North Vietnam comply with the agreement."

K: Right. In the Foreign Policy Report of May 1973, he [Nixon] said that we have told Hanoi privately and publicly that we will not tolerate a violation of the agreement and actions of aggression by North Vietnam. That is all we said about it.

R: You know he [Jackson] has been around long enough to know that the word secret agreement has a very special meaning going back to Wilson.

K: An agreement is a contractual obligation; this at least was an obligation, and you know what agony we were going through to get out of that war. Everyone wanted us to get out; public opinion was to get us the hell out of there. People think we had the opportunity to get the perfect agreement.

R: He [Jackson] keeps saying he did not pick up my call and that he made one to you. [Dorothy] Fosdick [administrative assistant to Senator Henry Jackson] said he had been trying to get to you for days and days before he put this out.

K: This is a total lie. He [Jackson] has made no effort to get in touch with me. A call like that would have reached me.

R: Just what we needed.

K: Right. He [Jackson] really makes it hard to get at.

R: If he were right, he would be insensitive. If he is wrong, it is not sensible.

K: Even if he were right, we have reached no commitment. I have stated publicly we only have a moral obligation, not a legal obligation, so what does that achieve?

R: Nothing but controversy, and some publicity. It is not even good politics from his point of view. What is the point of saying we have come across with a legal commitment?

K: That I don't know.

R: Okay, another day, thank you, Henry.

GENERAL SCOWCROFT–KISSINGER

Tuesday, April 8, 1975
6:45 P.M.

K: Have we put out a story on this thing?

S: No, I haven't. [Presidential Press Secretary Ron] Nessen wanted to wait till he [Nixon] got to the President.

K: I am getting deluged by phone calls. There was no secret agreement. And I am saying that there is nothing that goes beyond what was on the public record.

S: I think that is exactly right. The statements in the annual reports are at least as tough. There is no question. We will not tolerate violations, which is what it says.

K: Which is all it says. Can you have somebody go through the memcons [memoranda of conversations] to see if we promised anything [specific].

S: Yes.

K: Weyand told the Chiefs [about the letters].

S: Yes.

K: We must correct him on that.

S: I am waiting for him to call me back.

K: And will you ask him how he can give presidential letters to the Chiefs.

S: Yes. Nessen said he is going to try to get to the President as soon as he could.

K: And the President has our speech.

S: Yes.

K: Thank you.

RICHARD VALERIANI, NBC NEWS–KISSINGER
Tuesday, April 8, 1975
7:00 P.M.

V: We have some trouble with the Jackson charges. Tell us how to handle them.

K: How—

V: Some sort of statement by the Department.

K: I thought that we did respond.

V: On the secret agreement?

K: Well you know, there was no secret agreement. I am not going to get into a contest with McGovern again. I have had enough experience with him. There was no agreement. There were some, a number, of presidential letters, off the record, paralleling exactly what he said publicly at various press conferences and in annual reports.

V: From President Nixon?

K: Yes.

V: In a news conference?

K: Yes, privately and publicly, he said that he would not tolerate violations of the agreement by North Vietnam.

V: This was said in presidential letters to both sides?

K: South Vietnam essentially.

V: Don't you want to say this publicly to avoid contentions with Congress?

K: I want no contest with him [McGovern]. This is just for your guidance. There should be some kind of public statement.

V: A reiteration of the news statements in California?

K: No. My point—we made no agreements. There were a number of presidential letters. You can say your understanding is that nothing, in effect, is different from the various press conferences he gave.

V: And the letters were needed—

K: To get him [Thieu] to sign the agreement.

V: Nothing was said that goes beyond the public record?

K: Nothing, that I have been able to find.

GENERAL SCOWCROFT–KISSINGER
Tuesday, April 8, 1975
7:55 P.M.

K: Did you know that Nessen made a statement tonight that this [the issue of the nature of commitments in presidential letters] is being researched?

S: No, I didn't know that.

K: I told Bob [McCloskey] to call a number of people on this.

S: I don't know why he said that. He always says something.

K: Can you have Peter [Rodman] go through the memcons to see if there is anything we didn't say publicly?

S: There is one in December which shows what we are prepared to do in case of a violation. That is the worst one. It comes closer than anything to saying what we would do. But I don't think that this is a commitment.

K: No, it is just an indication of the sort of thing we intended to do. But then it became moot in 1973 [when Congress prohibited military action in Indochina].

S: Yes.

K: Okay. Good.

While Washington was conducting its permanent strife over Vietnam, the problem of evacuating Saigon became more urgent.

BEN BRADLEE, *WASHINGTON POST*
EXECUTIVE EDITOR–KISSINGER
Wednesday, April 9, 1975
2:40 P.M.

. . .

B: . . . I've got three guys in Saigon who concern me and worry me and the evacuation of whom is obviously important to me. They seem to doubt the implementability of the evacuation plans and I am worried about whether you are satisfied that—

K: Well, now what are you talking about? Americans or Vietnamese?

B: I was talking about both. Now I'm talking exclusively about Americans. I mean, I would love to make arrangements and I know that there are plenty of efforts, and I'm sure you've been involved in them, to get the Vietnamese employees out. Now I'm worried about the Americans themselves. Do you feel that the evacuation plans are okay?

K: Look, the evacuation plan—this you cannot use.

B: I'm not using it at all.

K: Our problem with [the] evacuation is to do it in such a way that we don't trigger: 1) total panic, and 2) anti-American riots.

B: Yeah.

K: This might then prevent anybody from getting out. So I can't give you—I think the evacuation plans are okay. And then, between you and me, we've got an Ambassador there who is maybe losing his cool.

B: Well, I think he is. And I've known that Ambassador for twenty-five years.

K: And so we are going to watch that situation. I'm not so worried about getting the Americans out unless the thing goes to pieces in a way that's going to be a total disaster.

B: Yeah.

K: What worries me is, you know, there are hundreds of thousands of South Vietnamese towards whom we must make at least a show of trying to save their lives. And those plans—that's tough.

B: Yeah. But I talked to Don Oberdorfer [*Washington Post* reporter] this morning and he is a responsible, cool man—

K: Where is he?

B: He's in Saigon. He says that the current evacuation plans require twelve to eighteen hours' notice and no opposition.

K: Well, let me put it this way: whatever isn't in shape—by tomorrow night will be in shape by then.

B: Okay.

K: I mean, we're going to reduce that readiness considerably.

B: You're going to reduce it twelve to eighteen hours?

K: Well, I haven't got the exact figures here but I can assure you it's one of the things—you know, unless the thing goes in twenty-four hours.

B: In the next twenty-four hours?

K: Yeah. I think we'll—by the weekend we'll have the evacuation plans in good order and we will be reducing people to a point so that it will become more manageable.

. . .

On April 10, Ford addressed Congress, asking for $722 million for aid to Vietnam—the figure recommended by General Weyand. How Weyand arrived at a figure of such precision is difficult to reconstruct at this remove.

PRESIDENTIAL PRESS SECRETARY RON NESSEN–KISSINGER

Thursday, April 10, 1975
3:05 P.M.

K: Ron?

N: Yes, Henry.

K: When I brief around 6:00, they will have read the speech.

N: I hope so.

K: Give them ten minutes with the speech.

N: I'm going to try to give them a little bit longer. I hope to get the speech to them by 5:00 maybe. That will give them an hour to read it, and think about it.

K: Good. And then I'll, well, I don't know whether I want them to think about it. I thought I'd do a conciliatory— You know, it's a fairly tough speech. And I thought I'd make a rather conciliatory briefing, explaining what he [Ford] is trying to do.

N: Okay. I think that's a good idea. I get the feeling that people are sort of leaning in that direction based on some of the things that the congressmen said when they left here yesterday. There was going to be a big pitch for bipartisan foreign policy and no finger-pointing and that kind of thing, so I guess that's what they're trying for, is that kind of approach.

K: But he's asking, in effect, the Congress to undo every legislation—

N: I know, that's going to be the toughest thing, and that's why I mentioned this morning this idea.

K: You've seen it, haven't you?

N: Yes.

K: What do you think?

N: Well, I think the toughest thing to deal with is going to be the request for American troops to go back in there. [Ford request that in emergency situations, American forces could assist in the evacuation of Americans.] And also for the money, and that's why I said this morning to you that you ought to explain that the money is—

K: Now what I will do about the money is to explain that whatever your assessment is of Vietnam, whether you think we ought to get out now, whether you think there should be a negotiation, or whether you think that you have to stabilize it, you've got to ask for the same amount. Because you can't get out now unless you've got something in place which helps you get out.

N: Well, that's the point. I mean that's a very persuasive argument. That these Americans are in great danger. And if you pull the plug now you're going to pull the plug on six thousand Americans. What ground rules do you want, Henry? A high American official, or do you want to go deeper than that?

K: What do you think?

N: I suspect it might be good to go deeper than that. You could speak more candidly and not have it attributed to anybody. Tell them that we want them to listen to you to gain some insights into what was behind the speech, what the future holds and they're going to have the President on record so they don't need any attributions for you.

K: That's fine with me.

. . .

As we briefed the media on the speech, we had to prepare the evacuation of Phnom Penh, whose defenders had run out of ammunition due to the congressional cutoff of American supplies.

AMBASSADOR HABIB–KISSINGER

Thursday, April 10, 1975
8:10 P.M.

H: The situation in Phnom Penh is getting very precarious. I don't know if we have time to wait to pull [Ambassador] John Dean and his people out. They're bombarding the airfield over there with howitzers and rockets. They've broken through some critical places.

K: What do you recommend?

H: That we tell them to get out by [unclear] rather than using the helicopters and Marines.

K: Which means the whole thing will collapse.

H: No question. They say it's highly possible the airfield will be closed by dawn. This [cable] is 5:00 P.M., local time zone.

K: I'll talk to the President. It's night anyway there now. I'll let you know by noon. The President in his speech is saying we're approaching all signatories of the Geneva Conference [of 1954] to arrange a cease-fire. Will you draft a note?

H: We'll get right on it.

THE PRESIDENT–KISSINGER

Thursday, April 10, 1975
8:23 P.M.

K: Mr. President, I just wanted to give you two things. One, we can no longer use Phnom Penh airport so we are going to do Eagle Pull [code name for final evacuation with helicopters] with the Marines on Saturday morning [April 12].

F: Right.

K: We can't do it tomorrow morning but we better not talk about that.

F: Well, Don [Rumsfeld] spoke to me and we modified that—he, by saying that it may be soon too late. Is that all right?

K: That is fine.

F: Okay.

K: The second thing is, I briefed both television and newsmen for about two hours.

F: Great.

K: You know, at first they started squawking about 722 [the amount of aid requested by Ford] and I said: If you were President, what figure is right for you? What would you do? Come up with a fictitious figure because if it's not 722, any of you could have picked any figure you wanted?

F: Right.

K: I thought they were in a very somber mood and not at all—

F: Belligerent.

K: No, not at all belligerent. The television people were not at all and the newsmen for them extremely respectful. I stressed the thing that you were not doing this in order to put the Congress on the spot, that the deadline was designed to put this thing behind us.

F: I think that's a good mood for them if they will reflect it in their commentaries and in their articles. And, you know, they are bound to do it if that's the way they acted. But I am going to be— to portray that attitude too.

K: I think the greatest strength you can show, the best it will be.

F: We will do our best.

K: Well, it's a good speech, Mr. President, and you led us all this week.

F: Okay. All right. We'll see you there tonight, Henry.

GENERAL SCOWCROFT–KISSINGER

Friday, April 11, 1975
7:38 A.M.

K: Two things: do you know there is going to be a joint State Department—Defense Department statement on the evacuation [of Cambodia] when it starts.

S: No, I didn't know. When it starts? Isn't that a little early?

K: Well, it will only be what is going to be done or what is being done at the time.

S: Okay. Well I guess nobody could react in that short a time.

K: I will tell them to put it out at 10:30. Okay?

S: That would be helpful.

. . .

GENERAL SCOWCROFT–KISSINGER

Friday, April 11, 1975
7:45 A.M.

. . .

K: What is the news on the evacuation?

S: Schlesinger will be on the phone constantly. Did you hear what [Israeli Defense Minister Shimon] Peres said this evening? [quotes from a news report about how the events that have just happened in Vietnam prove that Israel was right not to make any further concessions to Egypt during the abortive shuttle just recently completed.] The world is going up in flames (Peres talking) and I am convinced that our decision was the right one.

K: Excellent, suicidal, but excellent. . . .

. . .

As Phnom Penh was being evacuated, the tactical disagreements between the Pentagon and the State Department regarding the rate of evacuation continued.

SECRETARY SCHLESINGER–KISSINGER

Friday, April 11, 1975
9:01 A.M.

S: Henry. How's it go? Pochentong [Phnom Penh airport] was open all day yesterday. We had twenty flights in. They could have back-loaded people on. No problem. This guy [Ambassador Dean in Cambodia, who recommended using helicopters] is just acting like a loony.

K: Look. He claims—I checked it after our talk—that he, together with his, with all the military people there, felt he couldn't do it.

S: That's just plain flat wrong. Any advice he's getting from Tyler and from Palmer [Defense Department personnel in Phnom Penh] is just to the contrary, which is get moving. And he is in this position in which he wants to go out in a great wave of glory of helicopters to descend upon Phnom Penh. That's just a hairy operation—while he's got the fixed-wing aircraft he ought to be loading people on.

K: But, Jim, it is now dark. As I understand it, by daylight they're going to be ready to move, so— As I understand it, there is no further disagreement.

S: If he wants to stay on, he ought to load. Is he prepared to go out?

K: He's prepared to go out tomorrow.

S: Okay. His feeling is, he can't get to Pochentong, so we have to bring him the choppers.

K: That's his judgment.

S: Yes. But that was his judgment yesterday too. Pochentong was open all day. Okay?

K: You know, I just don't know what I can say. He claims that he and the military people he's got there feel it's got to be done by choppers.

S: He has been getting continued advice to the contrary—but, be that as it may. Now on Martin. Martin is doing a splendid job. He reduced the number of Americans by 570 yesterday. The way he did that was to fly out a few dependents and shift many of the so-called Americans to the role of aliens. [In other words, Martin, according to Schlesinger, was evacuating more Vietnamese than Americans, which was in the spirit of our policy.]

K: Jim!

S: He [Martin] needs a good kick.

K: Martin received instructions—the theory was that he would first help our AID [Agency for International Development] [people] and on the basis of that he would start evacuating people. And I think that should be going into operation today.

S: Okay.

K: You know, we also do have the responsibility not to collapse the whole thing.

S: I know. But, Henry, we could have gotten out 250 people a day or a hundred people a day or seventy-five people a day for the last ten days.

K: He is instructed now to get it down to about 1,200.

S: Okay. Well. Just keep him to the mark.

K: Okay. Thank you.

AMBASSADOR HABIB–KISSINGER
Friday, April 11, 1975
9:07 A.M.

K: Phil, in this maneuvering that's going on in the department—in the Defense Department—I've just had a call from Schlesinger and he claims that in his judgment fix-winged can do it. Now, I'm sticking behind you. I just want to find out why Dean believes it cannot.

H: Dean's specific words to me were, if you want to save lives, we'll do it with helicopters. If not—it is dangerous—we can't get to the airport. The airport is under fire. They lost another airplane there last night. They had a few people killed yesterday only two miles from the airport. Phil, if you want to save lives, do it this way. I said, John, you've got the hand on the throttle. You do it your way. Now, he did get some airplanes in last night. Yesterday with supplies and got them out but it's not the same thing as assembling hundreds of people, taking them to the airport across town, putting them on the airplanes and taking off. Dean believes this is the safest, cleanest way.

K: I'm backing you—look [Schlesinger] just wants to be able to say that he was pushing evacuation; if anything goes wrong, it's our fault. I'm behind you.

H: You know, I kept saying to them yesterday.

K: Phil, you stick to your cause. You've been a hero in this. I'm proud of you and I'm behind you. . . .

. . .

Sihanouk Interlude

While Cambodia was in its death throes, Prince Norodom Sihanouk, deposed in a 1969 coup, remained in Beijing. Ever since his
overthrow in 1969, he had shrilly supported the Khmer Rouge [the
Communist guerrilla force] and rejected negotiations with the
United States. At the last moment, however, he had second thoughts.
In the guise of asking American assistance in securing the return of
cultural objects he had left behind in Phnom Penh, Sihanouk opened
a channel of communication with the U.S. Liaison Office in Beijing.
It started just as Vietnam was beginning to unravel and Cambodia
was on the verge of collapse. It is presented out of time sequence
here to enable the reader to follow that particular incident.

AMBASSADOR HABIB–KISSINGER

Saturday, March 29, 1975
1:25 P.M.

K: On the Sihanouk thing.

H: I have a draft in the typewriter. We will have it up shortly.

K: ... I do not want a message passed through the Chinese. He
should put [it] in writing—he said this is what he was going to
tell you.

H: Let me try something else on you. We thought the message—
the guy has already got it fourteen times. We should ask him
some—I realize that you do not want to meet personally. But
how about designating a representative?

K: What I want you to do is to send a letter to him and say we will
take care of the cultural objects. We want his views on sending a
representative to discuss it and we are prepared to do it. Nothing
more. Do not ask him any questions. Just tell him the requests he
is making will be met. We are prepared to discuss with him his
ideas on the political events in Cambodia.

H: You do not want this to go through the Chinese?

K: You can inform the Chinese after it is done.

H: Okay.

Sihanouk had refused a political dialogue when it was offered in March. Now with American evacuation just hours away, Sihanouk suddenly came up with a scheme to return to Phnom Penh at the request of all the political forces there rather than in the train of the Khmer Rouge.

AMBASSADOR HABIB–KISSINGER

Friday, April 11, 1975
9:07 A.M. (continued)

. . .

H: Did you get my little note this morning as to what went on through the night on that [Sihanouk] thing?

K: Yes, but we couldn't get in touch with him.

H: Well, we finally did and he in a way raised the ante. But I've told Dean—

K: What does he want now?

H: He's talking now—it's not enough for them to call him back; he's got to get the bonzes [Buddhist clergy] and the populace, the peasants, and the army all to call for his return so that he can come back. Otherwise the Khmer Rouge—he'd have to come back with the Khmer Rouge. I—that's indirect. That's what his man is saying. The door is open. The Cambodians know about it and I've told Dean to go ahead with Eagle Pull [evacuation of Phnom Penh by helicopter]. Not to hold up.

K: You know, if we had a normal Secretary of Defense, I'd hold up on Eagle Pull.

H: I think, very frankly, that we can't. It's too dangerous now. They're very, very close in. And the final thing is: that if the Cambodians still want to do what we've opened the door for them to do with Sihanouk, they can do it without our presence now. Because we've passed all the messages that we need to pass.

K: Okay. It's not a proud day but we did the best we could.

H: Okay. Bye.

AMBASSADOR HABIB–KISSINGER
Friday, April 11, 1975
10:17 A.M.

. . .

H: . . . The latest message has just come in from Dean. Let me read it to you. Are you there—or here [White House or State Department]?

K: No, no, I am there.

H: In line with instructions, I informed [Sihanouk's go-between] of [the] state of play. He took notes, so on and so on. He took notes of the need to strengthen Sihanouk's answers. He deplored Chou So's condition for accepting prime ministership. In other words if Sihanouk agreed to in advance to a cease-fire, etc. Washington's 082755 [cable number] just received.

K: Who is Chou So?

H: He is the guy they [the Pnom Penh governmental forces] are going to make Prime Minister when they get rid of [Prime Minister] Long Boret. Dean says, appreciate your clear and precise instructions to the effect that latest developments regarding Sihanouk's return to Cambodia does not change Eagle Pull's schedule. He definitely wants to go ahead.

K: Well, what the President is wondering is, whether we should keep one or two officers and Dean there [to help Sihanouk if he returned].

H: He said specifically in a message—Dean said—that that was of no use whatsoever unless there was some guarantees of their safety—you are just leaving hostages. And he doesn't think it is necessary or desirable. He said that in a cable last night.

K: Well, could you—how long does it take to get flashes back and forth?

H: A couple of hours.

K: Would you get a message out to him and raise it [the idea of staying behind] with him? Say that the President wondered whether he could play a useful role and whether he thought he could—he leaves the decision up to him. It is not an order. But the President does want his considered judgment on that matter.

H: Wants—considered judgment up to him.

K: Yep.

H: Is it that Schlesinger's complaining about the method of extraction or the extraction at all?

K: Look, the President—

H: He is changing his mind now.

K: . . . The President is fully behind you. No, no, Schlesinger wants you out yesterday and Schlesinger wants to extract and the hell with the Cambodians.

H: Yeah.

K: No, no, no, the President wants to see, however, whether we could possibly arrange the turnover and maintain a presence there if there is a turnover.

H: What I was just doing was sending him a message saying let us know how you can communicate with them after you leave so that if there is any need to communicate we can still communicate with them. We will include that in the same message—okay? I think it will be well to do it in this same manner.

K: Can we get another message to Sihanouk? Asking how we can get in touch with him in Phnom Penh if we have to extract before—that we would like to be of some support to him.

H: If he gets to Phnom Penh?

K: Yeah.

H: There is a cable traffic, you know; whether it will still be running is another question. If he gets to Phnom Penh.

K: Yeah.

H: We have no word yet that Sihanouk has agreed to go to Phnom Penh.

K: Oh, we haven't.

H: I think that could be a next message to Sihanouk.

K: Can you flash that off too?

H: We will tell [head of Beijing Liaison Office George H. W.] Bush to have in mind that when Sihanouk comes back at him and says okay I am ready to go at that time, he should ask him—

K: No, he should ask him before.

H: Before?

K: He should inform him that we are thinking of extracting our Embassy.

H: Well, if we do that—I have been holding off telling him that because that would maybe tip Sihanouk to where he won't do a damn thing. Because he will think a) if we are not there he won't have any protection and b) . . . that it is all over, so why agree to anything? To hell with it.

K: Okay. He'll know by tomorrow morning.

H: Yeah, by that time we will be out, of course.

K: But then there will be no deal.

H: The deal is still there because the deal no longer depends on us. It depends on the Cambodians' announcing publicly what he wants them to announce—that is—

K: Look, you better figure out a means of communication—with Sihanouk in Phnom Penh and inform him of that two hours before we execute Eagle Pull.

H: Okay.

K: Saying we are pulling out but we want him to know this is a means by which he can get in touch with us and as soon as he can assure the security of Embassy personnel we will get them back in.

H: Okay.

K: Do you see what I mean?

H: Yeah. Yeah. Have Dean stand by in Bangkok, close by, ready.

K: Exactly. And Dean also ought to tell this to the others.

Ambassador Habib–Kissinger

Friday, April 11, 1975
10:25 A.M.

. . .

K: Sorry to bother you again. Just one other question: I am trying to refresh my memory because I am going in to see the President again in a few minutes—we authorized our Embassy to approach Sihanouk many weeks ago, didn't we?

H: Oh, yes.

K: What was his answer?

H: The answer was that—remember when he asked us to get his cultural records. We went back and said we would be prepared to discuss any political matter. His answer was it would not be appropriate for him to discuss political matters.

K: No, no, that I remember. But didn't we before then at one point—

H: Yes, we sent a message through the Chinese—this was in February or late—just a minute, Mr. Miller [desk officer] is in my office. ([To Miller] When did we approach the Chinese and say to them, give a message to Sihanouk that we would like to meet with him or one of his representatives, remember you did it—it was in February.) In February you personally—I had done it and then you personally told Han Xu [head of China's liaison office in Washington] to pass the message that we would be prepared to meet with Sihanouk or his designated representative.

K: We never got an answer.

H: We never got an answer.

K: Do you think they passed it on?

H: I am sure they did. [. . .]

K: So we didn't miss an opportunity to bring him back earlier?

H: No, sir.

K: Okay.

H: Of course, we had the French initiative in January.

K: Yeah.

H: In December.

K: Of course, you don't know what [they] passed on.

H: Oh, they passed it because remember then we passed the same thing.

K: Oh, that's right. We passed it how?

H: Through the Chinese.

K: Yeah. Okay. Fine.

H: All right.

K: Now my conscience is clear.

H: No, there is no lack of effort.

K: That's right. Now if your competence matched your loyalty we maybe wouldn't lose so many countries.

H: Yeah. Thanks.

. . .

K: Look, you have done a heroic job and the President is totally behind you. I explained the Eagle Pull to him this morning. He is totally behind it. So don't worry what leaks.

. . .

Implementation of Evacuation

TED KOPPEL, ABC NEWS–KISSINGER
   Friday, April 11, 1975
   1:04 P.M.

TK: I have gotten wind of the Cambodian evacuation and I know the critical aspects of the next few hours and I won't use the story till this evening at 6:00. But I do need to know the scope and who is involved. Do you have any idea of numbers?

HAK: It is several hundred. The remaining Americans and some Cambodians—whose numbers we do not yet know.

TK: Do you have any idea? Tens? Hundreds?

HAK: In hundreds.

TK: By air?

HAK: All by air.

TK: The other question, which relates to the Vietnamese evacuation: Do you have any conception of what kind of American military force would be necessary? How many divisions? It will take divisions.

HAK: I haven't got that yet.

TK: You are thinking in terms of divisions? It would have to be a fairly massive force.

HAK: We haven't thought it through yet.

TK: Thank you.

DONALD RUMSFELD–KISSINGER
Friday, April 11, 1975
1:12 P.M.

R: I've just been down listening to Nessen's briefing. He's using that statement on the secret deal things. We added something to the effect that if anyone suggests that because there were private communications, there were secret commitments, should indicate on what basis they're saying that. It's kind of going after Jackson on the things. I just listened to about half of it.

K: I had him [Nessen] in one [of] my discussions with people this morning.

R: That's what he said.

K: I'm considering doing it on a regular basis.

R: I think he's handling it well. I hope they play it well.

K: Don means to do the right thing.

R: You mean Ron.

K: Ron means to do the right thing. Don does not.

R: How do you feel about last night?

K: I think it was superb.

R: He delivered that thing as well as it could have been done.

K: I think he became President last night. I had breakfast with Hubert Humphrey this morning.

R: He patted me on the shoulder last night and said he thought it was good.

K: He said to me he was proud to be an American last night. He may not be able to support us but he really acted like a President. I had [Lee] Hamilton, [Clement] Zablocki, [John] Buchanan, and [Samuel] Stratton [members of the House of Representatives] in, really to talk about the Middle East, and while they're all saying we could not get the 722, they were all very complimentary about the speech. Then I said, what's the President going to do, and there was nothing like, how could he do this to us. I think he has to keep at it. He ought to go around the country and give the second part of that speech several times.

R: I agree.

K: I wanted to check with you.

R: You mean the Southeast Asia part.

K: And just enough about the Vietnamese part. He's going to look good on this. A year from now people aren't going to be so tired of Vietnam. People are sick and tired of seeing refugees on television. The mail in the department, which isn't decisive, last week 18 percent supported aid for Vietnam and this week, before the speech, 40 percent did. That isn't a majority, but it's interesting.

R: The other thing he did last night was exert leadership. The great thing about it is that the key thing about the speech, the President said what he deeply believes straight. He's comfortable with it. That's what he believes. You can't argue that.

. . .

R: The reason I wanted to talk to you, at 4:15 the President is thinking he would like to get together a small group to, one, to get a good idea on what's going to happen in the next three or four hours in Cambodia.

K: Could we do it at 4:30?

R: Four-thirty is fine, but then he has a 5:00 which we can push back a little.

K: He doesn't need a lot of time.

R: The second thing he said he want[s] to do is update him on the Cambodia political position and what's happening with Sihanouk, and the most important, the third thing, it's because I gave—

K: You cannot move into this office until you're sworn in.

R: The third thing, the Ambassador normally handles evacuation. You have Dean out there. The problem with that is that everything he does is accurate or inaccurate, there's going to be [inquiry] by the Congress, press, and public as setting a precedence for what might occur in Vietnam. Therefore such questions as the implications of the use of U.S. forces, the U.S. aircraft [unclear] the question of [unclear] Cambodia vis-à-vis United States and the destiny where they go. The thing to do is sit down at some point and review what is going to happen. What conclusions people will draw . . .

K: What we have not done is thought through where the Vietnamese are going.

R: That makes sense.

K: Schlesinger is posturing himself so he can get credit for evacuation.

R: I told Brent to talk and you should decide if you want Schlesinger to be there.

K: He has to be there. Keep in mind that Defense [incomplete] right on top of the pile and so forth. That doesn't affect that. That happens anyway. We need Habib there.

. . .

The President's speech requesting aid to Vietnam was formally well received. But Congress would not move on his recommendation. And congressional leaders were ingenious in finding ways to stall. One method was to delay testimony by me in support of aid to Vietnam. A conversation with Representative George Mahon (D.-Tex.), Chairman of the Appropriations Committee, and heretofore a strong supporter of the administration's security policy, illustrates this.

REPRESENTATIVE GEORGE MAHON (D.-TEX.), CHAIRMAN OF THE APPROPRIATIONS COMMITTEE–KISSINGER
Monday, April 14, 1975
3:11 P.M.

M: I have done some canvassing. I have talked to my subcommittee chairmen.

K: And they unanimously don't want me.

M: We don't want you tomorrow. We don't want to try to do anything on that supplemental bill. The groundwork has not been done. We are going to try to do everything possible to prevent anything being done on Vietnam. We'll try to prevent any consideration of Vietnam in a supplemental bill. With respect to having you, we may want to have you but we don't want to interfere with your meeting on Tuesday.

K: I could come on Wednesday, if you want me, Mr. Chairman. I was joking. I am at your disposal—if you want me to come, I will come.

M: I appreciate that. Will you get word to the President that we have decided it is too dangerous to do anything on this supplemental bill.

K: Even on the 300 million? You are going to wait for the authorization?

M: We are going to wait for the authorization; wait for a change in the climate and wait till we get a little support.

. . .

AMBASSADOR HABIB–KISSINGER

Monday, April 14, 1975
6:35 P.M.

K: When am I going to get material for [my appearance before the House Appropriations Committee] tomorrow?

H: I just got back from the Hill myself and it was all up there [Secretary of State's office].

K: I want questions and answers, breakdowns of figures; the sort of thing I can handle. Are you going with me?

H: Yes, if you want.

K: You have to go up there with me.

H: Okay. I will check to see what they have sent up there. I have to look at it and see, on the basis of my experiences there today, if it is all right. They really put me through the wringer today. They won't treat you the same way, I hope; they should still have some respect.

K: What is the major line?

H: They are uptight on the military aid thing. The sort of things that came out on the evacuation business are, Why does the President need or want this authority? How many Vietnamese are involved? etc. We could tell them how many Americans are involved. I talked in open session and I understand you are going to be in open session also.

K: Right.

H: How can we talk in open session about the evacuation? We went into executive session after I brought it to the chairman's attention that we couldn't talk about these things in open session. They took a vote and then we went into executive session.

K: I will just say they should be in executive session.

H: One other problem: we don't have good breakdowns on the military aid—especially for the open session. Are you going to handle military and economic questions?

K: I am. Why am I appearing before the Appropriations Committee?

H: Because McClellan [John McClellan (D.-Ark.), chairman of the Senate Appropriations Committee] said that is the one key committee you should appear before. The military budget starts usually in Armed Services. However, eventually they get the armed services stuff in the Appropriations Committee.

K: Can I have the breakdown fast?

H: In fifteen minutes to start and then we will decide whether it is sufficient.

JOHN CONNALLY, FORMER SECRETARY OF THE
TREASURY–KISSINGER

> *Monday, April 14, 1975*
> *9:47 P.M.*

. . .

C: You are a great man, working for your country, and don't let those bastards get under your skin.

K: If you don't have an alternative, you have no problem. I have to fight the battle.

C: That is right. You are performing in the interests of this country, that's one thing for sure.

K: I never thought the Secretary of State would have to go to a congressional committee and plead for money for an ally.

C: The hell of it is you plead, and you probably won't get it.

K: I don't know about politics, but I think there will be a horrible day of reckoning. They don't know what the Communists are like that are going to take over Saigon.

C: Yes, it will start problems in Malaysia and Thailand. Marcos [President Ferdinand Marcos of the Philippines] already has a war in his country.

K: We started the panic, that's the hell of it. There would have been no offensive if it wasn't for congressional debates on help to our allies.

C: They read the newspapers. They know poor South Vietnam has no choice but to surrender when their ammunition runs out.

K: I am going to read a letter before the Congress that Matak [Sirik Matak, former Prime Minister of Cambodia] wrote when we offered to take him out of the country. It is pitiful; he is a dead man, you know, but he refused to come out.

C: Well, I just don't know. Well, best of luck.

GENERAL SCOWCROFT–KISSINGER
Tuesday, April 15, 1975
8:55 P.M.

. . .

S: Have you seen the draft bill from the Foreign Relations Committee?

K: No.

S: It is lovely. They are proposing $200 million for humanitarian assistance; to assist the evacuation, to permit the use of troops to evacuate Americans, to permit the use of troops to evacuate Vietnamese if no more are needed than those needed to evacuate the Americans.

K: Just so we get the number of Americans down to two hundred.

S: That is right. They also added no more equipment. It is just unbelievable. It sums up the worst of what went on in the meeting.

K: Well, Indochina is gone but we will make them pay for it. In my whole testimony today, I said twenty-five times that it was Congress's fault.

S: I think we have got to do it for the self-respect of the country.

TED KOPPEL–KISSINGER

> *Wednesday, April 16, 1975*
> *12:35 P.M.*

   . . .

  TK: . . . Have you heard the latest report?

HAK: No.

  TK: The airport has fallen [in Phnom Penh] and the remains of the government is asking to negotiate a settlement—it is in effect a surrender.

HAK: Well, it is almost impossible today for me because I have to work on my speech.

  TK: Where are you speaking?

HAK: At ASNE tomorrow.

  TK: What is that?

HAK: The Society of Newspaper Editors.

  TK: Are you going to make a major address?

HAK: I hope so. I am working on it as if I were.

  TK: Can you slip me in for five minutes? Let me speak to you now for about five minutes. There is nothing that we can do at this point?

HAK: Nothing that I can think of.

  TK: Does it look to you as though Sihanouk will come back?

HAK: I wouldn't bet on that.

  TK: That would be a disaster if he doesn't.

HAK: That's right.

  TK: Where do we go? What if anything can we do? Are you active in any fashion?

HAK: We tried to get Sihanouk back last week. It is not easily explained.

  TK: What you are saying is there is nothing. Are you in touch with the Chinese or the Russians?

HAK: It is a great recommendation of Scotty's [Reston] but what the hell could the Russians do?

TK: I saw Scotty's piece, but what about the Chinese?

HAK: What could they do? We have been in touch.

TK: Have they been cooperative?

HAK: I don't think they could get him [Sihanouk] back. I think he may come back but he may be a figurehead.

. . .

JAMES "SCOTTY" RESTON–KISSINGER

Wednesday, April 16, 1975
4:30 P.M.

R: Where are we getting on cease-fire? Just between you and me.

K: Look we have to do on cease-fire in South Vietnam?

R: Yeah.

K: We are not getting anywhere, right now, but ah—well it is very difficult for me to talk about the diplomacy, but it is merely something we have in mind.

R: Well we are getting some—we are picking up some suggestions which we didn't put out on our own, but from two different sources, indicating that Hanoi wants to talk. I'm not surprised that they do—

K: Well, look, if Hanoi wants to talk it has been my experience they never have been very bashful about making that clear to us and if they want to talk, we certainly do our damnedest to facilitate it. Can you tell me, are these newspaper sources?

R: No, they are East German sources.

K: Well, we are certainly—I mean this is for your own guidance, we are certainly in touch with the Russians, and if anything is happening we will hear it soon enough.

R: What kind of help are you getting from Dobrynin?

K: Well, you know, I think these guys are as surprised as we are by what happened. What basically happened is that they kept their level of aid steady and ours declined for a variety of reasons including inflation, and oil prices, and after all since Schlesinger early in March gave a press conference which reflected our intelligence assessment that this would not be a year of a big offensive.

R: Yeah, well I heard your testimony on that yesterday. I just have a feeling that—nothing but a feeling that—maybe something can be done to avoid this really disastrous human carnage in Saigon—

K: Look, that is almost the only thing left to do.

R: Well, that is what seems to me ought to be—what troubles me, Henry, quite frankly, for reasons which I understand, obviously you have to give the impression that your first priority is the moral obligation to deliver arms, but certainly the higher priority is to—

K: Yeah, but you can't do one without the other.

R: You don't even have time to get the other there—

K: Probably, maybe not.

R: Schlesinger yesterday says six weeks before you can get really effective equipment in there—we haven't got six weeks, have we?

K: I think there is a certain logic of events that will unfold.

R: There is a kind of cynical idea around which is—and this is in our embassies saying in effect look what Washington really did—what it did was to negotiate a peace which got their POWs out and now they are negotiating an appropriation—got the rest of the Americans out.

K: No, I think the agreement could have held without Watergate and you know, in a reasonable atmosphere between the executive and legislative there wouldn't have been this sort of furor over the appropriations that developed this year.

R: You really think the Watergate thing was a factor in that—

K: I think the Watergate thing so weakened the executive authority and in May, as late as May '74 all the signals were that the Communists were digging in for the long pull there and then during the course of the summer they went to high points and in February of this year they decided to go all out—the vultures have had only about a month's training right now, so I think it is a casualty of Watergate.

R: Well, we will see, I just hope we can do something about—

K: But it is not an issue which we will pursue; I am giving a speech tomorrow to the newspaper editors—I'll send you a copy in the morning—I'm trying to make it a conciliatory speech.

R: Yeah, well I've been there all day and I'm just going down to the White House now for that bash down there. The President tried to deal with this, but you know he got into all kinds of trouble about, well—just give us three more years you know, Jesus Christ, nobody's got a stomach for three more years.

K: I haven't seen a transcript yet.

R: No, it wasn't a transcript, it was in response to questions.

K: No, no, I mean I didn't—I was at a lunch when he was—

R: What else is worrying you?

K: The big problem we have now is to change the world—there is nothing we can do about the world's perception of Vietnam, but there is a lot we can do about changing the world's perception about our reaction to it and that is our big problem right now.

R: Well, sure, but it is a perception of ours and what we are and what we stand for.

K: Exactly.

R: I agree. Well, off you go, you've got—

K: I think I'll see you tomorrow night—aren't you going to Rockefeller?

R: Yeah.

K: Good, and I'll see you there.

R: Great, all the best.

ROBERT McCLOSKEY, ASSISTANT SECRETARY FOR PUBLIC
AFFAIRS–KISSINGER

Wednesday, April 16, 1975
6:30 P.M.

M: Hello, Henry, I want you to know I had a very unpleasant conversation with [Bill] Atwood [Editor of *Newsday*] today.

K: I will get to that in a minute. I have agreed to appear before the
Appropriations Committee Monday afternoon.

M: We are also on for Friday morning before the House committee.
I had that unpleasant conversation—

K: You know, that is a guy I have done a lot of favors for.

M: He said that he had known you for seventeen years. When did
that start?

K: Probably under Kennedy.

M: He diverted the blame from himself to the extent that he said that
was an editorial in a series of four they have done on foreign policy.

K: You know, he has called for my resignation before.

M: Well, I told him that if you have facts and want to criticize the
Secretary it is all right, but we are going to give you hell for saying
he has misled the people. He then said that that was not his view,
but that the paper does not reflect his views but the consensus.
They are bringing up things like what is the legal commitment,
what are the other commitments. I reminded him of the time he
has spent in government and how that government works.

K: Everything in all those letters was said publicly, damn it.

M: I told him that. But he said that Nessen acknowledged that there
were communications between Nixon and Thieu, private ones. I
made the point with Bill, that it is on record and nobody paid any
attention to it at that time. Now when Jackson has brought it to the
public's attention, everyone has been fooled. I am really outraged
about what they are saying as far as the Secretary is concerned and
I let him know this. I think that by being nasty, I unsettled him.

K: I appreciate that. . . .

. . .

By April 16, the congressional leaders realized that they would not be able to avoid Ford's request by ignoring it and would have to hold hearings.

REPRESENTATIVE MAHON–KISSINGER

Wednesday, April 16, 1975
6:35 P.M.

M: It develops that we are going to have a meeting of the House on Friday. Normally they don't meet on Friday. Since we have a meeting scheduled, would you have the time to appear? It would be at 10:00 A.M. on Friday. Are you free at that time?

K: Unfortunately, I have just agreed to appear before the House International Affairs Committee.

M: I was taking a chance—

K: I would have given you first choice but I have already agreed.

M: Okay. We will keep it at 2:30 on Monday; that will be our target date. Do you think I ought to put it in closed session or open? You could be franker if it were closed. I will suggest it should be closed and see what happens from there. You will have to be more cautious in open session.

K: I have no strong preferences. They leak it out anyway.

M: You can't have fifty members and expect them all to keep quiet.

K: Don't bother to put it in closed session.

. . .

SENATOR JAVITS–KISSINGER

Wednesday, April 16, 1975
7:55 P.M.

J: I want to give you a conception on the Vietnam situation in the [Senate] Committee [on Foreign Relations]. I think it is important for you to understand. First, the negative point. We are concerned about the fact that we don't have any plan relating to the withdrawal [from Vietnam]. It is highly desirable that we get one.

K: I think that Eagleburger [Deputy Undersecretary for Administration] gave a schedule to you this afternoon.

J: We have received no such thing.

K: Well, wait a minute; he is here in my office. I will ask him. [Talks to Eagleburger] Eagleburger gave the figures to Moose [Richard Moose of the Senate Foreign Relations Committee staff] this afternoon and we have a meeting tomorrow to refine the full details.

J: The estimate that Moose gave us would leave a large number of people there by May 1. This is of grave concern to us. It is a matter of disagreement.

K: I have the figures here.

J: I don't want to talk on the phone. It is going to cause mischief now.

K: Let me see what I can do to speed up the process.

J: You should have a concept of the situation. We are all serving the same master, and we should work together to serve him well. I am dissatisfied with the pace of action. There will develop some disagreement between the [Senate] Armed Services Committee and the Foreign Relations Committee. The type of bill, which was made public today, I asked it to be reported on the floor, deals with that aspect which we are now discussing, but gives freedom in the use of resources. You have seen the bill?

K: No, I haven't.

J: I think you should. It was sent to the White House. I will send you a copy, if necessary.

K: No, I am sure I can get it.

J: The point is that the Armed Services Committee is likely to vote military aid. This committee is likely to vote on this particular bill, plus a resolution urging efforts to bring about political accommodation in the matter. When this hits the Senate my guess is the votes are going to be for the Foreign Relations Committee bill and not the Armed Services Committee's. However, they could be voted together. If they were, it would probably be affirmative.

K: The trouble with your bill is the figure of $200 million. It is just impossible.

J: What figure is good?

K: The figure we gave you.

J: I wouldn't be for that mess. The thing is, we are heading into a confrontation between the Congress and the President in which the Congress is likely to say withdraw and we will give you so-and-so with which to do it. And the President will say, I will accept no such position and they [the Vietnamese] deserve military and humanitarian aid.

K: That is probably what the President will do.

J: Unless some way is found to compromise.

K: How should we compromise?

J: That is the issue.

K: You have defined the problem well. The mood of the President is that he is very firm on this.

J: I said that on the *Today* show this morning.

K: He was firm on this thing before he knew me. He always voted the same way in Congress. As I read his mind, he will not accept the version of the Foreign Relations Committee bill. The amount is too small and it is given only for withdrawal.

J: That is not all.

K: That is in effect what he says.

J: Yes.

K: I will report to him first thing in the morning your sentiments and see if he will discuss a compromise.

J: Okay.

K: I will do the best to speed up the evacuation process.

J: It is the best thing to come to the committee today.

    . . .

GENERAL SCOWCROFT–KISSINGER
Wednesday, April 16, 1975
8:03 P.M.

. . .

K: Javits just called and he thinks we are heading for a confrontation. He said you are right. He said they are willing to compromise. What do you have in mind? I said. He said the figure you gave us is too high. He said the President is firm on this matter, he knows, but that there would be a confrontation. He says there is an Armed Services Committee bill which reports the thing out. Have you sent the cable to Martin on what steps to take if it collapses?

S: I have told him that we want a scenario.

. . .

By now the deteriorating situation in Vietnam was making discussions of aid requests substantially irrelevant. But we kept them going to avoid triggering a panic in Saigon and to preserve the principle of not abandoning an ally in distress.

THE PRESIDENT–KISSINGER
Friday, April 18, 1975
10:10 P.M.

. . .

K: . . . I wanted to bring you up-to-date on the military situation. It is deteriorating in Vietnam. You should be aware that we may have from four to ten days and we have to figure by next weekend, at the worst, it will be over. I would like to send a telegram to Martin. He has agreed to reduce the number of Americans to 1,730 next Tuesday.

F: Americans plus legitimate Vietnamese dependents?

K: Yes. I would like to tell him to get down to 1,250, which is one airlift. But we shouldn't announce that figure; it might cause panic.

F: As long as it is inevitable, let's do it, so we don't get adverse reactions.

K: If we can get it down to one airlift, there is no difference between 1,000 or 1,300, but we will be in trouble if we don't do that. I called in Dobrynin [Anatoly Dobrynin, Soviet Ambassador] tomorrow morning. I want to ask him for a temporary cease-fire to permit evacuation of Americans and Vietnamese.

F: Do they have control or the power to affect a cease-fire?

K: No, probably not, but I want to ask him not to ship in any military equipment during that time. I am for taking the two chances in twenty that they may help. I don't know whether they have the power, but they might want to assert themselves. Secondly, Hanoi may want a controlled takeover.

F: Did Martin see the President [Thieu]?

K: No. [. . .]
   [. . .]

F: [. . .] I hope for the best. It's a hell of a situation.

K: It is tragic. I testified before the House Foreign Affairs Committee today.

F: How did it go?

K: [William] Broomfield [(R.-Mich.), Republican ranking member], [Clement] Zablocki [(D.-Wis.), Democratic chairman] were not too bad. Some of the younger ones were obnoxious. They are talking tough language, but I am being very tough. I know that this is not in keeping with your policy of reconciliation, but I am being tough. I just want the record to show that we asked for it.

F: That is the point. The public should be able to see that it is on record. At the meeting I had with fifty newspeople from New England I took the same position.

K: How do you think it went?

F: Damn good.

K: Somebody was in today—oh yes, Elliot Richardson [U.S. Ambassador to Britain].

F: My successor?

K: No, he is measuring the walls in my office. He could be talked into taking your job, you know.

F: I am going to compete with you on this.

K: He said that the mood in the country was going to turn conservative.

F: That is right. In New England my approach on domestic and foreign policy [a major foreign policy speech defending détente] got a good response. And I really lit into the press group on the CIA and the intelligence community [refers to Church Committee investigations]. No President, including myself, can operate with a crippled intelligence community. It doesn't make sense to destroy the agency for one mistake they made.

. . .

As discussed with the President, on April 19, I delivered an "oral note" from Ford to Brezhnev via Dobrynin. (An oral note is a written document having the same status as an oral conversation but put in writing for precision and emphasis.) The note stated that a cease-fire in Vietnam was needed to accomplish the "evacuation of American citizens and those South Vietnamese to whom we have a direct and special obligation." We were approaching Moscow, because "it is in our long-term mutual interest that the situation be brought to its conclusion in a manner that does not jeopardize Soviet-American relations, or affect the attitude of the American people toward other international problems."

To give a more realistic cast to this essentially threadbare appeal, we stressed our willingness "to discuss the special political circumstances that could make this [a cease-fire] possible"—in other words, a change in the political structure in Saigon. We bluffed about the dangerous consequences of an attack on airfields and passenger planes—though so expert an observer of American congressional debates as Dobrynin was unlikely to take that threat very seriously.

While awaiting the Soviet reply, Graham Martin, on April 20, hinted to Thieu that the South Vietnamese President might consider resigning. Martin purported to speak in his personal capacity, though in fact the démarche had been approved by Ford on the slim hope that such an approach might lead to a negotiation, giving us a few extra days for evacuating our friends. Rather icily, Thieu replied that he would do what was best for his country. Martin ended his report to Washington on this poignant note: "I went home, read the daily news digests from Washington, took a shower, scrubbed very hard with the strongest soap I could find. It didn't help much." Ford, Scowcroft, and I felt the same way.

AMBASSADOR DOBRYNIN–KISSINGER
Saturday, April 19, 1975
12:10 P.M.

K: On that matter we discussed this morning.

D: On what matter—the first one?

K: The one on which I gave you a note.

D: Yeah, I already sent it.

K: I know, but what I wanted to add to it is that under the conditions we envisioned it would of course not require any substantial American forces to do the evacuation.

D: Not substantial.

K: No, just enough to prevent mobs at the airports.

D: I see.

K: Just a few hundred.

D: A few hundred.

K: Yeah.

D: Uh-huh. This is an important point. Thank you very much, Henry. I will add this and they will go immediately after—

K: And they will leave with the last airplane.

D: Okay. Thank you.

. . .

Secretary Schlesinger–Kissinger
> *Monday, April 21, 1975*
> *9:21 A.M. (secure voice)*

K: I'll see you after the WSAG meeting. You were away yesterday and I did not want to discuss it on the open phone.

S: Of course.

K: [. . .]

S: [. . .] It's obvious that we have considerable power but we are restricted in employing it. There are other reasons for moving that battalion up to—

K: As long as it was going to be moved— We don't have to say anything. We should just move it and say nothing.

S: I think that division at Okinawa deserves some reinforcement at this time. Aside from any signaling— As a signal is what I am concerned about in Southeast Asia. We have signaled many times before and, given the circumstances [congressional prohibition], we have not been able to do anything when our bluff is called.

K: In the case of the Tonkin Gulf I think we all agreed it would not be done [a movement of aircraft carriers to the Tonkin Gulf, which was cancelled when a media campaign questioned its compatibility with the congressional prohibition of use of force in or near Indochina].

S: —to move without justifying before Congress would have given us a chance.

K: It [the deployment] would have given us a chance.

S: No question. Our deployment kept them petrified for eighteen months— After Congress passed the new—

K: I just wanted you to know the background. We won't discuss it in front of the others but then you can come up after and I will bring you up-to-date.

. . .

I called Senator Kennedy because he had taken a special interest in refugees.

SENATOR KENNEDY–KISSINGER

Monday, April 21, 1975
11:35 A.M.

TK: Henry, how are you?

HAK: Okay. I am fine. Not lacking in action right now. . . . I called you last night to give you a little advance warning of what might be happening and to tell you I have asked Dean Brown [former Ambassador to Jordan put in charge of civilian evacuation from Indochina] here to keep in close touch with you on the refugee evacuation problem and before he does any other consulting on the Hill to talk to you first to get your advice if you are willing to do that.

TK: Fine.

HAK: Our problem is to prevent panic at the other end and we have an Ambassador there who might like to go out like [Charles] Chinese Gordon [British defender of Khartoum who was killed when he stayed until the city fell to the Mahdi] but I cannot say that publicly.

TK: I will be more than delighted. We have been following with Habib on the general movement of people.

HAK: I need help on congressional authority, on parole authority.

TK: Right. I was terribly hopeful that we might be able to see what kind of initiatives could be taken to try and see if we can get protection of the population there.

HAK: That is strictly for you—that is what we are working on now. We have some other countries involved. We have to weigh this again—the fact of panic starting spontaneously.

TK: I think it very important that as much restraint as possible is made in talking about a bloodbath. I am sure there are going to be some tough situations but I think the more it is talked about the more there might be. Obviously you have to gear up because of the possibility but as much restraint as possible should be used in talking against [a] bloodbath. I am hopeful they can do something. I just called [U.N. Secretary General

Kurt] Waldheim last week and also Jackson, who is heading
up the U.N. on the refugees and Waldheim has a personal
plea to get help.

HAK: I thought, when you said Jackson, you meant my expert on
immigration [Senator Jackson].

TK: Oh, no.

HAK: Get another amendment passed.

TK: I do hope that something—there is a tremendous—as you
can gather, concern of the massive movement.

HAK: Almost no possibility of massive movement unless there is
cooperation by the other side. We really owe it to the fifteen
years of effort to get some of the key people out.

TK: I think that is right.

HAK: And if we can get controlled conditions maybe more. If we
can get controlled conditions that will be very obvious and
there will be time for consultation. We are not going in with
a division or two and pull them out.

TK: Is there talk about that [Saigon] being declared a free city?

HAK: We are now waiting some possible moves and we are in
touch. How it is to be done, we have not begun to work out.
We have not got the principle established yet. That is what
we are trying to do.

TK: Is this real significant with Thieu going out?

HAK: I think it will lead to a negotiation.

TK: Not just window dressing.

HAK: I don't think so. Incidentally, this is strictly a private conversation.

The Vietnamese army, in the course of two decades, had ac-
quired and been given a great deal of advanced American military
equipment. James Schlesinger and I discussed moving as much of it
as possible out of Indochina to keep it from falling into Communist
hands.

SECRETARY SCHLESINGER–KISSINGER

Monday, April 21, 1975
7:59 P.M.

K: I have nothing; I just wanted to check whether you heard about the thing we talked about earlier. We haven't heard anything.

S: They have speeded up the evacuation. Dave Jones [Chief of Staff of the Air Force] told me that we were flying out some 130s from Clark [Air Force Base in the Philippines].

K: Right.

S: One thing, we have ninety airplanes that we got out of Cambodia and the Thai Foreign Minister—I don't know whether it was a superficial comment—says they belong to the government of Cambodia, which is the Khmer Rouge. We got them because we don't want to give them to the Khmer Rouge. After all, American law states that they remain under the control of the U.S. government.

K: Can you work with our people on a cable tomorrow? Get Ellsworth Bunker [former Ambassador to Vietnam now handling Middle East negotiations] together with Habib and I will strongly support it.

S: We may be able to get some equipment out of the country.

K: Can we fly to the Philippines?

S: You leave that to me.

K: I want it in the Philippines.

S: I am fairly sure. We will be able to move the stuff that we don't want to leave to our friends there.

K: The F-5s, can they reach it?

S: The F-5s and the 130s can get there.

K: Whatever you can do to get stuff out will be a great service.

S: We must work quickly.

K: I can't agree more. The more you can get out the better off we are. . . .

The maneuvering about the rate of evacuation did not end with that agreement on the removal of equipment. The bone of contention remained the rate of removal of civilians.

WILLIAM CLEMENTS, DEPUTY SECRETARY OF
DEFENSE–KISSINGER

> *Tuesday, April 22, 1975*
> *7:59 A.M.*

K: I want to congratulate the Defense Department for having put me on the front page of the *Times.*

C: On the front page of what?

K: On the front page of the *New York Times.*

C: Really?

K: Defense wishes total evacuation, but that son of a bitch Kissinger, who is thinking of national honor and dignity of the United States, won't permit it.

C: Goddamn—

K: You know, you guys over there really ought to be ashamed of yourselves. I'm trying to leave a little self-respect. You guys were the ones who had 57,000 people who were killed over there— you ought to defend them too—not just me.

C: You know, Henry—

K: I know you didn't—if I thought you did, I wouldn't be yelling at you—I'd be yelling at your boss.

C: That's a damn thing.

K: But don't you think—the disgrace of the United States of packing up and leaving everybody.

C: Well, I'm terribly sorry, Henry.

K: Besides, we worked out with your boss a precise procedure for evacuation of the personnel, and I had Scowcroft there—I have the verbatim notes. But if you want to get your goddamn personnel out, why don't you just pack up and get it out? My guys will stay.

C: Hmmm. I thought surely when you and Jim went off together yesterday, you all would solve that problem.

K: You know, there is a presidential order we are going to—first of all we might trigger the goddamnedest panic ever, if we pulled everyone out at once.

C: Jim—I mean, Henry, I couldn't agree more. I agree with that. Now, what do you want me to do this morning?

K: I just want you to let my extreme displeasure be known where it matters.

C: Okay—

K: That this is no way to run a crisis. I just wanted to put something on the record you can repeat.

C: I don't mind—I'm doing everything I can.

K: Bill, you are a great patriot. You don't play that way—you might say it at the meeting, but you wouldn't say it outside. Some others do the opposite—they don't say it at the meeting, but they will say it outside.

C: I will see him [Schlesinger] just as soon as I get to the building— I'm within five minutes of the office, right now.

TED KOPPEL–KISSINGER

Tuesday, April 22, 1975
2:30 P.M.

. . .

TK: I called about the Vietnam negotiations. Can you give me any kind of guidance.

HAK: I don't know that I can give you any guidance. I don't think anyone can have any real story floating.

TK: Has there been any contact? Is anything happening?

HAK: We're exploring some approach.

TK: Directly or through a third party?

HAK: I don't want to get into that.

TK: Did you see the story on the front page of the *Times* which talks about your favoring keeping some Americans in Vietnam while some in the State Department and DOD are opposing it.

HAK: I wish we could do something with a minimum of dignity. Everyone is covering their ass right now. Our problem is we want to get Americans out in a way that won't spark a panic. We've got it down to the 1,500 range.

TK: Do you plan to get them all out? I know up on the Hill you made a very passionate plea—calling it unreasonable that we are keeping them there as hostages.

HAK: It depends on what you're trying to achieve. The discussion is to get them out before they are jeopardized and that we are trying to do. We're also trying to save some South Vietnamese. You can't just leave everybody there.

TK: When you talked about South Vietnam—at one point you were talking about 200,000 people.

HAK: That is the minimum list of those that we can put together. I doubt if we can get that number.

TK: Do you have a realistic count. Can you give me some idea of a time frame. How much time do you think we have?

HAK: That depends on the efforts the North Vietnamese are willing to make.

TK: Is it your feeling that they want a battle at Saigon or do they want to avoid it?

HAK: I would slightly weight it against their wanting it, but not more than 50/49.

. . .

Disaster demands sacrificial offering in Washington. So it happened that amidst the increasingly gloomy news from Vietnam, I had to respond increasingly to rumors that my resignation would be demanded as a kind of sacrificial victim.

JERROLD SCHECTER, *TIME*–KISSINGER

Tuesday, April 22, 1975
5:50 P.M.

K: I am glad I made such an impact on you at the breakfast.

S: You did. I talked to Larry [Eagleburger, Deputy Undersecretary of State] and I thought the story came out well.

K: Well, except for the fact that it repeated all the things the President and I said were untrue. No one came to the President with these things, I am sure.

S: Well, two other people in the office reported in great detail on this. I spent most of the week trying to work out that this happened before anyone got back to Washington.

K: It is the least of my problems.

S: Hey, what happened also is that we got a version which stressed to a much greater degree that this was the President's thinking in this matter.

K: I am not staying in this job out of vanity. I have known since last year that we are now paying the price of Watergate. You cannot conduct foreign policy without authority. It is what we are paying for, so the longer I stay the worse it may get. I will expect our China policy to come apart next. They are not impressed by people who have no strength. I am staying because, well, for two reasons—it is not fair to pass along the problems I now have and, second, I am trying to rally what can be rallied.

S: I think we made that point.

K: It isn't just that I don't want to look weak. In an historical perspective, these things will be seen in a different focus.

S: I hope so. What can we do about that situation? There now happens to be something developing about the Pentagon wants to pull everybody out and you want to keep them there.

K: Look, Jerry, anybody can give orders to pull everybody out. We have two obligations, is all I am saying—one, to help the South Vietnamese and, secondly, to maintain the order in the situation.

We have got to stop speculating on who will take the blame. I don't think it is worth the debate. I would have to be demented to keep people there a day longer than is necessary.

S: Right.

K: I am trying to protect the negotiations and also to keep the maximum number of people alive and so far it is working. If we had given total evacuation orders before we got the number down to a manageable level it would have jeopardized, unnecessarily, a number of lives. There is a certain logic to these events. If one American breaks his toenail, someone is to blame.

. . .

Occasionally there were encouraging phone calls.

SENATOR STROM THURMOND (R.-S.C.)–KISSINGER
Wednesday, April 23, 1975
12:55 P.M.

. . .

T: . . . What the latest thing in South Vietnam?

K: We're continuing to reduce the number of people there. Between you and me, we're taking out many South Vietnamese.

T: I'm glad. They stood by us and we should stand by them.

K: Not everybody in Washington feels that way.

T: Okay. Thank you very much for clarifying that. I was concerned.

K: There's no reason to be concerned.

GENERAL SCOWCROFT–KISSINGER
Wednesday, April 23, 1975
7:35 P.M.

. . .

S: We got a cable in from Martin. I sent it over to you through Larry. He said he will bring it to you soonest. It says the Defense Minister [of Vietnam] wants to push Minh [Duong Van "Big"

Minh, perennial South Vietnamese presidential candidate and favorite of American peace activists] as Premier and he talked to the French Ambassador, who is also pushing Minh.

K: Had he [Martin] gotten our cable?

S: No, this was from his working day, yesterday. Then he talked to the Pole, Martin did, and asked whether he had been asked about the acceptability of Minh and what was the Pole's idea. He said he would try to find out. He will certainly report in the morning and he says I can report to the President and we can talk about it.

K: Okay.

S: Larry will bring it down to you.

K: Have we gotten any other advice?

S: No I don't think we have.

. . .

MR. LESLIE GELB, *NEW YORK TIMES*–KISSINGER
Wednesday, April 23, 1975
7:37 P.M.

G: Thank you for your call. A number of things. I found a story today saying that the only word we have gotten back from Hanoi and the PRG [Provisional Revolutionary Government—the South Vietnamese Communists] has been that they will not humiliate us and that they aren't prepared to negotiate and don't know the terms.

K: I won't go into the negotiations.

G: Should I tell you what I said?

K: Go ahead.

G: That essentially we are asking for two things. One, some sort of guarantees for getting Americans and their dependents out plus an unverified number of South Vietnamese; and two, that you are trying to signal to Hanoi publicly that if they will only wait that logic would come out of Saigon and a government would come to power that they would be able to deal with. Also that the intermediaries were not Moscow, Peking, or France. I didn't say that one of the intermediaries was not Romanian. I believe that is the only one.

K: I just— It is not totally wrong but there are some inaccuracies. You won't be disgraced.

G: I want to be lauded. If some of it is inaccurate—

K: I really can't tell you what. If you ask my opinion about something you ran by Scowcroft—really he told me that you did. He said you talked to him. Believe me, he said he restrained himself and didn't make many comments.

G: I would never comment on what anyone said or didn't say.

K: The only secrets to survive this mess will be those between journalists and their sources.

G: That isn't true, not in my case.

K: I can't force your opinion.

G: That is why I can't comment. One other thing: CBS is saying that the President gave a speech down in Florida without showing it to you.

K: When? Was it on CBS?

G: Just before the six o'clock news or just after, I can't remember which.

K: They have been running that lie all day long. The President and I discussed the subject matter of the speech. Have you read the speech? Unless he rewrote it on the plane, it is a very conventional speech.

G: I can't believe that this is the case.

K: It is absurd.

G: Of course, but they put it out.

K: And I don't know how I can comment on all these stories. What conclusion should I draw from it?

G: The one I am drawing. Certain people would like to see your influence with the President diminished. That is clear; that is the answer I would give you. It is foolish but who am I to say? It was CBS.

K: I don't know what it means to have my influence with the President diminished. I don't keep anyone from expressing his opinions and views from him.

G: It will probably affect your relationship.

K: Between the President and me?

G: It is a liability for any President to have one of his top advisers constantly criticized. It is a pain in the neck for the President to deal with and must weigh on him. The Chinese are chipping away also.

K: That is totally different.

G: It still contributes to the problem.

K: They [the Chinese] are saying that Schlesinger's role must be emphasized because we should have a strong defense posture. That is not a political game, or an internal political one.

G: Your interpretation may be right. But they are saying that the President is leaning more on Schlesinger than Kissinger. But it is another story about how you are perceived. I think that story basically will be chipping away, and whether it is successful, it certainly is an irritant.

K: Not to me. I am relaxed about it. It is totally out of my control. The only thing I worry about now is how can we progress out of it.

G: If you really have internalized what you said, that is the best thing to do about it.

K: There is nothing I can do about it. We are in a grave situation. Who knows today whether Rostow or Rusk [Walt Rostow, President Johnson's security adviser, and Dean Rusk, Johnson's Secretary of State] was up or down and years later this doesn't matter.

G: That is a terrific attitude.

K: That is my attitude now. We are in the last eighteen months of an administration and even if it gets reelected it will be reconstituted and will be totally different.

G: All you need—

K: I don't know who is doing the maneuvering. You might know.

G: I think I do and I think I know the motive. It is easy to figure out. It is a thing now that there is no question about.

K: It is your view that it is coming from the White House or else-where?

G: The White House and I think you know the source. Larry Eagleburger has got a good sense of this. . . .

. . .

By April 24, the debate was reduced to the number of Americans to be left in Saigon as a means to help us evacuate Vietnamese while South Vietnam was collapsing.

GENERAL SCOWCROFT–KISSINGER

Thursday, April 24, 1975
10:05 A.M.

S: I talked to the madman [Ambassador Martin]. It is being en-crypted and will be here momentarily. It gets us down under 1,100 by tomorrow night.

K: Is that his or our time?

S: His time.

K: That is tomorrow morning here.

S: He said the last thing in the world he wants to do is lose any Americans. He is not going to lose any Americans. There isn't any problem out there with the military/State team—the prob-lem is here in Washington.

K: That is probably true.

S: He said he was aware of our concerns but the last thing he wants is to lose anybody and he doesn't think he is taking undue risk and we should keep confidence in him. And, he added, that to cheer you up there is a typhoon brewing.

K: Then we won't get anyone out.

S: Right, but it means they probably won't launch an assault. That means it is another lever for Defense to use.

K: We have to have a talk with the President. . . .

. . .

While Saigon was disintegrating, the debate in Washington was the familiar one about the rate of evacuation and a mounting concern to evacuate as many Vietnamese who had cooperated with us as possible. The Soviet Union chose that moment to reply to our oral message of April 19 offering a dialogue on the end of Vietnam.

AMBASSADOR DOBRYNIN–KISSINGER
Thursday, April 24, 1975
4:00 P.M.

D: Hello, Henry. I received the following message from Brezhnev to President Ford. He asked me to go through you. First I will read it and then I could dictate to your secretary.

K: All right.

D: "As it has already been said to the President, immediately after the message of the President of April 19 was received by L. E. Brezhnev we took appropriate steps to get in touch with the Vietnamese side in this connection.

"As a result of these contacts now we can inform the President about the following: the position of the Vietnamese side on the question of evacuation of American citizens from South Vietnam is definitely positive. The Vietnamese stated that they have no intention to put any obstacles in the course of military actions to the evacuation of American citizens from South Vietnam and that now, in fact, favorable conditions have been established for such an evacuation.

"At the same time, it was emphasized that in the struggle for achieving a political settlement, the Vietnamese side will proceed from the Paris Agreement. We were also told that the Vietnamese do not intend to damage the prestige of the United States.

"Informing the President of the above in a confidential

manner, L. E. Brezhnev expresses his hopes that the President will duly appreciate such a position of the Vietnamese side and will not allow any action on the United States's part which would be fraught with a new exacerbation of the situation in Indochina."

K: What does it mean in practice?

D: There is no obstacles at all to evacuation of United States citizens. None at all and they have established conditions for this particular process and their attitude towards this is positive.

K: Okay.

D: And something on the political side too.

K: Can you explain that? They don't want to go further than the Paris Accords?

D: The basis for a political settlement is still the Paris Agreement.

K: Would you be prepared to ask them what they mean by that?

D: I would ask them—

K: No, let me check with the President first.

. . .

A State Department staff meeting assessing Brezhnev's message agreed that we should use it to gain a little time, though Bill Hyland, head of the Bureau of Intelligence and Research, estimated "a little" to be at most one week. I therefore instructed Martin to reduce the number of Americans to below eight hundred (the number that could be lifted in two and a half hours, according to the estimate of the Joint Chiefs), and thereafter to "trickle out" the remainder so that an airlift could be kept going to rescue the maximum number of Vietnamese.

In the afternoon of April 24, Ford held an NSC meeting to review the final evacuation plans. Schlesinger continued to advocate immediate evacuation of the remaining Americans, which would, of course, end the evacuation of Vietnamese as well. Ford put an end to the argument as he had at the meeting on April 9:

FORD: I understand the risk. It is mine and I am doing it. But let's make sure we carry out the orders.

ROCKEFELLER: You can't insure the interests of America without risks.

FORD: With God's help.

Grasping for every last possible extension, we replied to the Soviets at 8:25 P.M. on April 24. In our message, we posed a number of questions in the hope that the refugee airlift might continue while the Soviets prepared their answers. In our message, we noted that, in view of the "constructive [Soviet] reply . . . the U.S. side is proceeding with the evacuation of Americans under the assumption that conditions will remain favorable." We invited Hanoi's views on how to implement the provisions of the Paris Agreement "relative to the achievement of a political settlement." The President reassured Brezhnev that we would desist from military action, which the Congress was, in any event, prohibiting. So long as there was no interference with the evacuation, our note continued, the United States would "take no steps which might exacerbate the situation."

It was thin gruel but, as I said to the State Department staff meeting, all we had left to us now was a show of nerve. There is, however, a limit to what can be accomplished by diplomatic maneuvering, especially when dealing with the steely-eyed calculators from Hanoi.

GENERAL SCOWCROFT–KISSINGER
Friday, April 25, 1975
4:02 P.M.

K: Have you noticed Senator Clark [Dick Clark (D.-Iowa)] has now said he's against aid unless we reduce our numbers in Vietnam? It's (five hundred).

S: No.

K: Where do you think he got that number from?

S: That number sounds familiar.

K: It's sickening.

S: That's incredible.

K: Would you tell Martin I'm still waiting for a response to the message I sent with respect to the Soviets and the French.

S: Right. I don't think we ought to press him now on the numbers.

K: Tell him we want to know where he will be.

S: He sort of told us. We will be 1,090 minus thirty-five or forty plus whatever nonofficials he can get out.

K: Tell him we would like to know.

GENERAL SCOWCROFT–KISSINGER

Friday, April 25, 1975
8:06 P.M.

. . .

K: . . . Could you do a cable to Martin? He and I should be working on the same schedule with the same ideas. I want some idea by opening of business tomorrow of where we are going over the next week.

S: Going politically?

K: In general. What he is saying will happen. For example, if negotiations start, should we leave the Embassy open or should we get out? My own view is when the PRG comes in, we should leave, but I am open to different views.

S: It depends how they come in.

K: I want to hear his views.

S: Okay. Let me draft something. Do you want to see it before it goes?

K: Why don't you read it to me because I will be going home soon.

S: I will get on it right away.

. . .

GENERAL SCOWCROFT–KISSINGER

Saturday, April 26, 1975
10:10 A.M.

K: Have you read the Martin cable? Do you understand what he is saying?

S: Yes. He is not going to reduce any further for one thing, and another cable just came in. He has said that his staff is exhausted and he won't reduce the American staff any further as long as the airlift is still on. He said some reporters are coming back in because of the lack of military activity. He also said some businessmen are thinking of returning. We have about come to the end of the road, it says, and since you have left the decision up to me, I am not going to reduce American official community any further. I am, however, warning other Americans that they are staying at their own risk, he says.

K: I suppose he is right.

S: We have two problems now. What to do when pressures build up as Congress finds out and what to do with the Soviets when they find out [that we are taking Vietnamese out on American planes].

K: Yes.

S: But it is pretty hard to argue with him. He does have a lot of work to get done in terms of evacuating and everything.

K: Also he deliberately misunderstood my reference to the PRG.

S: Yes.

K: Could you straighten him out on this?

S: Yes. Let me draft something.

K: The political talks I was referring to were not between Saigon and the PRG but between the U.S. and the PRG. I want those conducted in Paris. He could conduct talks with the PRG on the technical situation in Saigon. He has yet to reply to any of the strategy in the negotiating cable we sent. I want his views so I can conduct policy; I don't want him conducting it.

S: He hasn't acknowledged any of that yet. I will have a draft cable for you when you get over here.

K: He is obnoxious, but he is doing well. He shouldn't slow down in getting people out.

S: I don't think he means that. He is pointing out that you let me control my part; you are not doing yours so well yourself. That is just one of his gratuitous slaps, that is the way I take that.

K: But he put something in about slowing down.

S: He says he could have operated more efficiently if we had been more prepared.

K: In Guam and Wake? But I will keep the heat on Dean Brown. [When Vietnamese were fleeing by the tens of thousands, temporary facilities for them were set up on Guam and Wake Island. Former Ambassador Dean Brown was put in charge of receiving the refugees.]

S: All right. Okay.

K: I wonder how he is going to get the people out with his own resources?

S: He is right about Americans in the north [in Danang]. We haven't lost a single American.

K: I would just leave him alone now.

S: We have, at least, got his attention anyway, which isn't easy to do.

    . . .

AMBASSADOR BROWN–KISSINGER
Saturday, April 26, 1975
10:15 A.M.

K: I have just gotten one of Martin's backchannels to me. He wants to slow down the evacuation because it is such a mess in Guam.

B: He can't do that. Even if Clark and Guam are overwhelmed. We have twelve thousand at Clark and more at Guam.

K: Don't put these figures out.

B: I haven't. There are thousands more on the way.

K: I thought he was bluffing me. That means we have gotten 25,000 or more out.

B: Right. Say, Martin hasn't answered the telegram we sent asking for his feelings and what the high-risk options are, etc., yet. It is near panic at the airport and they have no control over the situation, especially the issuing of certificates. What appears to be happening is that Americans are walking down to the planes with their Vietnamese friends and saying get on. Fifteen to 20 percent of the people have no papers and there is no proof that they are high-risk at all.

K: What can we do?

B: Nothing. Martin can't control the situation, because he can't be at the airport.

K: Can't anyone?

B: There are people who are trying to be at the airport, but it is difficult. Everybody is taking care of friends. Maybe they are sorting them somehow. But it is close to chaos. There is also a difficulty with California. I talked to Jerry [Brown, governor of California] a couple of days ago.

K: Is he against it?

B: No, but the federal government hasn't done anything for California and with their high unemployment, etc., he is saying it will be difficult. His impression is that we want to dump [the] Vietnamese on them. It is a political problem. I have Weinberger [Caspar Weinberger, former Secretary of Health, Education, and Welfare, later Secretary of Defense] set to call him today and talk to him. He will say that we will try to be helpful but we are going to have to start moving groups to the U.S. We need someplace in the U.S. to hold them until we can let volunteer agencies move them on. I have talked to the airlines and asked them if we can have free passages on planes because there is no money within the U.S. to move them.

K: Yes. It is a nightmare.

B: It is not going to come out very nicely. One of the things I wanted to say in the WSAG is how many people do we want to get out?

K: How many do you think?

B: Five to ten thousand more. If we could move them from Saigon to [unclear], we could alleviate a lot of pressure.

K: Let me think about it.

B: Okay. Also think about Hawaii or the possibility of moving them now directly to the States. We will talk about it.

K: Okay.

B: Defense has got to cooperate. Weinberger is calling Schlesinger and telling him to give the army a good name for once by letting them take an active part in the refugee movement. They are bucking us again. We need to let people use military bases as the next staging area to let the volunteer agencies have time to pick them up. It should work just like the Hungary thing [in 1956, evacuation after Soviet military move].

K: Okay.

B: Thanks, sir.

On April 28, Hanoi made Washington's debates irrelevant by launching a rocket attack on Saigon. Just two days earlier, at a speech in New Orleans, Ford had declared the war in Vietnam over, to the applause of the media. But the speech, which had not been cleared with my office, was asserting an irrelevancy. For by now the war was indeed over, and the sole remaining issue was whether the denouement could be postponed by diplomatic maneuvers to permit the evacuation of the largest possible number of Vietnamese, who, having cooperated with the United States, faced death or concentration camps. None of Hanoi's memoirists refers to the President's speech as having accelerated the North Vietnamese timetable, and Ford does not mention it in his own memoirs. The principal motive for Hanoi's final assault, paradoxically, may well have been the resignation of South Vietnamese President Thieu. Hanoi's leaders, having spent a lifetime at war to unify the country, did not want to see a government emerge that could make a new claim to international legitimacy—not even their own puppet, the PRG. Whatever the motive, the rocket attacks produced the final spasm: the total evacuation of Americans from South Vietnam.

On the evening of April 28 Washington time (April 29 in Vietnam), the final collapse of Saigon began with a rocket attack on Tan Son Nhut airport. Several thousand particularly endangered Vietnamese and four hundred Americans had been assembled there in order to enable the evacuation planes to be filled and turned around without delay.

Though the firing soon ceased, the refugees' very peril became their undoing. Panicked, they swarmed over the runways, and in effect stopped the airlift. At 10:45 P.M. Washington time on April 28, Ford very reluctantly ordered the final evacuation. Shortly before, we had talked not in the apocalyptic terms in which the occasion may appear in history books. Rather it had about it the feel of mourning for the unfortunate victims we were about to leave behind.

GENERAL SCOWCROFT–KISSINGER
Monday, April 28, 1975
5:10 P.M.

(missed first part)

. . .

K: I think we should terminate the C-130 operations if this keeps up. There's no excuse now. Then we should go to the helicopters by Thursday.

S: I think they decided—

K: That's the price you get for two days headlines [reference to Ford's New Orleans speech].

. . .

S: That's right. I hope they're happy, whoever got it in.

K: I don't think they're going to play.

S: It's becoming more and more useless.

K: Are there a lot of rockets hitting?

S: I don't know how many. It could be just a few. As soon as you get Americans killed. So far there's two been killed.

K: Americans?

S: Yes. We can no longer justify keeping them in even if it's a sporadic attack.

K: It's a DOD complex. I guess they ought to terminate operations tomorrow. Get this cable out. That just gives them the strategy. In an hour, send another cable in light of those attacks.

S: Are you going to call the President?

. . .

THE PRESIDENT–KISSINGER
Monday, April 28, 1975
5:28 P.M.

K: Mr. President, we have just had reports from Saigon that they have started rocketing the airport again and that two Marines were killed. I think we had better terminate the C-130 operations. We don't have enough leverage.

F: And not undertake to get the three hundred out?

K: I think we should let them conclude this C-130 run during daylight hours, which is our night, to get the three hundred out.

F: Yes, get all of that group out.

K: We can check with the military people but if you give your permission, we will do it without referring to you again.

F: Proceed on that. We will talk about the other four hundred tomorrow.

K: We should get the other four hundred out Wednesday or Thursday their time, which would be Tuesday or Wednesday our time.

F: All right, get going on that.

K: Okay.

The situation at Tan Son Nhut airport was chaotic. A multitude of refugees were at the airport seeking to get on airplanes. Seven hundred specially endangered personnel selected by the Embassy were there to be given priority on C-130s. These plans were now coming apart.

GENERAL SCOWCROFT–KISSINGER
Monday, April 28, 1975
5:32 P.M.

K: I just talked to the President. Have you got the revised copy [of the statement announcing shelling of Saigon airport]?

S: It is on the wire now.

K: Will you check with Clements and [Chairman of the Joint Chiefs of Staff George] Brown?

S: Brown wants to pull out right now. He called right after you did. He will check with the Embassy because he said they were given assurances that when they were taking fire, they would be able to leave.

K: Terminate without the whole day's run?

S: He did say that the C-130 runs were continuing to come in and that they would let them land or wave them off as the situation indicates.

K: I would prefer to let them operate through the day and let the Americans leave at the end of the day or it will be a panic situation.

S: That would be best. Graham was trying to [evacuate] up to three hundred people.

K: Let them do that. Will you do a cable to Martin for me saying this was ordered by the President. We need Martin's recommendations as to when the rest should go. We gain nothing by letting them stay there.

S: Maybe you are right.

K: Will you call Dobrynin and say that we have had reports that two Marines were killed at Tan Son Nhut and tell him that if this keeps up it will have a serious impact on Soviet-American relations since we have their assurances. . . .

GENERAL SCOWCROFT–KISSINGER

> *Monday, April 28, 1975*
> 5:50 P.M.

S: I am sorry to bother you, but George Brown called and said that he is compelled to do two things subject to your wishes. One is to let the DAO people [Defense Attaché Office] leave right now and secondly, to let the carrier planes coming in hit any rocket launching pads they find.

K: Did you call Dobrynin?

S: He is in town and will call me back.

K: Look, I am very reluctant to go along with any military action. I think that he can pull out DAO people and he should hold with the military action until I can talk to the President. Will you get the President to call me right after the meeting?

S: Okay.

GENERAL SCOWCROFT–KISSINGER

> *Monday, April 28, 1975*
> 6:03 P.M.

S: I just passed the President a note about what the Chairman [Brown] wants to do. He thinks if they are firing on Americans we ought to hit them.

K: I think they may be overreacting. We should let more planes take off and see if they are being fired upon.

S: They are still firing. According to the Chairman, it will be another thirty minutes before they will be in a position to attack at a minimum.

K: My instinct is against it. There is no sense in churning this up during the last two days of the war. Can they land on the field?

S: I don't know that. I don't know if they know that either.

K: Can you call out there or can somebody call there? It is the sort of reaction that we pay for [for] weeks; but then if we get more killed that will be bad too.

S: He [Brown] said that he won't let them cross the border without word from me.

K: What does Schlesinger say?

S: I haven't talked with him.

K: I think you had better call him and find out what he thinks and give him my views and then we will go back to the President.

S: Okay.

AMBASSADOR MARTIN–KISSINGER

Monday, April 28, 1975
7:05 P.M.

M: Hello, Henry, how are you?

K: Okay. I'd like to get a feel from you of the situation.

M: I was just going over it with Noel Gayler [Pacific Fleet commander], who has issued orders to immediately evacuate the DAO.

K: That's what we are having an NSC meeting on right now. So you better wait until that meeting is over.

M: I see. That's what I thought, but he went ahead and did it. Now the—

K: Hold on— [confers with Scowcroft]

M: [doesn't hear the Secretary's instruction to hold on]— now the situation is that the ground—still holding all right. The runways are questionable as to whether they will be usable a little later or not.

K: The runways are questionable?

M: Well, we don't simply know at this point whether or not some of the shells have impacted on one or both runways making them unusable. But we will know in about an hour, I think, whether the runways are usable, what the situation on the ground actually is, apparently the—off already. Now I don't mind the DAO's leaving, but I would hope it would be a little orderly way. For example, he [presumably General George Brown,

Chairman of the Joint Chiefs of Staff] ordered all flag officers to take a helicopter—the first one out—to one of the ships. That's all right, don't mind that. But if all the ground-handling people move out quickly, then we have a real problem, particularly since we were alerted last night to prepare ten thousand people here for movement out today. So the staff has been out most of the night and getting these people ready. Now I think this will probably be the last day it [evacuation] takes place. What I would like to—

K: But do you think you could operate?

M: —or to get a, the real facts, not just a hell of lot of uncollected rumors about what it is on the ground and get back to you.

K: Well, can you do that within the next hour.

M: [Martin doesn't hear] —clean out the DAO, using as much of the lift as possible today to get it out—I was supposed to slim the Embassy to sort of a really noncompletely essential but still a communicable office.

K: How many would that be?

M: [Martin doesn't hear] —and I'm not really frightened about getting those people out.

K: How many are you talking about?

M: I'm talking probably about a couple hundred in the end.

K: In the Embassy?

M: Yeah.

K: Okay and how about the civilians?

M: There aren't that many left—a couple of hundred, I think, mostly press.

K: Well, we have to get them out too, don't you think?

M: I would like to, but like in Phnom Penh, you know, some of them are going to stay, they've been through this before.

K: Yeah.

M: All we can do is make it available.

K: So you think you can get all of this done with fixed-wing aircraft today?

M: I'm not certain whether we can get it done with fixed-wing air-craft until we get a final reading on the runways, which we should have in about one half hour to forty-five minutes.

K: Okay. Well, you let me know—ah, what does Smith [General Homer Smith, Jr., U.S. defense attaché in Saigon] think of all of this?

M: Smith thinks there is a little bit of panic up and down the line, but when you are taking rockets out there, as he is, it gets a little—

K: Okay, now let me put Scowcroft on. I've got to go and see the President.

M: Okay.

Scowcroft: Hello, Graham?

M: Hi, Brent.

S: Go ahead, what were you saying?

M: I was saying that it makes sense to me to find out exactly what the runway situation is and whether or not we can bring in the C-130s today. The ground action is apparently died down a good deal. If we could move out in six increments part of the people that we have out there and part of the other high-risk people that we assembled yesterday at Gayler's request—to move ten thousand out—but if we sort of panic and vanish today, it is going to be a public relations thing of some importance, par-ticularly if it turns out not to have been really needed. This way, we ought to take a look, I think, in about—get back to you in about one hour, before finalization.

S: Okay, if you would, and work with Smith, because if we can get him on your side, you can kind of counterbalance [the] mili-tary back here, who are going crazy because their people are hurt.

M: Okay. Will do.

S: We'll be here, Graham.

M: All right.

S: Bye.

THE PRESIDENT–KISSINGER
Monday, April 28, 1975
10:25 P.M.

F: Yes, Henry.

K: Mr. President, the shelling seems to have substantially stopped. But now order seems to have broken down on the field and all the runways are full of people. It's getting to be like Danang, which is about probably what they wanted to create.

F: Right.

K: They are trying to restore order. We've talked to Graham Martin and we've told him that if the airfield becomes unusable, he's got to go to emergency evacuation.

F: I would agree in both places.

K: Yeah. Well, the major problem we will have now, Mr. President, is whether we can get the American personnel, if the order really has broken down at Tan Son Nhut [airport], off Tan Son Nhut and back to the DAO compound.

F: How much of a distance is there?

K: The distance isn't far. It's only about five minutes by car if we can get them off the— You know, we have no way of knowing how intermingled they are—

F: Right.

K: —with the Vietnamese and we will just have to sit it out now.

F: Are the C-130s getting in?

K: No, because the field seems to be flooded with civilians right now.

F: I see.

K: One of them was cleared for an approach but absolute bedlam broke loose when it got close, so they waved it off again. Now that shelling just created a sense of—

F: Frustration and panic.

K: So we may just have to go to emergency evacuation in a couple of hours. But the orders are absolutely clear. If the fixed-wing can't be used, we'll have to go to helicopter.

F: And just take ours out. Hope for the best.

K: That's right. I don't think they'll shoot it out. And I frankly don't believe that the Russians snookered us. I think that the North Vietnamese took another reading over the weekend and decided they were going to go for broke.

F: Well, let's see—it's 10:30, ten o'clock there, isn't it?

K: It's 11:30 there. Only about six hours left.

F: Apparently the ARVN [Army of the Republic of Vietnam—the South Vietnamese] are not able to do anything about it.

K: Well, we have General Smith on the ground there. He's out at Tan Son Nhut. We have Martin in town. They are in close contact and they'll just have to use their judgment. We can't run it from here.

F: No, I agree.

K: Both Jim [Schlesinger] and I sent the identical messages from you through our channels.

F: Right.

K: And I've talked to Graham Martin and I know that from Defense they have talked to Smith.

F: Right.

K: So everybody knows what he's got to do.

F: So it looks like—

K: To me, it looks like an emergency evacuation right now.

F: With the helicopters in the two places.

K: That's what it looks like to me. We'll keep you posted.

F: All right. I guess tragic as it is, Henry, we've got to leave those five thousand there and get our people out.

K: Yeah. Tragic because they are all selected for the North Vietnamese right there. They are all high-risk people but we can't do anything about it.

F: [long pause] Well, keep me posted and—

K: Well, we have no choice, Mr. President.

F: No. [It's] in the hands of the people out there.

K: That's right. And you've carried it to the absolute limit it could be carried and we have now just got to see how it plays out.

F: As I understand it now, Smith and Martin have the authority to order the helicopter operation.

K: Anytime they decide the field is unusable.

F: From what you tell me, it is, so we should anticipate that action.

K: Yes. It would be better for us if they could reopen the field, at least long enough to get the Americans off with fixed-wing aircraft from out there.

F: Right.

K: Because that's where all the commotion is. But since they are on the spot, they really have to judge it.

F: But they have full authority to do it.

K: They have full authority to do it and they are ordered to do it if they cannot get out by the end of the day.

F: Right.

K: They have no authority to stay another night.

F: Right.

K: They have the authority to call for the emergency airlift anytime tonight—our night—and they must call for it before the end of the day out there.

F: By the end of the day out there or by tomorrow morning here?

K: By tomorrow morning here. If the C-130s haven't taken them off, then the helicopters will.

F: That's a real shame! Twenty-four more hours—or twelve more hours.

K: Twelve more hours and we would have saved eight thousand lives.

F: Henry, we did the best we could.

K: Mr. President, you carried it single-handedly against all the advice and we played it out as far as it would play.

F: Well, I just hope Smith and Martin now understand where we are and will not hesitate to act.

K: Well, we checked with Martin. I talked with him fifteen minutes ago. I can't say that he's doing it willingly but he's going to do it. He wants to stay behind with two people to take care of Americans that might come out of the woodwork. But I just don't think we can justify it.

F: I don't think so either, Henry.

K: We can't give them any hostages.

F: No, no, no.

K: And incidentally, Mr. President, you may be pleased to know— I've told you already, the French have gotten kicked out of Cambodia too.

F: Well, isn't that some consolation? Well, Henry, we've done the best we could and you and I are taking it on the chin and can just hope the Good Lord is with us.

K: Well, we'll take it on the chin for a few more days. Just a minute, they are bringing me something. Yeah—all right. They are already working on getting the Americans back to the compound.

F: Right.

K: In the next thirty minutes we'll probably go to the helicopter evacuation.

F: Well, I'll be here. Be sure to call me and let me know how it's going.

. . .

GENERAL GEORGE BROWN, CHAIRMAN,
JOINT CHIEFS OF STAFF–KISSINGER

Monday, April 28, 1975
10:42 P.M.

B: This is George Brown trying to reach Brent.

K: Okay, he'll come on.

B: I was just telling him—you may want to know—that we've just been through to Smith in Saigon. Ambassador Martin agrees we should go to the helicopter evacuation and he's going to call your office.

K: Okay. I've got a call in to him and you hold on and then I'll get it from the President. And we'll have all of that within the next twenty minutes.

B: I was calling you to alert you he'll be calling too.

K: Good. Thank you.

AMBASSADOR MARTIN–KISSINGER

Monday, April 28, 1975
10:43 P.M.

M: Hello, Henry. I think the personnel security is disintegrating at Tan Son Nhut, more than the enemy action, and they tried to load a VNAF C-130 and got considerable interference from the ARVN [South Vietnamese army]. So I think the only thing to do is to go for execute on [helicopters].

K: Okay, how much time do you need? Well, you handle it from out there.

M: Yeah, okay.

K: Don't you think? We'll give you the approval back, which you will have within fifteen minutes, and then you schedule it, but then you do it during your daylight hours.

M: I'm not sure we can complete it all today, but we'll sure try.

K: Okay. No, you better complete it today.

M: Okay.

K: Okay, Graham, you did your best and it was excellent.

M: I don't like much A for effort, but—

K: Well, that's what all of us are getting. That's all we are going to get out of this.

M: Yeah, I know that.

K: Okay, we'll be back to you within twenty minutes. Thank you.

THE PRESIDENT–KISSINGER

Monday, April 28, 1975
10:45 P.M.

K: Mr. President. I've just talked to Graham Martin and he agrees that we ought to issue the execute for the evacuation.

F: From both places?

K: That's right.

F: Well, I think we should too. Shortly after you called, Jim Schlesinger called and I got the impression you and he were in agreement but I told him to call you to make sure that was true.

K: Yes.

F: And I— If Martin says so, I think we should move on it.

K: Right. And then I think that while this thing is going on, I think everything ought to go through Brent or me. We'll let you know in case anything happens but so that there aren't too many nervous Nellies running loose.

F: Right. Do you think I ought to come over to the Situation Room?

K: No. I don't think it's necessary. We'll keep you informed as soon as something happens. And it really doesn't require a presidential decision after the executes.

F: I'll be here, and by all means call me, good or bad.

K: We'll call you if there is anything at all to report. You first have to get the Americans back to the compound. That seems to be manageable from the little I've heard. But then we have to make sure Graham can get all the Americans together at the Embassy. That may take him a couple of hours. I told him he had to complete it during daylight hours.

F: There is six hours left.

K: About six and a half or seven hours left. I think it can be done. I just think we have no choice.

F: Well, tragic as it is, I think this is what has to be done and tell him to do it.

K: Well, he's under clear instructions. I'll now call General Brown and Jim [Schlesinger] and tell them that you've ordered the thing executed. They won't fight us hard.

F: That's an understatement.

K: The only thing is, they'll be so eager to get out they'll get the airlift in before the people are assembled.

F: You tell them to make damn sure every reasonable effort is made to get everybody out.

K: That's right.

F: So there's no question about that.

K: Right. And under these conditions we can't take any more Vietnamese.

F: No. Let's make sure that's in an order so that there is—

K: There is no physical capability, Mr. President, but I'll make that clear too.

F: All right. Get the order underway and it sickens me.

K: Mr. President, we carried it as far as it could be carried and maybe a few hours beyond it, and you know we need to have no regrets. It's the best that could be done.

F: Well, keep me posted but tell Graham to do it as quickly as possible.

K: Right, Mr. President.

F: Thank you, Henry.

GENERAL BROWN–KISSINGER

Monday, April 28, 1975
10:45 P.M.

K: How does it look over in Vietnam—I was just talking to the President.

B: Well, it doesn't look good. It doesn't look good because the airfield at Tan Son Nhut has a mob, which got pretty nasty when they [local personnel] tried to move two Vietnamese C-130s and we have had two C-130s overhead but have not been able to bring them in because of this mob on the airfield.

K: They've stopped shelling?

B: Yes, but the crowd is out of control and getting a little nasty and I recommended to Secretary Schlesinger that we go to the chopper thing and send our people back to the compound and to make the helicopters—

K: Yeah, but make sure that everybody is together and that—we can do the helicopters only once.

B: Well, we understand that and—

K: So that downtown they are also ready.

B: Oh, yes, they are talking to the Ambassador and I don't know what the reaction is—the Secretary is going to talk to the President, I guess.

K: You know, there are too many people making too many calls. Okay, I've talked to the President about it already.

B: Did you get a decision?

K: The President has [made his decision]. Defense has to make the decision if the airfield is closed—and can't be reopened—that he has ordered that we go to—

B: We don't want to wait to find out whether it can be reopened. That may be tomorrow morning, before we can conclude conclusively that it can't be reopened.

K: No, no, no. If it can't be reopened by the end of the day. I think, I'll check with the President, and I'll let you know. I think you can go to the helicopter [lift]. How long do you need?

B: What do you mean? Daylight to operate?

K: Yeah.

B: Oh, we would like at least two, three hours.

K: You have how much time?

B: We've got plenty of time—it is not even noon over there yet. About twenty minutes to eleven. So we've got a good seven hours of daylight. But I would hate to have us wait seven hours to conclude we can't reopen the airfield and plan on doing the chopper lift tomorrow.

K: No, no, no. That's out of the question. If we do the chopper lift, we'll do it this afternoon, their time.

B: I'm sorry, sir, I didn't hear you; there is a lot of—

K: You do it before the night is over.

B: Yes, sir. Here's the Secretary.

Schlesinger: Henry?

K: Yes, Jim.

S: The President just wanted to be sure that the stories he is getting are all in sync—I indicated to him we had the VNAF [Vietnamese Air Force] C-130s that have been pinned down by a mob with a fair amount of shooting—F-5s on the taxiway with the engines running have been abandoned. There is a car that's been driven across the runway to block the 130s and so on. He indicated as long as our stories are the same, that he was prepared to proceed, but he wanted first to be sure that the stories—the evaluation was the same, and secondly that to proceed, that the orders to emanate from Martin and Smith—

K: Let me talk to him.

S: The President?

K: Yeah. I've just talked to him a few minutes ago, but I think you must have talked to him in between.

S: Yeah, it was just after you talked to him. He mentioned that he just talked to you. In any event the feeling is we will not be able to restore security in Tan Son Nhut.

K: So you feel we ought to go to the helicopter lift?

S: Yeah. Gayler and Brown have both recommended. Smith is now seeking from Martin an order to go ahead from that quarter.

K: Okay, let me—I'll do two things. I'll talk to Martin and then I'll talk to the President and then I'll be back to you.

S: Righto.

K: It couldn't take more than a half hour.

S: Okay, time is going to get short. We've got about seven hours of daylight there.

K: You'll have it settled within—I'll get Martin right away.

S: Okay.

K: I'll call you right back.

S: Bye, bye.

Secretary Schlesinger–Kissinger

Monday, April 28, 1975
10:51 P.M.

K: Jim. I just talked to the President and he said to give the execute.

S: They're on the way.

K: And the problem now is to make sure we get everybody assembled. We just had a report from CBS. Somebody called Nessen saying that over five busloads of Americans have been stopped on the way to Tan Son Nhut by the South Vietnamese police. I think we've got to let Martin and Smith tell us when they've got everyone together and when they want the lift.

S: Yes.

K: I don't think we can do it from here.

S: No, it's in their hands now.

K: Okay. Will you take care of—? I've told Martin to go ahead.

S: Right. Okay. It was already executed.

Ambassador Martin–Kissinger

Monday, April 28, 1975
11:00 P.M.

M: —Okay, fine, we'll execute—

K: You'll execute and you have the control now when you get everybody together.

M: Okay, fine.

K: We have had a report that the police have held up a group of Americans trying to get to the airport—is that true?

M: It may have been a checkpoint at a gate, but I haven't heard anything else.

K: Okay, but you think you can assemble everyone in time to get out today?

M: Yes, I think so.

K: And you better be on the chopper yourself.

M: I would like very much to stay on a few days longer.

K: The President doesn't approve it.

M: Well, as you say.

K: We need our heroes back in Washington—there aren't too many of them.

M: Oh, my God, you know. That's talking about—

K: You've been heroic, Graham, and I admire what you've done.

M: Thanks a lot, Henry.

K: And you get everybody out now and we'll talk to you soon—

M: Okay, fine.

K: And God bless—

M: Okay.

LAWRENCE EAGLEBURGER, DEPUTY UNDERSECRETARY OF STATE FOR MANAGEMENT–KISSINGER

Monday, April 28, 1975
11:06 P.M.

K: Larry?

E: Yes, sir.

K: We are going to this emergency evacuation, will you tell Phil Habib?

E: Yep, right away.

K: Did you have anything else?

E: No, I was just wanting to check on whether that was what would happen.

K: Yep.

E: Okay, I'll call him right away.

VICE PRESIDENT ROCKEFELLER–KISSINGER

Monday, April 28, 1975
11:11 P.M.

K: I just wanted to tell you the order has broken down at the Tan Son Nhut airport, we are now going to helicopter evacuation.

R: That's a tragedy, so that the five thousand didn't get out.

K: No, and they are sitting there all selected.

R: What group was that?

K: Well, they were high officials—from families of foreign service personnel.

R: Boy.

K: Eight thousand or nine thousand.

R: No kidding.

K: Yeah.

R: Did they get any of them out in helicopters?

K: No, because we are not going into Tan Son Nhut with helicopters.

R: You're not?

K: No, we are going into a compound nearby. We'll be lucky to get the Americans out now.

R: Really?

K: Well, you know, it depends how quickly the mob, if there is one, can get out of control.

R: What did they do—did they close the airport by shelling?

K: No, they stopped the shelling as I thought they would, but the ARVN [South Vietnamese army] at the airports is out of control.

R: Oh, the ARVN themselves?

K: Yeah.

R: What did they want to do, get out on the airplane? Same thing as up in the north.

K: Yeah.

R: Well, it's a sad chapter Henry. You've done your part, you've done it nobly, you've fought right to the end. If you stand for principle, you can do something.

K: I told the President that he's got nothing to regret, he fought to the end.

. . .

AMBASSADOR HABIB–KISSINGER

Tuesday, April 29, 1975
Midnight

K: I tell you, Phil, if you had a good heart, we'd really work you.

H: As a matter of fact, I asked Larry [Eagleburger] if I could come in and he said he'd let me know. After he gets done.

K: You know we are evacuating tonight.

H: He told me.

K: We had no choice, did we?

H: You're absolutely right.

K: You know Graham was bitching but I figured—

H: You're absolutely right. I say that with a degree of positive knowledge, as I know that situation.

K: I just thought that it would come apart in Saigon.

H: There is no circumstance in which there is any reason to leave them there. What can they do?

K: Exactly.

H: If there was a function to perform, then you could leave some. The only alternative he has is to take everything except a handful. If there is a function to perform—

K: He wanted to stay behind with three people, but I don't know what he would do.

H: Heroics. But I would have said no.

K: I ordered him out. I told him he had no choice. It was a presidential order. But, Phil, what we need is a joint Defense-State statement like we did in the Cambodia thing. Which should be issued in the middle of the operations. And then we need a presidential thing. For the end.

H: You'd better issue it fairly quickly because as soon as he [Martin] starts to move, the last thing the press will do will be to file stories out of there that they're moving.

K: Well, then do it as soon as the operation has started.

H: What time has it started—does it start?

K: In an hour or two.

H: All right. I'll come down.

K: I'm in the White House but I—

H: I'll be in the Operations Center.

K: Will you call me with a statement?

H: I shall call you.

K: Good.

LARRY EAGLEBURGER–KISSINGER

Tuesday, April 29, 1975
12:16 A.M.

K: —to draft a statement, you know, to be released when the operation starts.

E: Okay.

K: And as soon as you have an agreed text, call me.

E: Right.

K: And then we are drafting one here that the President can issue when it's completed.

E: I'll have it for you in a few minutes.

K: Good.

After Thieu's resignation, Big Minh had been appointed as President. As his first act, he ordered all Americans to leave the country.

THE PRESIDENT–KISSINGER

Tuesday, April 29, 1975
12:22 A.M.

K: Mr. President, I just want you to know that Big Minh [just appointed as president to replace Thieu] has just ordered all Americans out of the country within twenty-four hours.

F: That's helpful, isn't it?

K: Well, he must know we are leaving, because they are doing it on open radios to collect the civilians and I think he is trying to make some points with the Communists.

F: I would gather that too.

K: But actually it may be sort of a protection for the Americans too—at least they are not bugging out under these conditions. They are being ordered out.

F: You ordered out—

K: After all we have suffered there, it is a hell of a way to leave.

F: Yeah, big friend of ours.

K: I think probably on the whole it will have a tendency to save lives.

F: I would think so. Outside of the fact you don't like it as a comment that will go down in history, but on a practical basis tonight, it might be helpful.

K: Okay. I won't call you again until the operation has started.

F: All right, thanks for calling me on this, Henry.

K: And then I'll read you also the statement we are drafting you.

F: That will be fine.

K: Right, Mr. President.

F: Thank you very much, Henry.

THE PRESIDENT–KISSINGER

Tuesday, April 29, 1975
12:39 A.M.

K: Mr. President, I just wanted to tell you the helicopters are about five minutes out and I'll send over the statement or bring it over. Are you up still?

F: I'll—

K: I'll read it to you after. I just want Rumsfeld to get a look at it and make sure.

F: Why don't you read it to me?

K: Can I call you in five minutes?

F: Sure.

K: I'll call you after Rumsfeld has had a chance to take a look at it.

F: Okay.

K: And then I won't bother you again until it's all over.

F: Well, don't hesitate one bit, Henry.

K: Unless there are some complications.

F: All right. You call me in about five minutes.

K: Right, Mr. President.

LARRY EAGLEBURGER–AMBASSADOR HABIB–KISSINGER

Tuesday, April 29, 1975
1:00 A.M.

. . .

E: Mr. Secretary, Phil's on. He doesn't want to issue anything.

H: Hello, Mr. Secretary. My feeling is—I was just talking to Defense—that the later you can issue a statement, the better, rather than issuing it before the evacuation starts, or even at the beginning of it. Official confirmation it's going on will get a different kind of play out there than the kind of rumors and news reports that are now being used. It seems to me—the news reports are already carrying it's going to take place—all that we need now is this kind of a statement say about toward the end of the actual lift. There are about three thousand Vietnamese out at that airport right now [who were, in effect, being left behind].

K: Yeah.

H: And there could be a mad scramble for additional ones to get on. Who knows what's going to happen out there. And I think it would be better to hold off on this sort of thing until you are a little way into the operation.

K: Okay. Well, why don't you do it midway through.

H: All right. When we get some idea that it's about halfway through or that there's no trouble developing. If there's real trouble developing, then I think we should call you.

K: That's right. And don't say "is being protected as necessary." Why don't you say, "is being protected by security forces," isn't it—of U.S. Marines or by a security force?

H: "Is being protected by a security force." Then we'll use the word "necessary" down below about force. We'll say, "and is being protected by security force of U.S. Marines. Force will not be used unless necessary."

K: And I would say "tactical aircraft."

H: Well, that's another one we cut out of it deliberately because if we put that in, then you've just given away what's overhead. They might [not] even know what's overhead if we don't tell them.

K: Well, if we do it well into the operation—

H: —make any difference.

K: Put in "tactical aircraft."

H: All right. "Tactical aircraft are in the vicinity in the event they are needed" or "are in the vicinity."

K: We don't have to say so. "By a security force of U.S. Marines and tactical aircraft."

H: All right. Fine. We'll hold up on this awhile and when we do it, we'll have Bob start calling around.

K: Bob who?

H: Anderson [State Department spokesman].

K: Yeah. Well, once you know it's well underway, then you better let it go.

E: Okay, sir.

K: I'm afraid we may have waited too long.

H: No, the word is out already because the newspapermen are filing from Saigon that—

E: We waited too long to do it or to announce it?

K: To do it.

E: That may be.

H: Yeah, that may be. That's why I'm a little reluctant to announce formally too soon.

K: Yeah, but once it's underway— Look, Defense is leaking this stuff like crazy.

E: That's frankly what worries me.

H: Look, Defense is leaking it but the press out there are filing stories too because they've been notified—

K: Yeah, but I'd like State to come out with something.

H: All right. Fine. All right, we'll put it out fairly soon.

K: Okay.

H: All right. Bye.

THE PRESIDENT–KISSINGER

Tuesday, April 29, 1975
1:06 A.M.

K: Mr. President, we still have no confirmed report that any helicopter has actually landed—they are having a little trouble coordinating the TAC [Tactical Air Command] air and the helicopters. It isn't due to any problems. There is a problem—or maybe—one on the ground, in the sense that a few thousand South Vietnamese have gotten into the compound at the airbase. But we'll just have to see this now.

F: They are planning to land in both places. [In the end, the evacuation was conducted from the Embassy as the only site.]

K: I think what is holding it up is, as I understand it, is some problem of coordination between the—they want to have the TAC air and the helicopters coordinated so that the TAC air can give support.

F: Well, you keep me posted, Henry.

K: Well, if you don't hear from me it is going smoothly.

F: All right, then let me know when it is completed under any circumstances.

K: That in any event. Can I read you the statement? I have shown it to Don [Rumsfeld] and also to Habib. [reads the statement]

F: I think that is good, Henry.

K: I think that is all we can—

F: I think it speaks for itself and we'll stand by it.

K: Right, and then we will issue that when we know it has been completed. Or about six or seven in the morning, so they can run it on the morning shows.

F: Right. Of course, if there are any complications we will have to change—otherwise, we will go with that.

K: I will call you when the operation is completed or if there is some major difficulty.

F: Okay, Henry. Thank you very much. See you tomorrow.

After weeks of debate about the rate of evacuation, the airlift was delayed by an unexpected difficulty: that of synchronizing the efforts of the airlift, largely navy-controlled, and of the fighter escort, under air force command.

AMBASSADOR HABIB–KISSINGER
Tuesday, April 29, 1975
1:25 A.M.

K: We just got another urgent backchannel from Martin. He has been asked to pull out the defense attachés within twenty-four hours by Minh and [Martin responded] that in view of the above, I repeat my request to permit me and about twenty of my staff to remain behind, at least for a day or two, to at least give some dignity to our departure and to facilitate an orderly disposition of our extensive properties here. I can keep two Air America [airline used by the CIA] helicopters and we can depart within a moment's notice. I seriously recommend this course and hope for your prompt approval. And then he mentioned that Minh's request will permit the announcement of departure be by [Vietnamese] request not from our own panic. What do you think?

H: Well—

K: What could he do there?

H: What he could do there is, he could sit in his building, he could put the three choppers on the roof and he could make a few phone calls and go down the street and see somebody. You don't need twenty people to do that. Well, it is not a question of whether it is twenty or three—it does make a difference. If he says he is going to stay, then give him what he needs to stay, but the idea that this is going to be dignified whereas if they all get out now it won't be dignified doesn't strike me as being reasonable. It seems to me that it is quite clear that it is time to leave.

K: It does.

H: It is time to leave in the interest of safety and everything else.

K: And, in fact, the other twenty could more easily become hostages.

H: Well, that is a possibility—it doesn't worry me. I think if he puts them on the roof of the building he can close the doors downstairs and get off the top. Of course, they could shoot him down. But I don't see any reason to keep people there. What would they do to dispose of properties? I mean the place is going to be looted inside fifteen minutes as soon as he walks out. That is what happened in Phnom Penh and that is what will happen here. Every house that every American ever lived in [in] Vietnam will be looted inside of twenty minutes.

K: Really?

H: Of course. . . .

. . .

H: . . . Our remaining interest is the safety of about eight hundred Americans. That is all our remaining interest in this, especially when the government—the alleged government—has asked that we take out three or four hundred of them [the military personnel]. The only way you can take out those three or four hundred is with the helicopter lifts. The helicopter lifts should not be played around with. It should be in and out as fast as it can be done, with whatever security force is necessary.

K: Okay. Do you have any reports on that goddamn lift?

H: The mil rep just came in and said that they are still orbiting at their initial point, they have not yet been told to go in and land.

K: And why is that?

H: He didn't know, sir.

K: Well, they will be running out of fuel.

H: Well, they won't spend much time there—they are due in a minute but it is not clear why they have not been ordered in. You can't tell—there may be something going on at the airfield which makes it difficult for them to get in. Well, I take it your instinct is to tell them to stay within twenty people.

K: No, my instinct is to tell him to come home.

H: That is my instinct too.

. . .

AMBASSADOR HABIB–KISSINGER

Tuesday, April 29, 1975
1:55 A.M.

K: I just want to find out what's going on.

H: I wish I knew. They [the helicopters] were late getting off by at least an hour and fifty minutes. The last ETA we had, estimated time at the landing in Saigon, was 3:00. It is now 3:07, and we just talked to Saigon again and they've seen no helicopters. Now, we've had one report—

K: You're sure you're not using the Danang plan [sarcastic comment regarding use of plan to evacuate Danang a month earlier]?

H: No, we thought we were using the—

K: We've screwed up everything else in this war—why not that?

H: This is screwed up all right; I just hope they show up. I'm worried [unclear] but can't do a thing but worry. We've got an open line to the Sit Room. As soon as we know anything— Are you in your office? Or at home? Or where?

K: I'm in my office but I'm going home now.

H: Well, if anything dramatic occurs we'll give you a call.

K: Right. Well, you keep the Sit Room informed and they'll get to me.

H: Yeah. We've got an open line to them. But nothing to report.

K: But you don't really know what's happened.

H: We don't know a thing. We don't know where the choppers are. They're overdue in Saigon.

K: They're overdue in Saigon?

H: They are, yes, they were due at—

K: But would they be shooting at American helicopters?

H: There's been no shooting reported.

K: That we would know?

H: I think we would know that. But we do know that the fighter escort has not expended any ordnance. That's the only fact we've got.

K: Right. Okay. Well, good. We gave it a good effort.

H: They'll be in there in a minute, I'm sure.

K: Okay. Good. Good-bye. Thank you, Phil.

H: Good-bye.

By the next morning, the airlift was at last in full operation, though with an inexplicable delay of five hours.

Ambassador Habib–Kissinger

Tuesday, April 29, 1975
8:42 A.M.

K: Phil, I think you ought to call a few of our congressional people and tell them what is going on. I know the White House is doing a lot of this—but we ought to call some of our key committee people.

H: Who have they called, do we know? Why don't I at the minimum call—

K: I'm sure they called the chairman.

H: They will have called the chairman and the ranking minority—why don't I call some of the key guys who have been after us like Kennedy and Clark [Senator Dick Clark].

K: Let me call Kennedy.

H: You call Kennedy, all right, I'll call Flint. And Clark.

K: Just call a few of the key members; I'm assuming Mansfield [Mike Mansfield (D.-Mont.) Senate Majority Leader] and—

H: How about Humphrey, will you call him or will they call him?

K: No, you call Humphrey, say you are doing it on my behalf.

H: Okay.

K: You'll know who the people are—McCloskey will—let McCloskey do a little calling.

H: I'm going to come over to a meeting with you in five—I'll have McCloskey—

K: Don't make a huge problem of it—just get somebody to make the calls.

H: Right.

SENATOR KENNEDY–KISSINGER

Tuesday, April 29, 1975
8:48 A.M.

TK: Oh, Henry, how are you?

HAK: Ted, how are you? I just wanted to tell you what's going on—we are evacuating all Americans from Saigon. There was shelling during the night their time at Tan Son Nhut—which was end of the afternoon yesterday here in Tan Son Nhut airport—we tried to operate out of Tan Son Nhut and we have about eight thousand high-risk Vietnamese there, but panic developed on the field and all the runways were closed, so we moved as many people as we could to the DAO compound and into the Embassy and we have been operating out of there during our night, their day. Now they are still operating—it is dark there now—we have evacuated about

45,000 people up to now, there has been no opposition. And we expect to continue this evacuation for the next two hours; after that there will be no Americans that we know of left in Saigon. That will end the Vietnamese evacuation, also, except for whoever gets out by boat.

TK: Yeah.

HAK: So, that is the end of that chapter.

TK: What was the problem with Minh—they couldn't—did it just take too long to get the—or did they just refuse to negotiate with him?

HAK: Well, we thought we had something set with the Russians that included a political process, but apparently, the North Vietnamese were prepared to only let us evacuate without interference and they just wanted him in a position of total impotence. Now I suppose now they will start negotiating with him and I think there will be a sort of a government set up— a tripartite government which they will control.

TK: What is your reading, Henry, of have we had any kind of flexibility in terms of the resources to try and bring the monies that have been appropriated—can any of those funds be used to in terms of the coalition government or—security people and that sort of thing.

HAK: Well, I have the impression, I saw a breakdown of it, and I had the impression that something near $100 million might be available. And we could continue in Cambodia, but right now in Cambodia, they seem to be engaging in mass executions— they don't respond to any approaches.

TK: Is that right.

HAK: You know, the U.N. have approached them and we informally told the U.N. that we would be sympathetic, but they are even kicking out the French. In Cambodia, it is pretty bloody right now.

TK: Is it?

HAK: Yeah. But in principle we are open-minded on that subject. And then for your information, we established contact with the PRG in Paris so they know how to talk to us.

TK: Yeah.

HAK: We just thought it was too dangerous to keep some Americans sitting in Saigon in a situation that for a while nobody might control.

TK: Yeah, yeah. I think you are absolutely right.

HAK: We then might turn out to be hostages. If we do give relief, it should be a free act.

TK: Yeah, that's right. Okay, well I appreciate it. . . .

. . .

AMBASSADOR BROWN–KISSINGER
Tuesday, April 29, 1975
10:22 A.M.

K: Rog Morton [Secretary of the Interior and in charge of the Trust Territories (Guam and Wake Island) to which the refugees were being brought] says that he may be able to take up to four thousand Vietnamese into the Trust Territories.

B: The Trust Territories?

K: For clerical work and so forth.

B: Oh, that'd be great.

K: Will you get in immediate touch with him to see whether you could really work that out?

B: We'll be in touch with him right away, sir.

K: Okay.

B: Looks like we are still moving quite a few people out—down to about 750 still left in the compound.

K: Seven hundred fifty total?

B: Yeah, total.

K: Including Americans.

B: Yeah. This was just a fast flash figure in from—

K: Oh, but that's pretty good.

B: That's right.

K: That means—that they can move in less than an hour, probably.

B: That's right, sir. It is one third of what we were talking about earlier.

K: Okay, good work.

SECRETARY SCHLESINGER–KISSINGER
Tuesday, April 29, 1975
1:45 P.M.

K: Jim, I have just talked to the President and he sees no choice except to terminate the thing.

S: Okay. He [Martin] has about 700 between 750 people there [at the Embassy compound] now. Five hundred Vietnamese—what we can do is give them a number of choppers to go in or tell him there is a time limit—he must be out by 3:30 or something like that.

K: Well, how many choppers can you give him?

S: We have in train eight choppers plus eleven. Eight are on the way and there are eleven more that are standing in the wings, as it were.

K: Eight would get out how many?

S: Approximately 450.

K: Four hundred fifty and we have altogether 750.

S: Right. I would say, goddamnit this is the end—you know.

K: Why don't you give him, say, all together twelve helicopters and say that is a presidential order.

S: Okay.

K: Would twelve do it?

S: I think so; we may jiggle that to thirteen or something. We will have to do some careful calculations.

K: Well, give them what you think it takes of what is on the ground now and that's it.

S: Right.

K: I take it you have got communications to the ship [aircraft carrier from which helicopters were launched] now?

S: We are concerned whether or not we can still go through by crypt [encryption] but what we will do is give a pilot a message to hand to him [Ambassador Martin].

SECRETARY SCHLESINGER–KISSINGER
Tuesday, April 29, 1975
2:09 P.M.

K: Jim.

S: Yeah, Henry. We are sending a message to them [the officers handling the evacuation]—because of the 46s as well as the 53s [helicopters]—that the nineteen choppers, which should handle 760 people, are all that he gets and we expect them—him out on the nineteenth chopper at the latest at the pace to terminate around 3:30.

K: All right. Now, you tell him, Jim, if you don't add that this is a presidential order he won't come out.

S: Right. We shall do that.

K: That's what I wanted to make sure that you add.

S: Shall do. He is a man with a mission.

K: Well, he lost a son there.

S: Yes. You have got to admire the bugger.

K: Look, his thoughts are in the right direction.

S: That's right. Dedication and energy.

K: And, I think—

S: You weep.

K: I think you and I will be glad we went this way.

S: There is a certain slobbiness in the American soul now that Martin has—

K: That's right.

S: That's why he repels so many people.

K: That's exactly right.

S: But he sure can be insubordinate.

K: I know. I know. Will we have total figures when this thing terminates?

S: Yes, sir. Yes, sir. We will—as a matter of fact we can give you a very good approximation now and I'll get the figures over to Brent [Scowcroft].

K: Good. I would be very grateful.

S: Okay.

K: So you call me when it is finished.

GEORGE MEANY, AFL-CIO PRESIDENT–KISSINGER
Tuesday, April 29, 1975
3:08 P.M.

. . .

K: . . . I just wanted to call you to let you know that the labor leaders that you were particularly concerned about have been taken out of Vietnam.

M: Mr. Bhu and his people.

K: Mr. Bhu and I think all of his people. But certainly most of his people. And I think we got—I think there were two hundred—said we got all of them, but it is sort of a messy situation. But Bhu is definitely out and his closest associates are out and I wanted you to know that.

M: Thank you. I'm glad to hear that.

K: And when you feel better, if you have the time, I'd like to get together with you and bring you up-to-date where we stand on various things.

M: All right, sir. . . .

. . .

DEPUTY SECRETARY CLEMENTS–KISSINGER
Tuesday, April 29, 1975
4:14 P.M.

K: Bill, for a layman like me, what the hell is making this thing move so slowly?

C: Well, it's just impossible for me to understand it, Henry. I've just been raising hell over here and I'm disgusted with it and so forth and so on. We've got nine helicopters to go.

K: I mean, the President is raising holy hell with me.

C: I don't doubt it. He ought to be. I mean, I think it is just a damn poor performance by everybody concerned and the biggest single block in this, Henry, is our communications and they are just miserable. Just absolutely miserable.

K: You know after—I'm talking to you as a friend now. But after two weeks of preparation how the hell is that possible?

C: I know it and there is that kind of a question mark on it and I'm eleven thousand miles away from those bastards and I can assure you that George [Brown] is even more disturbed than I am and there is going to be some changes out there with about two or three top people.

K: I think that's right.

C: And we're going to hold those people accountable, Henry. Because I don't want to leak it but—and I don't [mean] to say anything publicly at all—but it is really a miserable performance.

K: And you know if we lose anything in the last hour—

C: That's right. It's going to be bad. No, I think— The helicopters are in the air. We've got three redundant ones standing by in case we get a motor failure—engine failure—something like that. And we ought to have those people out of there within the hour at this point. But it is going to take us another hour.

K: Because you know the President has been standing by here. He thought it was all over by 3:00. We told the legislative leaders it would be over by 2:00.

C: I know. I agree with you, Henry. I'll feel every bit as bad as you do and I wish there was something that I could do about it. Now I've talked to Gayler on the phone myself. He knows how unhappy I am with him. . . .

K: Well, after all the bugging of us he did, you would have thought he had it worked out.

C: That's right, so— There we are. It's just an unfortunate set of circumstances and I'm just praying that we are going to really get everybody out of there and keep our fingers crossed. Because it goddamn sure doesn't have anything to do with how smart we are. We're just lucky.

. . .

Lew Wasserman, MCA chairman–Kissinger
Tuesday, April 29, 1975
4:30 P.M.

W: The purpose of the call is to tell you that with all the problems you're having that there are a lot of your friends out here that are thinking about you and that love you.

K: Aren't you sweet.

W: I'm going to hang up and let you go back to work. That's the only reason I called you.

K: Lew, you're a good friend and I won't forget this.

W: We're all rooting for you, Henry.

K: Thank you.

W: It goes without our saying that if there is anything we can do we're available day or night.

K: Well, I can't tell you how much this call means to me. Especially today.

W: Well, hang in there. We're with you.

At 5:00 P.M., when I was informed that Martin had left on what was assumed to be the last helicopter, I briefed the press.

Returning to my office, I found that Vietnam still would not let go easily. While Graham Martin and the remnants of the Embassy staff had indeed departed at 4:58 A.M. Saigon time, elements of the 9th Marine Amphibious Brigade guarding the evacuation—comprising 129 Marines—had been left behind for some reason that we could never discover. Huge credibility gaps had been manufactured from far less than this, but those of us in the White House Situation Room had no time to worry about public relations. The helicopter lift was resumed. As a result, the last conversations about Vietnam left no scope for commenting on the tragedy of what would now occur. They concerned instead technical quibbling about how to rescue the Marines inexplicably left behind.

VICE PRESIDENT ROCKEFELLER–KISSINGER

Tuesday, April 29, 1975
7:06 P.M.

K: We've just heard that there are 138 men still there.

R: Is it true?

K: Nelson, I cannot explain it to you. We had heard both from NMSC [National Military Command Center] and Clements it was over. Now we hear we are down to thirty-eight. What did you think of the briefing? You don't think it was too defensive, do you?

R: You were marvelous. You explained the past and the future. And you got this message just as you were leaving? What is Defense saying?

K: They blame it on six other guys.

. . .

THE PRESIDENT–KISSINGER

Tuesday, April 29, 1975
7:20 P.M.

K: I just wanted to tell you they are down to one helicopter load; to thirty-eight and the helicopters were reported five minutes out,

but probably fifteen minutes out, because they black out for a period.

F: So they are down to one helo.

K: No there are two. There will be thirty-eight to lift off and
each helo can take forty-six in one load—but they will land simultaneously—they should be loading, but we have no confirmation.

F: Let me know as soon as they are in the air.

K: Mr. President, we have come too far, not to get this. They didn't
have to fire.

F: Okay, let me know as soon as we have something.

K: Right, Mr. President.

DEPUTY SECRETARY CLEMENTS–KISSINGER
Tuesday, April 29, 1975
8:01 P.M.

C: We finally got those people out.

K: Is that absolutely certain now?

C: Absolutely certain. Yes. The last deal they changed the numbers
on us three times. They finally told us all three guys left. And we
went in to get out the [last] ten and there were eleven instead of
ten. It is unbelievable. I called not only for that reason but to tell
you that I am damn sorry about any crack you are in now because
of that. When you said the evacuation is now complete—has it
caused you some problems?

K: It is causing me some problems and when your people are briefing over there it will be worse.

C: Can I say something that would be helpful.

K: We must see how it breaks tomorrow. But if you want to tell your
press that you gave us the information that is the only way left.

C: I'll do that in the morning. I'll do it.

It was 7:53 P.M. Washington time (and already daylight in
Saigon) when the helicopter carrying the last Marines left the Embassy roof.

Two hours later, North Vietnamese tanks rolled into Saigon. One of the first smashed through the gates of the Presidential Palace. There was no turnover of authority because that would have implied the existence of an independent, or at least autonomous, South Vietnam. Instead, Big Minh and his entire Cabinet were arrested and disappeared from public view.

The Provisional Revolutionary Government (PRG), the reincarnation of the National Liberation Front (NLF)—advertised in the West for a decade as the putative centerpiece of a South Vietnamese democratic coalition government—disappeared with Big Minh. Within a year, the two Vietnams were unified along the traditional Communist pattern. Not a shred of autonomy remained for the South. Hundreds of thousands of South Vietnamese, including all those who had been in the government or armed forces, were herded into so-called reeducation camps—a euphemism for concentration camps—where they stayed for the better part of a decade. Tens of thousands fled as boat people.

For the sake of our long-term peace of mind, we must someday undertake an assessment of why good men on all sides found no way to avoid this disaster and why our domestic drama first paralyzed and then overwhelmed us. But, on the day the last helicopter left the roof of the Embassy, only a feeling of emptiness remained.

Acknowledgments

This was an unusual volume to assemble. It required culling from material that had been prepared as it was occurring those items that dealt with the subject matter, identifying names often only cryptically mentioned, and explaining references whose significance had become obscured by the passage of time. It required also shepherding the material through the clearance procedures of the National Security Council. All of this was in addition to the more routine tasks of editing the explanatory text and supervising the stages necessary for producing a book.

On my staff, Theresa Cimino Amantea performed all of these responsibilities with indefatigable energy, dedication, and efficiency, assisted by Jody Williams. Jessee Incao held down the fort in running my office and helped with research and collating. Peter Mandaville and Christopher Long assisted with research.

I am indebted to Dr. Condoleezza Rice, Assistant to the President for National Security Affairs, for facilitating the clearance process and much appreciate the assistance of David Travers in her office. In the office of Records and Access Management at the National Security Council, William H. Leary, Senior Director, and Rod Soubers, Director of Access Management, were friendly, helpful, and implacable in insisting on the prerogatives of security.

At Simon & Schuster, I dealt with the by now familiar cast of helpful individuals, beginning with Michael Korda, whose advice contributed to my decision to produce this book and who improved it with his ever incisive and understanding comments. John Cox ably assisted with the editing. Gypsy da Silva oversaw the copyediting process with firm efficiency, a cheerful disposition, and undeserved good humor; Fred Chase was a relentless and thoughtful copyeditor. Jim Stoller, Barbara Raynor, Joshua Cohen, and John Morgenstern were indispensable proofreaders. Sydney Wolfe Cohen prepared the index; George Turianski supervised the production; and Amy Hill did the interior design.

As always, my wife Nancy was there when needed with advice, review, and encouragement.

Needless to say, I alone am responsible for the shortcomings of this volume.

I have dedicated this book to my grandchildren—Sam, Sophie, Will, and Juliana—of whom I am very proud, in the hope that when they grow up, the problems described in these pages will no longer be relevant to their lives.

Index